Sarah Osborn's Collected Writings

Sarah Osborn's Collected Writings

Edited by

Catherine A. Brekus

Yale UNIVERSITY PRESS/NEW HAVEN & LONDON

Published with assistance from the Annie Burr Lewis Fund.

Yale University Press books may be purchased in quantity for educational, business,
or promotional use. For information, please e-mail sales.press@yale.edu (U.S. office) or
sales@yaleup.co.uk (U.K. office).

Designed by Mary Valencia.
Set in Fournier type by Integrated Publishing Solutions.
Printed in the United States of America.

Library of Congress Control Number: 2016956007
ISBN 978-0-300-18289-7 (hardcover : alk. paper)

A catalogue record for this book is available from the British Library.

This paper meets the requirements of ANSI/NISO Z39.48-1992 (Permanence of Paper).

10 9 8 7 6 5 4 3 2 1

In memory of
Liliana Lawrynowicz
and
Gertrude Emma Kneeland Brennan

For the former things are passed away.
—Revelation 21:4

CONTENTS

CONTENTS

WHOSE LIVES DO WE CHOOSE to remember, and why?

This book collects the writings of Sarah Osborn, an evangelical woman who lived in Newport, Rhode Island, during the eighteenth century. Osborn was a published author, a rarity for early American women, and she became well known during her life for leading a religious revival at her house during the 1760s and 1770s. In many ways she was an extraordinary person. But she was also poor and female, two characteristics that are rarely associated with the makers of history, and in the decades after her death she was gradually forgotten. This collection of her writings, along with my narrative history of her life, *Sarah Osborn's World: The Rise of Evangelical Christianity in Early America*, demonstrates why she deserves to be remembered and, more broadly, why women's stories are crucial to understanding historical change.

A book like this probably would not have been published before the 1960s, or at least not by a major academic press. Perhaps a Christian publisher would have been interested in marketing Osborn's story as devotional reading, or a local press in Newport might have wondered whether Osborn's writings could have antiquarian appeal. But most publishers—like most scholars—would have questioned whether a relatively obscure woman's life could tell us anything important about American history. Earlier generations of historians acknowledged the significance of a few exceptional female leaders like Elizabeth Cady Stanton and Harriet Beecher Stowe, but they seem to have assumed that ordinary women were so caught up in the cycles of pregnancy, childrearing, and housekeeping that they stood virtually outside of history. Since early American women could not vote, hold political office, go to college, be ordained, or own their own property after marriage, how could they have been the agents of historical change?

Today there are still many historians who share Thomas Carlyle's conviction that "history is the biography of great men," but these scholars no longer have a monopoly on our understanding of the past. Because of the rise of women's history and social history during the 1960s and 1970s, we now have a broader understanding of who "makes" history. Most historians now argue that change comes not only from the top down but also from the bottom up. Though leaders are important, they become leaders only when large numbers of ordinary men and women share their vision. For example, George Whitefield would not have become one of the most celebrated preachers of the eighteenth century if not for the thousands of men and women, including Sarah Osborn, who embraced his ideas as their own. *His* agency was largely dependent on *theirs*. Without understanding the concerns and aspirations of people like Osborn, we cannot explain how and why historical change takes place.

Like all of us, Sarah Osborn both made and was made by history. She was deeply shaped by the eighteenth-century world into which she was born, and in many ways she perpetuated its beliefs and practices. Most of us uphold the verities of our world more than we challenge them, and Osborn was no exception. Much of her agency involved upholding the social, political, economic, and religious structures of her day: for example, she assumed that women had been created subordinate to men, and for most of her life she did not question whether monarchy was God's favored form of government. From the distance of more than two hundred years, we can see the ways in which her life, even her very sense of selfhood, was shaped by ideas that she inherited as the truth. There were limits to how she and other eighteenth-century Americans could imagine their lives.

Yet Osborn did not simply reproduce the assumptions of her culture; she also challenged them. When we read her writings we can see a world in motion, a world that was changing as she and thousands of other colonial Americans made new discoveries and sought new answers to enduring questions about human life. By the time that she died in 1796, she had rejected many of the ideas that she had once taken for granted. Rather than accepting slavery as God's will, for example, she eventually denounced it as a sin. And rather than adhering to the faith of her parents, she devoted her life to a new kind of Christianity that emerged during the revivals of the Great Awakening, a Christianity that emphasized a personal relationship with God, the joy of being "born again," and the call to spread the gospel around the globe. Though she was too immersed in her own time to recognize it, she helped to build the religious movement that today is known as evangelicalism. Of all the ways in which Osborn made history, she most wanted to be remembered for her evangelical faith.

Reading Sarah Osborn's writings can help us come to a deeper understanding of the changes that took place in eighteenth-century America, including the spread of Enlightenment ideas, the rise of humanitarianism, the emergence of antislavery sentiment, the expansion of women's religious authority, the advent of the American Revolution, and most important to her, the rise of the evangelical movement. All of these transformations took place because of the agency of men and women, most of them now forgotten, who dreamed of creating a different world. When we remember Osborn, we remember that historical change always emerges out of the hopes, fears, and strivings of ordinary people.

In 1743, Sarah Osborn, a schoolteacher in Newport, Rhode Island, decided to write a memoir. Inspired by the emotional revivals that historians have called the Great Awakening, she wanted to share the dramatic story of her conversion, the religious crisis that had changed the meaning of her life. Looking back, she remembered longing for God's grace because of her feelings of hopelessness and worthlessness, but fearing that she was too sinful to be saved. She had felt as if there were an immense gulf separating her from God. She was depraved; he was perfect. She was empty; he was full. She was helpless; he was all-powerful and free. And yet just at the moment when she felt most broken in spirit, he had healed her. "It is not possible for me . . . to make anyone sensible what joy I was instantly filled with," she testified, "except those that experimentally know what it is." She had been born again, "restored, as it were, from the grave."[1]

Lost but now found, doubtful but now sure, dead but now reborn—this was Sarah Osborn's story, the story that she treasured as the defining moment of her life. A deeply religious woman, Osborn believed that her life illustrated the power of God's grace, and she spent many hours reflecting on the meaning of her experiences. She wrote about her suicidal crisis in adolescence, her conversion, and her fear that the "Antichrist" would be victorious during the French and Indian War. She wrote about her work as a teacher, her religious meetings for slaves, and her hope that the American Revolution would usher in the millennium, the thousand years of Christ's reign. She wrote about her love of God. Many of the questions that she asked in her writings are timeless, especially about the definition of happiness, the nature of God, and the meaning of suffering. But because of her faith in divine providence, she also searched for evidence of God's will in the dramatic political and economic changes taking place around her. God, she believed, controlled all things, and as she poured out her heart to him in written prayer, she tried to make sense of his plan for the world.

Reading Osborn's writings can help us to answer many of our questions about religion and everyday life in eighteenth-century America. How did Osborn think about herself and God? How did she make sense of poverty, illness, and war? How did she understand her gender? How did she answer perennial human questions about the meaning of life and the nature of happiness? Though few people today have heard of Osborn, her story was shaped by many important events in eighteenth-century America, including the revivals of the Great Awakening, the French and Indian War, and the American Revolution. Her writings offer a fascinating window onto both her private life and the tumultuous world in which she lived.

Amazing, Astonishing Grace

Born in 1714 in England, Sarah Osborn was a mother, a wife, and a schoolteacher who moved to the colonies as a child, eventually settling in Newport, Rhode Island. She is remembered today only because she left an extraordinary record of her experiences in thousands of pages of letters, diaries, and a spiritual memoir, more than two thousand pages of which still survive. (According to her minister, the Reverend Samuel Hopkins, she wrote as many as fifteen thousand pages during her life.)[2] In addition to these manuscripts, there are a few of Osborn's writings that were published in the eighteenth and nineteenth centuries. In 1753, after a minister read a letter of spiritual advice that she had written to a friend, he arranged for it to be published anonymously as *The Nature, Evidence, and Certainty of True Christianity.* (It appeared in 1755.) Two collections of Osborn's writings were also published after her death: Samuel Hopkins's *The Memoirs of Sarah Osborn,* which included extracts from her diaries, and Elizabeth West Hopkins's *Familiar Letters, Written by Mrs. Sarah Osborn and Miss Susanna Anthony,* which reprinted some of her correspondence with her closest friend.[3]

Sarah Osborn had much to write about. At her birth in 1714 she seemed destined for an ordinary life, but no one's life, when viewed up close, looks ordinary, and hers has all the ingredients of a novel: a turbulent childhood, a suicidal crisis in adolescence, early widowhood, the loss of an only son, poverty, the brutality of two American wars, and, through everything, debilitating bouts of a chronic illness. Though it is impossible to diagnose her across the span of almost three centuries, her symptoms suggest that she may have suffered from either rheumatoid arthritis or multiple sclerosis. During the last twenty years of her life she was unable to walk and nearly blind.

Yet despite these tribulations, Osborn never lost her faith in God's goodness, and she was so charismatic that many people in Newport sought her spiritual counsel. During the winter of 1766–67, she emerged as the leader of a religious revival that brought hundreds of people—including large numbers of slaves—to her house each week. Although she remained poor, strangers from as far away as Canada and the West Indies sent her money to help defray expenses. By the time of her death in 1796, she had become virtually a Protestant saint. In her memoir, she described her extraordinary life as proof of God's power to save even the worst of sinners. "It is all of free grace," she testified, "amazing, astonishing grace."[4]

Osborn's writings are a rare record of a woman's life in early America. Few women in the eighteenth-century colonies could read, and even fewer were taught how to write. Writing tended to be identified as a "masculine" craft because it was particularly useful for keeping accounts and signing legal documents. In New England, however, women's literacy rates were relatively high because of the Puritan insistence that all Christians should be able to read the Bible for themselves. As measured by counting how many women could sign their names on wills or other legal documents, women's literacy ranged from under 40 percent in rural New England to more than 50 percent in Boston.[5] Ministers encouraged women as well as men to keep a record of their religious experiences, and many educated women, especially those who were the daughters or wives of ministers, seem to have written diaries. In a sermon that he delivered in 1711, the Reverend Cotton Mather claimed that many women "have wrote such things as have been very Valuable; Especially relating to their own Experiences. Many Volumes of the Works which have been

Two pages from Sarah Osborn's diary, March 15, 1758. She cut pieces of folio paper into squares and sewed them together to make individual books. (Her stitching is visible along the side of the second page.) Each diary page measured approximately 6 × 4 inches. Courtesy of the Newport Historical Society.

for thy Glory and my future
Encouragement yt I may not
ver sink under a Prospect
of the frowns of Mortals
Let faith be strong and then
nothing can disquiet me but
when faith totters nothing
can Establish me Lord increase
my faith this is thy glorious
Gift and by this thou wilt
be Glorified faith will work
by Love and Purifie the Heart
and influence to beter obedience
and thou shalt have the Glory
while worthless I reap the
comfort o guard me against
accursed Pride my Shield my
Rock and Sure defence Save
me Here because this will
displease and dishonour thee
o Let all the world be against
me rather then Suffer me
to displease and dishonour
thee o Hold me by thy almighty

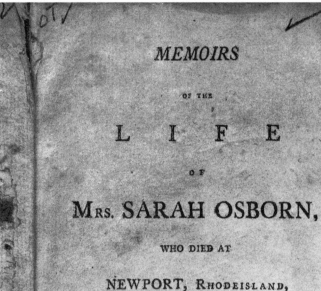

MEMOIRS

OF THE

L I F E

OF

Mrs. SARAH OSBORN,

WHO DIED AT

NEWPORT, Rhodeisland,

ON THE SECOND DAY OF AUGUST, 1796.

IN THE EIGHTY THIRD YEAR OF HER AGE.

By SAMUEL HOPKINS, D. D.

PASTOR OF THE FIRST CONGREGATIONAL CHURCH IN NEWPORT.

PRINTED AT WORCESTER, MASSACHUSETTS,
BY LEONARD WORCESTER.

1799.

The title page of Samuel Hopkins, *Memoirs of the Life of Mrs. Sarah Osborn* (Worcester, Mass.: Leonard Worcester, 1799). The Reverend Samuel Hopkins published extracts from Osborn's diaries three years after her death. Courtesy of the Newport Historical Society.

wrought and write, by these Dorcas's, are to be seen in the Private Hands of their Surviving Posterity."[6] Most women's writings, however, have been lost.

One might imagine that a woman in the eighteenth century, especially a woman who had received only three months of formal education, would write mostly about her daily routine. Yet even though Osborn was a teacher, she rarely wrote about the curriculum that she followed in her school. Nor did she write about the domestic chores that she did every day, whether scouring floors, making beds, or kneading dough into bread. Instead she filled thousands of pages with her earnest prayers to God. If not for her desperate prayers for money, for example, we would not know about her poverty, and if not for her prayers for resignation, we would not know about her chronic bouts of illness. When she mentioned details about her everyday life, she usually squeezed them into the margins of her text as an afterthought. After praying that God would deliver her "from oppression or extortion," for example, she wrote in the margin, "Re: raising my price for schooling." If not for this note, we would not know that she was fearful that raising her tuition might be unjust.[7] Both literally and figuratively, God is at the center of her pages.

Like other early Americans who kept detailed records of their daily lives, Osborn wanted to preserve her memories against forgetfulness, but what she most wanted to remember was her relationship to God. Though sometimes she felt as if God had "hidden his face" from her, she loved him passionately. No single word or image could contain him: he was the bleeding Christ who had died for her sins, a physician who could heal her wounds, a warrior who would crush her foes with a rod of iron, the only food that satisfied her craving soul, a bridegroom who loved her with boundless love, and a faithful shepherd who protected her from harm. Often she switched from writing about him in the third person to addressing him directly by name, praising him for his power or pleading for his help and care. Quoting from the Bible, she described him as her "portion"—her inheritance, her legacy, the reason her life bore meaning.

Evangelicalism and the Enlightenment

Osborn's writings offer fascinating insights into many different aspects of early American life, but they are especially valuable as a record of the rise of the movement that we now describe as evangelical Christianity. Osborn was deeply affected by the First Great Awakening, the religious revivals that took place in New England during the 1740s and 1750s, and she believed that she stood on the brink of a new era in Christian history. Today evangelicalism has become such a familiar part of the American religious landscape that it seems virtually timeless, but like Christianity itself, evangelicalism has a history, and when it emerged in the mid-eighteenth century it represented a distinctive turning point in the history of religion. The word "evangelical" was not new, and its roots stretch back to the Greek word *evangelion*, meaning "gospel."[8] The sixteenth-century Protestant reformers used *evangelical* as an adjective to emphasize their reliance on the Bible alone. Yet during the eighteenth century the word became increasingly identified with the popular preachers of the Great Awakening, including the celebrated George Whitefield, and by the early nineteenth century it had become a noun. In his *Letters from England*, Robert Southey explained, "The countess of Huntingdon was a great patroness of Whitefield, and his preachers were usually called by her name,—which they have now dropt for the better title of Evangelicals."[9]

In the years before the American Revolution, most evangelicals in America traced their heritage to the Calvinist wing of the Reformed tradition, and they fiercely denied that humans were free to choose their own destinies. (In England, by contrast, the Wesleyan wing of the movement preached a gospel of free will.) Emphasizing the doctrine of original sin, they described humans as inherently inclined to evil. Osborn's writings are filled with descriptions of God's sovereignty, her sinfulness and "depravity," and her inability to earn salvation through good works.

Explaining the rise of evangelicalism is not an easy task, but it is clear that the movement emerged in response to momentous changes in politics, economics, intellectual life, science, and technology that laid the foundations for our modern world, especially the Enlightenment. Even though evangelicals resisted the skeptical and rationalist strains of the Enlightenment, they could not help being influenced by the new ideas that increasingly permeated the eighteenth-century Atlantic world, and they absorbed parts of Enlightenment thought as their own. The Enlightenment took place not only *against* Protestantism but also *within* it. While liberals were affected by its emphasis on free will and divine benevolence, evangelicals absorbed its focus on personal experience as the foundation of knowledge, its elevation of the individual as the most important source of religious authority, its faith in progress, and its humanitarian sympathies.[10]

One of the most striking features of the new evangelical movement was its empiricism, a reflection of John Locke's profound influence on eighteenth-century American culture. According to Locke, experience was the foundation for knowledge. "All our knowledge is founded" on "*Experience*," he explained. Describing the mind as "White Paper, void of all Characters, without any Ideas," he asked, "How comes it to be furnished?" His answer was simple: "from Experience."[11] The Enlightenment was not only an "Age of Reason" but also an "Age of Experience," and Enlightenment thinkers insisted that knowledge must be based on empirical proof rather than clerical authority or inherited tradition.

This emphasis on experience was not new, and it had deep Christian roots stretching back to Bernard of Clairvaux and the Protestant reformers. But under the influence of the Enlightenment, the language of experience became more widespread, and it also gained a greater association with scientific authority.[12] Unlike earlier generations of Protestants, who had been hesitant to appear too confident about their salvation (lest they be guilty of pride), evangelicals insisted that they could empirically feel and know whether they had been spiritually reborn. According to Sarah Osborn, true faith was not a matter of abstract reason but the palpable experience of being born again. "How do I know this God is mine, and that I myself am not deceived?" Osborn asked. "By the evidences of a work of grace wrought in my soul." She described her faith as "experimental": it could be validated by concrete, measurable experience. Writing about her conversion, she explained that most people would not be able to understand her sense of joy "except those that experimentally know what it is."[13]

Evangelicals did not trust personal experience in the abstract, and in fact they assumed that most people viewed the world with eyes clouded by sin. But they insisted that Christians gained new powers of perception during conversion. According to Osborn, she had been overwhelmed by a new "sense" of God's "excellence, glory and truth" that was as real as the sense of seeing, tasting, or touching. Critics of the evangelical movement complained that this sort of language was arrogant, and as Osborn admitted in her memoir, she was accused of being "puffed up with spiritual pride" and "holier than thou." Nevertheless, she insisted that her faith was "sensible."[14]

Though Osborn did not realize it, her image of a "new sense" came from Enlightenment thinkers like the third Earl of Shaftesbury and Francis Hutcheson, who argued that all humans have an innate "moral sense" that helps them to distinguish good from evil. Although evangelicals rejected this positive view of human nature, they agreed that knowledge comes from sense perception, and they appropriated the Enlightenment language of sensation as their own. When Jonathan Edwards searched for words to narrate his conversion, he described it as "a sense of the glory of the divine being; a new sense, quite different from anything I ever experienced before."[15] According to Osborn, God had given her not only a "sense" of his mercy but a deep "sense of the odious nature and bitter evil of sin."[16]

In addition to being influenced by the Enlightenment language of experience, evangelicals also absorbed its individualism—one of the most enduring legacies of the eighteenth century. In earlier periods of history it had seemed almost inevitable that children would grow up to follow in their parents' footsteps: a farmer's son would usually become a farmer, and a goodwife's daughter would live in the same neighborhood as her mother. But because of social and geographical mobility and the expansion of political and economic choices, personal identity no longer seemed as fixed in the eighteenth century, and individuals gained a new sense of self-determination. According to Enlightenment philosophers, the sovereign individual had the right to choose his own government, to pursue his own economic interests in the marketplace, and to worship according to the dictates of his own conscience. Although Enlightenment thinkers almost always imagined the individual as a white man, Native Americans, African Americans, and women of all races gradually laid claim to this individualistic language as well.

Evangelicals were ambivalent about the individualism that was enshrined by the Enlightenment, but in response to the challenges of their time they crafted a new form of Protestantism that was based more on the converted individual than on the covenanted community.[17] Earlier generations of Puritans had emphasized the morality of the entire commonwealth, imagining New England in collective terms as the people of God, the "new Israel." In contrast, even though evangelicals agreed that both personal and communal transformation were important, they put their pronunciation more on the individual, arguing that one could not be a Christian without a personal experience of grace. As a minister explained, "True religion is an inward thing, a thing of the heart." Sarah Osborn's *Nature, Certainty, and Evidence of True Christianity* overflowed with the words *I* and *me*. "I'll tell you truly what God has done for my soul," she declared at the beginning of her letter. "God the Father manifested himself to me." "God made with me an everlasting Covenant."[18]

Finally, the nascent evangelical movement was also influenced by the stream of Enlightenment thought known as humanitarianism. Humanitarians were a loose coalition of thinkers who were involved in many different causes—including prison reform, antislavery, and poor relief—but they were linked together by their faith that humans were essentially good and were called to alleviate suffering and create a better world.[19] On one hand, evangelicals refused to see human happiness as the greatest good, and they defended doctrines that humanitarians found abhorrent, especially eternal punishment. Yet on the other hand, evangelicals were fervent about creating a kinder, more compassionate world, and ultimately they forged an understanding of "benevolence" that was uniquely their own. Although Sarah Osborn believed that she was called to give charity to the poor, minister to the sick, and visit the imprisoned, she thought there was no greater act of charity than saving sinners from damnation. Evangelicals became renowned for their missionary work, placing more emphasis on evangelism than virtually any other group of Christians before them. The evangelical version of humanitarianism was evangelism, preaching the gospel to as many people as possible.

No historical turning point is ever completely divorced from what came before it, and in many ways evangelical Christians revitalized an older Puritan tradition.[20] Evangelicals were strongly committed to the doctrine of original sin, and they had a vivid sense of the reality of hell. They also believed in examining themselves for signs of God's grace. Yet evangelicals looked forward as well as backward, and they crafted a new religious movement in response to the unique challenges of their day. Evangelicalism was a heart-centered, experiential, individualistic, and evangelistic form of Protestantism that emerged in dialogue with the modern world.

A Writing Life

Osborn's desire to convert others to her evangelical faith provides one answer to the question of why she spent so much of her life writing. Though she usually kept her memoir and her diaries private, she occasionally shared them with friends, and she hoped that her manuscripts would be preserved for others to read after her death. Because they were not only a record of her personal life but also evidence of God's goodness, she felt as if they did not belong to her alone. She wanted to give others the gift of seeing God just as she did: "infinitely wise, holy, just, merciful, truthful, unchangeable," and "the same yesterday, today, and forever."[21]

It is hard to imagine how Osborn ever found either the time or the privacy to write so many pages. After the death of her first husband at sea in 1733, she became a teacher in order to support herself and her son, supplementing her meager salary by baking and sewing. After she married Henry Osborn in 1742, he suffered a breakdown that left him unable to work, and she continued to work long hours in her school to pay her family's bills. In an era before supermarkets, dishwashers, and microwaves, she was also burdened with grueling household chores that kept women busy from dawn to dusk. Doing laundry, for example, required filling huge tubs with water, gathering wood for a fire, scrubbing out stains (or adding stale urine to the pot as bleach), stirring heavy loads of wet clothing with a washing stick, and wringing them out to dry. The whole backbreaking process could take the better part of a day.[22] Although Osborn recruited neighborhood women to do some of her chores, educating their children for free in exchange for their cleaning, ironing, sewing, and baking, she often deprived herself of sleep in order to write.

Depending on which house Osborn and her husband were renting, she sometimes had a private "closet" where she could write without interruption, but when space was limited she found other ways to be alone. For at least a dozen years in the 1750s and 1760s, she used her bed as her retreat. After her husband had risen and dressed, she pulled the bed curtains shut for privacy, propped herself up with bolsters, and then knelt in front of her desk with pen and paper. (Kneeling must have seemed like the right posture for communicating with God.) "There I read and write almost everything of a religious nature," she explained to her friend, the Reverend Joseph Fish. "Thus I redeem an hour or two without which I must *starve*."[23]

It is not clear when Osborn first began writing. Although she seems to have composed three volumes of diaries before 1743, all of them have been lost. (We know about them only because her memoir is entitled "fourth book.") After 1743, though, when she was twenty-nine years old, she made writing a regular part of her spiritual life. "O, blessed be God that I have been taught to write," she recorded in her diary, "since that is the means that God has made the most effectual of all other to fix my thoughts on eternal things." Though she spent many hours reading the Bible and meditating on the life of Jesus, she felt closest to God when she had a pen in her hand. With every exclamation of praise, cry for help, or plea for understanding, she wrote herself more deeply into his presence. A blank page was an invitation to draw near to him, an opportunity to experience his grace. "'Tis in this way of musing that the fire burns," she explained, echoing a verse from Jeremiah: "His word is in my heart like a fire, a fire shut up in my bones. I am weary of holding it in; indeed, I cannot."[24] Writing was almost a compulsion for her, an unquenchable fire in her heart.

Other than a single letter that she wrote in 1742, Osborn's memoir is the earliest piece of her writing to survive. Composed in 1743 during the height of the Great Awakening, it traces the story of her spiritual pilgrimage from her childhood, when she learned to fear God, until her awakening during the revivals, when she committed her life entirely to his care. Though she wrote briefly about her family and friends, her story revolves almost entirely around two main characters: herself and God. Of all the stories that she could have told about herself, she thought the most important was her discovery of God's love.

After finishing her memoir, Osborn continued to narrate her life in thousands of pages of diaries. By recording her experiences, she seems to have hoped to see how God was guiding her life. In a poignant diary entry that she wrote at a time when she had little money or food, she reminded herself that her past experiences offered convincing proof that a loving God would never abandon her. Addressing him directly, she wrote: "My own experience has ever proved to me that thou art the God who has fed me all my life long, the God that didst never leave me upon the mount of difficulty, but that always appeared and wrought deliverance."[25]

By recording her prayers, Sarah hoped to keep track of when (and if) they were answered. For example, at some point after asking God to help her and Henry pay their debts, she added in the margins, "blessed be God, good success." Sometimes her prayers were answered almost immediately, for example on the day when she anxiously wrote about the scarcity of firewood in Newport, and fifteen minutes later someone arrived at her door to tell her where to buy it. But even if she had to wait months before a prayer was answered, she returned to her original entry in order to make a notation. In case she was ever tempted to forget it, her diaries "proved" that God was a God "hearing Prayer."[26]

Sarah seems to have struggled throughout her life with episodes of depression, or what she called "despair," and writing seems to have helped her to cope with her moments of darkness. When she felt as if God had "hidden his face from her," she tried to bring him into her presence by the sheer power of her words, making him visible on a page. When she recorded her experiences she could see that God was everywhere in her midst: in the neighbors who brought her firewood when her family was destitute; in church, where he fed her with his "broken body" and his blood; in the meetings of her women's prayer group, where he warmed their hearts with praise; and especially in the Bible, where he spoke directly to her across time and space.[27] Writing about God was like lighting a candle in the dark. Suddenly, she could see him.

Osborn seems to have wanted to transform her life into a text that could be read when she struggled with doubts. Poor and often ill, she sometimes found it difficult to keep her faith, but writing helped her to remember God's goodness. By recording her religious experiences in her memoir and her diaries, she could examine them for rational "evidence" of divine providence. When she looked back over the whole story of her life, she hoped to reassure herself that even when she had felt most alone and vulnerable, God had arranged everything for her own good.

Osborn's diaries are best described as written prayers or letters to God.

Just as she had signed a covenant with him after her conversion, she sometimes signed her entries as if they were letters. "I am thine forever," she promised him, and then, with a flourish, she added her signature, "Sarah Osborn."[28] Her voice is sometimes melancholy and sometimes joyful, but always immediate. Unlike her memoir, which tells the story of her entire life up until the age of twenty-nine, her diaries take place in the urgent space of *now*.

Osborn wrote letters for many of the same reasons as she wrote a memoir and diaries, but with a twist. Exchanging letters with friends and ministers allowed her to see God's hand not only in her own life but in theirs as well. When her friend Susanna Anthony praised God as "our reconciled friend and Father, our covenant God; and everlasting portion," or when the Reverend Joseph Fish affirmed that "our happiness lies in being able truly to say, not our will but thine be done," she felt as if she could see God's grace in their hearts.[29] "Your dear manuscripts," she wrote to Anthony, "have so often refreshed me, and warmed my heart."[30] She recognized the presence of God in Anthony's life even when she was blind to him in her own.

Most of Osborn's letters have been lost, but an edited collection of her correspondence with Susanna Anthony was published after her death, and many of her other letters survive in archives, including more than seventy to Joseph Fish. Her circle of correspondence seems to have been large, including the Reverend Guyse in England (her uncle), the Reverend Samuel Buell of Long Island, the Reverend Gilbert Tennent of New Jersey, and the Reverend Eleazar Wheelock of Connecticut. "My pen, as well as myself, have long, I trust, been solemnly given up to God, to be used by him and for no other," she wrote in 1769. "And when, through sore conflicts, I am tempted to lay it aside, the sin of the slothful servant stares me in the face, and I dare not."[31]

Like other evangelicals, Osborn saw letter writing as a way to build the kingdom of God. Imitating the apostle Paul, who had sent letters throughout the Greco-Roman world, evangelicals developed vast networks of correspondence that stretched across the ocean to include the West Indies, England, Scotland, Wales, and, by the end of the century, Africa. John Wesley, the founder of Methodism, counted more than sixteen hundred correspondents.[32] Because of their belief that the transatlantic revivals represented a remarkable outpouring of the Holy Spirit, evangelicals were hungry for news of other

O Sir Pray for me yt god will strengthen my faith
and resigne my will for my trials are great in many
respects as to my health I am in a Low state and my
Dear in no better for some months Past scarce able to
keep up half this time and I fear the consequence
Poverty as an armed man has been coming on us
ever since he was with you Last but this Last winter
especially it has made such Ravages for my business
where the sickness of children the Latter Part of summer
and fall and bad weather in winter and measles now has
fail'd So yt our income Has not been Half Equiv
alent to our unavoidable expence yt we both Labour
+ but to Lessen our change or increase our income all
is at a course of providence is so precarious
as to means yt holds up our heads above water as at
Dear yt it is but Little we got by them at ye most
Our Son has with this family teen children Some Sul
and others Some Seen no way to the
during circumstances if they have Said, Suld from
them they were hungry naked and drang up as her
when in a gospel Land real objects of charity
which Should my compassions towards us them and
I cant represent it now cast them off So Long as tis
Possible for me to grapple with them when Such
on them I am most through Gods Psalm yt am yet
off Supports me — their Father is gone into the ar
my and there is a poor Slothful wife and two
more poor children as they can to lub
I Pretend to do for themselves I have given
them up to Shift for themselves I cant hold out
any Longer to do for them I am Tired to keep
Help for I hant strength of body to go thro the
business of my school Small as it is and family
affairs too yt I have Fire to maintain wholy
and now Dear Sir Judge am I as a poor overgrown
breath animal groveling and Emitting underneath
burden or do I only indulge my Self So

at that Price they wash for them and find them flour

Besides all the Difficulties I have mentiond I have
had five in my family Down with the measles four
at once yt my business was quite broke up for Some
weeks and since that end of my business has fled
the Runway — Yet if I stop away as quire my trials
Concerning you with my complaints tis with a view
to your going excited to Pray for your afflicted friend
and old Dear Sir Pray for faith they for resigned to
cant Support my Does and tis very happy avery
of yt the fruit of all may be to take away my
Sin or yt I may be Reserv'd from Murmuring
against my Precious god for he does me no
wrong tis All this mercy to me — not to say
Pure I am Determind to medfine him Till I die
and if he will but stay my undelief the sea he slay
me S yet Put my trust in Him oh yt god may (a
Glorify Cause in me what will or what Seemeth
Him good but oh beg yt he will May me more our
pere than he was tenable me to Learn Its Livng
Dear Sir I Hope to Have never to Dear the race
and miss Bokey be but I cant accomplish it I may
make my Records regards acceptable to the Rece how
note and Ingrate and respond with them Say for
me oh How Glad Should I be to See you at Cloge
then but I quest Submit it cant be interceed with
both daughtons Sir for Letters for me that them Long
to Hear them Speak to me again and Pray Sacour
your Prosiff Soon if your Boffiting cause the promisu
Interview once since my affectionate regards to whom
Fifth I believe Dear Sir writes you and I must
come in these shatterd Lines with wishing you
and yours the best of blessings in christ Jesus
Oh I want to get to Heaven where I may Praise Him
forever for He is altogether Lovely my dear Saint
with me in all sincere affection which Pray acct

From yours till Death Sarah Osborn
my compliments my Cess and Some
Love to cousin Jemmes

people's religious experiences, and often they read letters aloud or passed them to friends as evidence of God's grace. In a fascinating example of the epistolary links among evangelicals, Osborn sent a letter to Joseph Fish in 1766 that quoted the correspondence of Samson Occom, a Native American preacher, to Samuel Buell a year earlier. It is not clear whether Buell had sent her a copy, but somehow Osborn knew that Occom had referred to his journey to England as a "strange providence."[33]

Sarah's closest friend and most frequent correspondent was Susanna Anthony, or Susa, as she called her, whom she seems to have met around 1740.[34] Since Newport was a compact city of six thousand, they may have been acquainted before then, but they were separated by both age and religion. Susa was twelve years younger than Sarah, meaning that she was only about fourteen years old when they met, and she had been raised as a Quaker. But in 1740, when George Whitefield came to Newport, she joined the throngs who gathered to hear him preach, and in 1742 she joined the First Church as well as Sarah's prayer group. She was a troubled woman who suffered from episodes of melancholy, self-loathing, and even self-harm (she remembered biting herself, gnashing her teeth, and throwing herself on the floor during an episode of religious distress), but Sarah loved her as the closest of friends. "Lord, thou knowest there is no creature upon earth more dear to me," she testified in her diary. "Thou hast made her, as my own soul, precious to me."[35]

Osborn also corresponded frequently with Joseph Fish, whom she also may have met during the revivals. He preached in Newport in 1742, and his wife, Rebecca Pabodie Fish, was the half-sister of Benjamin Pabodie (spelled "Peabody" by Osborn), the deacon of Newport's First Church.[36] Though Osborn had always admired and respected ministers, she felt especially close to Fish, who became a trusted friend. As she wrote in 1753, "There is, as Mr. Whitefield expresses it, a sacred something that has knit my heart to you with stronger bonds than that of natural affection."[37] Fish was only eight years older than she, and she grew to love him as a brother. In return, Fish called her

(*Opposite*): Two pages from one of Sarah Osborn's letters to Joseph Fish, dated May 3, 1759. Her letters were written on folio pages measuring 14 × 9 inches. Courtesy of the American Antiquarian Society.

his "dear sister" and assured her that she was always in his prayers. Over the years their friendship grew to include their families, and Osborn visited him and his wife Rebecca in Stonington. Mary and Rebecca, his two daughters, boarded in Newport in order to attend her school. "In my thoughts I am with you daily," she assured him, "and sometimes till thought itself is swallowed up and I am as it were forced to break off abruptly."[38] Even though they lived a day's ride apart, she felt as if they were linked together by their letters.

Notably absent from Sarah's correspondence—and from her writings as a whole—is her husband Henry. Sarah occasionally mentioned him in a letter or a diary entry, but he remains a shadowy and somewhat mysterious figure. Based on her brief references to him, however, it is clear that he shared her Christian faith and supported her even when ministers questioned whether she had gone "beyond her line." Perhaps her silence about him reflected his access to her writings. Knowing that he might read her manuscripts, she may have hesitated to write too much about him. Or perhaps she simply wanted to keep private her intimate relationship with her husband.

Osborn kept the letters that she received, storing them carefully, because they seemed to point towards the communion of saints, the unity of all Christians in Jesus. Even though her friends had their own distinctive stories, they shared so many of the same religious experiences that she felt as if they were tied together by invisible bonds of grace. When Sarah signed her letters "your sister in Christ," she meant her words literally. Someday, she believed, she would sing God's praises in heaven with her friends, and the love once expressed in their letters would last for all eternity. If anyone read their letters in the future, they would catch a small glimpse of the cloud of witnesses waiting beyond the grave.

Literary Influences

Sarah Osborn had little formal training as a writer, and because of her meager schooling, she never learned the rules of spelling, capitalization, or punctuation. Her manuscripts can be difficult to read because her sentences run into one another without any pause or break. Yet Osborn developed a forceful writing style by imitating the books that she admired the most, especially Puritan and evangelical memoirs and the King James Version of the Bible.

Osborn was a voracious reader. Since she had little money to spend on luxuries, she could not afford to buy the many tempting titles she saw in Newport's shops, and when she died in 1796, the inventory of her possessions listed only seven books: two copies of the Bible (a small octavo edition and a larger, more imposing quarto one), four unidentified "pamphlets," and the Reverend William Patten's *Christianity the True Theology, and Only Perfect Moral System in Answer to "The Age of Reason."* (Since Patten was the pastor of the Second Congregational Church of Newport, he probably gave her this book as a gift.)[39] Yet this small number of books did not reflect either the breadth or depth of Osborn's reading. Despite her poverty, she was able to satisfy her intense craving for books by begging friends and ministers to lend her interesting titles, dropping by neighbors' houses to read their books (as she did when she went to Deacon Nathaniel Coggeshall's house to read Daniel Defoe's *The Family Instructor,* an advice book about family relationships), and borrowing books from her church.[40] Her minister, Nathaniel Clap, had tried to spread "books of piety and virtue" through his congregation, and beginning in 1756 and continuing into the 1770s, the First Church of Newport bought "good books for the use of our Society."[41] These included Puritan classics like Nathaniel Morton's *New-England's Memoriall* (1669), a providential account of New England's founding, as well as popular evangelical titles like Samuel Hopkins's *Life and Character of the Late Reverend Mr. Jonathan Edwards.*[42] Although Osborn never mentioned going to the Anglican Church's free library, which was open to everyone in Newport regardless of denomination, she may have also borrowed books from their impressive collection.[43]

True to her Reformed heritage, Osborn enjoyed reading the works of seventeenth-century Puritan authors like John Bunyan, whose *Pilgrim's Progress* (1678) and *Grace Abounding to the Chief of Sinners* (1666) became newly popular during the revivals. Inspired by Bunyan's account of his spiritual pilgrimage, she was touched by his insistence that God had saved him despite his sinfulness. Like him, she expressed her longing to "lie low at the foot of grace while 'tis abounding to the chief of sinners."[44] Osborn also read James Janeway's *Token for Children* (1671), a book of children's conversion narratives that she frequently read aloud to her school, and Charles Drelincourt's *The Christian's Defence against the Fears of Death* (1651).[45] Though Drelincourt was a French Calvinist, his works were widely translated into English in the seventeenth and eighteenth centuries.

Osborn also pored over the new books that emerged out of the Awakening, including Jonathan Edwards's *Life of David Brainerd* (1749) and Samuel Buell's *A Faithful Narrative of the Remarkable Revival of Religion* (1766).[46] Reflecting the transatlantic reach of the revivals, her reading included works by British, American, French, and German authors. For example, she greatly admired Karl Heinrich von Bogatzky, a German hymn writer and Pietist who was influenced by Augustus Hermann Francke. In 1762 she spent the month of April copying down passages from Bogatzky's book *A Golden Treasury for the Children of God, Whose Treasure Is in Heaven* (1754) into her diary. "I bless thee that I dare appropriate this precious text," she wrote to God.[47] She also read James Hervey's *Theron and Aspasio; or, A Series of Dialogues and Letters, upon the Most Important and Interesting Subjects* (1755).[48] Hervey was a well-known British minister who had been a member of John and Charles Wesley's Holy Club at Oxford, but instead of following the Wesleys into a new Methodist church, he remained a Calvinist. After reading his book, Osborn commented, "Have been much pleased in finding man's nature and performances laid in the dust, their proper place."[49]

Perhaps because Osborn spent so many hours writing about her life, she particularly enjoyed reading other people's spiritual narratives. In addition to David Brainerd's published diaries and John Bunyan's memoir, she read the memoirs of Cotton Mather, Elizabeth Bury, and Hannah Housman. Even though she always judged herself to be inferior to these great men and women of faith, their stories strengthened her conviction that her own "evidences of grace" were real.[50]

Osborn was strongly influenced by these narratives. As she explained in her memoir, "I have always reaped much benefit myself by reading the lives and experiences of others. Sometimes they have been blessed to convince me of sin; sometimes to scatter doubts; and sometimes raised my affections into a flame." The "I" in her writings reflected not only her own personal experiences

but her immersion in a transatlantic culture of Puritan and evangelical literature. "When expressions has been warm," she wrote, "they have put me upon
imitating them as well as I could by breathing out my soul in like manner." And
"imitate" she certainly did. For example, when she lamented in her diary that
"my ways are, as Mr. Eliot expresses it, hedged up with thorns and grow darker
and darker," she explicitly borrowed a turn of phrase from Joseph Eliot's 1725
book, *A Copy of a Letter Found in the Study of the Reverend Mr. Joseph Belcher*.
She also repeated Eliot's evocative description of his sense of union with God:
"I lie becalmed in his bosom adoring his sovereignty, rejoicing in his infinite
justice, power, truth and faithfulness."[51] After reading David Brainerd's lament
that he was under a "fatal necessity" to break God's commandments, she reflected in her diary on "the corrupt bias of my nature whereby I am under such
a fatal necessity of grieving and offending God."[52] Though she refracted his
language through the lens of her own experiences, she clearly wanted to sound
as much like him as possible.

Because Sarah believed that souls (unlike bodies) had no gender, she did
not hesitate to use men's writings as a model for her own. When she read
Brainerd's diary, for example, she seems to have approached it as a universal
story about God's grace to sinners—a story that was not only about him, but
about her. Remembering one of her favorite books, James Janeway's *Invisibles, Realities, Demonstrated in the Holy Life and Triumphant Death of Mr. John
Janeway*, she prayed to God, "As thou hast with Moses, as thou was with
Joshua, as thou was with Janeway, so thou art with me."[53] Each Christian's life
might be different on the surface, but ultimately each told the same story about
human sinfulness and divine grace.

Yet because of her belief that God had ordained women to be subordinate
to men in the family, church, and state, Osborn took pains not to carry her
identification with male Christians too far, fearful of sounding too "masculine" or assertive. As Jonathan Edwards explained, men had been created to be
"strong in body and mind, with more wisdom, strength and courage," whereas
women were "weaker, more soft and tender, more fearful, and more affectionate, as a fit object of generous protection and defense."[54] Women were taught
to see themselves as "weak," "passionate," and in need of men's "protection"—
a euphemism for women's subordination to patriarchal authority. Although

Osborn could admire David Brainerd's relationship to God, she could not try to imitate him in other ways unless she was willing to appear radical or deviant. As a woman, she faced limits to the kind of Christian she could be.

Because of these entrenched ideas about women's subordination, Osborn cultivated a "feminine" voice in her writing. By reading books like Elizabeth Bury's *An Account of the Life and Death of Mrs. Elizabeth Bury* and Mrs. Housman's *The Power and Pleasure of the Divine Life*, she learned how to sound properly humble and deferential.[55] Like Bury, for example, an intelligent, accomplished woman who frequently referred to herself as "weak," "unworthy," or "a child," Osborn lamented her "weak mind" and described herself as "poor, weak and feeble."[56] Since Osborn and her closest friend, Susanna Anthony, often read each other's diaries and wrote spiritual letters to each other, she was also influenced by an example closer to home. Because their writings sound so much alike, two different archives, the Newport Historical Society in Newport, Rhode Island, and the Beinecke Library at Yale University, catalogued Anthony's manuscripts under Osborn's name. Yet even though Osborn certainly could have written the words, "I saw myself, as in myself, to be infinitely vile and wretched, utterly unable to help myself; [and] most unworthy that God should help me," the sentence was actually written by Anthony.[57]

Although Osborn never mentioned reading any of the sentimental novels that were popular during her day, they may have influenced her as well. She wrote in an emotional, fervent voice that was filled with the word "O." "O, subdue my passions," she wrote in a typical diary entry in 1753. And a day later, she wrote, "O, may I do much good in my day and generation."[58] She also experimented with flowery phrases worthy of a sentimental heroine. Imagining her death, for example, she wrote, "It can't be long before the welcome messenger death will have its commission, and then adieu to sin, adieu to Satan, adieu to interposing clouds. Farewell, alluring world; farewell, sleep. Ye shall never be able more to separate my God from me."[59] Since devotional writers like Elizabeth Rowe were also fond of sentimental language, Osborn may have been imitating religious books, but given how many other evangelical women read sentimental novels, it seems likely that she may have occasionally indulged in their pleasures as well. The daughters of two prominent ministers—Esther Edwards Burr, the daughter of Jonathan Edwards, and

Sarah Prince Gill, the daughter of Thomas Prince—corresponded about their reading of Samuel Richardson's novels *Pamela* and *Clarissa,* and even Susanna Anthony ruefully admitted to spending a day with a novel. "I blush, Lord; I am ashamed that such amusement has engrossed almost all my thoughts this day," she confessed in her diary in 1749. (She, too, may have been reading *Clarissa,* a tearjerker published in 1748 that was wildly popular on both sides of the Atlantic.)[60] Although most of the authors of sentimental novels were men, their focus on women's lives and struggles strongly appealed to a female audience. It probably is not a coincidence that Osborn and Anthony decided to exchange heartfelt letters to each other (despite living in the same neighborhood) at the same time as epistolary novels like Richardson's *Pamela* and *Clarissa* were selling thousands of copies in both England and America.

Of all the influences on Sarah Osborn's writing style, the greatest was the King James Version of the Bible. Consider, for example, a few sentences that Osborn wrote in 1757 when she was so poor that she did not know how she would support her family. Insisting that she had not lost her faith, she wrote, "But the God that has fed me all my life long does know what I need and will supply all my needs, too. Let Satan or unbelief say what they will, he never yet made me ashamed of my hope, nor he never will. He has said he will never leave me nor forsake me." Though this passage is brief, it is filled with biblical allusions. The words "the God that has fed me all my life" allude to Israel's blessing of his son Joseph after a life of many afflictions, including being sold into slavery. When Osborn applies these words to herself, she implies that she, too, has been blessed by God and is part of his covenanted people. Osborn also refers to Paul's comforting words to the Philippians, "My God shall supply all your need according to his riches in glory by Christ Jesus," and David's plea in the Psalms, "Uphold me according unto thy word, that I may live: and let me not be ashamed of my hope." Rewriting David's words to be more assertive, she testifies that she will *never* be ashamed of her hope or regret her faith in God's promises. Remembering one of her favorite passages in the Bible, she also quotes Paul's words to the Hebrews, "Let your conversation be without covetousness; and be content with such things as ye have: for he hath said, I will never leave thee, nor forsake thee." This passage, in turn, points to other biblical stories, including God's promise not to forsake Joshua.[61]

Sarah's facility with the Bible enabled her to connect her own experience to scripture. Her language is so biblical that it is sometimes hard to tell which words are her own. Because she understood her life as the biblical story in miniature, a story about sin and redemption, she wrote her diaries *over* the Bible.[62] Joseph, David, the Philippians—the Bible contained an abundant store of characters whose experiences had foreshadowed her own. She could be Jabez, who begged God to "keep me from the evil," or the Virgin Mary, who "magnified the Lord" in praise.[63] There was only one story—the biblical story—and all Christians lived within its pages. The Bible was the living, breathing word of God, the place where a hidden God revealed his will.

Osborn compared herself to many biblical figures, but several particularly captured her imagination, including Job, Habakkuk, Jacob, and Esther. As part of the Calvinist wing of the Reformed tradition, Osborn emphasized her sinfulness, and she closely identified with Job, who was afflicted by an all-powerful, inscrutable God. Like Job, she often denigrated herself as "vile" and a "worm," and she asked God to take pity on her weakness. During an illness, for example, she began a diary entry with Job's words, "O my God, as a father pities his children, so pity me." Like many other Christians, she also invoked Job when struggling to cope with overwhelming grief. After her son died, for example, she quoted Job's somber words of resignation, "The Lord gave and he has taken, and blessed be the name of the Lord."[64]

Osborn admired the prophet Habakkuk for the same reason she identified with Job. Even when God's mercy seemed to have failed, Habakkuk refused to give up hope. His lament was her own—"How long will I cry, and you will not hear?"—but, she hoped, so was his trust. "Grant me a Habakkuk's faith," she wrote in her diary, "that although all should be cut off, yet I may trust and rejoice in thee."[65]

Osborn's emphasis on her childlike dependence on God did not mean that she imagined herself as passive or helpless, and her allusions to Job and Habakkuk were coupled with references to Jacob, who wrestled with God for a blessing, and Esther, who saved her people from destruction. Even though Osborn attributed her agency to God, insisting that he "enabled" her to pray, she often portrayed herself as a "wrestling Jacob" who refused to let go of God until he granted her request.[66] She also imagined herself as Esther, who begged the king not to destroy the Jews. "Hold out the golden scepter," Sarah pleaded with God. "Let me touch the top, and grant my petition."[67]

In addition to Esther, Osborn was particularly drawn to the stories of three other women in the Bible: Hannah, Mary Magdalene, and the unnamed woman who had been plagued with an "issue of blood" for twelve years. In the nineteenth century, evangelical women would compare themselves to out-spoken female evangelists like Phoebe or Philip's four daughters, but Osborn identified most closely with biblical women who emphasized their humility.[68] Like Hannah, she had given birth to a child, Samuel, whom she had dedicated to God, and like Mary of Bethany, she longed to worship Christ at his feet. "Let me lean on his sacred breast and lie at his blessed feet," she wrote in her diary, and "bathe or wash them with my tears and wipe them with the hairs of my head."[69] Perhaps because of her health problems, she was also drawn to the story of the woman who had crept behind Jesus to touch the hem of his gar-ment, hoping to be cured of her hemorrhage. In response, he promised that she had been made "whole." Influenced by Calvinist images of humans as polluted with sin as well as gendered stereotypes of women as weak and un-clean, she imagined herself clinging to Jesus's hem in order to be healed of her "plague."[70] Writing was an act not of self-assertion, but self-abasement. Only by emptying herself could she make room for Christ, a fountain of overflow-ing love, to fill her.[71]

The result of Sarah's extensive reading was that she developed a writing style that reflected the narrative conventions of her world. When we read her words, we can hear the echoes of many different voices: Puritans examining themselves for signs of grace, sentimental novelists reflecting on the power of compassion, female authors lamenting their weakness, and evangelicals pro-claiming their rebirth in Christ. Most of all, we can hear the echoes of the Bible, the book that Osborn read virtually every day of her adult life. Even when she lost her eyesight and could no longer read, she asked friends and acquaintances to read the Bible aloud to her. By then she knew large parts of it by heart, speaking and writing its language as her own.

It is not clear who decided to preserve Osborn's writings, but they seem to have been passed around as devotional reading after her death in 1796. Several people wrote their names on the inside cover of her 1757 diary, including "Cabel J. Tenney" of Newport, Rhode Island, and "Miss Clara Allen" of Northampton, Massachusetts.[72] At some point in the nineteenth or early twentieth century, some of the owners of her manuscripts realized that they were too precious not to be preserved. Her memoir, diaries, and letters eventually ended up scattered in archives on the East Coast, including libraries in Rhode Island, Connecticut, Pennsylvania, Massachusetts, and New Hampshire.

Osborn had always hoped that her manuscripts would be read by future generations. On the cover of one of her diaries, she bequeathed her words to "the disposal of providence," hopeful that her story of transforming grace would live beyond her.[73] Remembering her own struggle to believe that God loved her, she wanted to encourage others not to give up hope, certain that if they read her writings, they would see that a mighty, compassionate God could triumph over their despair. Even in her darkest hours, God had never forsaken or abandoned her.

"My life," she testified at the end of her memoir, "has been a life of wonders."

A NOTE ON THE TEXT

THIS BOOK REPRINTS a selection of Sarah Osborn's manuscripts, including the full text of her memoir, more than twenty of her letters, and excerpts from her diaries. I have tried to make my transcriptions of her writings as accessible as possible without altering her style.

Osborn did not use punctuation (except for an occasional exclamation mark), and she capitalized words haphazardly. For the sake of clarity, I have added punctuation, capitalization, and paragraphing. Although I have chosen not to correct her grammar, I have modernized some of her words: for example, I have changed "hant" to "haven't," "het" to "heated," "oft" to "often," and "ant" to "is not" or "am not." In some places I have also silently filled in missing words in order to make the text more comprehensible. This is especially true in chapter 9, which includes selections from Osborn's 1767 diary. This manuscript is crumbling at its edges, and if I had indicated all of the instances in which I added the missing ends of words, the chapter would include hundreds of brackets. Throughout the manuscript, the words that I have added most frequently are "I," "so," "to," "of," "it," and "that." As a general rule, I have kept my additions to a minimum.

Unfortunately, Osborn crossed out many sentences and paragraphs in her writings, especially in her memoir. When I have been able to decipher her cross outs, I have included her original words in the text with a notation; otherwise I have used ellipses to indicate where words or lines are illegible.

Many of Osborn's writings include marginalia. I have indicated these marginal comments either in the text or in the notes.

Sometimes Osborn indicated the time of day that she wrote a diary entry or a letter. I have included these notations in the text whenever they appear.

Osborn was remarkably fluent in the Bible, and her writings are filled with thousands of biblical citations. When she calls attention to a scriptural verse that she quotes verbatim—for example, "Thee hast said, 'I will never leave thee nor forsake thee'"—I have placed quotation marks around the text, and I have included the scriptural reference in the endnotes. (Since there is significant repetition in the Bible, some quotations have multiple citations.) However, when Osborn paraphrases or alludes to biblical stories or verses, I have chosen not to use quotation marks, and I have not included the scriptural reference in the notes. Providing a full guide to all of Osborn's biblical citations would add many pages to this book. Those who are interested in identifying her biblical citations can see a full list of them at http://yalebooks.com/sarah-osborns-writings.

The majority of Osborn's writings collected in this book have been taken from her manuscripts. However, I have also used material from two collections of her writings that were published after her death: Samuel Hopkins's *Memoirs of the Life of Mrs. Sarah Osborn,* which reprinted extracts from her diaries, and Elizabeth West Hopkins's *Familiar Letters, Written by Mrs. Sarah Osborn and Miss Susanna Anthony,* which reprinted some of her correspondence with her closest friend. Since both Hopkins and his wife, Elizabeth West, seem to have edited Osborn's writings to conform to their view of an ideal Christian, I have reprinted material from their books only sparingly. But since they transcribed extracts from many of Osborn's diaries and letters that no longer survive, their books are an invaluable resource for her writings. Like me, Hopkins had to make difficult decisions about how to add punctuation, paragraphing, and capitalization to Osborn's manuscripts. Though I have preserved most of his choices, I have also made minor changes to his transcriptions in order to clarify Osborn's meaning.

Though I have kept the occasional exclamation points in Osborn's original manuscripts, I have chosen to delete them from the diary entries copied from Hopkins's 1799 edition. Hopkins added large numbers of exclamation marks to Osborn's diary entries, perhaps to make her sound more fervent. Unfortunately, the effect is to make her sound overwrought. I have also chosen to remove some of the exclamation marks that appear in the 1755 edition of Osborn's published tract, *The Nature, Certainty, and Evidence of True Christianity*. Although the original letter does not survive, it is likely that either the editor (Thomas Prince) or the publisher (Samuel Kneeland) added the numerous exclamation points. Interestingly, the 1764 edition of her tract includes fewer exclamation points than the earlier edition.

Unlike Hopkins, who sometimes published only a section of a particular diary entry in his *Memoirs of the Life of Mrs. Sarah Osborn*, I have chosen to transcribe the full text of each entry.

I have included brief introductions in each chapter to contextualize Osborn's writings, but readers who want to know more about her life and her beliefs should consult my companion volume, *Sarah Osborn's World: The Rise of Evangelical Christianity in Early America*.

The locations of all of Osborn's manuscripts can be found in the appendix.

Sarah Osborn's Collected Writings

ONE

That Precious Promise, 1742

THE EARLIEST PIECE *of Sarah Osborn's writing that survives is a letter to the Reverend Eleazar Wheelock that she wrote after hearing him preach in Newport. Wheelock (1711–99) was a Congregationalist minister who later became famous as the founder of Dartmouth College.*

In this letter, Osborn thanks Wheelock for convincing her to confess a sin that she had committed against her parents. In 1731, when she was seventeen years old, she had stolen thirty pounds from them after they had refused to give her the customary "marriage portion." They had hoped to prevent her from marrying Samuel Wheaten, a sailor, but she had disobeyed them, and it was not until hearing Wheelock's 1742 sermon that she decided to confess her theft. By then both Samuel and her father had died: Samuel in 1734 of unknown causes at sea, and her father in 1739 of tuberculosis. Her mother, however, was still alive, and Sarah pleaded for her forgiveness.

This letter was written on the day she married Henry Osborn, a tailor. He was a fifty-seven-year-old widower with three sons—Edward, eighteen, Henry, seventeen, and John, fourteen. She was twenty-nine years old, and her son, Samuel, was ten.

Sarah Osborn to Eleazar Wheelock, May 5, 1742

Most dear and venerable Sir,

I have but just opportunity out of gratitude to return you thanks for all your labors of love and to let you know that the glories of God did not suffer them to be lost on me. O, dear Sir, you little thought what a wound you gave me when you stated some particular cases and adjured conscience to do its office in your sermon on Tuesday afternoon. Mine convinced me of concealing a sin I had many years been guilty of against my parents and bitterly bewailed before God, but pride, fear of making a breach that could not be made up, and hopes that God did not require it of me prevented me from confessing it to them. But blessed be God, as soon as you told me I was guilty of that sin, so that day, notwithstanding my lamenting it before God, he gave me strength immediately to resolve to confess it, whatever difficulties it exposed me. For I humbly hope had I been sure it would have taken life itself, I would not have dared to conceal it any longer. I was made willing to sell all I had in the world to make restitution. But my dear mother, instead of being angry, received her returning prodigal with the utmost tenderness, and I trust the separating wall has been broken down between Christ and my soul more than ever. Surely I have had more constant sweet communion with Christ than ever before.

O, may not I hope that in me is satisfied that precious promise "All things shall work together for good to those that love God."[1] O that I could live more to his glory. O, for an eternity to praise that God that is so good to so vile a monster in sin as I am. O, I long to be more like him and so be swallowed up in love. O, when shall it ever be that the things that are in part shall be done away? When shall I be free from sin, the worst of evil? I long to be dissolved and to be with Christ, but this power I am willing to wait his time, for I may yet live to his glory here.

Dear Sir, I would acquaint you that God in his providence has once more blessed me with a companion, which I have reason to believe is a Christian, one whom I can go to the house of God with, and set down with the Redeemer at his table with. I was satisfied I was doing God's will in this weighty affair by these words, when with great agony and vehemency of soul, pleading with God to let me know by some token what would be most for his glory, even these: "Go forward; fear not, for I am with thee." They come with so much power and sweetness that I was convinced it was an immediate answer of prayer, and taking my Bible to look for the words further to confirm it, I opened to these: "Why criest thou to me? Speak to the children of Israel that they go forward."[2]

O Sir, I know not how to write to you without telling you how wonderfully God has of late indulged such a worthless, ungrateful wretch as I, that have abused so many thousands of former mercies. Once of late, more enlarged than usual in pleading with God for some comfortable promise that I might plead in behalf of my dear child, this was given me: "All thy children shall be taught of God and great shall be the peace of thy children."[3] This is so large I can plead it not only for my own, but in behalf of the dear offspring of my yoke fellow. He has three sons.

O dear Sir, besiege the throne of grace for me that God may make me faithful to each soul of them as well as to my dear companion. One more remarkable answer was, when begging that I might carry no guilt with me, whether sins of youth or others, this promise was constantly set home for many days: "Thou shalt forget the shame of thy youth and shalt not remember the reproach of thy widowhood any more."[4]

Nine of the most serious of our society with myself set apart a day of fasting on my account. We experienced much of the presence of God with us. Satan still rages dreadfully here.

I long to see you, dear Sir. Pray write to me if possible. I would have wrote more particular about others but the bearer waits, so beg your acceptance of these.

With wishing you the best of blessings in the dear Lord Jesus, and begging your prayers, I subscribe with humble duty,

Your sincere though unworthy friend and sister in Christ,

Sarah Osborn

TWO

A Memoir, 1743

QUILLS, A PENKNIFE *for sharpening them, ink wells, stacks of foolscap paper wait-ing to be cut into squares, a portable writing desk. Besides her Bible, an imposing quarto edition, these were among Sarah Osborn's most cherished possessions. The act of writing stood at the heart of her devotional life, helping her to draw closer to God.*

Most of Osborn's writing took place in diaries and letters, but in 1743, at the age of twenty-nine, she decided to undertake the ambitious task of writing a mem-oir, narrating the story of her entire life from birth to adulthood. Though she may have been daunted by the challenge of placing her experiences into a single, coher-ent plot, she seems to have wanted to come to a deeper understanding of her spiritual pilgrimage. How had she arrived at her life in 1743? What was God's plan for her?

Osborn wrote her memoir in the wake of two events that had changed her life: her jubilant decision during the revivals of the Great Awakening to commit herself completely to Christ and, more painfully, a financial crisis that forced her and her husband, Henry, to declare bankruptcy in 1743. Torn between conflicting feelings of joy and loss, she struggled to understand how God was guiding her. By writing a memoir, she hoped to remind herself of who she really was: not simply a twenty-nine-year-old woman facing destitution, but a beloved child of God.

Osborn began her memoir by insisting that she was "impartial in this work, declaring the truth and nothing but the truth," but she inevitably made choices about which stories to include and which to leave out. Instead of recording her whole life as it was actually lived, her memoir reveals the "self" that she chose to share—and on a deeper level, the self that she wanted to be.[1] She hoped that writing the story of her life would help to strengthen her new identity as a Christian. By fixing her identity on a page, she tried to bring her old self into line with the new person she had become and, even more important, to determine the self she would be in the future. She never wanted to forget that a loving God had redeemed her, claiming her as his own. "Thou art mine," she testified in her memoir, quoting from the Bible, and "I am thine."

Whenever Osborn was tempted to doubt the reality of her conversion or to question God's goodness and mercy, she read her narrative again, determined not to forget the ultimate meaning of her life. "This book I have reread again and again," she wrote on the cover.

Since Osborn seems to have returned to her memoir many times with a quill in her hand, the surviving text of her manuscript is complex and multilayered. Although she let most of her words stand on the page, she also crossed out sections, squeezed new words into her sentences, and added comments to the margins. Without changing her main plot of sin and redemption, she tried to make small changes to influence how her story was interpreted. For example, she crossed out two long descriptions of marriage proposals, perhaps embarrassed by the fact that she had considered marrying men who were not committed Christians. Although it is possible to read some of her crossed-out words with patience and a magnifying glass, other passages are crossed out so darkly that they cannot be deciphered.

Even in places where Osborn did not cross out sentences, she seems to have feared that she had revealed too much. Next to the account of her suicidal crisis, for example, she asked in the margin, "Is it duty to let this criminal affair stand recorded?"

If Osborn was concerned about her self-presentation, it was because of her hope that others might read her memoir after her death, especially those in search of Christ's grace and forgiveness. Every word of her memoir was aimed at glorifying God, and she dreamed of a day when her description of his power and compassion would inspire others to seek him. As she testified on virtually every page of her memoir, she had been "a monster in sin" who did not deserve his mercy, but his blinding love had eclipsed her sins.

Of all the stories that Osborn could have told about her life, she thought that only one mattered. She had been born again, transformed by God's irresistible grace.

Having been for some years under strong inclinations to write something of what I can remember of the dealings of God with my soul from a
child, hoping it may consist with the glory of God—at which I trust, through
grace, I sincerely aim—and the good of my own soul as a means to stir up
gratitude in the most ungrateful of all hearts, even mine, to a glorious and
compassionate Savior for all his benefits towards so vile a monster in sin as I
am, and for the encouragement of any who may providentially light on these
lines after my decease, to trust in the Lord and never despair of his mercy,
since one so stubborn and rebellious as I have through the sovereign riches
of free grace obtained it, [I have begun this memoir]. But O, let all tremble
at the thoughts of abusing a savior so lest God should say, "let them alone";
"they shall never enter into my rest."[2]

Lord, humble me for my base ingratitude and help me by affording me
the assistance and influences of thy blessed Spirit that I may be impartial in
this work, declaring the truth and nothing but the truth and, in all that, have
a single eye to thy glory. O, for Jesus's sake, suffer me not to do anything that
will tend to puff up self. O, remove all spiritual pride and keep me low at the
foot of Jesus. Fill me with admiring and adoring thoughts of thee, O God—
the Father God, the Son, and God the Holy Ghost—who hast so wonderfully contrived and wrought out my redemption. And though thou hast
through infinite wisdom hid these things from the wise and prudent, yet thou
hast revealed them to babes and even to me, the most ignorant and vile of all
creatures, whose deep-rooted enmity against thee and thy laws broke out into
action as soon as I was capable of any.

The first I can remember of actual sins which I was guilty of was telling
a lie.[3] But that text of scripture often rung in my ears: "All liars shall have
their portion in the lake that burns with fire and brimstone."[4] I was frequently
under the strivings of the Spirit of God, pressing me to forsake sin, repent,
and to perform duties, but sometimes found them very burdensome to me,
such as praying and saying many other good things, which I was frequently
taught. Blessed be God, however, for such instructions. *Sometimes I loved
them and was much affected with them,* but my corruptions prevailed dreadfully. I remember I partook of an angry, ungrateful temper stirring in me,
especially when corrected by my mother, but must acknowledge to the

glory of God that he preserved such a tenderness of conscience in me that if at any time my mother convinced me that she did it because it was her duty for my sin against God, I could bear it patiently and willingly, yea thankfully.[5]

Thus I continued till I was about seven or eight years old, when my father, being in New England, my mother put me to boarding school in a place called Peckham about three miles from London, where everything was delightsome to me.[6] I was constantly taught things that was religious and they all become sweet to me, so that I verily thought I lived a heaven upon earth. O, how sweet was Sabbaths, and for secret prayer I would not have omitted it for all the world. Nay, the sin appeared so monstrous that I durst not lie down without it, for I should have been afraid the devil would have fetched me if I had; it seemed such a dreadful thing.[7] I was frequently much enlarged in that duty and used to weep much when pleading for the pardon of sins and for the confessing of them and for an interest in Christ. The name of Christ was sweet to me, and sin more hateful.

I often used to reprove others when guilty of it, but once in particular, I remember when I was at Hertford, where my grandmother lived, and my brother with her, a little before I came to New England. My brother did something that I thought was wicked, and I reproved him sharply for it, but was much perplexed with this text of scripture: "Thou hypocrite, first cast out the beam out of thine own eye and then thou shalt see clearly to cast the mote out of thy brother's eye."[8] But at last told my grandmother of it, who encouraged me to go on, telling me it was my duty so to do, and if I was faithful God would bless me and love me.

So I continued for awhile, as I thought, to delight in the ways of holiness, but alas, alas, how soon was it over. My goodness was like the morning cloud and early dew, which soon passeth away. For when I was in my ninth year, my father sent for my mother and I to come into New England to him, and on board the ship I lost my good impressions and grew vile so that I could play upon the Sabbath then.[9] But I was convinced of that sin by an accident that befell me, or rather what was ordered by infinite wisdom to that end.[10] For as I was busy a boiling something for my baby [a doll], I fell into the fire with my right hand and burned it all over, which I presently thought was just upon me for playing on a Sabbath day. And I was ashamed and sorry I had done so.

But after this I remember no particular conviction for some years, but ebbed and flowed: sometimes quite careless and then more diligent in performance of prayer. I had always, as I thought, a great love for any that I thought was good people, *especially ministers.* My very heart would leap for joy when I could see or come nigh enough to touch them, and thought I could do anything in the world to serve them.[11]

About two years and a half after we came to Boston, my parents moved to Freetown and I with them, and when I was about thirteen years old my mother came from thence to Rhode Island and went to visit Mr. Clap, who gave her a little book of spiritual songs for me, and bid her give it to me and tell me that it came from one that was a hearty well-wisher to my soul.[12] These words immediately seized me and filled me with shame, to think that one I never knew should take such care of my precious soul and I so careless myself. And from that minute, I thought I dearly or gratefully loved Mr. Clap and longed to sit under his ministry.[13]

I was then for some time under strong convictions. Had such a sense of the hardness of my heart that I often thought it was impossible for me to be sufficiently awakened by any ordinary means.[14] Prayed God would do anything with me, though ever so terrible, so that I might be drove from my evil courses and turned to God. Some change, I thought, there must be wrought in me or I should never get to heaven, but after what manner I knew not.

However, I resolved to persist in a way of duty, as I called it, and to forsake my sins and lead a new life. But fool that I was, I made resolutions in my own strength and built upon my own works and so soon fell again. O, amazing grace that God should spare such a wretch as I, such an abuser of mercy.

After this I found myself dead and to have no heart, as I thought, to pray; nor no sweetness in it when I did. Then, O, how I longed for the return of God's Spirit, imagining it was withdrawn from me. Sometimes I should agonize in prayer and plead with God that he would return to me by his Spirit once more, but was often answered by these words, "My Spirit shall not always strive with men."[15] Then I would beg and promise that if God would try me this once I would never grieve or resist his Spirit again. O, wretch that I was, thus to lie to the glorious God who was then striving with me to bring me to his Son, for I did—I did—quench his motions, and soon forgot my promises. O, deceitful, desperately wicked heart. Who can know it? Lord, I am amazed at thy patience that I am out of hell.

Sometime after this, contrary to my parents' commands, I got into a canoe to paddle about and could not get on shore again. It being in the night, I expected no other but to be drowned.[16] Once I attempted to get out and pull the canoe on shore, but tried first if I could reach the bottom with my paddle, and finding I could not, durst not venture. Then I could see no possibility of escaping death, so I kneeled down and prayed, and all my former convictions revived, and the sin of disobedience to my parents especially appeared odious. I thought it was just with God to bring me into this distress for it, and with great vehemency and self-abhorrence confessed and aggravated my sins before God, pleading for an interest in the blood of Christ and for pardon for his sake for that [sin of disobedience] with all my other sins. And while I was thus praying I felt a secret joy, verily believing that I was forgiven and that Christ had loved me with an everlasting love and that I should be happy with him, and longed for the time. I was immediately resigned, as I thought, to the will of God—quite willing to die, and willing to live, begging that God would dispose of me as most consisted with his glory.[17] And after I had thus resigned myself, as I thought, soul and body, into the hands of God to do with me as seemed him good, I was as calm and serene in the temper as ever in my life.[18] But at last bethought myself that self-preservation was a great duty, and therefore I ought to try to get on shore.[19]

So I hollered as loud as I could to the neighbors, who with much difficulty heard and came to me some hours after. There was not another canoe within two or three miles, so I had drove with the tide some miles first up and then down the river. How it would have been with my soul if God had taken me out of the world at that time, he only knows. Some *Christians* have thought the change was then wrought and I should have been happy.[20]

After this I was more diligent in pursuing, as I thought, the ways of holiness in the means God had appointed, and watchful against sin.[21] My life was sweet and pleasant. I had great enlargements in duties, but at length grew cold again. O, ungrateful soul, to forget such a remarkable deliverance from death.

The next winter I was as wonderfully preserved. The weather being exceeding cold, the river was froze so that people, horses, and carts went over. But while it was hard and slippery I durst not venture on it for fear of falling, but after a great thaw so that the ice looked quite black, I—contrary to my parents' orders again, they being from home—went quite over to the other side, which was a mile. But the tide was rising so I could not get on shore, and when I looked round me I could see nothing but great holes as big as houses or larger—some of them. There was no way for me but to go straight back again, which I did, but the water was almost over shoes all the way, and the ice, it seemed to me, bent every step I took.[22] And when I got back, the water was so risen I was much beset to get on shore, and it was dusk of the evening. But at last, with much difficulty, found a strip of ice that, as a narrow bridge, reached the shore, and I got off.[23] But when I was landed and see the imminent danger I had exposed myself to by my folly and presumption, it made me tremble exceedingly. I presently thought again how just God would have been if I had been drowned for my disobedience to my parents, and wondered at his patience in sparing me.[24] But do not remember that it left any abiding impressions, so great was my woeful stupidity.[25]

As to the river, the wind rise [*sic*] presently and blew very hard, but south, so that it—with the tide—broke it up, so that before bedtime there was not a bit of ice of any bigness to be seen within sight of our house, which stood almost by the river. I am amazed when I consider how miraculously God preserved me, a poor sinful worm, so unworthy of the least mercy.

The next March we moved to Dighton, where we lived one year.[26] I remember of but one awakening in that time and that was by hearing of the death of one of my old associates in Freetown, a young girl about my age. Then again I was astonished at God's patience in sparing me alive and out of hell. Then I renewed my resolutions to lead a new life, but instead of that, in the spring we moved to Rhode Island, where I soon got into company and was full of vanity. But conscience would not let me be easy.

One day—O that I could mention it with weeping eyes and a bleeding heart and after such a manner that glory may redound for the glorious God, while I with shame confess my monstrous, God-provoking, and hell-deserving sin. My mother's being very angry with me and, as I thought, for no reason at all, my passion was raised to a dreadful degree, but durst not vent it by saying anything to her. I reflected upon many such seasons and thought myself exceedingly wronged. Satan took the advantage of me at this time, and tempted me to believe that there was no one upon earth lived so miserable a life as I did. *Neither was hell worse.* I had therefore better take away my life and so know the worst at first, for that hell would be my portion sooner or later, for my sins was so great they could never be pardoned.

At first I started at the temptation and thought it a dreadful thing to murder myself, but Satan hurried me on till at last—monster that I was—I yielded so far as to think how to accomplish so hellish a design. And being in a garret, there was seemingly a voice, which said, "there's a rope and there's a place," which was one of the crosspieces in the roof. "What hinders you now?" And being thus drove by the violence of temptation and my own corruptions, I thought to do it.[27]

But while in the utmost hurry, anguish, and distress, these words came to me with great power, "Resist the devil and he will flee from you. Draw nigh to God and he will draw nigh to you."[28] O! How then did I fall down prostrate on the floor and adore the infinite goodness of a compassionate God, and when I had with floods of tears returned thanks for so great a deliverance and, as I thought, committed myself to God's keeping, I came down rejoicing and perfectly calm in my temper.[29]

O, let parents be entreated to be very careful that they don't provoke their children to wrath by being too severe to them, since a subtle adversary will take the advantage of such seasons. And O, that children, for whose sakes I write these lines, would be advised to take warning by this awful circumstance and submit to and obey their own parents or other superiors in all things right, and not suffer passion to rise in their breasts, lest they should provoke God to permit Satan to suit a temptation to their condition and leave them to theirselves to comply with it so as to be past all recovery, as I had certainly done if left to myself a few moments longer.[30] And everyone has the

Osborn's memoir includes an account of a suicidal crisis (see the bottom right) written in large, agitated handwriting. She seems to have been distressed while remembering her temptation to kill herself. In the margin she asked, "Is it duty to let this criminal affair stand recorded?" Courtesy of Beinecke Rare Book and Manuscript Library, Yale University.

same seeds of corruption in them through the woeful fall of our first parents and the same criminal inability to help themselves, however they think they would not do so.[31] O, that all might learn to know that it is all owing to restraining and special grace that they are kept from running on with violence to sin while they have a fountain of corruption in them that is ever flowing, and a subtle devil who is like a roaring lion seeking whom he may devour.

But I would not be understood to justify myself in this or any of my vile sins. No, far be it from me, for if God had withheld that grace he was no ways bound to give and left me to have wrought my own ruin—soul and body—to all eternity, he and his throne had been spotless forever, and his justice had been glorified in my damnation. But O, astonishing grace! He has glorified his mercy in making me the monument of it without disparagement to justice.[32] Lord, let this consideration humble me to the dust before thee, and fill me with gratitude—flaming love, too—and praise of thee, my God and King, who like a mighty conqueror appeared for me in the mount of difficulty and put to flight the grand enemy of my soul's salvation. O, help me, dearest Lord, forever to put my trust in thee.

After this my life was more sweet to me, and I had a great desire to forsake *all sin* and to comply with every commanded duty. I longed to join to the church but thought I was unworthy. O surely, I thought, I thirsted for communion with God in that ordinance of the Lord's Supper and used to think if I was once come up to *that,* it would certainly be a restraint upon me, so that I should not dare to sin as others. And when I stayed to see the ordinance administered, I used to think I could give all this world. I was fit my spirit would even sink within me for the longing I had. Sometimes I should weep so that I could not conceal it.

One Sabbath, I went to hear Mr. Clap preach at his own house where I inclined to go constantly, but my parents went to the other meeting and did not care I should go from them, so I went but seldom.[33] But at this time there was a girl of about fourteen years old baptized, which so affected me that I could hardly refrain crying right out in meeting, when I thought how I had broke my covenant engagements which my parents had made with God in my behalf in my infancy, and so long abused so great a privilege as being a child of the covenant, and she, who had not had so much done for her, should now come to desire it herself. I see, as I thought, such a beauty in her that I loved her entirely and wished to be as good as I thought she was.[34]

I made new resolutions to live answerable to the mercies I had received, but being made in my own strength, I soon fell again. I thought I trusted in God and used frequently in time of trials to go and pour out my complaints to him, thinking he was my only support, but I durst not now be positive or really conclude that I knew what it was to put my trust in God, for my conduct after this seems so inconsistent with grace that I durst not say I had one spark, but rather think I was only under a common work of the Spirit— though sometimes I think I had true grace, though very weak. God only knows how it was. O, that he would enable me now to give diligence to make my calling and election sure that I may not be deceived in a matter of so great importance.

But to go on, after all this—O, that with deep humility of soul, with sorrow and shame, I could speak of it—I relapsed again and was full of nothing but vanity. I used to sing songs, dance, play at cards with company as oft I could get opportunities.[35] And kept company with a young man some-thing against my parents' will. But that was owing to false reports raised of him, for at first they liked him, but while they was angry with me they often threatened to give me nothing, which I thought was very hard, for, I thought, I had been very diligent to work to help get it.[36] So was tempted by Satan and wicked companions to believe it was no sin to take anything I wanted, for it was my own by right, my parents having no other child here but me. And accordingly I did—in trifling things to the value of thirty pounds total as I cast them up afterwards—and was exceedingly perplexed when I found how much they amounted to.[37]

And should have restored them all again, but those who had persuaded me to take them and had kept them for me pleaded with me not to do it, for I must discover them and it would be base ingratitude in me so to do, when they had done it all for my good. And more than that, it would make a breach between my parents and me that would never be made up, for they knew they would make me a public example. And still insisted upon it: it was *no sin*. So, at last, all these things prevailed over my resolutions, and I kept them [the goods] with this thought: that if ever I was able, I would make restitution. But it has cost me thousands of tears since.

O, let children tremble at the thought of doing any such thing, and be entreated to shun all such company as will persuade them to it, for the scripture plainly says: "He that robs his father or his mother and says it's no sin is a companion of a destroyer, and he that wasteth his father is a son that causeth shame."[38] Proverbs 28:24 and 19:26.

But to go on: after marriage I made resolutions that I would lead a new life, flattering myself that *then* I should not have the hindrances as I then had.[39] I used bitterly to reflect upon myself when I gave myself liberty to be merry, for though I appeared outwardly so, I had no real pleasure but still put off repentance, or an entire breaking off from vanity, till a more convenient season, and so resisted the Spirit of God.[40] O, how just hadst thou been if thou hadst left me entirely to myself, and if thou hadst, nothing would have been too bad for such a vile wretch as I to have committed. But blessed be God that withheld me from such sins against strangers as would have brought me to open justice and exposed myself and family to disgrace and shame.

In prospect of time I was married, being in my eighteenth year, October the 21st, 1731, and went with my husband the first winter to see his friends in the country, where I stayed almost five months and was almost all the time under strong convictions.[41] The sin of disobedience appeared monstrously odious to me, so that I thought I could have laid down my very life to have recompensed my parents for the wrong I had done them. Then that sin was more clear to me than ever before. I could no longer flatter myself with hopes that it was no sin, but in bitter agonies of soul pleaded with God to forgive me for it, and to give me a competence of this world so that I might make restitution. I was not yet convinced fully that it was my duty to confess it to my parents except I could restore what I had taken, which was then out of my power.

O, how I should sweat and tremble for fear my convictions should wear off again, and plead with God to set home strong convictions and *never, never* suffer them to cease till they ended in a sound and saving conversion—till I knew and was sure that I had a saving interest in Jesus Christ and was freely forgiven for his sake. And this was the substance of my frequent prayers ever after, when I could pray at all with earnestness, that I might never rest more till I was sure my peace was made with God.

From this time, I had a hope again at times that Christ was mine, but it was some years after before it pleased God to answer it fully by giving me an assurance of it. But then again I longed for the ordinance of the Lord's Supper, though sometimes shocked by that awful text, "He that eateth and drinketh unworthily eateth and drinketh damnation to himself."[42] But resolved at last if I lived to get home I would venture *in obedience to Christ's command* and throw myself into the arms of mercy. I longed to commemorate the death and sufferings of a crucified Jesus.

I thought nothing should tempt me to delay any longer, but O, my sinful soul, must I yet add to the number of backslidings? Could not the time passed suffice that thou hadst provoked a compassionate God? Was it not enough—more than enough—that thou hadst so long rebelled against a glorious Christ and grieved his blessed Spirit? But must I go on again after such awakenings as these, when one would have thought it was impossible? But, O, deceitful heart: thou didst. Thou didst forsake thy God again.

Lord, I blush and am ashamed when I remember my notorious ingratitude. O, break this heart of flint, dearest Lord, that it may melt into tears of contrition. And never suffer me to forgive myself because thou hast forgiven me.

After I came home, I met with much affliction in many respects. My parents are more set against me than ever, but it was not for anything that

. . . .

[*Osborn crossed out seven lines here.*]

In short, it seemed to me that the whole world was in arms against me. I thought I was the most despised creature living upon earth. I used to pray to God in secret to relieve me but did not, as I ought, see his hand in permitting it so to be as a just punishment for my vile sins, and therefore was not humbled under it as I ought, but let nature rise and acted very imprudently in many respects.

I was then with child and often lamented that I was like to bring a child into such a world of sorrow, but sometimes found a disposition to dedicate my babe to God while in the womb and did so at all seasons of secret prayer.[43] And after it was born, my husband being at sea, I could not rest till I had solemnly given it up to God in baptism. I met with many trials in my lying in, it being an extreme cold season. My child was born on October the 27th day of 1732.

[*Osborn crossed out four-and-a-half lines here.*][44]

The next spring my husband returned, and I thought I had been like to have had another child, which made me very sorry, but while I was pondering about it, these thoughts came into my mind: How do I know but I may bring forth an heir of Christ's kingdom and one that might advance his glory and interest in the world? This peradventure filled me with so much satisfaction that I thought I could endure anything in the world if it might be so, and though it was a considerable time by reason of indisposition of body before I was undeceived, yet I never once wished it to be otherwise. However, God for wise ends otherwise determined.

My husband went to sea again, but died in November of the year 1733. I was then in my twentieth year. The news of my husband's death came to me the first of April after, and I was prepared the evening before to receive it by being more than ordinary exercised in my thoughts about spiritual things. And this text in Hebrews was continually in my mind: "How shall we escape if we neglect so great salvation?"[45] This put me upon pleading with God that I might not be found amongst the neglecters of it. I went to bed in a house all alone, my child being at my father's, and about eleven or twelve o'clock at night was waked to hear the heavy news.

But God wonderfully appeared for my support. I see his hand and was enabled to submit with patience to his will. I daily looked around me to see how much heavier God's hand was laid on some others than it was on me, where they was left with a great many children and much involved in debt, and I had but one to maintain and, though poor, yet not so involved. Others, I see, had their friends snatched from them by sudden accidents. The consideration of these things, together with the thoughts of what I deserved, stilled me, so that though the loss of my companion, whom I dearly loved, was great, yet the veins of mercy I see running through all my afflictions was so great likewise that, with Job, I could say, "The Lord gave and the Lord has taken, and blessed be the name of the Lord."[46]

I had then the promises of a widow's God to plead and seemed to cast myself more immediately upon his care, verily believing, as I thought, he would provide for me with my fatherless babe, for whom I oft pleaded for covenant blessings to be bestowed on him since he had been cast upon God from the womb.[47] O, how much comfort do those parents lose that never gave their children up to God in baptism in their infancy, and how sad for children themselves to be deprived of the privilege of pleading with God for covenant blessings. My being dedicated to God in my infancy always put an argument into my mouth to beg of God that I might not cut myself off since I was a child of the covenant: from a child, given to him in baptism.

But to go on: as before this affliction, every one seemed to be enemies to me, so now from that time all became friends. My parents used me very tenderly, and God inclined everyone that knew me to be kind to me. My brother was come into New England, and being a single man, we went to housekeeping together. But in three months after, he married, and I soon found it would not do to live as before, and began to be thoughtful how I should do. I could see no way at all how I could get a living. All doors seemed to be shut. But I verily believed that God would point out a way for me, and accordingly the very day I came to a resolution to move as soon as I could, a stranger to my case that kept a school a little way off, came to me and told me she only waited for a fair wind to go to Carolina, and if it would suit me I should have her chamber, scholars and all together, which I joyfully accepted. Thus the widow's God remarkably provided for me. This was November the 19th, 1734.

I was then placed in a family that discovered a great deal of affection for me and, in all respects, used me as tenderly as if I had been a near relation. It pleased God the next May to lay his afflicting hand on me by a sharp humor that broke out in my hands so that for three months every finger I had was wrapped up in plasters, and could help myself but very little. And under the doctor's hands in the fall, I was taken with violent fits and was quite deprived of sense by them five days. I was blistered almost all over by the doctor and my hands and arms was all raw from my fingers' ends up above my elbows and a great fever.

But all my friends was exceeding kind to me, and those in the house took care of me and my children, too, so that my school was not broke up till I was able to take care of it myself again. But my fits, the humor, continued at times very violent for some years, and indeed, still returns at some seasons, but all this time of illness God wonderfully provided for me. I wanted for none of the comforts of life; neither was I cast down, for his mercy held me up.

Once, I remember, after this I was more than ordinarily concerned about my rent, the time drawing nigh that it was due, and I could see no way that I could possibly get it. But went that evening to visit my mother, who told me as soon as I came in that she was glad to see me, for a gentlewoman had been with her to get me to make her two shirts, which seemed very remarkable to me. And accordingly I did, and had the money to a penny the day my rent was due, which was the time she set for them to be done—and that made it so much the more remarkable.

One day after this, I was sitting very melancholy. I had not one penny in the world and knew not where to get one morsel of victuals, but thought at last: God would find out some way or other for me. And accordingly the very minute I thought so, one come to the door from a stranger that never sent me anything before, with a plate heaped full of chicken pie—enough to serve me for two or three dinners, which so overcame me with a sense of God's goodness that I knew not how to contain myself. The many instances of God's remarkable hand of providence in ordering my temporal affairs is innumerable.

But O, vile wretch, after all this I grew slack again and got into a cold, lifeless frame. As I grew better in bodily health, my soul grew sick. I daily laid up a stock for repentance.

[*Osborn crossed out seventeen lines here.*][48]

But at length, through rich grace, I was again convinced of my stupidity and began to be more diligent in attending the means of grace, but found I could not profit by the word preached. Nothing reached my heart, but all seemed but skin deep, and the more I went to meeting the more I found it so. Then I began to think I must take some other course.[49]

In November of the year 1735 I went to [the Anglican] church. The family I lived with, high church folks, though I cannot say they persuaded me to it, bade till I went with them.[50] And I seemed to be much affected both with the manner of worship and the sermons, too, as I thought, and from thence concluded it was my duty to go where I was most affected. On Christmas day I stayed to see them receive the sacrament, and thought I would join with them next time, resolving to lead a new life. I was more diligent in the performance of duties and generally wept much when I performed them.[51]

[*Osborn crossed out thirteen lines here.*]

Thanks be to God that these did not suffer me to rest here, though I thought I was in the way of duty. N.B.: absence of thought was my infirmity.[52]

[*Osborn crossed out four more sentences here.*][53]

I had now gone to church about seven weeks, but the latter day night after Christmas I went to visit my mother, who after some usual questions begun with me thus: I hear, daughter, you are turned church woman.[54] I told her I was not come to a full resolution yet, but thought it was my duty to go where I was most affected. But upon enquire, could give her no rational account what it was that affected me, but seemed as ignorant as a mere babe. We had a great deal of discourse (which is needless to mention), but at last my mother asked me if I had anything to object against the principles I had been brought up in. I answered no: as for that, there was but little or no essential difference.[55] Then she asked me if it was because I thought that those I was about to join to lived more circumspect and agreeable to the rules of the gospel than the Presbyterians did. But I could not say it was. All the plea I could make was this: that I could not profit by the preaching I had sat under. Then she asked me what was become of Mr. Clap, whom I used to admire so much. I knew not what to say then, for I had been so bewildered that I had forgot him as much as if I had never had any value for him.[56]

When she perceived I was silent, she said to me thus: "Child, I would have you seriously consider what you are about to do, for it is my opinion you are under a strong delusion, and as sure as you turn church woman *without knowing upon what grounds you turn, so sure you will turn reprobate.*"[57] These words seized me immediately. O, thought I, can I do nothing but sin? I thought I had been in the way of duty now, and is all this sin? O, what shall

I do? Then my conscience was laid open to convictions. I got home as soon as I could but got no sleep that night.

The next day I went to hear Mr. Clap, who told me the very secrets of my heart in his sermon as plain as I could have told them to him, and indeed, more so. His sermon was very terrible to me. All my sins from my cradle was ranked in order before my eyes, and my original sin, as well as actual, appeared doleful.[58] I see the depravity of my nature and how I was exposed to the infinite justice of an angry God. All my former convictions was brought to my remembrance. I see how I had stifled the motions of the blessed Spirit of God and resisted all the kind invitations of a compassionate savior. I was heartsick of all my works, and as Satan had often before lied in telling me it was time enough for me to repent, now his tone was turned, and he told me it was too late for me to find mercy.[59] Once I might have had a Christ, but now my day was past. He told me likewise I had committed the unpardonable sin because I had sinned against light and knowledge, even against the convictions of my own conscience. This I knew I had done, and therefore believed I had committed that sin that could never be forgiven.

In this distress I went to my Bible but could find nothing but terror there. All I could see was such texts as these: Rom. 2:5–6, "after thy hardness and impenitent heart treasurest up wrath against the day of wrath and revelation of the righteous judgment of God, who will render to everyone according to their deeds"; "all liars shall have their part in the lake that burns with fire and brimstone"; and this, "depart from me, ye cursed, into everlasting fire, prepared for the devil and his angels"; and this, "consider this, ye that forget God, lest I tear you in pieces, and there be none to deliver"; and this, "he, that being often reproved hardens his neck, shall suddenly be destroyed, and that without remedy"; and this, "ye have set at naught all my counsels, and would none of my reproof—I therefore will laugh at your calamity and mock when your fear cometh"; and this, "it is a fearful thing to fall into the hands of the living God"; and this, "who among us can dwell with everlasting burnings?"[60] All these and many more such terrible texts of scripture I found whenever I opened the Bible. My eyes was open to nothing else. No, not one word of comfort could I find, and if I thought of complying with any commanded duty I seemed to be frowned away by these words: "What hast thou to do to take my covenant into thy mouth?"[61] O, the distress and anguish of soul I then felt, neither my tongue or my pen can express, when I was brought to believe there was no mercy for such a monster in sin as I, and expected every moment that hell would open its mouth and swallow me up, amazed that God had kept me out so long.

When Satan had gotten the victory over me so far as to make me despair of God's mercy and verily to believe hell would be my portion, he went on to tempt me to try to get the easiest room there, and to that intent to keep myself as ignorant as I could, telling me that the servant that knew not his Lord's will would be beaten with few stripes, while he that knew it, and did it not, would be beaten with many stripes. And as my time was over for doing his will, I had better leave off reading, praying, or hearing the word preached any more, for I should fare better if I did. And O, vile wretch as I was, I yielded to the subtle adversary of my soul's salvation.

[*Osborn crossed out two lines here.*][62]

O, astonishing grace that God did not strike me down into hell the very moment I thought to do so, where I could never have had the opportunity to all eternity.

[*Osborn crossed out one line here.*][63]

God had been, however, just, if he had done so, though I would have melted under the scalding drops of his wrath forever and ever. But O, what shall I say or hope? Shall I, with gratitude enough, express the wonderful goodness of that God who preserved me even when I was—according to my own apprehension—upon the very brink of hell, weltering in my blood when no eye pitied me, nor no created arm could save me. Even then did he spread his skirt over me and said to me: live.

After I had been nigh a week in this distress, my very soul wracked with fears of what I must undergo to all eternity, those words—"depart from me"—sounding in my ears, and I uttering the anguish of hell—"there is no hope; there is no help; the door of mercy is shut against me forever"—all at once I was alarmed by these words: "Who has told you that your day of grace is over? Is not the meetinghouse doors open? Can't you hear the offers of salvation? Haven't you your Bible to read? And you may pray. Therefore, you see your external day of grace is not over, and how do you know but you may yet obtain mercy? It is the devil has told you all this, and he is a liar from the beginning."[64]

Then I realized it was the devil that had been tempting me to despair of God's mercy, which before I did not perceive, but really thought those things he had protested to me was true: to wit, that there was no hope for me. And during the time of this distress, which was from Saturday night to Saturday night, I slept no more than just to keep me alive, and when I did at all it was filled with terrors. It was the same with my necessary food. I thought myself so unworthy of the least mercy that I knew not how to eat. Well is it expressed that "the spirit of a man can sustain his infirmity, but a wounded spirit who can bear?"[65] For sure I am, no affliction or pain of body whatsoever is to be compared to what I then underwent.

[*Osborn crossed out four lines here.*][66]

O, how terrible must it be for those poor souls that are lying on a deathbed to have such hard work to do. I have often thought that if I had not been in bodily health, I could not have lived through it. But blessed be God, it was when I was as well as to any bodily weaknesses as I have been this many years, which has been a comfort to me on all accounts, and particularly because sickbed repentance frequently wears off.

But to proceed: after I see that I was tempted by Satan, and knowing that he was a liar, I began for a few minutes to have some glimmerings of hope that it might possibly be that Christ would receive me, because he had spared me hitherto this side of the grave and out of hell. Who knows, thought I, but I may yet be a child of God? Immediately upon these thoughts, Satan assaulted me furiously with new temptations and told me not to flatter myself with the thoughts I should be a child of God, for I was not elected and therefore could not be saved, and besides, God did not leave his children to be tempted so by him. I might be sure if I was one of God's chosen, he would not have suffered him to tempt me so.[67] But I was his and he was sure of me. Thus did that cruel tyrant tyrannize over me in misery and I, O fool that I was, believed him again, forgetting his monstrous impudence in tempting the Lord of Life himself and many of his dear children. I at once cast off my hope again, verily believing it was impossible I could ever be a child of God.[68]

And now I was plunged in as deep an agony as ever, but thought I would open my Bible once more to see if there was no relief for me in it. O, then I was brought to the greatest extremity. I see myself utterly lost without a Christ. I thought I could have suffered any or all the torments in the world for an interest in Christ. If I could have but purchased him with doing anything—though ever so hard—I should then have thought it nothing. But O, base, proud, unbelieving heart, I could not take him freely upon his own terms, because though I did see him able to save me for the uttermost, yet I could not see him willing to receive so vile a wretch. O, how was that scripture verified which says, "By grace are ye saved through faith and that not of ourselves; it is the gift of God."[69] Sure I am, I can never boast, for it was as much then impossible for me of myself to believe as it was for me to create a world.[70] Neither could any less power than that which raised Jesus from the dead cause me to venture upon Christ and accept him upon his own terms.

But O grace, forever to be adored, now the clouds of darkness was so thick, the glorious savior just ready to appear and expel them all, for as I said, I was in a dreadful agony. I opened my Bible and immediately cast my eye upon these words in the tenth chapter to the Corinthians, thirteenth verse: "There hath no temptation taken you but such as is common to man, but God is faithful, who will not suffer you to be tempted above that you are able; but will with the temptation also make a way for you to escape that you may be able to bear it."[71]

As before it is not possible for me to express how great my distress was, so it is as much impossible for me to make anyone sensible what joy I was instantly filled with by this gracious promise, except those that experimentally know what it is. For God was pleased that moment, I see it, to give me faith to lay hold on it and claim it as my own. O, how it did fill my heart and mouth with praises and my eyes with floods of tears. I was humbled to the dust and amazed as I paraphrased upon every branch of the text—first, to think there had been no temptation taken me but such as is common to man, when but a minute before I had been thinking that there never had any been tempted like me. This part, I say, surprised and comforted me, too, but as I perused the other part—to wit, that God was faithful and would not suffer me to be tempted above that I was able, but would with the temptation make a way for me to escape that I might be able to bear it—my transport of joy was so great that it was more than my poor feeble frame was well able to contain, for my nature even fainted with excessive joy. Then I see Christ not only able but willing to save me and could venture my soul in his hands. My Bible appeared quite different from what it did just before. I could find cordials in great numbers of texts of scripture, and all—as well as the first— looked to me as if I had never read them in all my life till then. I think I slept none that night but continued praising God.

The next day I went to meeting, and it being sacrament day I stayed to see the ordinance administered. But O, what a condition I was in when I viewed the dear children of God sitting with the Redeemer at his table, and see by faith a crucified savior pouring out his precious blood to redeem his people *from their sins,* and believing that I, through grace, was one of them. O, how did my heart melt and my eyes flow with tears when I thought I saw my dearest Lord in his bitter agony in the garden and then crowned with thorns, spit upon, buffeted, beaten black and blue, and at last nailed to an accursed tree, and all to free me from the torments I had so lately dreaded. *It caused me bitterly to reflect upon myself and cry out: "My sins! My sins, O Lord, have been the procuring cause* of all thy bitter sufferings!"

O, how odious then did sin appear, and especially the monstrous sins of ingratitude and unbelief I had been guilty of, in refusing so long the kind invitations of a bleeding, expiring Jesus. O, when I considered how often he had stood knocking till his head was filled with the dew and his locks with the drops of the night but could have no entrance into my hardened heart, I was astonished at myself that I could possibly be so cruel, and astonished at free grace and redeeming love that I was spared to see that happy day.[72]

O, then I begged that the everlasting doors of my soul might be lifted up that the King of Glory might enter in and take full possession. O, how gladly did I embrace a savior upon his own terms as my prophet, priest, and king. He appeared lovely, the chiefest among ten thousands, and was ten thousand times welcome to me. And I was enabled through grace to own the covenant and give up myself in an everlasting covenant never to be forgotten, resolving—God's grace assisting me—to comply with every command of my dear savior. And these words loudly sounding in my ears: *this do in remembrance of me,* adoring my dear Redeemer for his infinite goodness in appointing such a glorious ordinance for the nourishment of his dear children where they might have intimate communion with him. I promised, God enabling to keep it, that I never would omit that duty once more, nor never did.

In this condition I remained during the time of the ordinance being administered, filled with such a mixture of joy and grief that I was not able to contain myself but was obliged to get down on the floor and to lean on the bench, for I could neither sit nor stand, but my being in a pew in the gallery alone, my condition was not discovered by any, as I had no desire it should, for I strove to conceal it as much as possible. Thus through rich, unlimited grace was I brought to lay down my arrows of rebellion, which I see I had held as long as I could. Blessed be God that I was there compelled to come in and list under Christ's banner. *Sure I am, whatever others may boast of a free will, I have none of my own but to do evil, for I resisted to the last moment. O my God, I adore thy sovereign power that made me willing in the day of it. If ever there was a monument of mercy, sure I am one.* O, let me remain forever and ever for Jesus's sake.

The next day I went to see Clap with an intent to acquaint him with my desires to join the church, these words—do this in remembrance of me— still sounding in my ears. *But I appeared so vile in my own eyes that I know not how to ask the privilege of him.* But when I came after some usual questions concerning my welfare, he asked me when I had been to see him before, I answered: not in a great while. Then he asked me the reason. *I durst not now make any formal excuses* as usual, *only burst out into tears and told him I had been too wicked.*

He now perceived what my condition was, but like a tender father to a little child, bid me not grieve. If that was the reason, I was welcome to him now, and he would do all he could to help me forward. And after some more talk, contrary to my expectation, asked me if I did not desire to join to the church. I said yes: that was part of my business. I had had many hindrances and particularly that awful text of scripture—"he that eats and drinks unworthily, eats and drinks damnation to himself"—had made me afraid to approach the Lord's table.[73] *But now resolving through grace to rely upon Christ alone for assistance and acceptance, renouncing all my own righteousness, believing it to be a positive commanded duty, I durst not omit it once more if it might be received.* At this he told me that he should inquire into my character, which I said I expected, but could tell him more of myself than any could say of me, *having been through restraining grace kept from open scandalous sins.* Then he told me I had great cause to be thankful. He bid me come as often as I had a mind if it was morning, noon, or night, and I should be always welcome to him, and lent me a book entitled *But They Seek a Better Country, Even an Heavenly.*[74] I was so delighted with it that I sat up all night to read it two or three times over.

I visited Mr. Clap very often and he as often expressed his willingness to do me good, and once in particular after he had done so, *he lifted up his hands, giving me his blessing and said, "You see I am willing to do you all the good I can, and if such a poor sinful creature as I am willing to do so, think with yourself how much more willing your glorious Lord is to receive you."* These words, having so much reason in them, filled me with a joy unspeakable and full of glory. I hardly knew how I got home, but see Christ willing and I, through grace, made willing. I could utter no other language but: "come in, Lord Jesus, take full possession"; "I will come to thee"; "thou art mine and I am thine"; "even so, Father, for so it seemed good in thy sight."[75]

I immediately retired as soon as I got home to give vent to my passions, but O, what a rapture was I in when I renewed *my solemn engagements to be the Lord's,* enabled, I trust, through grace, sincerely to take the Lord Jehovah for my covenant God; the Lord Jesus for my prophet, *priest,* and king; the Holy Ghost for my comforter, guide, and sanctifier; the scriptures for my rule to walk by *giving up myself soul and body, all my faculties and members, as instruments of righteousness.* O, how could I sing of redeeming love and free grace. Surely my heart reached forth in burning desire after the blessed Jesus. O, how was I ravished with his love, and when examining myself thrice, putting the question to my soul as Christ put to Peter—tell me, O my soul, lovest thou the Lord Jesus?—how did my heart melt and my eyes flow with tears in appealing to him. Lord, thou knowest all things; thou knowest I love thee. And when inquiring into the cause of this love I felt and from whence it flowed, it still overcame me more because I could say, "Lord, I love thee because thou first loved me."[76] This caused me to loathe myself and cry out, "Lord, what a traitor have I been, and yet thou hast freely loved me."[77]

O, why me, Lord? Why me? Why not in hell? Why among the living to praise thee? Lord, there can be no other reason but because where my sins has abounded, thy grace has much more abounded. O, amazing grace, hast thou snatched me as a brand out of the burning? *O, hast thou ransomed my soul from destruction and delivered me from my own lusts and out of the clutches of a cruel tyrant who had so long suffered me and tyrannized over me in misery?* O, then how sweet was a savior. I could heartily subscribe to that text which says to them that believe, "He is truly precious, the fairest of and chief of ten thousands, altogether lovely."[78]

Thus I continued from day to day in such ecstasies of joy, *thirsting for full sanctification and more intimate communion with God,* daily asking what I should render to him for all his benefits towards such a hell deserving sinner as I, *earnestly begging that God would find out some way for me that I might be made instrumental for the advancing of his kingdom and interest in the world. O, how I dreaded being an unprofitable servant.* The employment I still followed seemed to encourage me to hope God intended to make some use of me for the instruction of little ones, which caused me often to bless God for placing me in that calling. And though I know that in everything I offend and in all come short of God's glory, so that every performance has need of washing in the blood of Christ, yet it is a comfort to me to this day that I was enabled through grace to labor with the little souls thou committed to my charge, but desire to be humbled that I did no more. O, that I had been more faithful. Surely I longed that all the world, but more especially those dear to me by the bonds of nature or friendship, might be convinced of sin and come to a glorious Christ. I thought I could even spend and be spent for them. I thought I could travail in birth till Christ was formed in them, and when I see any giving themselves a liberty to sin, I could not at some times refrain from reproving them.

Some would tell me I was turned fool and distracted when I said that I had been a vile sinner, for everybody knew I had been a sober woman all my days, and yet I used to do such things far as well as they could. What was the matter now? Sometimes they would say, "This fit will be over quickly." But all such answers as these, of which I had a great many, *would serve to humble me yet more, and put me upon pleading for persevering grace that I might never bring dishonor to God's name.*

And indeed, all the trials I met with, which were various, had through the abundant goodness of God this effect: *to quicken me yet more.* And Satan had still a desire to sift me as wheat. He assaulted me daily, but these words of the blessed Jesus were frequently applied for my support: "*I have prayed for thee that thy faith fail not.*"[79]

One night in particular, when watching with a dear friend that was sick, Satan assaulted me in as furious a manner seemingly as though he had appeared in bodily shape, though with my bodily eyes I see nothing. I believe the combat lasted at least two hours, as fierce as though I had talked with him face to face. He again ranked all my sins in order before my eyes, telling me it was impossible—notwithstanding all my great hopes—for me ever to be saved. He was still sure of me and would not let me go. *I should surely turn back again and be worse than ever.* It is impossible to relate a tenth part of the fiery darts he flung at me, but I was composed—not in the least daunted— but could prove him a liar by scripture in everything he said, which flowed into my mind as though I had learnt it all by heart. Never had I such a variety of scripture texts at my command in all my life, neither before nor since. There was nothing he could allege against me but, if I knew it was true, according to Mr. Doolittle's direction I immediately subscribed to it and then flew to the particular properties of the blood of Christ, which I found sufficient for me.[80] Thus I overcame him by the blood of the Lamb and was left at last filled brimful of the consolations of the blessed Spirit, triumphing over Satan, blessing and praising God for delivering me out of the hand of this cruel tyrant, adoring the Lovely Jesus. And thus I spent the remainder of that night. O, how sweet was it for me. I longed for more strength to praise and love and even to be dissolved and to be with Christ. Thus I continued for some time rejoicing, and resolving by assisting grace to press forward and by all means give diligence to make my calling and election sure. Then I wrote my experience to the church.

[*Osborn crossed out three lines here.*]

I was admitted February the 6th, 1736/7, to partake of that glorious ordinance of the Lord's Supper. But it is impossible for me to express the ecstasy of joy I was in when I see myself *that was by nature a child of wrath, an heir of hell, and by practice a rebel to God, a resister of his grace, a piercer of the lovely Jesus,* unworthy of the crumbs that fall, yet through free grace compelled to come in and partake of children's bread. It was indeed sweet to me to feed by faith on the broken body of my dearest Lord. Surely it did humble me to the dust and filled me with self-abhorrence as I meditated on his death and sufferings and knew my sins to be the procuring cause. But when I come to take the cup, and by faith to apply the precious properties of the blood of Christ to my soul, the scales of unbelief seemed all to drop off and I was forced to cry out, "my Lord and my God," when I behold the hole in his side and the prints of the nails, and appealing with Peter to him, "Lord thou knowest all things, thou knowest that I love thee."[81] O, then I was with the beloved disciple prevailed to lean on his breast. O astonishing grace and unspeakable joy to see God reconciled to me, in and through him, and he bidding me welcome to his table.[82] The Holy Spirit by his powerful influences applied all this to my strong consolation. O, what a feast is this when intimate communion with the glorious God is thus obtained, when strong covenant engagements with him renewed, God assuring me he was mine, and I giving myself soul and body to him forever and rejoicing in him for my only portion forevermore. Surely, I thought, I could never enough adore the lovely Jesus for appointing such an ordinance as this, but I cease to say any more here, for it is impossible for me to describe the thousandth part of what I then felt. O, that I could always live as one that had thus been upon the mount with God.

The next morning I was as much refreshed by meditating on the 32nd psalm from the first verse to the end of the fifth.[83] This caused me yet more to adore distinguishing grace and even to be swallowed up with love to the immaculate Lamb and resolve more and more with full purpose of heart to cleave to the Lord. The frequent language of my soul was this: "Whom have I in heaven but thee? And there is none upon earth I desire besides thee."[84]

I daily kept my covenant engagements with God, but that they might be more inviolably kept, I resolved to write them, and accordingly began so to do in Mr. Doolittle's form, and went on comfortably until I came to these words: "*that I will leave, lose, and deny all that was dear to me when it stood in competition with God, even life itself, if he should be pleased to call for it rather than to forsake him and his ways.*"[85] Then Satan in a rage flew upon me and furiously assaulted me. He told me that I was now a lying to God, for I had nothing in me that would stand by me when an hour of trial come, but with the stony ground hearers would cast away. This gave me a dreadful shock at first and caused me to stop awhile to plead with God for a discovery of my state, and that he would search me and try me and see if there was any wicked way in me and grant me real and persevering grace. And in answer to my petitions, this portion of God's word was powerfully set home: "My grace shall be sufficient for thee." And then my heart filled with joy and praise, firmly believing he was faithful who had promised, and therefore would perform so.[86] I proceeded to write with more fixed resolution than before.[87]

But O, when I had finished it, which I accomplished March the 26th, 1737, and came to spread it before God, and with prayers and tears to deliver it to him as my own act and deed, it verily seemed to me that all heavens rung with acclamations of joy that such a prodigal as I was returned to my God and father. And my joy was so great that my bodily strength failed, and I was for some time as one whose soul was ready to break loose and wing away into the bosom of my God.

O, how welcome a messenger would death then have been to me, but my great petition was that I might with patience wait my appointed time upon earth. Once more (I am not sure whether before or after this transaction between God and my soul) Satan with great fury assaulted me and *told me my hope would surely perish and I should turn back and be worse than ever. I should be brought to shame, and again ranked in order my sins of youth.* But I immediately opened my Bible, being dreadfully shook with fear lest it should be so, and the first lines I cast my eyes on was the fourth verse of the fifty-fourth of Isaiah:

> Fear not; for thou shalt not be ashamed: neither be thou confounded,
> for thou shalt not be put to shame: for thou shalt forget the shame of
> thy youth, and shalt not remember the reproach of thy widowhood

any more. For thy Maker is thine husband, the Lord of Hosts is his
name, and thy Redeemer the Holy One of Israel; the God of the
whole earth shall be called. For the Lord hath called thee as a woman
forsaken and grieved in spirit, and a wife of youth, when thou was
refused, saith thy God. For a small moment have I forsaken thee; but
with great mercies will I gather thee. In a little wrath I hid my face
from thee for a moment; but with everlasting kindness will I have
mercy on thee, saith the Lord thy Redeemer. For this is as the waters
of Noah unto me: for as I have sworn that the waters of Noah should
no longer go over the earth; so have I sworn that I would not be
wroth with thee, nor rebuke thee. For the mountains shall depart,
and the hills be removed; but my kindness shall not depart from
thee, neither shall the covenant of my peace be removed, saith the
Lord that have mercy on thee.

These gracious promises were so adapted to every particular of my circumstances, and applied by the Spirit of God with such great power, that they
strengthened me exceedingly.

But I find upon further reflecting it was when writing, before I finished
my covenant engagements, that I experienced this, for after I had so solemnly
delivered that to God under my hand and seal, I went on my way rejoicing,
this being the language of my soul: "Who shall separate me from the love of
God?[88] Shall tribulation or distress or persecution or famine or nakedness or
peril or sword? No, I am persuaded that neither life, nor death, nor principalities, nor powers, nor things present, nor things to come, nor height, nor
depth, nor any other creature, shall be able to separate me from the love of
God, which is in Christ Jesus, my Lord."[89]

And I am astonished when I remember the amazing condescension of
my God. He granted me near access to the throne of his grace continually.
And in almost everything I earnestly prayed for, I was remarkably answered,
and so surprisingly at some times that I was afraid to think it was so. Once in
particular, in that same month of March, one morning as I lay sleeping in my
bed I was awaked with the most terrible wind that I ever knew. The first I
knew of it, both my casements was ripped off and carried away into the

street. I got immediately up and looked out, but I think I never see the heavens and the water look so dreadfully in all my life, and the wind blew exceeding hard so that it looked as if all the vessels in the harbor would presently be wracked to pieces. But I thought of those poor souls that were exposed to its fury, and my heart was filled with tender pity and compassion for them.[90] I retired for security into a garret. After I got there, I expected every moment the roof would be ripped off, but I was very earnest with God to abate the violence of the storm and to have compassion on the poor souls in distress. And while I continued pleading with God, I had a great discovery of the sufficiency of one word of Christ to do it. It was only for him to say, "'Peace, be still,' and the winds and the seas would immediately obey him."[91]

And after I had for some time thus wrestled with God in prayer, I went down. I had been so earnest that I had not perceived any abatement, but looking again out of the window in my chamber, I was surprised out of measure. The sea looked as calm and pleasant to me as if there had been no storm at all. I immediately retired again and returned thanks for it as a remarkable answer of prayer. But have often since heard that it was a piece of pride and presumption for me to think it so. However, this I know: God is both the hearer and answerer of prayer for Jesus's sake.

I could not avoid, when there was opportunity for it, expressing my love and thankfulness to God for snatching me as a brand out of the burning. And once, doing so to my mother with tears of joy running down my cheeks, she said to me, "O child, you will not always find your love thus flaming to the blessed Jesus. After awhile you will be more cool again." But I hastily answered, "It was impossible I could be such a monster for ingratitude."[92]

[*Osborn crossed out two lines here.*]

She told me she did not mean that I should in reality love him less, but compared the first espousals of a soul to Christ to the first espousals of man and wife, which were generally attended with a more fondness and joy than afterwards, though the love might be the same or stronger.

I continued to go on my way rejoicing some time before I ever knew what it was to be deserted one hour together; or entirely to lose sensible communion with God in any duty, special ordinance; or ever to lie down without God; or to awake without some sweet and refreshing portion of

God's word in my thoughts. My very sleep was filled with pleasant thoughts of divine things. Surely I enjoyed some foretaste of heaven in this season.[93]

But thus much for happy days of this time. And now, how shall I speak?

O, that with a heart truly broken for my sins I may. After all this I began by degrees to grow more conformed to the world. Things that while I was thus lively appeared insipid, and indeed odious, to me now began to grow tolerable and by degrees in a measure pleasant. And nature and Satan together pleaded for them thus: there was a time for all things, and singing, dancing now and then with a particular friend, was all innocent diversions.[94] Who did I see besides myself so precise and penurious? Other Christians allowed themselves in such things that I had reason to think was far superior to me in grace, especially one with whom I was very intimate. Sure, if it was sin, she would not allow herself in it. It was for extraordinary Christians—such as ministers and others that were eminent for piety—to stick at such things and not for *me*. Who did I think I was that I should pretend to outdo other Christians? They could talk of worldly things; what ailed me? Thus the devil and carnal reason argued me out of a great part of my resolutions for strict godliness and, in short, made me, as it were, believe that it was only pride and hypocrisy to be seen of men that had ever made me pretend to it.

Thus I sunk by degrees lower and lower till I had at last lost almost all sense of my former experiences. I had only the bare remembrances of them and they only seemed like dreams or delusions at some times. At others, again I had access to the throne of grace, and obtained some communion with God, and resolved to be more circumspect, and renewed my covenant engagements with God. But I knew I was a dreadful backslider and had dealt traitorously with God and sometimes dare not with any boldness look up to him, guilt would so stop my mouth.[95]

At other times, gracious invitations to backsliders to return would revive me, so I continued, sometime revived, and sometimes sunk, for a great while. In May of 1739 my father was sick of a consumption, and I expected his death in a short time. I was not yet fully convinced that it was my duty to tell him of the sin I had been guilty of in defrauding him in the days of my youth, but in general begged of him to forgive me for everything I had offended concerning him in from my cradle, which he readily did, and begged of God to forgive me, and bless me with the best of blessings in Christ Jesus, telling me I was a dear child to him. About this time I was pretty comfortable, and my father talked greatly to my satisfaction, several times assuring me he knew on whom he had believed and he was now going to take a sweet sleep in Jesus. And on the 29th of May I stood by him and resigned his departing spirit into the hands of God.[96]

I trust this rod was in a measure sanctified to put me upon preparing for my own change. I cannot say that I had no natural affection working in this affliction. Nevertheless, God quieted me and resigned me to his will in it in a wonderful manner.

Immediately upon this, the smallpox broke out in town, and I, living next door to where the Indian was that others catched it of, but knowing nothing of his distemper, out of pity went in to see him. He was light-headed and strove much to get out of bed, and I stooped much upon the bed and held down the clothes, persuaded him to lie still, but he got out of bed close by me and he was much broke out. The room was small so that I was, as it were, wedged up—he being betwixt me and the door. And as I stood so, one that had had the smallpox came up to help him to bed, and said if there had been anything of the smallpox here, he should think he [the Indian] had it. With that, I trembled like a leaf and thought I should have sunk down where I stood, and immediately I thought: what a poor creature am I? How little do I know my strength till tried? For I had thought the smallpox would not sur- prise me. However, they still concluded it was the measles he had, but when it proved otherwise I expected no other but to have it. There was two carried out of the same house I lived in, and I was much not well and thought every hour I should go.[97] I got all things ready and was, I think, truly resigned—as willing to go as stay—but God had otherwise determined.

I escaped. Surely this was a remarkable deliverance or preservation. After this I was some time pretty comfortable and lively.

[*Osborn crossed out more than a page and a half of her memoir here. The following words can be deciphered:*]

I had then the offer of marriage with one that, as to this world, was likely to maintain me comfortably, but not so sober as I wanted one to be and therefore could not consent.[98] And yet his arguments at some times was so weighty, I could not get rid of him. I earnestly pleaded with God to direct me. I often told him if he would secure his interest in Christ, he might have an interest in me, but not else. But one night he was exceeding earnest with me to assent, pleading with me that the unbelieving husband was sanctified by the believing wife, and he believed I should be a mercy to him in God's hand to make him happy, soul and body. But if I refused, it might get all that was light, too, and be ruined forever after.

Since he used such discourse and earnest entreaties, his person not being disagreeable to me, and he had been two years begging at times to gain my consent, I gave it. I thought we was to be published on the next Sabbath and married the next week, it being Michaelmas and he going directly to sea, which was his calling.[99] But after I dismissed him in the evening I betook myself to the throne of grace, begging of God to take me and his affairs into his own hands, and if it would not consist with his glory for me to proceed, to find out the way to prevent it. And that text was oft in my mind—"be not unequally yoked"—that it terrified me exceedingly.[100] I could not bear the thought of having an enemy to God [as a husband]. I slept none that night but resolved in the morning to forbid pursuing that voyage, which I did, and with much ado, he consented.

And he went out and proved a very bad husband. Spent all he got in extravagancies and in his absence had a child laid.

Bad lives have often been turned sweet. When he returned . . . . He was ashamed to pretend anything . . . .

[He] died.

I mention this to show the wonderful goodness of God in preserving me upon the very brink of ruin as to this world.

O! How many deliverances has God wrought out for me, both in spiritual and corporal things, but alas, O ungrateful soul, I backslid, got cold after this, and by degrees got so low and formal that in short I differed but little from an Edomite. I fell fast asleep with the foolish virgins.[101]

[*Osborn's cross out ends here.*]

And so continued till September 1740. God in mercy sent his dear servant Whitefield here which something stirred me up, but when Mr. Tennent came soon after, it pleased God to bless his preaching so to me that it paused me.[102] But I was all the winter after exercised with dreadful doubts and fears about my state. I questioned the truth of all I had experienced and feared I had never yet passed through the pangs of the new birth, nor never had one spark of grace. And what confirmed it to me, my dear aged pastor frequently preached that those that had real grace had growing grace. This used to make me tremble because I could perceive no growth, but thought I rather went back and grew worse. Thus I was covered over with thick clouds for months together. O, the dreadful fruits of backsliding.

At last I applied myself to Mr. Clap and begged of him that if he knew of anything I had left undone by what I had told him or wrote for my admission into the church. By it [her written covenant], I could not be denied an admission there, yet I begged him to let me know it, that the mistake might be rectified before it was too late. I was indeed possessed with the thought that he see so clearly into my state that he knew I was a hypocrite, though I did not till then. I told him of this, but he said he never thought so, and put me upon renewing my covenant engagements with God, and giving myself up to him then, and maybe I should find I had done so before.

This I endeavored to do and did get some relief, but was not yet satisfied. The tokens of a woeful backslider were upon me. I had forsook my first love and God justly deserted me.[103] Sometimes that text would refresh me, "Return ye backsliding children and I will heal your backslidings." My heart would answer, "Behold, I come unto thee, for thou art the Lord, my God."[104] And sometimes that [text]: "I, even I, am he that blotteth out thy transgressions, and as a cloud, thy sins: return unto me, for I have redeemed thee."[105] But yet this time I could not get free of doubt, but thought such formality and hypocrisy as I perceived to be in myself could not consist with grace. I labored along thus all the winter, unresolved how the case stood between God and my soul. And a dreadful, uncomfortable life it was. At some times I was so covered with darkness that I seemed to be sure I had not one spark of grace. At other times, afraid of ingratitude; afraid to deny what God had done for my soul. O, that was the dreadful fruits of backsliding and losing my first love. The Lord in mercy preserve me that I never may do so anymore.

I continued thus till March 1741, and then it pleased God to return Mr. Tennent to us again, and he preached twenty-one sermons amongst us successively. But while he was here I was more than ever distressed I had lost the sensible manifestations of Christ's love. I had no more but a bare remembrance of some things, and yet I was afraid to draw up a conclusion one way or the other. I applied myself to him, and he discoursed very suitably with me. But still I was not quiet but exceedingly distressed. The next day he stated in a sermon that in the espousals of a soul to Christ it was much as it was with a woman and her sucking child. She fondled it and dandled it upon her knee, but as it grew older and stronger, she ventured it alone to walk by itself, but still her love to it was the same. And so it was with Christ and the soul: in its first espousals he frequently manifested himself and kissed it with the kisses of his love, but afterwards did not usually do so, but ventured the soul to walk by faith. Nevertheless, his love to the soul was still the same. This refreshed me more than anything I had met with for a little while, but my darkness returned again and I sunk very low. I was so afraid of presumption that I durst not conclude my state was good, and he struck directly at those things I had so foolishly and wickedly pleaded Christian example for, such as singing songs, dancing, and foolish jesting, which is not convenient.[106] He said he would not say there was no such thing as dancing Christians, but he had a very mean opinion of such that could bear to spend their precious time so, when it is so short and the work for eternity so great.

Then, and not till then, was I fully convinced what prodigal wasters of precious time such things was, and through grace I have abhorred them all ever since, and for the glory of God be it spoken, for it is only his wonderful goodness to me.[107]

[*Osborn crossed out the following words:*]

Notwithstanding, I could sing a hundred songs, of which I had wrote the first lines in a list, and used to be frequently worried with them even when I desired myself free. Upon Sabbath days they would crowd into my mind so that they grieved me very much. And it is now two years and eight months since Mr. Tennent was here, and I have lost them all so out of memory, as well as esteem, that I never could sing one since if I had tried.

[*Her cross out ends here.*]

And I am indeed now astonished to think how I myself, or any other Christian who has once known what one moment's sweet communion with

God means, can have any relish for such vanities as singing, dancing.[108] O, how much greater is the pleasure in the exercise of religious duties than any such thing can afford. Not only so, but I am amazed to think how I could possibly want such things to pass away time, for I now find the precious moments fly so fast and my work so great that I am often hard beset to know how to spend my time as God requires, between the immediate exercises of religion—public, private and secret—and the calling God has placed me in. I know the same God who has bid me hear and pray and search the scriptures has bid me work—and both, in their place, is my duty.

And I find it very difficult to yield a uniform obedience, to give to God what he requires for himself, and to the world: what is required as a duty and no more. Besides all this, my heart is so perverse that I have enough to do to watch against pride, sloth, wanderings, formality, hypocrisy, and Satan's temptations, who is ready enough to disquiet in. All these, I find, is employ-ment enough to bring about the days without these former recreations. If I am cheerful, a song of Zion is more sweet and refreshing to me than all the vain songs in the world ever was or can be. And sure I am, whatever any may plead that there is a time for all things, God never yet allowed time for sin.

O Lord, humble me for the bad example I have set since I called myself a Christian, and forbid any should ever again be able to plead my example for vanity. And O, that all that name the name of Christ may be enabled to depart from iniquity and abstain from appearance of evil. And if we pretend to be in Christ, O that we may walk even as he walked, for I am persuaded the careless walk of Christians lulls more consciences asleep when the devil, and flesh and blood, sets in to plead their examples than the vices of all the world besides that makes no profession. And O, what a dreadful thing for Christians to be a means to ruin precious and immortal souls and diminish that kingdom and interest which they should be forever engaged to promote —his kingdom and interest against which they should always proclaim an open war. O, dreadful indeed that Christ should be so wounded in the house of his friends. Lord, make me more circumspect for Jesus's sake.

But to proceed: as I said, I still continued in very dark and melancholy circumstances between hope and fear, afraid to conclude one way or the other. And having no opportunity to speak with him [Tennent] again, I wrote to him, as well as I could, briefly what I had experienced, and begged of him to try it by scripture rules and judge of it accordingly and give me his opinion, that I might not sin by denying the grace of God if I had it nor speak peace to my soul if God did not. To which he returned me this answer:

> My dear friend, I like your experiences well. They seem to be scriptural and encouraging, and I think you may humbly take comfort from them and give God the glory of his pure grace. Those who have been so humbled and distressed for sin as to be divorced from the governing love and practice of it, and have been by the Spirit of God made willing to embrace the Redeemer deliberately, unreservedly, and resolutely upon his own terms, have a sure interest in the great salvation. John 1:12: "to as many as received him, to them he gave the power to become the sons of God, even to them that believe on his name." And whatever involuntary defects they are guilty of, they shall not break the everlasting covenant between God and their souls. Though they have played the harlot with many lovers, yet they may return to their first husband. Though God may hide his face for a little moment, yet with everlasting lovingkindness will he return. Though they be sometimes easily beset with sin, yet he who was the author will be the finisher of their faith. I add no more but love, and remain your real friend, G.T., March the 22nd, 1741.

This letter I have wrote at large, that if Providence should ever cast these lines into the hands of any in like circumstances, it may, if the Lord will, have the same happy effect on them as by God's blessing it had on me, which was this: the letter itself was exceeding sweet and refreshing, but the precious texts of scripture he quoted were so powerfully set home that they scattered all my clouds immediately, and I was one restored, as it were, from the grave.[109]

Then with life and courage I again renewed my written covenant engagements with God and became more lively and zealous for God than ever. O, the amazing goodness of God to me. Some Christians, I have heard, never recover from such backslidings all their days, but I have not ever lost my evidences since then.[110] Though I have sometimes been under desertion, yet I could live by faith when I could not by sense so that I could frequently say, "Why art thou cast down, O my soul, and why art thou disquieted within me? Hope in God, for I shall yet praise him who is the light of my countenance and my God."[111]

After I was thus revived, my longings to be made useful in the world returned, and I earnestly pleaded with God that he would suffer me to live no longer an unprofitable servant, but would find out some way that I might be useful in the world, and that I might now be as exemplary for piety as I had been for folly. And it pleased God so to order it, that I had room to hope my petitions were both heard and in a measure answered, for presently after, a number of young women who were awakened to a concern for their souls came to me and desired my advice and assistance and proposed to join in a society, provided I would take the care of them, to which I trust with a sense of my unworthiness, I joyfully consented. And much sweetness we enjoyed in these meetings. And blessed be God, it is yet kept up by some, though others are married and cannot come.

About this time, it pleased God to lay his afflicting hand on me by the removal of my only brother by death. As to the loss of his person, I found I could quietly submit and say, "The Lord gave and he has taken, and blessed be the name of the Lord."[112] But I had a sinful curiosity to know how it was with his precious soul, and being filled with fear about it, was very much sunk. But I see and knew my curiosity was sinful, and I pleaded earnestly with God that he would not suffer me to pry into the secrets of his will but to give me a quiet submission. I continued wrestling with God for resignation to his will till about 2 o'clock in the morning, and then I went to bed, still begging that I might never spend another day unresigned. And just about break of day, I was awakened by seemingly a voice, which roused me up, saying, "Secret things belong to God, but those that are revealed belong to us. Search no further. My will is done; my will is done; my will is done."[113] I would not be understood that this voice was vocal, but the words seemed to be set home with as much power on my soul as if they had been so, and they quieted me, so that I rose as cheerful, composed, and thankful as if I had met with no affliction at all, and I think more so.[114] And never did, from that hour to this, mourn one moment, nor never could. This I can look upon as no other but a remarkable answer of prayer.

After this, my business failed, and I found I could not keep my room where I lived, and which way to turn I knew not but was persuaded God would point out some way for me. I had several offers in the country to keep school in credible families where I had a prospect of wanting for nothing of necessaries of this life, but I could not bear the thought of going from the means of grace and other precious privileges I then enjoyed, and the society of young women often begged me not to leave them. I had double ties every way and yet knew not what to do. But I was not distressed, believing God would provide for me, and accordingly he did so, though by an afflictive dispensation. It pleased him to remove a dear friend by death with whom I was very intimate. Her companion was a very sober, good sort of a man and wanted me to keep his shop for my board and work for myself.[115] This offer suited me very well, for thereby I was not likely to be deprived of any of my religious privileges. So on the first of July [1741] I went there to live and indeed had much comfort. Dear Mr. Clap met with the society at his house twice every week, which I earnestly entreated, and religion seemed to be the chief business of my life.[116]

[*Osborn crossed out twenty-seven lines here. The following words can be deciphered:*]

In the fall I had again a great trial concerning a young person that had expressed a desire for me above others. I did not doubt his affection. He was in every respect a respectable . . . .

Then I had reason to expect myself passionate, I thought, and was really . . . .

But one thing was needful to make it all complete, and that was he had no reason to think he had any interest in Christ . . . whether could he be persuaded to . . . all the time we had been acquainted I had . . . .

[He] always expressed thankfulness for the pains I took and desiring not to leave off but still seemed . . . .

if God had decreed he should be damned. But I could not help it.

[*Osborn's cross out ends here.*]

I wrestled with God in bitter agonies for him from day to day and from night to night, cried, pleaded for myself that God would never suffer me to let my affection overcome my reason so as to act inconsistent with his glory. This I feared exceedingly.

[*Osborn crossed out three sentences here.*][117]

Once in particular, when praying for him and therefore myself that I might not be left to dishonor God in this weighty affair, these words seemed very sweet: "Be not afraid, only believe."[118] I took some encouragement from this time to hope God had designs of mercy for him, but at last, when I found I could by no means prevail with him to take care of his precious soul, I thought it my duty to part wholly, for I could not bear the thoughts of being espoused to one that was not for Christ. This I found to be a great piece of self-denial, but through God's grace I overcame my reasonings, which were not few, and his, too, which were many. This was the second time God preserved me from dishonoring him in this case. Blessed be his name. O, that all single persons would be persuaded earnestly to look for God for direction in all their affairs, but especially in this. Surely they would find the time spent in prayer to God for his protection and blessings is not lost time, and the testimony of their consciences that they did aim at his glory in it would greatly sweeten their lives and quiet them under any troubles they might meet with afterwards.

But as I said, in November we parted quite, and I went on my way rejoicing, enjoying much comfort in all the duties of religion—public, private, and secret—and had as much time to spend in them as I could desire. In March, the Rev. Mr. Wheelock came to preach amongst us, and exceedingly glad I was.[119] I heard him with much delight and satisfaction, but in one sermon he pierced me to the heart because I had not confessed the sin of my youth against my parents. I was so sunk under a sense of my vileness that I could not act faith upon Christ in his fullness and sufficiency, and in a dreadful, distressed condition I was.[120]

But resolved to conceal it no longer, and therefore wrote to my mother, who lived at South Kingstown, as follows.

Honored mother,

With trembling and great humility I would plead with you to have patience with and compassion for me while you read these unexpected, surprising lines. I do with the prodigal confess I have sinned against thee and am no more worthy to be called thine. O, be entreated to forgive me for a sin long ago committed and bitterly bewailed before God, though not till now confessed to you. Sure I am, if you could but have seen the dreadful agonies and the thousands of tears I have shed on that account, though you was never so angry it would move you to pity me.

The cause of my distress is this: when I lived with you before marriage, while you was angry with me and often threatened to give me nothing, what with the corruptions of my own nature, the temptations of Satan, and the advice of wicked companions—*and some that I thought was good people too*—I was brought to believe it was no sin for me to get anything from you I could, without your knowledge, and accordingly did at convenient seasons take such things as I thought I should want. But did not imagine I had any great value till, after my marriage, I cast them up, for which I am now thankful, and as you sold them in the shop I found they amounted to [*crossed-out word*] pounds, at which I was exceedingly terrified. But I had ingenuously confessed and restored all when you found out that of Block Island.[121] But poor Mrs., who is dead and gone, who kept them for me, pleaded with me to keep my own counsel, persuading me that you would make me a public example and I must betray her and all my other friends who wished me well, still urging that it was no sin, but my just due.[122]

O, dreadful—it is too late now to beg forgiveness for her, and it is because God's compassions fail not, that I am not consumed. But O, how often has my concealing it rushed into my mind and robbed me of sweet communion with God. It has at some times been like a separating wall between Christ and my soul, and yet of self-denial I was not able to learn, a cross I could not take up till now. My pride and fears was so great. Sometimes I have resolved to confess it to you, but I have conferred with flesh and blood—I mean with Christian friends—who thought God did not require it of me except I had wherewith to make restitution, and that, I thought, I could not do. And I was afraid it would make a breach between us that would never be made up. I have laid such a case before you when I have been sunk in my spirits, to know whether persons were required to confess to man what they could not make amends for, and you was of opinion it was not.

Thus I have been from time to time burdened, but strove to still my conscience by repairing to the precious blood of Christ for the remission of that with all my other sins. But when God's dear, faithful servant Wheelock came in one of his sermons to state exactly such a case as if I had told him, and loudly to adjure conscience in the name of the great God to do its office, and tell that man or woman, whoever they were, that they were guilty of that sin to this day, notwithstanding all their lamenting it before God, mine flashed crimson in my face immediately and made me resolve to conceal it no longer, come on it what would.

And now I throw myself at your mercy and at the foot of a sovereign God, begging I may be disposed of as most consists with his glory. I have prayed more to have a competency of this world that I might pay that debt than for all other things in this world beside, and have never had a prospect of prosperity but that was uppermost in my thoughts. But never was convinced, till now, that it was my duty to sell what I have to do it. But blessed be God, I am now made willing to do that if you desire it, and with Zacchaeus and Peter to forsake all and follow Christ. My fears, my shame, pride, are all through God's goodness so far subdued that I am determined to know nothing but Christ and him crucified. And though I was sure the discovery of this sin would take away my life itself, I hope I would not dare to hide it any longer, for I am resolved, God's grace assisting me, to leave, lose, and deny all that is dear to me when it's inconsistent with God's glory, even life itself if he shall call me to it.[123] And I trust he will enable me to account all things as loss and dung that I may win Christ. Without him I can do nothing. Without reconciliation and peace with God, fellowship with God—the Father, Son, and Holy Ghost—*I cannot live*. As the hart pants after the water brooks, so pants my soul for thee. O God, I thirst for God, for the living God. O, when shall I come and appear before God. Search me, O my God, and try me, and see if there be any wickedness in me and lead me in the way everlasting. O, what shall I render to the Lord for all his benefits, and especially for sending his dear servant to discover to me my sins and giving me resolution and strength to confess and forsake them. O, that he would root out every root of bitterness and suffer me not to spare an Agag.[124] O, that all my sins were nailed to the cross of a sweet, bleeding savior who I trust has loved me and washed me in his own blood. O, amazing grace, that such a monster in sin could obtain mercy, that have crucified the Lord of Life afresh and put him to open shame. But through grace, thus it is.

I hope, dear mother, if you will suffer me to call you so, that you have the opportunity of hearing the dear Mr. Wheelock. He was to preach on Thursday at Tower Hill. He kept at our house, and a delightful Christian to converse with he is, as ever my eyes beheld. He is meek as a lamb but thunders out the awful and evangelical truths of the gospel with the courage of a lion. I trust he has not altogether labored in vain.

And now, dear mother, I have through the goodness of God obtained peace of conscience, and I trust peace with God through the merits of the dear Redeemer, and I do renew my petitions to you, most honored mother, for the forgiveness of my trespasses against you, and beg you will be reconciled and at peace with me for the sake of him who has said, "if you forgive men their trespasses, your heavenly Father will forgive you your trespasses."[125]

Be entreated to pray for me and write to me as soon as possible, and accept this with humble duty from your once rebellious but now obedient daughter till death,

Sarah Wheaten[126]

After I had wrote this letter and sent it away, I was much refreshed, and resolved with a great deal of cheerfulness to sell my household goods to make restitution, on having nothing else in the world. But on Saturday I received a present from my mother, and she had not received my lines.[127] This so overcame me with a sense of my unworthiness to receive any favor at her hands, or the least mercy from God, that I was not able to contain myself. It seemed to me the whole creation did not afford such a vile sinner. Surely with bitterness I possessed the sins of my youth, and my faith in the fullness and sufficiency of my dear Redeemer staggered, so that I was almost ready to conclude I was too vile to be forgiven, but durst not, neither. I continued thus all the remaining part of the day and evening, but in the morning just at break of day was waked with these words: "O Israel, thou hast destroyed thyself, but in me is thy help."[128] I clasped Christ in this promise immediately and was wonderfully filled with joy and praises, adoring free grace and redeeming love. I renewed my covenant engagements and laid myself under fresh obligations to be the Lord's, resolving with full purpose of heart to cleave to the Lord. I went to his house, being Sabbath day, and with great delight sat under his shadow and his fruit was sweet to my taste. I seemed like one recovered from a bed of sickness. I walked up and down in the light of God's countenance every day.

The next Wednesday, the man who is now my husband came to see me, but I could not harbor any thoughts of entertaining him. I was not sure how things would be betwixt my mother and myself. I received no answer to my letter, and at length, growing impatient, on the 19th day [of March] I wrote a second as follows.

Honored mother,

After humble duty, this comes to acquaint you I have impatiently waited for an answer to my letter, but have none, which grieves me so I don't know how to subsist. Are my fears in good earnest come upon me? Is there such a breach made by my confessing my sin that it cannot be made up? Has not God said: "whoso covers his sins shall not prosper, but who confesses and forsakes them shall find mercy"?[129] I do with shame confess. I do judge and condemn myself, and I hope freely forsake.

But O, dear mother, will you shut up your bowels of compassion towards me? Can't you forgive me? Must I suffer your displeasure now which I have so long dreaded? Please to consider, the sin was the same before as now, and though I don't desire to lessen my crime, yet if you think with yourself if I had not done as I did, you would have lost that, with the rest, by [*crossed-out word*], it may serve to moderate you a little.

O, what shall I say or do? Have I wasted your substance? Did not the prodigal, too? And yet when he returned, his father's arms was open to embrace him. And when the servant could not pay his lord without all that he had being sold, his lord frankly forgave him the debt. But if you desire it, I am still willing to part with all to make restitution. As for depending any longer upon future prosperity, to do it I cannot, for I never expect to be able while single, and if I should have a prospect of altering my condition, I should not know how to desire one that was now the better, for anything I had, to pay such a debt for me. Neither should I know how to mention such a thing, and to think of doing it after a clandestine manner and so add sin to sin. That, I should not dare to do, even if you would accept it, which you would not. I am resolved to carry no moth or guilt of conscience with me to blast the prosperity of another. I hope if God should ever see it good to give me a competency of this world's goods, I shall not be left to be undutiful or ungrateful to you, but I beg you will be pleased to let me have an answer from you now that shall put a final issue to this thing, that I may by some means be clear from my iniquity, this burden that has so long oppressed me.

O, I trust God's anger is appeased for the sake of the sweet Lord Jesus, who has made up a complete righteousness for me that have none of my own to plead, and has, I trust, justified me freely and washed me in his own blood. And will you not be entreated to forgive? O do, pray, pity me since I cannot recall what is past, and none but God and my own soul knows how terrible my distresses have been on this account.

Consider, dear mother, this is an ingenuous confession. If you had found it out by any other means, you would not have had that room to believe my repentance was sincere, as now you have.

I return you a thousand thanks for the presents you sent me and acknowledge myself unworthy of them. It seemed to be so ordered by Providence, I thought, to humble me yet more than you should happen to send them at that time. I was so overwhelmed with a sense of my own unworthiness to receive them that I was not able to contain myself or conceal my grief from the family. O, that I could always be so sensible of how unworthy I am of all God's mercies. I do again beg to be forgiven by you and earnestly beg an answer that will finish this business forever, for I can't be easy till it is entirely done with. If I have an answer of peace, I hope it will always be gratefully acknowledged as a great favor by your very affectionate and dutiful daughter till death,

    Sarah Wheaten

    I beg your prayers.

In keeping the copies of these letters, I had nothing in view but to peruse them myself occasionally, that I might always be humbled. But fearing there is too many children—by the advice of wicked, false friends, the prevalency of their own corruptions, and subtle suggestions of a cruel adversary—who have been brought into the same distresses and fears, I have wrote them here, that if Providence should ever cast them into the hands of any such poor, burdened creature, they may possibly be useful to them. And for their encouragement to venture to ease their burdened consciences by an ingenuous acknowledgment of their sin to those they have wronged, I will write the copy of my mother's answers, which were exceedingly comfortable and sweet to me. They were as follows.

March the 20th, 1741/42

    Dear Child,

    I received yours on the 13th instant dated the 4th. Dear child, this has increased my comfort and love for you beyond expression. Indeed, I cannot but think . . . , according as things may be for circumstanced, it may not be always the duty of a person to confess to somewhat they are never able to repair. Were it to some persons void of true grace and, it may be, to others that know not what it is to be born of God, they might take advantage by it and so cause the name of Christ to be evil spoken of and thereby dishonored.

Notwithstanding, my dear, since you were convinced it was your duty now, and in obedience to Christ was willing to follow his example, who was really harmless, undefiled, and separate from sinners, who or what a wretched creature should I be to have any manner of regret towards such a sweet child, who, through rich grace, is made able rather to instruct me than to receive from me. I desire to bless God for this unspeakable gift. O, what manner of love is this that the father has bestowed upon us that we should be called the children of God. Let us prize our privileges and endeavor in all things to adore the doctrines of the Lord, our savior.

My dear child, I long to see you. I beg you would be thoroughly easy, for assure yourself, I do as freely forgive you as I pray God to forgive me all my trespasses, and beg that if I have failed in my duty to you, either by temporal or spiritual assistances within my poor capability, that you would forgive it likewise. And let us be followers of Christ, as dear children rejoicing in hopes of the coming kingdom of our Lord Jesus Christ, to whom be glory forever. Amen.

The remembrance of me in your prayers will be grateful to your affectionate mother,

Susannah Haggar

No one can possibly think, except those that have experienced anything of the like nature, how I was overcome when I received this letter. The goodness of God appeared so great in inclining my mother thus tenderly to treat me that nature was ready to faint under a sense of it. And so, contrary to my fears, the very thing that I thought would alienate, increased my mother's affection. I was then ashamed of my hard thoughts and sorry I had wrote my second letter, the answer to which was as follows:

March the 29th, 1742

Dear child,

It was above a week after the date your letter, March the 9th, come to hand, and as soon as I had opportunity I wrote to you on the 20th instant, which I hope you have received. Yours on the 19th instant came to me this afternoon.

I am, dear child, grieved exceedingly to think that you should entertain such a thought that I could be so cruel, so hard-hearted, so barbarous, so far fallen from grace, as not to be as ready to forgive you as you to ask it. No, child. I bless God, I can truly say, if my heart don't deceive me, if it had been all I possessed and what had exposed me to work for my bread as I do, I hope I neither could nor durst have denied your forgiveness, and should be ready—were I able—to put a ring on your hand and shoes on your foot.[130] Your confession is too much, and more than I can well bear, and beg you would not mention it anymore, nor once think or endeavor to make me any further recompense. You have done enough and more. I neither expect nor will receive. I make no question but the same kind God, which hath hitherto provided for me, will still by his good providence take care for me, and you, too, and though my circumstances will not allow me to do for you according to my inclination in this world, yet I trust we shall at last come to our inheritance uncorruptible, undefiled, that fadeth not away, reserved in heaven for us. That this may be our hope, our comfort, our exceeding joy. And rejoicing in Christ Jesus, this is the desire and prayer of, dear child, your affectionate mother,

Susannah Haggar

P.S. My mind hath been very much discomposed for some time, and this letter almost too hard for me. I long to see you but cannot add more now. Only beg your prayers for me that the Lord would please to refresh me with the dews of his blessed Spirit, and that in the multitude of my thoughts his comforts may delight my soul.

I have omitted some passages in each of my mother's letters wherein I think her affection causes her to speak more highly of me than I deserve. But as she ascribes all to the rich and free grace of God, I feared it might be rather a wrong to her, than a piece of humility in me, to leave them out. Lord, in mercy grant I may be enabled to live answerable to her opinion of me and for the many mercies I daily receive.

And now, if any of these should ever come into the hands of any parents, or others that have been wronged by children, servants, or any, that God shall thus convince of their sin and incline them to confess them to you—O, be entreated to follow the example of my mother in this case. Forgive them for Jesus's sake, and in so doing you will be Godlike and Christlike. O, I could plead for such poor souls as upon my knees that you would not add your displeasure to increase their distress. O, believe it: if their repentance is sincere, it is a bitter one, but bitter as it is, happy are they that obtain it in this world. Blessed be God that I was not left to repent of this sin in hell, where it would have been too late to seek forgiveness–forever too late. O, what shall I render for all his benefits towards me.

But to proceed: after I had received these sweet letters from my mother, I was lively. I seemed like one released from a dreadful burden, which I would not have upon my conscience again for all this world. Now I had peace in my own breast and peace with God, and sweet communion I enjoyed in almost every duty. God in a wonderful manner poured out upon me a Spirit of prayer and thanksgiving. My heart was in a measure filled with gratitude, and my lips declared his praise. Surely I never lived nearer to God in my whole life. Many a gracious visit and sweet manifestation of his love I enjoyed, even such as strangers intermeddle not with.

And now I began to take into serious consideration this third offer of marriage. My inclination did not much lead me to it for several reasons, such as *his age*, his children, and the like. But the *main thing*, for which I had always prayed, I trusted was in him—namely, a principle of grace—and I found this to be a strong motive. Nevertheless, I was in a great strait, fearing

I could not have affections enough to be found in the way of my duty and should dishonor God and break his commandment. I had multitudes of thoughts and reasonings for and against, but was every day admitted to have nigh access to the throne of grace and mercy to spread my case before God and implore his direction, throwing myself entirely upon his care, pleading with him that if it was his will I should proceed, he would grant that my affections might be so far placed upon the man as might consist with his glory. And the more I prayed, the more I found it so.

But one day in particular, when more than ordinarily engaged in this duty of prayer, crying mightily to God for direction,

[*The following paragraph is crossed out.*]

I vehemently begged that God would condescend to give me some token that I might know if it was his will I should go forward, and the very instant, while I was pleading, these words was with amazing power and sweetness set home upon my soul: "Go forward, fear not, for I am with thee."[131] I instantly felt a calm in my spirit and turned thanks to God for his wonderful condescension, and after this heart prayer, I took my Bible to see if I could find any such portion of scripture. The first I cast my eye on was the words of God to Moses when the children of Israel were pursued by the Egyptians and knew not which way to go and Moses prayed to God for direction. The words were these: "Why cryest thou to me? Goest to the children of Israel that they go forward."[132] This confirmed it much to me and [*Osborn's cross out ends here*] eight of the society at my request kept a day of fasting.[133]

From this time my reasonings all ceased, and my regard for his person was greater than before, so that I had no fears but I could love him so as to be found in the way of my duty to him. And his circumstances as well as mine seemed to call for a speedy marriage.[134] My business failed so that I had no work to do, and indeed it looked very remarkable that God was this way providing for me, for I had had some fears I must quit my station, having no other dependence there but my board, and without work that would not do. But I foresee there was difficulties which I must unavoidably encounter, and many duties would be incumbent on me which I was hitherto a stranger to, particularly on account of my being a mother-in-law to three sons my husband had by a first wife.[135] But God continued to enable me with great earnestness from day to day to unbosom myself to him, and plead with him for grace sufficient to my day, and that he would not suffer me to be useless amongst them but make me an instrument in his hand to promote their everlasting good. And to that end, to give me a room in their hearts and affections so that we might always live in peace and love, that the God of peace and love might delight to dwell amongst us.

One day, I was more than ordinarily enlarged in wrestling with God for blessings for my only son, who had been cast upon God from the womb. I had a great sense of the worth of his precious immortal soul

[*The following words are crossed out.*]

and entreated that God would put some particular praise into my mouth that I might plead with him on his behalf all my days, and continued as if I could not give over pleading or be denied something that would encourage me to hope God would be merciful to him. O, I think I felt the pangs of the new birth for him, and having

[*Osborn's cross out ends here.*]

had such a sense of his miserable state by nature, and what it would be if he died Christless, and such a discovery of the all-sufficiency of Christ for him, I continued agonizing with God in prayer for a considerable time.

[*The following words are crossed out.*]

And at last was quieted by this portion of scripture, adapted and sweetly applied: "All thy children shall be taught of God, and great shall be the peace of thy children."[136] O, this caused me to bless and praise my God that he had naturally put this poultice into my mouth to plead on behalf of my own son. But I . . . .

[*Osborn's cross out ends here.*]

And could plead in behalf of those he was about to give me, and, indeed, I do find to this day much sweetness in pleading for them with God when I can get so near him as to fill my mouth with arguments.[137]

Surely I never did live nearer to God than from the time of writing mine and my receiving my mother's letters to the time of my marriage. And as that drew nigh, my earnest desire from time to time was that Christ would honor me with his presence at that time, and enable us both afresh to give ourselves to him as well as each other, that so the marriage union might be complete for soul and body. And sure I am, God did hear me and answer me, too, in this respect.

On May the fifth, 1742, I was married, and during the whole time of the ceremony I did enjoy much of God's gracious presence and was enabled to renew my engagements with the blessed Jesus and to give my whole self to him while giving myself to my husband. O, surely Christ did sweetly manifest his love to my soul. A happy marriage this was indeed, and I have great cause to think God was with me of a truth from first to last and, blessed be his name, has answered all my petitions throughout the course of my widowhood by giving me one who I trust is united to Christ and is

[*The following words are crossed out.*]

in all respects almost

[*Osborn's cross out ends here.*]

a tender and indulgent companion, and my affections are so much pleased on him as I desire they should be on anything here below. And as to the children, they have always treated me with the most tender affection, both in sickness and in health, that I can desire, and are not unwilling to hearken to my counsels

[*The following words are crossed out.*]

with respect to spiritual and temporal things and, blessed be God, are sober, well-inclined, yea, in no ways addicted to the vices of the times, that I know of.[138]

[*Osborn's cross out ends here.*]

And God has preserved that peace I prayed for, now a year and seven months. O, that I could sufficiently praise him. May it yet be continued for Jesus's sake. O, that our house may indeed be a Bethel, and every soul in it a temple for the Lord Jehovah to dwell in.

But to return: after I was married in July, I went with an intimate friend to Little Compton on purpose to keep a fast, which was there appointed, to implore the outpourings of God's Spirit upon that place, which was attended with much solemnity. The next day, the 29th of the month, my friend and self was riding to a meeting, and my horse stumbled and threw me over his head. My stomach came first to the ground and yet was comparatively but little hurt, and close by, where my head came, was a large rock, which must in all probability have ended my days if I had fell upon it. This gave me a sense of God's goodness in preserving me.

I got safe to the house I purposed to go to, and in the evening Mr. Tyler preached a close but moderate sermon—I mean, not much terror in it.[139] However, it greatly affected the people who were under concern before, but they with much difficulty kept silence till sermon and prayer was done, and then cried in vehement agonies, lamenting their lost condition without a savior and pleading with God to have compassion on them and give them an interest in Christ. At this time I had an awful sense of the state of the damned, who were screeching under their torments but past remedy. Then a number of young women with myself withdrew into a chamber in order to settle a society there. We spent some time in praying, reading, conversing, and singing. The meanwhile, in another room was a company of young men engaged in the same exercises. We happened to sing in both rooms at once. The melody was very sweet and gave me lively apprehensions of the glorious employment and blessed enjoyment of the saints in the New Jerusalem, and filled my soul with adoring thoughts of God.

But on my return home, it being late in the night, we were overtaken in the most awful thunder and lightning that I ever heard or see. During the terrible claps of thunder, my horse stood still trembling, and as soon as they ceased, ran full speed. I was then filled with a greater sense of the awfulness and majesty of a God than ever I had before experienced, and more moralizing thoughts of the solemnity of the great and last day. I did not imagine that was the time, but thought it a great resemblance of it, and I expected every moment to be called to appear before my judge, whether by the thunder and lightning or a fall from my horse. This put me upon examining myself to see where my foundation for hope was laid, and whether I had real grace and a sure interest in Christ that he might then be my advocate. I earnestly pleaded this might be my very case. Upon strict search, I found such evidences as kept me from all fears of hell, though I did not then feel the manifestations of God's love as at some other times.[140] But just after the last thunderclap, my horse, turning swift round a corner, threw me off backward. My right temple came first to the ground as I fell. I committed my spirit into the hands of my savior, expecting death, but was wonderfully preserved so that I was but little hurt.

Thus God showed me, in this day and night of large experience, what he could do with me in a way of judgment, and what for me in a way of mercy, in wonderfully preserving me when in imminent danger of death. Lord, for thine own name's sake, write a law of gratitude in my heart for this with all thy other mercies. O Lord, what am I that thou art thus mindful of me, the chief of sinners?

[*The next pages have large Xs through them, but are still readable.*]

September the 9th, 1742.[141] One told me that she had heard I was accounted a bold pretender for saying I was sure of heaven as if I was there, and it had given so much offense that one minister had preached very smartly against it, so that several that heard it knew who he meant.[142] At first I did not know but it might be surmise—that people might only think he meant me—but I have since heard of his speaking of it himself in this tenor, and in others, too, and that I likewise said that God must cease to be God if he damned me.

Now how far I may have spoken in vindication of that doctrine that holds the saints' perseverance in grace—that those that are once united to Christ are always so—when I have been talking with any that believed it is possible to fall from grace, I cannot tell. But I might say that *those* that are once interested in Christ are sure of heaven as if they were there, and I firmly believe it still. And again, doubtless I may have said, when speaking of the justice and faithfulness of God, that he could as soon cease to be God as to act contrary to his promises, made in Christ Jesus, in damning those that had accepted him for their savior upon gospel terms. But positively to say to any person that I was sure of heaven as if I was there, or that God could as soon cease to be God as damn me, I do not remember expressing myself in any such terms to any person on earth. Neither can I find out, by those that I have most freely conversed with about such things, *that I ever did once say so.* When I was first told of this, it gave me a great shock, but the answer I gave my friend was this: that I did not remember my saying so; however, my comfort was, "The foundation of God stands sure, having this seal, sure the Lord knows who are his."[143]

But when I come to be alone, I thought much more on it. I bless God it was not useless to me, though it perplexed me very much, for it put me upon a strict search into what I had experienced and where my foundation was laid, *that I might know, if I had unwarily dropped such a speech, whether it was truth* or not. And in searching the scriptures to see where my evidences for heaven were grounded, I was much comforted and confirmed by some verses in the eighth to the Romans with astonishing sweetness applied to my soul:

> And we know all things shall work together for good to them that love God, to them who are called according to his purpose. For whom he did foreknow, he also did predestinate to be conformed to the image of his son, that he might be the firstborn among many brethren. Moreover, whom he did predestinate, them he also called, and whom he called, them he also justified, and whom he justified, them he also glorified.[144]

I *was enabled here to prove my calling,* and from that judged I might safely conclude it was really so, that the work would be complete in heaven. The first verse of the chapter was likewise very sweet to me: "There is therefore no condemnation to them that are in Christ Jesus, who walk not after the flesh but after the Spirit."[145]

I was then enabled, with all my faculties engaged, I trust sincerely, to renew my written covenant engagements to be the Lord's, and was filled brimful of strong consolation, being with the apostle persuaded that "neither death, nor life, nor angels, nor principalities, nor powers, nor things present, nor things to come, nor height, nor depth, nor any other creature, shall be able to separate me from the love which is in Christ Jesus, our Lord."[146]

Thus it pleased God to bless this trial to me. Indeed, things of the like nature were not uncommon with me from the time that God in much mercy revived me by Mr. Tennent. For after this, I grew heartsick of my conformity to this world, as Dr. Watts expresses it—tired with visits, modes and forms, and flatteries paid to fellow worms. However, I endeavored to treat my friends with civility as much as ever when with them, but could not content myself to spend whole afternoons in such company as I could hear nothing of God or have opportunity to speak of him freely.

This set their mouths open. Some said they should hate such religion as caused people to forsake their friends. Others said, in a way of derision, they supposed I thought they were monsters now, I thought myself so good. And almost every word, anything I spoke in their hearing, though ever so innocently and without the least thought of giving offense, was presently carried about, and much game was made thereof.

But this never grieved or disturbed me on my own account. I resolved if this is to be vile, I will by God's grace be more so, but little did they know how I was concerned for *them*. My love to their persons or souls was not in the least decreased, though their speeches and actions was not pleasant. And while I have a day to live, I desire gratefully to acknowledge all former kindnesses, and did it lay in my power, should rejoice to serve them by night or day.

One day, calling to see some that I had been acquainted with, but not very intimate, they urged me very much to come and stay an afternoon, and thinking no harm, I answered: I durst not promise for I had but little time to visit, and several of my acquaintance was sick, and I thought it my *duty* to visit them. The woman replied, if I spent my time in going about to do good, I should come there that they might get some by me. Laughing, I said I was a poor creature and durst not say I did any good, but I knew it was my duty to do all I could.

Sometime after this, my old friend, who in years past I had been more conversant with and enjoyed many sweet hours in discussing of our experiences and the abundant goodness of God to our souls, but now, I being convinced that such things—as I had before pleaded for example for—was sinful, I forsook them wholly and could not speak favorably of them, though I never did reproach her nor speak uncharitably of her, but thought if she was convinced as I was, she would forsake them, *too*.[147] But she took occasion to show her dislike to most or all of my conduct at all opportunities. Sometimes she would say she wondered how I could form myself to visit ministers, intimating it was a piece of boldness or rather impudence, and what she could never set herself about. Sometimes she said she thought my religion chiefly consisted in meats and drinks. Thus, by the by, she would frequently give me to understand she was displeased with me.

But once in particular she came on purpose to talk with me and told me plainly that she did think I was dreadfully puffed up with spiritual pride, and it was a dreadful thing for me to go about boasting that I must spend all my time in visiting the sick and doing good, and I had no business to speak of what I experienced. Religion was chiefly carried on betwixt God and the soul. All this, I told her, I acknowledged. Nevertheless, I believed it to be justifiable, and a duty for me at convenient seasons, to give God the glory of his grace in telling what God had done for my soul.

I was very much affected to think a Christian friend should reprove me for doing too much, when my own conscience told me I did not far enough. I endeavored to prove it a duty from the example of the Psalmist, who said, "Hearken unto me and I will tell you what God has done for my soul."[148] But she said that was pride in me again to endeavor to imitate the inspired Psalmist, alleging there was a vast distance betwixt him—that was immediately inspired by God's Spirit—and me. I said I acknowledged that, but if I was a child of God, I was guided by the Spirit of God as well as he, and I thought my obligations was great as well as his. And in hopes of convincing her they were so, I made a parallel betwixt his case and mine, telling her my thoughts was, that it was a sense he had of what he was by nature, and what he was by grace, that [*crossed-out word*] him thus speak. And said, I think I know of myself that I was by nature an heir of hell, a rebel to God, a despiser of his grace, a woeful sinner by practice and liable to everlasting torments, and yet he had through rich and sovereign grace snatched me as a brand out of the burning and made me a monument of his mercy. And should I altogether hold my peace, it appeared to me such a monstrous piece of ingratitude that it seemed as if the very stones might cry out against me.

I wept some and pleaded much with her to put on bowels of charity and believe that as the apostles spoke, the love of God constrained me to speak. I told her had she reproved me for my cowardly ingratitude to my God in being so backward in matters of religion, I would have subscribed to it with all my heart, and acknowledged it just, but I could not think I did too much. At last I brought her own example and asked her how many times I had heard her speak of God's remarkable goodness to her soul, and say, "O, that I could so speak of it *as to excite others to put their trust in him*." And if she did so, upon this privilege, why could she not charitably hope I acted upon the same as well? As to ascribe all to spiritual pride, I told her it was true: I durst not say

I had *none of that*. But I could appeal to the searcher of hearts that whenever I perceived it, it was my grief, and what I deeply strove to mortify.

But all I could say seemed to give her no satisfaction. Then she insisted much on my being against such things which other Christians had practiced. I told her if they did so, I durst not follow their example *now* that *I was convinced it was sin for me*, for that would not stand me in [good] stead in the great and last day. She said our savior himself sharply reproved the Pharisees of old for tithing mint, anise, and cumin. I told her I knew he did, for their depending on such things and omitting the weightier matters of the law, justice, mercy, and truth. But at the same time, he said, "These things ought you to have done and not have left the other undone."[149]

But after all, I could say I have reason to think she believes me to be, as others have said I am, one of that number that say, "Stand by thyself, for I am holier than thou."[150]

The trial I met with in this friend, and one more who I hope is a Christian, was more grief to me than all the scoffs and ridicules of those that plainly appear not to be acquainted with spiritual things. While I was talking with her I had a great sense of my vileness, and of the astonishing riches of free grace, and the great obligations I was under to devote myself to the glory of God. After we parted, I set myself to the work of self-examination and begged of God that if I did not act with right aims and upon right principles, he would discover it to me.

The next morning I was much refreshed by providentially opening to the 131st psalm in Dr. Watts's version, entitled humility and submission:

> Is there ambition in my heart
>> Searcheth, gracious God, and see
> Or do I act a haughty part?
>> Lord, I appeal to thee.
> I charge my thoughts, be humble still,
>> And all my carriage mild
> Content, my Father, with thy will,
>> And quiet as a child.
> The patient soul, the lowly mind

Shall have a large reward

Let saints in sorrow lie resigned

And trust a faithful Lord.[151]

After this I had many conflicts, fearing that, as my friend had said, my zeal was rather prompted by pride than by what I had thought it was. And sometimes Satan and my vile heart set in hand to persuade me to return to my former careless walk, but by God's grace I was preserved from complying.

I had no thought when I began of multiplying words about these sorts of trials, though I have not found them small ones. Yet all this is by way of digression and out of place, [these events] being before my second marriage.

[*Osborn replaced her large Xs with dense cross outs here. She crossed out approximately fifty-seven lines of her memoir (roughly two pages). Only a few words can be deciphered.*]

In September 1742, I was much perplexed with the cares of the world rushing in upon me. My husband had unavoidably contracted debts, having a ship, and the debts was due. The creditors wanted their own and business failed.

And indeed, month in and month out we could raise no more cash. Then, cash to provide, [we sold] the house.

I was afraid of involving ourselves further in debt lest we should not justly and honestly pay, and by that means should bring dishonor on God and a scandal upon our profession. So I cast up all we owned and took an inventory of our goods at price to sell and found they amounted to . . . .

And proposed to my husband [to give them to a] shopkeeper to trade them, which would be quick. And by that we might pay every debt. Till he consented, and we attempted it but could not succeed.

And what to do, we knew not. Then I proposed to him to sell them at a vendue for . . . but found things sold so much under price, he was discouraged, and so sold but few. Then sometime after, we, having but little, to answer demands were obliged to expose the rest to sale, and lost so much by them that instead of having enough to pay every one, we owed a hundred pounds or more.

And almost everything we did, did likewise turn out much the same.

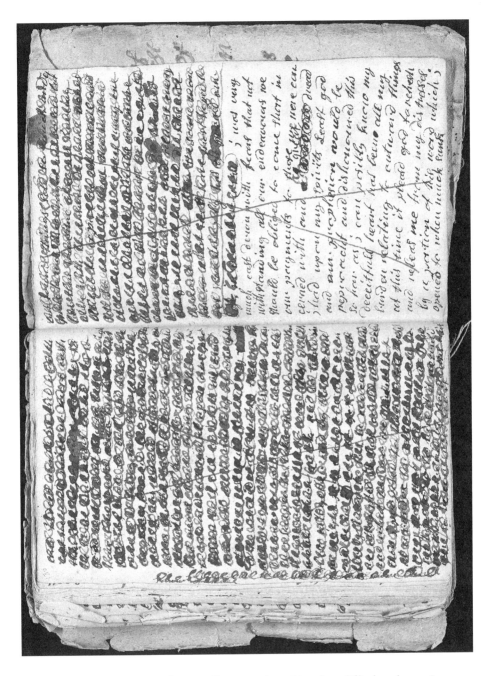

Osborn crossed out several pages of her memoir, making them difficult and sometimes impossible to read. Though she wanted her memoir to be read by others in the future, she decided not to share everything that she had originally written. Courtesy of Beinecke Rare Book and Manuscript Library, Yale University.

What we have most hoped to get something by, has oft proved our loss. In December 1742

[*Osborn's cross out ends here.*]

I was very much cast down with fears that, notwithstanding all our endeavors, we should be obliged to come short in our payments to those we were concerned with, and a great dread I had upon my spirits, lest God and our profession would be reproached and dishonored. This, so far as I can possibly know, my deceitful heart, has been all my burden relating to outward things. At this time, it pleased God to refresh and release me from my distresses by a portion of his word, which I opened to when much sunk: "Let your conversation be without covetousness, and be content with such things as you have. For he hath said, I will never leave thee nor forsake thee."[152] Upon this promise I lived cheerfully till the next June, and then Satan and my own unbelieving fears suggested to me that God would certainly be dishonored by us, and we should wrong those that were concerned with us.

The particulars of this distress from day to day, and my deliverance, is already set down in my diary, which began June the 28th, 1743, so think it not proper to enlarge here, only to say, in brief, my conflicts was very great.[153] I desire always to realize the all-sufficiency of my God to bring about things for us far better than we can think. But I wrote this particular account of our worldly affairs that if God, for wise ends, should see meet to sink us still lower in the world, so that we should not be able, according to our desire, to pay everyone to the last mite their due, they may be convinced it does not proceed from carelessness about it. For I can appeal to him that knows all hearts that it has been my constant care to do justice as well as love, mercy, and to walk humbly with my God, equally regarding the duties of first and second table.[154] I would therefore beg if this should be the case with any, that they would eye the hand of God in it, and look on it as a frown of his providence for just and holy ends, both on us and them.

I have often thought God has so ordered it throughout my days that I should be in an afflicted, low condition, and inclined the hearts of others to relieve me in all my distresses, on purpose to suppress that pride of my nature, which doubtless would have broke out greatly to his dishonor had I had health and prosperity, and so, as it were, lived independent upon others. I will think it best for me, for the tenderness of my friends to me has always had a tendency to humble me greatly and cause me to admire the goodness of God to me. That while others was daily complaining, "the rich has many friends but the poor is despised by his neighbor," I could never say but I had as much love and respect showed me as if I possessed thousands, and by the rich as well as poor, *so that on account of poverty* I never was despised.[155]

And now I have, according to my desire, committed some of the many thousand of my experiences to writing, and will give my reasons for so doing. The first motive, as I mentioned in the introduction, was that I might be excited to praise and glorify that God who has wrought such wonders for me. And through the influence of his blessed Spirit moving me thereto, it has hitherto had this effect in some measure throughout the time of my writing of it. The Lord grant it may continue so throughout my days, and then my first great end will be answered.

Secondly, I have always reaped much benefit myself by reading the lives and experiences of others. Sometimes they have been blessed to convince me of sin; sometimes to scatter doubts; and sometimes raised my affections into a flame. When expressions has been warm, they have put me upon imitating them as well as I could by breathing out my soul in like manner. And though I fall ever so short of the excellencies which others have been endowed with, yet I know with God all things is possible. He can bless a word from the weakest, meanest, and unworthiest of all creatures—even me. If a word in these lines ever proves useful to one soul after my decease, it is ten thousand times more than I deserve from the hands of a bountiful God. To him alone be all the glory.

It is his glory, I trust, through rich grace I sincerely aim, and if it does not consist with that, that these lines should be ever seen by any, either before or after my decease, I heartily desire—so far as I can possibly fathom that unfathomable deep, my own deceitful heart, and know it—that these may be all buried in oblivion. Surely, I had far rather my name and all belonging to me should be forgotten among men than remembered to the dishonor of my God. I am an ignorant, short-sighted creature, but God knows what will be for the best. To him I commit it, begging that in his all-wise providence it may be disposed of as he sees meet.

I make no doubt but some people would be ready to blame me for being so particular as to the sins I have been addicted or drawn into by the violence of temptation. As to the first that I mentioned, through God's grace it has cost me much sorrow, and I have been enabled to watch and pray against it, and hope I don't indulge it on any account. And my intent has been all along to show how God's glorious grace has triumphed over my sins and temptations, infirmities, and everything that has rise in opposition to it, and so free grace may but be magnified. I care not how much I am abased. If any can possibly find anything relating to me worthy of notice or imitation—O, give God all the glory. It is all of free grace—amazing, astonishing grace.

But I would beg as for my life that none would take example by me to abuse such tender love and dear compassion of God as I have done, for if you do, the happiest portion you will or can have will be introduced by a severe and bitter repentance if ever God bestows his grace upon you. Surely my sins has never been so sweet, but my repentance has been as bitter.

In particular, I would beg of young people to refrain from all such company as will endeavor to persuade you that your parents or other superiors deal hardly with you, for however great their friendship may seem to be, they are only instruments in the devil's hands to stir up discontent in your hearts. And then if God withhold you not, you will be ready for all manner of wickedness. And beware of all such as will persuade you to defraud them and pretend to you it is no sin. O, flee from such, as you would from serpents, for they are false friends—or rather private enemies—doing the devil's drudgery and laying snares for your precious souls. I am not insensible that this is a common thing amongst many, which make me give these warnings and bear a testimony against all such. And sure I am, they have not the mark of those whom Christ pronounces blessed, even peacemakers. Owing to such false friends was most of the breach between me and my parents, which in the time of it was too well known. Had we on both sides conversed with those that would have strove to reconcile us, we might have been at peace, and that dreadful sin I was guilty of in defrauding them had been prevented, for which—though I trust God and my mother has forgiven me—I shall never forgive myself so as to think of it without shame and regret. Again, be entreated to beware of slighting Sabbaths, stifling convictions. O, watch and pray that ye enter not into temptation, and be very careful and circumspect.

[*The end of Osborn's memoir is damaged. The next four pages are ripped, and many of the words are crossed out. It is not clear whether Osborn did this herself, or someone else did it at a later date.*]

I have prayed that God would preserve [me from] being led by impulses, but this I know: God is the hearer and answerer of prayer. Once more, I would mention that wherever I have spoke of seeing such or such things, I meant no other but with the eyes of my understanding or seeing by an eye of faith. Likewise, of hearing as it were a voice, I would not be understood any real voice. No, I pretend to no visions or revelations. And as to what I have mentioned of outward things, which may be called meats and . . . .

Nothing but union with him by faith will be of any value at all, for except his righteousness is imputed to me, I must be miserable, notwithstanding all I can do.

If these lines, after my decease, should come into the hand of any judicious Christian that may see anything I have wrote will be hurtful to the interest of religion, I desire it may be concealed. Blessed be God, he has carried me thus far through seas of sorrow towards the New Jerusalem, I trust for Jesus's sake alone.

[*On the inside of the back cover, she wrote several sentences in large handwriting, which suggests that she may have added them in the last twenty years of her life when she was nearly blind.*]

As to a particular application of scriptures adapted to my case, as an individual of that church for whom they were wrote, I trust I have a right to them.

My life has been a life of wonders, but the greatest wonder is that am out of hell. Three times God preserved my life when through my folly and presumption there was not a step between me and death.[156]

THREE

A Son's Death, 1744

PERHAPS THE GREATEST TRAGEDY *of Sarah Osborn's life was the death of her only child, Samuel, at the age of eleven. He was serving an apprenticeship in Rehoboth, thirty miles outside of Newport, when he became gravely ill with consumption (now known as tuberculosis).*

Twelve days after his death, Osborn wrote an account of her grief at losing him and her anxiety over whether he had been saved. During the last days of his life she tried to convince him to repent and seek Christ, but to her sorrow he did not show any evidence of a deathbed conversion. Yet at the moment when she felt most alone and forsaken, she experienced an overwhelming sense of God's love and presence. Though she did not know whether Samuel's "naked soul" had gone to heaven, she was certain of her own enduring covenant with God.

Friday morning, September 22, 1744

On Thursday afternoon, the sixth day of this month, I had the sorrowful news that my only son was sick unto death.[1] God in his providence provided presently for me: my dear Susa Anthony to keep my house, a horse for my husband and myself to ride, and all other things comfortable. And on my way God gave me such a sense of his goodness to me in a thousand instances, that instead of sinking under my sorrow, my mind was employed in attention to, and blessing God for my mercies. Sometimes, that he was not snatched from me in a moment by some awful accident; that he was not at so great a distance but I might be allowed to go to him with hopes of finding him yet alive. And those precious promises, which in the morning had supported me,

still continued as a refreshing cordial, even these: "Call upon me in the day
of trouble, and I will hear thee."[2] "This poor man cried, and the Lord heard
him; and saved him out of all his troubles."[3]

On Friday morning we got to Rehoboth, where I found my son much
swelled with a dropsy and pined to a mere skeleton with the jaundice, scurvy,
and consumption, all combining. He rattled in his throat like a dying person,
laboring for every breath. He was given over by the doctors and all friends,
who lamented him and did the best for him in their power as to the body.
But alas! My great concern was for that precious jewel, his immortal soul. I
endeavored to improve every opportunity to discourse with him, and read to
him such portions of scripture as I thought suitable, with passages out of Mr.
Alleine's *Alarm*, etc.[4] And I was enabled to pray all the day by ejaculatory
breathings, and sometimes to plead and wrestle with God on his behalf,
though alas, God was pleased to hide his dealings with him altogether.[5] For I
could discern no evidence of a work of grace wrought on his soul, for which
I did plead from day to day. I did not so much as once, in all his sickness,
pray for his life, but for some evidence that his soul might live. And for want
of this, I sometimes seemed to be crushed down, having a sense of his doleful
case if not reconciled to God. On Thursday, Sept. 13, the day before he died,
I was just ready to give up and sit down discouraged. My heart even almost
died with fear of what would become of him. But just in this juncture, God in
his providence ordered it so that I received a letter from my dear Susa, which
was a cordial to my drooping spirits.

In his dying moments I had an awful sense of his deplorable condition, if
his naked soul should launch into a boundless eternity without a God to go
to. I had also a view and sense of his and my utter inability to help ourselves,
and utter unworthiness that God should help us. And with the woman of
Canaan, I cried out, "Truth Lord, I am unworthy as a dog!" But I pleaded
for the crumbs that fell, one of which would be sufficient for me and mine.[6]
I had a clear discovery of the fullness and sufficiency of Christ to make satisfaction. I pleaded that he would have mercy, as on the thief of the cross, then
at the eleventh hour; apply but one drop of his precious blood, and it was
enough.[7] Thus I was enabled to fill my mouth with arguments, and in bitter
agony of soul I wrestled with God for mercy for him.[8] Surely the pangs I

then endured for his soul far exceeded those that brought him into the world. But as soon as the soul had taken its flight, I was eased of my burden. I immediately cast myself, and my burden too, on God. I adored him as a sovereign God, and blessed his name, for he had given, and it was he who had taken.[9] Surely he was better to me than ten sons.

I then arose from my dead child and was quieted, for the will of God was done, and my work was done as it respected my child.[10] And God was pleased to give such evidence of his love that my mouth was filled with praises. But when I looked on the young people who stood round lamenting him, I felt bowels of compassion for them and besought them to take warning and make their speedy flight to the blessed Jesus before sickness and death overtook them.[11]

While friends were putting on his grave clothes, I went out into the field and walked, where, with more secrecy and freedom, I could breathe out my soul to God. And the sweetness of that season I cannot express. God discovered himself to be my God, my covenant God, my Father, my Friend, my only portion and happiness, my sovereign, my all in all, my infinite fountain of all fullness.

And these were some of the breathings of my soul after him. "Lord, I adore thee as my all. I rejoice in thee as my only portion. Lord, if I have thee, I have enough. Though all the streams were cut off, yet the fountain remains; I cannot be poor. Whom have I in heaven but thee? And there is none on earth I desire besides thee. Though my flesh and my heart fail, yet God is the strength of my heart and my portion forever. Blessed God, though death separate from all things here below, it cannot separate between thee and me."[12]

O, here I rejoiced again, chose my God again, and again renewed the dedication of myself to him, my whole soul and body, with all I have, am, or can do. O his word comforted, his *rod* comforted me. I saw no frown in it, no, but the kind chastisements of my indulgent Father. This portion of scripture was very sweet, "If ye be without chastisement, whereof all are partakers, then are ye bastards, and not sons. For whom the Lord loveth, he chasteneth."[13] Therefore I cried out, "I know, O Lord, thy judgments are right, and in very faithfulness thou hast afflicted me."[14]

But I must cease, for such blessed seasons are better felt than expressed. I continued so composed and comfortable that I feared those who knew not the cause would think me void of natural affection, till my taking my last farewell at his funeral. And then I found the bonds of natural affection very strong, and I wept much. But as I followed to the grave, I pleaded thus with God, "Lord, I adore thee still as my sovereign. I do not repine at thy hand. But, dear Lord, pity me, and suffer me to weep under the smart of thy rod; it is my *only son*." Then I thought on Psalm 103, "As a father pitieth his children, for the Lord pitieth them that fear him."[15] This comforted me. But as I inquired again, if my tears were not sinful and the effect of an unresigned will, which I dreaded most of all, I was comforted again by reflecting that when Martha and Mary wept for their brother Lazarus, the blessed Jesus was not angry but wept with them.[16] O, then I again adored a sympathizing Savior, a glorious high priest, who was sensibly touched with the feeling of my infirmities. These and such like were the exercises of my mind, while following and laying my dust into the grave. And ever since I have been kept composed and cheerful.

The Lord in mercy grant that I may more and more glorify him in affliction. O that my sins may be more mortified. Lord, grant I may come out of this furnace as gold purified and fitted for my master's use.[17] If I have behaved in any measure as becomes a child of God, and any resignation has appeared in me, Lord, it is all owing to the riches of thy glorious and special grace. For had not thou by that compelled me to act otherwise, I should have flew in thy face, murmured, fretted, and repined at thee, cast away all my other comforts and mercies, and said I had none left because thou had taken *one* from me. Lord, these, and more than these, would have been the effects of my perverse nature. Therefore, not unto me, not unto *me*, but to thy glorious name be all the glory forever and ever, Amen.

[*We do not know whether Sarah Osborn ever gained a sense of assurance that her son had gone to heaven. But at some point after she finished writing her memoir in 1743, she crossed out several sentences about her hopes for his salvation. Besides scratching out the words, "O, I think I felt the pangs of the new birth for him," she also crossed out her description of being "quieted" when he sent a "portion of scripture, adapted and sweetly applied: 'All thy children shall be taught of God, and great shall be the peace of thy children.'" (See chapter 2.)*

She seems to have been unsure about his fate, fearful that he might have been damned.

Osborn never mentioned Samuel by name in any of her extant writings after 1744, but in an undated letter to her friend Susanna Anthony and in a 1756 diary entry, she made it clear that she interpreted his death as a stroke of divine punishment. She feared that she had sinned by loving him too much, setting him up as an "idol" in competition with God.

Just as a jealous God had demonstrated his absolute sovereignty by taking away her first husband, her brother, and her father, he had taken away her only son. Osborn believed that Christians were called to love God more than anything else in the world.]

Letter from Sarah Osborn to Susanna Anthony, undated

Daily encumbrances, necessary visits, bodily indisposition, and a backward heart join to prevent my writing so seasonably and full as I should be glad to. However, I now in haste will try to write a little.

And first, I would tell you that the late shock I have met with, has hitherto been blessed for quickening me to greater diligence in making my

(*Opposite*): Two pages from Osborn's memoir. Osborn crossed out several sentences expressing her hope that her son Samuel had been saved. Originally she had written, "One day, I was more than ordinarily enlarged in wrestling with God for blessings for my only son, who had been cast upon God from the womb. I had a great sense of the worth of his precious immortal soul and entreated that God would put some particular praise into my mouth that I might plead with him on his behalf all my days, and continued as if I could not give over pleading or be denied something that would encourage me to hope God would be merciful to him. O, I think I felt the pangs of the new birth for him, and having had such a sense of his miserable state by nature, and what it would be if he died Christless, and such a discovery of the all-sufficiency of Christ for him, I continued agonizing with God in prayer for a considerable time. And at last was quieted by this portion of scripture, adapted and sweetly applied: 'All thy children shall be taught of God, and great shall be the peace of thy children.'" Osborn crossed out most of this paragraph, leaving only the words, "I had a great sense of the worth of his precious immortal soul . . . had such a sense of his miserable state by nature, and what it would be if he died Christless, and such a discovery of the all-sufficiency of Christ for him, I continued agonizing with God in prayer for a considerable time." Courtesy of Beinecke Rare Book and Manuscript Library, Yale University.

three these more difficulties which
I must unceasingly encounter in
many duties would be incumbent
on me which I must hitherto been
stranger to particularly on account
of my being a minister viz. here to
three find my sins bound up by a
first if he but god continued to
enable me with great earnestness
from day to day to exercise my self to
him and plead with him for greater
proficiency in my day and that he
would not suffer me to be useless
amongst them but make me an instrument in his hand to promote
their everlasting good and he that
and to give me a name in their house
and affectations so that we might all at
once live in peace and love that
the god of peace and love might
delight to dwell amongst us and
oh how great were these endearing
engagements with god
from feelings for my entering to him who
had been cast upon god from the
womb; had a great sense of the
worth of his precious immortal
soul and ...

and for his interest the state by nature and
what it would be if he died thus he
and real discovery of the proficiency
that first his sins continued except the
my with god in prayer for or prayed
over the time ...
...
...
...
...
...
...
... could plead ... in behalf of
those he and ... cast to give me
and indeed I do find to this
much proficiency in ... to ...
... with god when I can get
to near him as to tell my mind
with enlargements freely I never ...

calling and election sure. O, I have cause with you to cry out, all God's ways are truth and faithfulness. O, how much wisdom and goodness hath he manifested in his dispensations towards rebellious me. How often hath he recovered my wandering soul and brought me nearer to himself, when I have been, in my own apprehension, on the very brink of ruin.

Sometimes he will visit me with affliction. He will take away the husband of my youth, and thereby cause me to fly to the widow's God and rejoice in him as the best of husbands. At another time, he will take away a tender father, and enable me to acquiesce in his dispensation and rejoice in him as my father's God, as my God, and a father of the fatherless. Then he will remove an only brother and thereby cause me more fully to know what it is to be resigned to his will and to adore his sovereignty.

Again, lest my heart should be joined to idols, he will have an only son, and show me at the same time that he is better to me than ten sons.[18] Ah, than ten thousand sons and all earthy enjoyments. Then, when my heart gets entangled with the world, full of plots and contrivances how I shall get this or that, pay one and another, etc., God will utterly dash all my schemes, hedge up my way with thorns, cross all my endeavors, and bring me to the greatest extremity, that I may know assuredly the work of my deliverance must be all his own. And when he hath subdued my stubborn will, brought me to leave all with him to work in his own way, then he appears on the mount of difficulty, preserves his own honor, causes his name and ways to be *well* spoken of, instead of *evil*, as I had feared, delivers me from all my fears, and makes me to rejoice in him. He inclines all my friends to minister to my comfort, smiles upon my endeavors, and makes me as cheerful and happy as I can be in this *life*. But if my poor foolish heart abuses these mercies, grows cold and indifferent and, need be, I shall be in heaviness through manifold temptations, corruption shall break out. Satan shall be let loose, and God will make his arrows sharp as though I were his enemy. Thus it has been of late. Justly is he styled a wonder-working God.

It is sweet, my friend, thus to trace him in his footsteps here, for surely he appears lovely and faithful. But O, what will it be when we have a more full discovery in glory, when we shall see him as he is? O, eternity shall then assist our praises.

FAMILIAR
LETTERS,

WRITTEN BY

Mrs. SARAH OSBORN,

AND

Miss SUSANNA ANTHONY,

LATE OF NEWPORT,

RHODE-ISLAND.

PUBLISHED ACCORDING TO ACT OF CONGRESS.

NEWPORT, (R. I.) PRINTED AT THE OFFICE OF
THE NEWPORT MERCURY.
1807.

The title page of *Familiar Letters, Written by Mrs. Sarah Osborn, and Miss Susanna Anthony, Late of Newport, Rhode-Island* (Newport: Newport Mercury, 1807). Osborn's letter to her friend Susanna Anthony about her son's death was reprinted in this volume. The original letter does not survive. Courtesy of the American Antiquarian Society.

You ask if I ever find such substantial joy as when my whole soul is devotedly fixed on God? I answer, no. I have no idea of any happiness compared to this. This is the utmost of my desires, to be made holy as God is holy. To have his image enstamped on my soul makes me happy here. But O, what shall I be when I wake in his likeness? O, even from the *thoughts* of this flow *rivers* of pleasure.

But shall such polluted worms as *we* be brought to this, the enjoyment of a holy God? Let us stand and wonder—stand and adore our glorious Mediator who hath purchased all these blessings for us at the expense of his *own* most precious blood. Here, I am lost in admiration.

Yours, in the sweetest bonds,

S.O.

November 14, 1756, Sabbath evening

Blessed, forever blessed, be my gracious God, for he is good and his mercy endureth forever. Yesterday, and Friday evening also, God took me near to himself in meditation, prayer, and examination; this morning, also; and adored be his name, he keeps me in his fear all the day long, habitually so. Blessed be his infinite wisdom, love, and faithfulness, for all the dispensations of his providence, that he by his mercies hath led me to repentance; not only so, but hath used the rod to reduce my wandering soul, breaking off my dependence on creatures, weaning my affections from things below, that they may be more steadily fixed on himself and his Christ, his Spirit and grace, that these may be all in all to my soul. What wise and blessed steps hath he taken, though once afflictive. When in my young and tender years, my heart was much set on the husband of my youth, he rent him from me, and likewise bereaved me of almost all that was dear to me according to the flesh, whereby he broke off my dependence on those streams for comfort and led me to the mountain. O "happy rod, that brought me nearer to my God."[19] He hath abundantly made up to me, in himself and in his Christ, the loss of all of these. But alas, still the world, its pleasures, profits, and cares, threatened to engross and entangle my affections. Infinite wisdom saw this and therefore dashed all my schemes, disappointed all my hopes and expectations from friends and means—though, blessed be his name, he did not leave me wholly destitute. By this, through his grace, he brought me to cast my care on himself and rely more immediately on his providence to provide for me, and mine, ever since. And here I have lived secure and at rest, amidst many ups and downs, frowns, and flatteries from creatures. The less reason hath had to work upon, the more freely faith has cast itself upon the faithfulness of God, and here my expectations have never been disappointed. God hath comforted me when creatures have failed and proved vanity and vexation of spirit.

But still my foolish heart must needs seek something below to go out freely after, and hath been exceedingly attached to Christian friends. And here, because I hoped I loved for Jesus's sake, I have indulged excess; here have my affections twined; these have been as the apple of my eye, or even as my own soul. In these have I rejoiced; from these, my expectations of future comforts have been raised. I was ready to say, surely *these* will not fail. But rather than my dependence should be placed on these, and they prove rivals in my heart, God will embitter them, every one, at some time or other, even to the breaking of my very heart. I shall find a sore thorn under every one of these sweetest roses upon earth.

And now, blessed be God, I am more than ever convinced that all things under the sun are vanity and nothing but God alone a substantial good. Adored be thy name, O my God, for every twig of thy rod. Help me now to cease from man, whose breath is in his nostrils. Now let me be effectually weaned from the world, and all my hopes, expectations, desires, love, delight, and joys terminate in thee. Yes, let me forever be for thee and for one other. Lord, thou hast won my heart. Take it to thyself, fill it with grace, and possess it to eternity. Go on, I beseech thee, to rend away every rival. I stand divested of all the world; give it to whom thou pleasest. Give me my chosen portion— thyself, thy Spirit, and thy grace—and I have enough. Here I am: do with me what seemeth thou good.

FOUR

A Hidden God, 1744–1754

DURING THE TEN YEARS *between 1744, the year of her son's death, and 1754, the beginning of the French and Indian War, Sarah Osborn continued to search for evidence of a "hidden God." She faced many hardships during these years, including the deaths of two of her ministers: Jonathan Helyer (1719–45), a recent Harvard graduate who died after serving her congregation for only a year, and the venerable Nathaniel Clap (1669–1745), who had welcomed her into full church membership. Though she and Henry were never forced to declare bankruptcy again, they remained poor, and Sarah struggled to pay their bills on her meager schoolteacher's salary. She also continued to suffer from a chronic illness that left her tired and weak. Often she felt as if God had "hidden his face" from her, leaving her in spiritual darkness. "Hide not thy face from me in the day when I am in trouble," she read in the Psalms. "Incline thine ear unto me: in the day when I call answer me speedily" (Ps 102:2).*

There were many ways that Osborn tried to make a "hidden God" visible. Besides praying to him throughout the day and reading the Bible, she attended church regularly and developed close relationships with many clergy both in Newport and elsewhere, including the Reverend William Vinal (1718–81), who became her pastor in 1746, and the Reverend Joseph Fish, who corresponded with her for more than thirty years. Describing Fish and other ministers as Christ's "ambassadors," Osborn depended on them for spiritual advice during times of doubt.

Osborn's life revolved around spiritual practices that were designed to bring her closer to God. Besides writing to him in her diary, she met every week with the women's society in order to praise and glorify him, and she fasted before her church's celebration of the Lord's Supper each month, emptying herself in order to be filled with the real presence of Jesus in the bread and the wine.

Part of Sarah's glorification of God included berating herself for her sins. Like other evangelicals in the Calvinist tradition, she portrayed herself as innately and profoundly sinful, and she cultivated a stance of self-abasement as a way of exalting God. While he was pure and infinitely powerful, she was the opposite: weak, corrupt, and loathsome, nothing more than a "worthless worm" who was helpless to accomplish anything without him. She was despondent when someone accused her of being "lifted up with spiritual pride" because this was the sin that she most feared. True Christians were supposed to be humble and self-effacing, not arrogant.

Despite her focus on her sinfulness, Osborn also wrote about the parts of her life that brought her joy: her friendship with the Reverend Joseph Fish; her close spiritual ties to her "brothers" and "sisters" in her church and the women's society; her deep love for Susanna Anthony, who was like a sister to her; and her work as a teacher. Although she sometimes found her students "noisy and unruly," she spent many hours praying for their salvation. As one of the few jobs open to women in the eighteenth century, teaching tended to be low-paying, and Osborn probably earned only half as much as male teachers. Yet despite her poverty, she hesitated to raise her prices because of her fear of appearing covetous. Teaching was not just a job to her, but a vocation—a way of serving and glorifying God. Joseph Fish sent his two daughters to her school because he knew she would teach them not only reading, writing, and needlework, but also the meaning of a Christian life.

What sustained Sarah Osborn during her moments of spiritual darkness was her faith that God would never abandon her. "He will never leave me nor forsake me," she quoted from Hebrews. Even when she cried out in despair that God had hidden his face from her, she knew that he was still invisibly present, holding her world in his hands.

1744

May 10, 1744

I desire to record it with thankfulness that God in his providence gave me an opportunity last evening to advise with my dear aged pastor (Mr. Clap) about praying with my scholars. He rejoiced much in the proposal and advised me, by all means, to proceed and let nothing discourage me; and fear no scoffs, for it was God's cause, and he who had put it into my heart to do it would take care of his own glory. He likewise reminded me how highly Christ resented it when his own disciples would have deprived little children of privileges. He advised me to be brief and plain and often to mention those words in Matthew 6, "Ask, and ye shall receive; seek, and ye shall find; knock, and it shall be opened unto you."[1] And those in Proverbs, "I love them that love me, and those that seek me early shall find me."[2] And to make confession of sin, and plead for pardon for Christ's sake; endeavor to follow him in plainness, so that the little ones might understand what I mean, &c.

As I think I never saw him more joyful and pleased with me, so I know not when I have come away more comforted, for my scruples all vanished. And now, by assisting grace, I determine to proceed as God shall enable me. Blessed be God that I enjoy so great a privilege as my dear pastor, who has thus encouraged my faith, obedience, and joy, and helped me in my strait. And now, O my God, I am convinced it is my duty to pray with my dear children. I fly to thee again for assisting grace. Lord, without that, it will be only a piece of formality, and will never prove serviceable to any. I beseech thee, O Lord, pour out on me a spirit of prayer and fill me with bowels of compassion to poor little ones.

1745

May 27, 1745, Monday evening

This morning it pleased the great and glorious God to take to himself my dear, dear Mr. Helyer. O, he is gone from me. I shall never more hear any of his precious sermons or solemn counsels. O my God, preserve me from murmuring at thine holy hand. I desire to bless thy dear name, that thou didst lend worthless me so sweet a pastor so long. And now thou hast in infinite wisdom bereaved me of my shepherd, I would give myself wholly to thee, thou great shepherd and bishop of souls. O, be thou my all. Now, Lord, thou hast laid thy hand heavily upon me; thou hast touched me in a tender part; thou hast cut off a stream from which much comfort has flowed to my poor soul. Now, my God, appear for me and refresh my soul with streams more immediately from the fountain.

Lord, sanctify thine hand to me, to his dear consort and all relations, to my dear aged pastor [the Reverend Nathaniel Clap], to the whole church. O, let this awful dispensation of thy providence awaken secure souls and quicken the awakened. O, let the fruit of all be to take away sin. Lord, I confess thou might justly deprive me of all precious means. But pity me, dear Lord, and still afford us the means of grace.[3] O, give us a pastor after thine own heart. Blessed be thy name, the residue of the Spirit is with thee. Lord, I desire to trust thee for all future events, but I beg, I beseech thee, bring me nearer to thy blessed self by this great turn in the wheel of thy providence. O Lord, enable me to be, in good earnest, preparing to follow him, who through faith and patience is gone to inherit the promises. O Lord, hear me; Lord, answer me for Jesus Christ's sake, in whose name I beg all, to whom be glory forever. Amen.

July 28, 1745, Sabbath day

This week past I have through God's goodness been carried safely to see my mother, where I saw a letter to her from ———, in which he seems to intimate his fears that I am much lifted up with spiritual pride and stand in great need of caution from Christian friends.[4]

Lord God Almighty, thou searcher of hearts, thou trier of the reins, convince me, I beseech thee, if this be the principle I have acted upon, in communicating to others thy remarkable, gracious dealings with my soul. O Lord, the jealousies of thine own experienced children make me jealous, too. O, search me and try me and suffer me not to deceive myself. O, is it indeed so? Have I been practically saying to any, stand by thyself, for I am holier than thou? Boasting myself as though I were something of myself? Lord, if this has been the case, O convince and humble me, for thou knowest I thought I boasted in none but thee. Thou knowest I thought it was thy love constrained me thus to speak and declare thy wonderful works. O Lord, pity me, for thou knowest how often conscience reproves me for being so ungrateful to thee, so little speaking to thy praise and glory, and I think justly, too. But O, how shall I behave? If I speak, I stumble and grieve even thy dear children and servants. Lord, direct me, and O, hasten the time when I shall find no more backwardness to praise thee, nor fear of giving offense or grieving any, but shall chant forth thy praises throughout an endless eternity.

I bless thee, O my God, that there is a day of judgment appointed wherein the secrets of all hearts will be disclosed, and I trust it will appear that the little zeal and gratitude I have shown did proceed from right principles, through the infinite riches of thy grace in Jesus Christ. In the meantime, help me daily to approve myself to thee, who infallibly knowest my heart, and grant I may be a stumbling block to none in any respect. O, quicken me, Lord, in thy way for Jesus's sake.

November 1745[5]

Now, with sorrow of heart, I am again going to record the repeated blow of God's hand, in bereaving me, and the mournful church to which I belong, of our dear aged pastor, the Rev. Mr. Clap, who died on Wednesday evening, October 30, 1745. The Lord in mercy sanctify this rod, and enable us all to see it, and who it is who hath appointed it, and with truly resigned humble souls to say, "The Lord gave, and the Lord hath taken away: Blessed be the name of the Lord."[6]

Lord, help us to bless thee that thou hast indulged us so long with so eminent a man of God, and O, for thy mercy's sake, pardon our iniquities and go on still to be gracious to us, and give us another pastor after thine own heart. Lord, direct thy people in choosing such a one as thou wilt delight to bless, and incline the heart of thy servant to accept the invitation. O, keep out all contestation, thou God of peace and love. Unite thy church in peace and concord. O blessed Jesus, thou great shepherd and bishop of souls, suffer us not to be scattered as sheep without a shepherd. O, preserve us from wolves in sheep's clothing. O King Jesus, thou great head of the church, we trust we are a vine of thine own right hand's planting. O, delight to build us up and not to pluck us down. Lord, help us to cast all our care upon thee. But O, pour out upon us a spirit of prayer and supplication, that in everything thereby, with thanksgiving, we may be making known our requests to God, and O, hear for Jesus's sake.

On Monday, November 4, the dear and venerable Mr. Clap was decently interred, attended by a numerous throng of people of all ranks and denominations. O, that all who followed him sorrowfully to his grave might joyfully meet him in the morning of the resurrection. And O my God, grant that I, thy poor worm, may then see his face with joy. Lord, forgive me that I have improved his precious counsels and solemn warnings no better. Lord, humble me for this, and at the same time accept of praises, that thou didst make him so dear and helpful to me. Thou, Lord, knowest how oft thou hast set home thy word, dispensed by him, with power irresistible upon my poor soul— sometimes to arouse, convince, and awaken me, sometimes to strengthen and establish my faith, sometimes to encourage me in the way of duty, sometimes to remove doubts and fears. Lord, thou knowest also how sweet it was to me to have recourse to him in all times of difficulty and trial, and how ready he was to afford me his counsels. For all these favors, Lord, I would humbly bless and adore thee, thou blessed author and bestower of them, and since thou, in thine all-wise providence, hast deprived me of all these former privileges, and I can never more in this world have recourse to thy servant for any solemn counsels, I beseech thee, dear Lord, I beseech thee, that I may have more free recourse to thy blessed self.

O, give me access to thy throne that in everything, by prayer and supplication, with thanksgiving, I may be making known my requests unto thee. O, now thou art removing the means and instruments by which thou was wont to convey the graces and comforts of thy blessed Spirit to me. O, now refresh my weary sin-sick soul with streams more immediately from the fountain and guide me by thine unerring counsel. Lord, in thine own time restore the means of grace, I beseech thee, and grant I may be made meet for heaven, and receive me to glory for Jesus's sake.

1748

Sarah Osborn to Joseph Fish, February 4, 1748

Very dear and Reverend Sir,

I cannot well express how much I was rejoiced when I received your letter, for which I had so much longed. I am also thankful upon one account I did not receive one before. This, dear Sir, may seem strange, but I'll give you my reason for it. I am apt to think had you answered more fully, it would have prevented some free conversation I have had with my own reverend pastor, which has endeared him much to me, as I'll acquaint you by and by. God is infinitely wise and orders all things well. I cried, "All these things are against me."[7] I passionately longed for a letter or to see you. But I beseech you, dear Sir, let not my mentioning this prevent you from writing for time to come, since now I can freely converse with my own minister, though before I could not use that freedom I wanted. I am happy in dear Mr. Vinal far beyond what I ever expected and think I can never be enough thankful that I am allowed such precious means as I enjoy.[8]

And now, dear Sir, according to your desire I proceed to give you some account of the dealings of God with me since I wrote last. I remained much as I was then all this summer and fall—sometimes pressed down with sinking discouragements and unbelieving fears that it would never be better in this world, and seemed to be looking out on every side for some sore judgment, or to be left to commit a scandalous sin greatly to the dishonor of God's name. My path seemed every way hedged up with thorns, and what to do I knew not, for I could not pray. And though I hope I was not ignorant that I could not merit anything by my prayers, yet I knew that was a means of God's appointed, and I never expected to grow till I could pray, since in that way God usually bestows his mercies on me.

Dear Mr. Vinal had been going through a course of sermons to awaken the unregenerate and then through another to align them to Christ, beginning with the compact with his Father and so on, all his offices. In short, he begun at the foundation and went up to the topstone. But all this while I sat untouched except in one sermon on Christ's kingly office, where he shewed his power to subdue all his and our enemies, and in one [sermon] on those words, "and of his fullness we have all received and grace for grace," where he shewed that there is a fullness of sanctifying grace in him.[9] When he had finished these two courses he thought meet to turn to the believer, and mentioning that he should first begin with the weak believer, I hoped with those to take my portion. His text was, "O thou of little faith, wherefore didst thou doubt?"[10]

But before he began to deal out the children's food, he gave a solemn warning to all hypocrites to stand off. And amongst the rest—to those that could not produce the evidence of growth in grace—[he said that] whatever their hopes were for true grace will be growing grace. These words were like a pointed dart, for I knew I could not produce that evidence, and I was ready to sink right down. And though I could not deny the rest of the marks laid down for trial, yet I dare not apply them or take comfort in them. And now my distress increased. I was extremely puzzled for I could not let go my hold of God as mine, and yet the possibility of being deceived made me tremble.

In this perplexity I applied myself to my dear pastor who used me very affectionately and tenderly and gave me good counsel and put me in mind that Mrs. Bury said she did not think it worthwhile to pull down her foundation every time it rains in at the roof, which proved a word in season to me.[11] And when the clouds were thickest the glorious sun was just ready to appear, for God revived me and shewed me that he was the same faithful God still and would never leave me nor forsake me; no, nor never suffer me to leave him. And now, blessed God, I am again going on my way, rejoicing in hope of the glory of God.[12] And trust I shall be kept by the mighty power of God through faith unto salvation. The path of duty is made much more plain and easy to me than before. God permits me now to get near him and pour out my heart before him. O, amazing grace, think you there ever was a greater monument of it than worthless I?

Take courage, dear Sir. I make no doubt but that, though you walk in the midst of trouble, he will revive you in his own time. O, may the joy of the Lord be your strength. Though you have enemies within and without, yet he that is for you is stronger than all. O, when we can realize it that we are marching forward and fighting under the banner of the great captain of our salvation, how easy it is to bid defiance to earth and hell, but when once we lose sight of him, everything is dreadful. If he were changeable as we are, we might well sink, but he is the same compassionate savior still, a God nigh at hand in time of trouble. O, who that knows his name would not put their trust in him? I can't pretend to know how great your trials are, but I know God has said, "All things shall work together for good to those who love him, even to those who are called according to his purpose."[13] It is hard for us to realize this in a time of distress and darkness, but we often find it so afterwards, even in this world. Surely God is an infinitely wise sovereign, and he knows better than we do what is best for us. And if he is pleased to exercise us with troubles all our lives, yet if we are united to Christ by faith there is good news for us. We must die if Christ is ours. Death is ours also, and then we shall bid a final farewell to all sin and sorrow. All tears will then be wiped from our eyes, and one moment's enjoyment of God will richly make amends for all we undergo.

How my heart aches for you, and I heartily pity you under all your sorrows. O, that in the multitude of your thoughts within you, God's comfort may delight your soul. I don't wonder if you think your case singular. I believe there be few Christians under desertion or sore trial but what think so.

Dear Sir, forgive my freedom in writing this to you, I who am so weak and unworthy, and accept it as coming from one who wishes you the best of blessings, however incapable of giving you advice. O, pray for me that I may be kept humble, love much, praise much, and do much for the glory of that God who has done so much for me.

Dear Susa is still alive, but I have not seen her since I received yours. I hear, Sir, you have some thoughts of sending your little daughter here to school, and if you conclude so to do and will commit her to my care under God, you shall be heartily welcome to what schooling I am capable of giving her, and I should be exceedingly glad it might be ordered so that I could have her to board with us altogether.[14] I would endeavor to make it as easy for you as possible. I think it would be a great pleasure to do anything to serve you, whom God has made very dear to me.

My paper fails,[15] so must beg your acceptance of this, with hearty respects from your sincere friend and sister,

Sarah Osborn

1752

February 9, 1752, Sabbath evening

Ah, Lord, how deceitful do I find my heart to be. How often have I thought I desired nothing more of this world's goods, but just daily food and raiment and wherewith to render to everyone their due. Yea, I have once and again told thee so. And thou hast in thy good providence granted me all that I asked of thee; yea, thou hast given me to the utmost of what I then desired. And now, ere I am aware, I find myself busy in providing for futurities, want to lay up a little of this and a little for that. And from thence, I begin to want a great deal, to provide for sickness and old age, and whatnot.

Lord, I am afraid of this worldly mindedness. I know not where it will end. O, I pray thee, subdue it by thy grace, or all my strivings against it will be ineffectual. O, do I begin to lay up a treasure here? Then I fear my heart will be here also. Lord, I dread being glued down to the things of time and sense. I pray thee, give me no unsanctified prosperity, but sanctify my fancy, and let not my vain imaginations carry my heart off from God and bury it in this world. O, for some discoveries of eternal things. That this vain, empty world, with all its enjoyments, may shrink into nothing compared with that more durable substance, that one thing needful: an interest in the blessed Jesus. O Lord, help me more and more to lay up all my good in God so that it may overbalance the sweetness and bitterness of all creatures.

Lord, I would not ungratefully forget to thank thee for the care of thy good providence in so providing the comforts and conveniencies of life for me. But O, I deprecate having these as my portion. This is not the portion I have chosen, O no, but thyself, thy Christ, and the sanctifying influence of thy blessed Spirit, that I may be enabled to live to thy glory here and to all eternity. O, grant these desires; give me this portion, I beseech thee, for Jesus's sake.

1753

Sarah Osborn to Joseph Fish, May 29, 1753

Much honored Sir,

Yours of April 17 (big with gratitude) came to hand last week. I think, dear Sir, your acknowledgments far exceed the deserts of any of my poor endeavors to serve you. If I have in any degree acted as becomes a Christian, may God have all the glory. Sure I am, I have done no more than my duty and yet remain an unprofitable servant.

May God in his all-wise providence find out and bless means for the recovery of you and yours out of every difficulties, both inward and outward. Yea, and in his own time, he will, too, when his most glorious ends are accomplished, for truth and faithfulness will not willingly afflict or grieve his dear children. If God has put any tenderness and sympathy in a heart so hard as mine, as I must acknowledge to the glory of his name he has, insomuch that I think I can truly say, in all your sorrows, so far as I am acquainted with them, I am afflicted and mourn with you. In your comforts I do rejoice. There is, as Mr. Whitefield expresses it, a sacred something that has knit my heart to you with stronger bonds than that of natural affection.[16]

And if so, O how do the bowels of our great High Priest who has had feeling of your infirmities, and in like manner been tempted, care towards you? O does he not, when he afflicts you, touch even the apple of his eye. And yet if need be, ye must be in heaviness through manifold temptations. O precious promise: all things shall work together for good to those that love God. O how sweet being in covenant with a God who is truth and faithfulness in the abstract and who never, never will leave the soul once united to Christ by faith.

Earthly comforts may and will fail; these springs may be cut off, but can you be poor who have the eternal Jehovah for your portion? O no, it cannot be. O, let this raise your drooping spirits amidst all your trials, that since you are founded upon the rock, Christ Jesus, though the rain descend and the floods come, the winds blow and beat upon the house, it shall not fall. Nor shall all the united force of earth and hell ever be able to pluck you out of his hand. Who is he that condemneth you? It is Christ that justifieth. May this be your comfort. To your own master you stand or fall, and I trust integrity and uprightness shall preserve you all your days. Christ will guide you by his word and unerring Spirit. He will help and strengthen you; he will uphold you by the right hand of his righteousness. Has he not said he will be your God—lo, I am with you always, even to the end of the world, to and through death. He will openly acknowledge and acquit you in the day of judgment in the presence of men and angels; yea, and before the accuser of the brethren, too.

The Lord support and comfort you with daily communications from himself, the spring and fountain of all consolations, and renew your strength that you may mount on the wings of faith towards heaven and take a view of the promised land. O, may faith bring home some clusters of grapes for you to feed upon while you travel through this wilderness, this vale of tears. May you always lean on our beloved and rest your weary head on his dear delightful breast. O, my very heart is melted within me with ardent desires for you, and happy shall I think myself if God will own and bless the poor weak endeavors of a feeble worthless worm to refresh you, who knows she is not worthy to wash the feet of the servants of my Lord and blushes at the review of the freedoms I have used with one so much my superior in all respects. But I am persuaded, dear Sir, you will forgive them, accept of my honest intention, and cover my failings with the mantle of love.

I was much pleased, dear Sir, with the hope of seeing you, Madame Fish, friends, and any as well as your dear children, and thought much of the satisfaction in conversing with you. But alas, I am for the present disappointed. Well, God knows what is best for us. Perhaps I depended too much and raised my expectations too high. If it may consist with the divine will, I shall much rejoice to have an opportunity to wait on you and yours. But if this is not to be granted, I trust we shall ere long meet where there will be no interruption nor separation forever. O, refreshing thought. Then we shall be able to communicate to each other what we enjoy and shout forth the riches of redeeming love and grace. There we shall be sure that the glory of God is the end of all—that the tyrant pride cannot lurk under anything.

And O, that God would preserve me from that hateful and accursed sin while I tell you that you may bless God with me and for me, that he has for some months been exceeding gracious to a worthless wretch who has a thousand times forfeited all her comforts into the hands of his justice—and who deserved to be kept under desertions and at a distance all her days, yea, to be spurned from his presence forever. Yet he has not dealt with her according to her sins, nor rewarded her according to her iniquities, but on the contrary has graciously healed her backslidings, recovered her from her declensions, and caused her to return to her first husband and given her larger discoveries of himself, perhaps than ever before, as a God of infinite perfections—self-sufficient, self-existent and independent, before whom angels and seraphim do bow and veil their faces—and the only proper object of choice and adoration till the soul has been much enamored with his beauty (and especially as a holy God).

[My soul] renewed its choice and dedications and rejoiced exceedingly in him and its portion, in and through a glorious Mediator for time and eternity. Strong desires after sanctifying grace excited a spirit of prayer poured out more than for years past. As great discoveries of indwelling corruption as ever, but at the same time, see Christ all-sufficient and his grace sufficient to work all in her and for her. Meditations on death, judgment, and eternity exceeding sweet. Blessed earnests and foretastes of the full enjoyment of God forever, the heaven of heaven itself. But I have not yet attained [heaven] (though at some times loathe to descend hither again); I am still in my enemy's country and a thousand snares await me.

Therefore, dear Sir, pray hard for me, that I may not lose the precious relish for divine things nor let my beloved go. No, nor yet be high-minded but fear, remembering 'tis by grace I stand. And O, pray for greater degrees of grace, for it is to be attained. O, why should I sit down with low degrees since grace is absolutely free and sovereign? I cannot be willing always to remain a dwarf in religion. Truth, I am utterly unworthy of all the mercy and truth God has already shewn to his handmaid, but Christ Jesus is infinitely worthy, in whose name I come; yea, and he has died to purchase this very blessing. O Sir, pray in hope, and pray in faith, that the prayer of faith may prevail for there is a "maybe"; there is a "who can tell?"[17] But God will give me grace in strength as well as grace in truth. I ask not riches, honors, or long life, but Christ and his grace, and all is well.

Forgive my intruding on your patience, and pray let me hear from you as soon as you can without its adding to your difficulties. I would write to Miss Molly if I had time.[18] I beg she will not wait, but write to me. Her letters are always welcome. Miss Susa has been too poorly to write a great while and is now out of town for her health, but intends to write as soon as she can. Mrs. Vinal has been ill and exceedingly exercised in mind all winter and spring and so remains.[19] The Lord deliver her in his own time.

'Tis time to conclude with humble service to yourself and love to the dear offspring from your sincere though unworthy friend,

Sarah Osborn

July 12, 1753

O, what a clog is this poor crazy body. How much time must be bestowed on it in sleep to make it in any measure active in the service of God. If 'tis denied the refreshment it requires that way, it utterly refuses to afford me any assistance and hangs as a dead weight to bear down my spirits. Its ails and complaints are almost all that can be attended, and I am unfit for everything. O blessed be God, I shall ere long shake off this clog. And then, my soul, thou shalt be forever active; then thou mayest fly swift to execute his commands; adore, gaze, praise, exult, and triumph! And drink in as much of God as thou canst hold. There is no weariness in thy Father's house: no, there the weary are at rest. Then the full end of thy first and second creation shall be answered, even to glorify God and enjoy him forever.

O my God, I bless thee for these hopes of glory, but O, make me active even here. Let the influence of thy Spirit and grace be lively and strong, and it shall animate even this lump of clay and make it at least for a season forget its infirmities. O, be with me and assist me in duty this day, I pray thee, for Jesus's sake.

July 15, 1753, Sabbath evening

I have this day been admitted to wait on God in his house and at his table, and there, blessed be God, had my heart enlarged. I trust sacramental graces was really drawn forth into exercise, and I was enabled to say "my beloved is mine and I am his."[20] Sin as the procuring cause of my dear Redeemer's suffering appeared exceeding bitter. Assisted in pleading for its utter destruction by the blood of Christ, which was shed for the remission of sin, and in pleading for strengthening and quickening grace. Adored the wisdom and goodness of God in appointing such an ordinance, and I, who so long ago deserved to have had the cup of trembling put into my hand, should be brought to drink of the cup of divine consolation, even the blood of the Son of God. Was satisfied I was an invited guest and came there in obedience to my dear Redeemer's command, to do this in remembrance of him. Was persuaded he had answered all the demands of justice in my room and stead; had drunk the very dregs of the cup of divine indignation that I might be free in him; had cast over me the wedding garment, even his own spotless righteousness, that the shame of my nakedness might not appear, nor I be found speechless when he came in to view the guest. Neither was I, blessed be God, but was bid welcome there.

O, amazing grace. O, astonishing love and condescension! There, there, I solemnly renewed my choice and dedications, and solemnly resolved, by grace assisting, to follow hard after God, to be for him and for no other. I rejoiced to think how I was going from ordinance to ordinance, and from strength to strength, and should ere long arrive where there is no need of ordinances. O! What a feast have I had today—a feast of fat things full of marrow, of wines on the lees well refined.

And now, my soul, remember the vows of God are upon thee. I fly to thee for strength to live answerable to these solemn transactions betwixt thee and me. O, hold me fast by the bonds of thy Spirit and grace, and then I will perform my vows; then I will hold thee fast and will not let thee go. O blessed Jesus, stand by me and strengthen me, and I will clasp the arms of my faith around thee. I will obey thee with my whole soul and body, which are thine own. O, how sweet to tell thee they are thine own, and Lord I repeat it: they are thine own forever to all intents and purposes. Therefore possess them. O, accept them and use them as most consists with thy glory, and all is well, infinitely well.

But Lord, remember, I promise thee nothing at all in my own strength. No, no, I will not, I dare not, for if thou leavest me I shall surely leave thee, turn apostate or do everything that's dreadful. O, keep me from temptation. Keep me from sin. Carry on thy own work in opposition to earth and hell. O adored be thy name. Thy power is infinite. If thou wilt work, none can let, and thou art faithful, too.

Therefore by grace I will rely upon thee for everything I want, for I am thine and thou art mine,

Sarah Osborn

July 28, 1753, Saturday evening

Last evening straitened and confused in prayer. This morning waked with sick headache, much out of order every way, and my spirits sunk exceedingly. A gloomy veil cast over everything: my school was to be all confusion; my spirit of government being lost, the children be sure would not profit from me and so would by degrees dwindle away and come to naught. These and the like things Satan or unbelief took the advantage of my indisposition to suggest. I reward the trial that I may see the hand of Providence providing and overriding all things well for me, as faith tells me it will.[21]

O my God, pity me, and help me to break through the entanglements of this world. Thou seest of myself I cannot do it. Lord, I thought carking care, distrust of thy providential care, had been a conquered enemy. O, have I too confidently believed it to be so. O, forgive me, I pray thee, and for thine own honor's sake subdue this hateful sin. Lord, I would fain rely on thee at all times for I do believe; help thou my unbelief—thou wilt do all things well for me.

And I am thine own,

Sarah Osborn

July 29, 1753

This morning I have again been exercised with despondencies and seemed to be sinking in deep waters. Lord, save me. O save me from the prevalence of this sin of distrust. Save me from pulling on me the evils of a tomorrow, which may never come. O, save me from this sin, I beseech thee, for in me it is attended with a thousand aggravations! For I know it is in direct contrariety to thy positive command "Take no thought for the morrow."[22] 'Tis contrary to all my resolutions and determinations, by grace assisting, to commit all my concerns into thy faithful hands and to cast all my care upon thee. Besides, my own experience has ever proved to me that thou art the God who has fed me all my life long, the God that didst never leave me upon the mount of difficulty, but that always appeared and wrought deliverance. Thou hast been my tried friend in six and in seven troubles, and thou hast said thou wilt never leave me nor forsake me.

August 12, 1753, Sabbath daytime

By taking some medicinal snuff night before last, I am (contrary to my expectation) by its operation deprived of the opportunities of waiting on God in his house today. My head is much stupefied, eyes and nose run—mouth, gums, and throat sore, and indeed, disordered in every part. Will God give a blessing to these means, that my sight, hearing, and memory may be repaired, pains abated, and I more fitted to serve thee and my generation according to thy will. Lord, if it may consist with thy sovereign pleasure, grant a blessing upon this medicine. Let it accomplish the desired effect. But this I ask with submission to thy will and only in subordination to thy glory.

O Lord, let me not with holy Basil be too earnest with thee to remove this inveterate headache lest I should provoke thee to remove it and let loose some lust upon me.[23] O Lord, let thy will be done. Continue what bodily disorders thou pleasest—yea, afflict me in any way thou pleasest—rather than let loose one lust. O! I deprecate this; I tremble at the thought of this. Let sin be crucified; let that gasp and die; let grace grow and flourish; let union be more complete and sensible communion with thee be more obtained. Lord, make me holy and all is well, infinitely well. I, with importunity, ask no more. I desire no more but to be like thee—thou knowest is all my joy and all my salvation.

Let flesh and heart fail; let it cry out or shrink from pains as even the innocent nature of Jesus did, but if God is the strength of my heart and my portion forever, I am not only safe but happy, too. O, thou God of ordinances, send me a blessing, a portion out of thine house this day. Bless me, even me, with thy gracious presence. Thou art not confined to house or means. Blessed be thy name forever and ever. Amen and Amen.

August 18, 1753, Saturday evening

I have been this afternoon a little scrupled about my taking so many scholars and told in plain words by one that he feared I loved the money better than the children. If so, I am no better than a pickpocket and my case is sad indeed. The Lord humble me under this censure and make me yet more faithful. Lord forbid that the love of money, that root of all evil, should ever influence me to do what is contrary to thy will.

O assist me in the duties of my calling, I pray thee, and Lord, revive thy own work in my soul. O! Hold me not at a distance, I pray thee, Lord. Art thou about to depart from me? O, stir me up to run and cry after thee and help me to stretch forth the arms of faith and lay hold on thee and not let thee go. O, hast thou not said thou wilt never leave nor forsake me? O Lord, return and leave me not comfortless and forlorn. Lord, what can I do without thee? What shall I do? Everything is dreadful if thou art absent. O return, return, forgive my sin, heal my soul, and bring me nigh thyself for Jesus's sake, whose I am and will, by grace, forever be.

September 2, 1753, Sabbath evening

Last evening and this morning, blessed be God, I was assisted in drawing nigh to God, my desires after communion with him at his table and for increase of grace enlarged, and I hoped for a refreshing season. But alas, alas, when I came there I was afflicted with a thousand impertinencies and idle imaginations washing in upon me almost every moment, insomuch that I dare not say my heart was fixed.

O my God, it was easy with thee to have put to flight these foes, though I could not suppress them. O show me wherefore thou didst suspend the influences of thy Spirit. Art thou angry with me? O, remember thou hast sworn thou wilt not be wroth with me nor rebuke me. Lord, look in the face of thine anointed and grant peace and pardon, and for his sake be at peace with me. Did I provoke thee by self-confidence? Lord, humble me to the dust before thee, or whatever the cause was, O, show it me and take away my sin.

Lord, thou art just in all thy dealings with me, for I have a thousand times forfeited this and all my mercies, but O, take not the forfeiture at my hands, but according to thy tender mercies, heal my soul. O, didst thou withdraw, in a way of adorable sovereignty, to show me my own weakness and insufficiency and to make me follow hard after thee? O, let this be the effect—yea, and by grace assisting, I will follow thee. I will not let thee go: I cannot live without thy light, cast out and banished from thy sight. O, hasten the time when all these intervening clouds shall be done away, and I shall see thee as thou art and enjoy thee without interruption. O! This is not my rest. What are means or ordinances to me if the God of ordinances is not found? Lord, grant they never may content me.

But what hast thou done, O my soul? Have not thou charged God foolishly or dared to murmur? Dost not thou unwarrantably claim that privilege which God has nowhere promised to his children? Namely, that they shall always be favored with the light of his countenance here and enjoy his sensible presence. If God has graciously promised for Jesus's sake that he will not finally be wroth with me nor rebuke me, he has never promised that he will never hide his face at all. Is not grace absolutely free and sovereign? And who am I, and what am I, that I should dare as it were to lay the blame on God, even on a just and holy God? O, let me rather take shame to myself; lay my hand upon my mouth and blush before him; yea, and tremble, too, because of my sin, because so unholy and unlike to him, a bitter fountain of indwelling sin, O wretched one, because of this body of sin and death that so oft betrays me and separates between my God and me. Lord, I acknowledge before thy sacred majesty, the fault is all my own. On me let the blame lie where 'tis justly due. And O, humble me for this pride and presumption, I beseech thee, while I acknowledge thou hast already bestowed on me unmerited grace and mercy.

September 19, 1753, Wednesday evening

All this week hitherto, I have been more than usual confused about the badness of my natural temper because I am so hasty, passionate, and apt to take things hard, which perhaps are no ways meant to distress me. O, does my desire of vindicating and justifying myself to everyone that I think suspects I do wrong proceed from an overweening opinion of myself or proud self-conceit?

Lord, convince and humble me and let me not run into an extreme this way under a pretense of duty. O, whether this does proceed from workings of corruptions in the heart or from natural temper or from bodily indisposition, I know not, or whether they all combine together to rob me of my peace.

Be it as it will, for that I know 'tis high time to mortify and not to indulge such things: the Lord give me strength to overcome and wisdom to direct me, and make me thankful for all the tokens for good thou hast bestowed on me, an ill-deserving wretch, and thankful for all the kindness of friends to me. Lord, 'tis thou hast given me favor in eyes of so many notwithstanding all my imperfections.

O, make me humble and courteous to all my friends, and may the law of kindness be ever in my mouth. And let me not be as a churlish Nabal that I must not be spoke to lest I be offended in a moment and resent it.[24] O, make me candid and generous to my friends at all times. May the Golden Rule be mine.[25] As I would they should put favorable constructions on my words and actions and bear with my infirmities, so may I always do by them. And may God be glorified for time to come by my meek and quiet behavior.

Lord, I bewail before thee everything that has robbed thee of thy due and fly to the cleansing, healing blood of my dear Redeemer. O, pity and pardon for his sake alone, for I am thine own forever,

Sarah Osborn

October 30, 1753, Tuesday morning; October 31, 1753, Wednesday morning[26]

I have been perusing my writings and find that this year has been a year of singular mercies. God has revived his own work in my soul from time to time in a surprising manner. A thanksgiving is this week proposed, but methinks I need not wait for the day but begin the work of thanksgiving this day and carry it on every day, for sure I have work enough cut out for me to last me all my days. O my God, how shall I ever enough praise thee who so far exceeds all praise. O! I cannot sufficiently do it, nor can the tongues of angels, yet Lord permit and assist a worthless worm: touch her lips as with a coal from thine altar. Blow up the sparks of love thou hast implanted in her soul. Clear the eye of faith that it may behold thee in all thy beauties and excellencies, and then my soul will soon be enamored with thy beauty, for thou art all glorious and lovely in and for thyself—beautiful in holiness, fearful in praises, doing wonders.

Lord, I would fain dive after thy perfections but I am lost and language fails. Who can by searching find out God? Who can find out the Almighty unto perfection? Thou art the God whom angels adore but cannot comprehend. Well then, my soul, let me imitate them, fall prostrate, and adore! Adore him because such a God; adore him because infinitely wise, holy, just, merciful, truthful, unchangeable; yea, so that in him there is no variableness or the least shadow of turning, but he is the same yesterday, today, and forever, omnipresent, and at one perfect view sees everything from eternity to eternity. With him 'tis always one everlasting now. He is omnipotent, all power is in his hands, and nothing too hard for him to do. When he will work none can hinder, for he is absolutely sovereign, too, and rules with uncontrollable sway all the affairs of the upper and lower worlds; yea, he does his will in the armies of heaven and amongst the inhabitants of the earth, and none can stay his hand or say unto him, what doest thou?

O! Who or what but stupid mortals—rebel man—could help being ravished with his beauty, his adorable perfections? O, what a covering is unbelief, what a veil does it cast over all the perfections of the blessed God. Lord, rend it away; O, rend it from top to the bottom, and unveil thyself. Let me gaze a little longer, for 'tis good for me to be here.[27] O, that thou wouldst keep me near thee here, or take me into thy immediate presence that I might always behold thee. Lord, my soul even breaks with longings for the full enjoyment of thyself. O! When shall the day break and the shadows flee away? O, if it may consist with thy will, hasten the time. But Lord, glorify thyself either in my life or death, and all is well.

I submit to thy sovereign pleasure and again commit myself to thee, for I am thine own forever,

Sarah Osborn

November 16, 1753, Friday morning; November 17, 1753, Saturday morning[28]

Yesterday and the day before, my children were out of measure noisy and unruly, so that they brought me to my wits' end, raised my passions, and confused me so that I knew not how to carry on my business at all. The Lord pardon me for whatever I uttered rashly or foolishly. And O, subdue my passions and preserve me from speaking unadvisedly with my lips to the dishonor of thy dear name, and will God undertake for me and guide me in this difficult calling by thy prudent counsel. Lord, thou seest my trials and knowest my weakness. O, let me not be more exercised than I am able to bear, but let thy grace be sufficient for me and thy strength be made perfect in my weakness. Lord, remember I am but dust. O, pity me under my weakness and infirmities, and as my day is so, let my strength be. O, leave me not to my own strength. I am weak as an infant and cannot stand alone. I shall fall and dishonor thee if thou dost. Lord, did not even the weakest man that ever lived, except the man Christ Jesus, speak when provoked? O, give me wisdom from on high.

Lord, if nothing more than my own private character or the wounding my own soul lay at stake, the matter would not be so great if I slipped and fell. But 'tis thine own honor, the interest of religion, that also will be wounded if I am not circumspect, and, Lord Jesus, hast not thou too many wounds already in the house of thy friends which dishonor thee and sink thy interest in the world? More than all that the unregenerate can do, O, this I lament and mourn over before thee. And shall I also tear open thy bleeding wounds and put them to open shame? O, forbid it, gracious God. Are not thou the vine? Am not I a branch in thee? O, purge me that I may bring forth more fruit to the glories of thy sovereign grace.

Forgive the children and restrain them, I beseech thee, that he [the devil] may not accomplish his designs either against them or me. O, bless the children, dear Lord, and seal instruction to them. May it be as bread cast on the waters to be seen many days hence. Lord, I cannot reach their hearts. 'Tis thou alone canst do that. To thee I commit them. O, deal graciously with them that their precious souls may live before thee.

And as for me, give me grace to be found faithful to the great trust thou hast committed to me. O, may I never account it a light thing to have the care of so many precious souls in a measure committed to me, one of which is worth more than a million worlds. Lord, I thank thee that thou in thy providence has so ordered it that I may not live a useless life. O, may I do much good in my day and generation. Give me patience and prudence, and may I evidence it even to the children, as well as to others, that faith purifies the heart, works by love, and is productive of good works.

O heavenly Father, glorify thyself in me and all is well, for I am thy own. All my opportunities, gifts, and talents are thine; yea, my whole soul and body, with all I have or can do, is thine own. O, in this I will rejoice that I am not my own but thine. Lord, use me for thyself. I am the purchase of the precious blood of thy own son. Lord, my soul has cost thee dear since it was ransomed at no cheaper rate. O, is it not a precious soul, since redeemed with precious blood? Let it still be precious in thy sight. Lord, delight to dwell in it by thy blessed Spirit, for Jesus's sake, and it will be more holy and a more fit habitation for thee. None but thyself can make it fit for thyself. Lord, I can and shall rejoice the more it is so, but I cannot make it so. No, no, the work is all thy own and the glory all thy own forever, and I rejoice it is so. O, be thou everything to me in time and eternity, and it is enough. I ask no more; I desire no more but to be full of God.

O my soul, what canst thou desire more? Dear Lord Jesus, dost thou say I have chosen that good part that shall never be taken from me?[29] Amen, Amen, Amen, Amen, Hallelujah. The Lord God omnipotent reigneth. None shall be able to pluck me out of thine hand, for I am thine and thou art mine forever,

Sarah Osborn

1754

March 26, 1754, Tuesday morning

[*In the margin she wrote: Re: raising my price for schooling*]

I have for some time been easy, and as I thought, in the exercise of faith, relying on a covenant God for all supplies both for soul and body. But why this gloom now? Have I been too self-confident? Lord, convince and humble me if so. Have I erred in my affairs? If so, Lord, forgive. And O, from oppression or extortion, Lord, deliver me for thy name's sake. O, do I not abhor it! Lord, preserve thine own honor in this affair. I beseech thee: may the Golden Rule be always mine, and O my God, suffer me not to be over careful about the speeches of others.

O my God, conquer by thy grace this excessive self-love that creeps into and clings so fast to me in every performance. O, grant me humility—that dear and lovely grace—and let me not be proud and haughty, nor yet expect to escape the censure of those that think I do amiss. Do I think myself perfect, that none must espy or speak of a fault in me, but it immediately sinks my spirits when at the same time I can see others' failings? O, have I not a beam in my eye that must first be cast out? Lord, convince and humble me and keep back thine handmaid from secret or presumptuous sins and make me faithful and successful in my calling. O, assist me for thine own name's sake, for I am thine forever.

March 28, 1754

A considerable degree of hysteric disorders are working, which strikes at all my comfort, and though I do know what ails me, yet my spirits are so sunk I know not what to do with myself. O thou Great Physician for soul and body, help. I am unfit for everything.

Lord, help, and sanctify this rod. Let it accomplish the end for which thou sendest it, whatever it be, ere thou remove it, for sure I am I need it or thou wouldst not use it. For thou dost not afflict willingly nor grieve the children of men. O, discover it to me: what is the particular lesson thou wouldst have me learn by this? Is it sympathy with others distressed in the same way? Am I too apt to forget my own weakness and blame others for giving way to the discouragements such ails expose me to? O forgive me, and make me more compassionate than ever. I entreat thee, Lord, make me more merciful to every failing in others, seeing I am as a reed shaken with every wind and shall surely become a prey to every enemy, except upheld by thy grace.

O preserve me from sin and Satan. Hold me in thy own hands, and do with me what seemeth good, for thou hast an absolute right to do what thou pleasest with thy own. O let me fall into the hands of God and not the hands of Satan or my own inbred lusts. Lord, they are tyrants: they will have no mercy. They will drive me from thy gracious presence, as they did my first parents out of paradise, and hide thy lovely face from me. O I deprecate spiritual judgments, hardness of heart, blindness of mind, and unbelief.

O, strike in what way else thou pleasest. I'll adore and kiss the hand, the dear hand, that smites. Lord, I really fear nothing but sin. The devil himself cannot hurt me if thou wilt only preserve me from sin. O, let this be the fruit of every dispensation to take away my sin. O, purge and purify me though in a furnace of affliction. Thy will be done. All things shall work together for good. Lord, I believe; help thou my unbelief.

And O, remember I am thine own forever and ever,
S.O.

Sarah Osborn to Joseph Fish, May 16, 1754

Much Honored and Reverend Sir,
'Tis with pleasure I once more sit down to write to such a valuable friend, but think of seeing you with still greater. May Providence favor your design of coming here. My heart is often at Stonington, though Providence has hitherto let my going thither, for wise ends without doubt, but I almost long to see you all.

O Sir, bless God with me and for me, for I know not whether my whole life has produced larger experiences of God's goodness than the two years past. O, who would not choose such a God for their portion, did they but know him? Verily none could do otherwise, for he is in himself altogether lovely. O! What cruel enemies are ignorance and unbelief, that spreads such a veil over the perfections of the great Jehovah and the dear Emmanuel, that the benighted soul can see no form or comeliness in him. O, were these removed, how soon would the soul be enamored with his beauty, how eagerly would it gaze till it was swallowed up and lost in admiration! With what vehemence would the arms of faith and love be clasped around the dear object and absolutely refuse to let him go.

Well, though these seasons are rare in this vale of tears, and I have reason to cry out, "O, how little do I know of thee," yet while I bewail my ignorance, I find a disposition to rejoice in hope that it will ere long be entirely done away, and I shall see him as he is and be transformed into the same likeness, be made holy as he is holy. O, then shall I be satisfied, when I awake in his likeness. O, transforming thought!

But does not adorable sovereignty appear in all its luster, dear Sir, while you hear such a wretch as I expressing such hopes as these? Sure it does, for who am I, and what am I, that God should thus look down on me?[30] O let sovereign grace be magnified, for I am utterly unworthy of all the mercy and truth that God has hitherto shewn to his handmaid, much more [unworthy] of such great things to come. Forgive my freedom in speaking, for if I write at all, I must tell you, that fear God, what he has done for my soul. And though I hope God's grace is the motive, if you fear pride and ostentation, look at the bottom. O, pray hard for me that those hateful sins may be forgiven and subdued. O, when shall it once be that I shall shout aloud the riches of redeeming love without any degree of fear of selfish principles? In God's own time, I trust I shall, since the foundation of all my hopes is laid on the Rock of Ages.[31]

But I must not talk on this delightful subject any longer at present. Time fails. And now, Sir, I would inform you that we have thoughts of putting our Negro boy into the country for some time if we can get a place to our minds where he may have his victuals and clothes for his work. And if it would suit you, Sir, to take him, it would be most agreeable to us of any place whatever.[32] He is in his tenth year, capable of doing chores indoors and out: he can read, sew, and knit sufficient at least to mend his own clothes (if fitted), and knit his stockings in the evenings. He loves play very well and is heedless, antic, &c., but I think he is not addicted either to pilfer, lie, or call names. But I fear his want of business with us will be a hurt to him, for we have not wherewith to employ him, and I know idleness is an inlet to everything that's bad. And I can't be willing he should be brought up in it: I want he should learn to labor. Bad examples prevailing here, also, to which he is exposed, gives me uneasiness.

These, Sir, are the reasons why we incline to part with him for a season, and if he might be serviceable to you, I should be exceeding glad, and I desire if he does come, that no favors may be showed to him because he belongs to me. For I choose rather he should know his distance. For his being brought up with us as our own from the cradle, and we having no other child, has doubtless made him use some freedoms with us, which with strangers he would not pretend to. I hope he will be a good boy. Be pleased to consult with Madame Fish and let us know your minds.

If it will not suit you, Sir, to have the boy, if you know of anybody near you that you think would be likely to care for his soul as well as body, and allow him the privilege of attending public worship (for without such a prospect I could by no means part with him), I should be obliged to you if you would mention it. I should be quite satisfied with a place of your choosing, Sir. I have thought of Mr. Eels, as I was acquainted with his spouse, but know nothing of the circumstances of his family, so leave it with you, Sir, whether to speak of it or not.[33] I talk of other places only in case it will not suit Mr. Fish, for I repeat it again, that I had rather he should come to you than any person living, though I would not urge anything to your disadvantage.

And now, Sir, earnestly wishing you the best of blessings, and begging the continuance of your prayers for me and mine, I beg leave to subscribe with all due respects to yourself, spouse, and daughters, your sincere though unworthy friend and humble servant,

Sarah Osborn

P. S. I wish you a refreshing meeting with our reverend pastor and worthy deacon, both in body and soul. The Lord grant that all your health and comfort in both may be furthered.

Pray, Sir, excuse my old patched up letter. 'Tis shattered to pieces, much like its author. I had not time to transcribe.[34]

Sir, as I said before, I would urge nothing to your disadvantage, but if it would suit you to take him a little while, if only this summer, I should be glad, and whenever you choose he should return, only write to us and we will take care to fetch him soon. He never was sick to lie by in his life, but I do not think him hitherto very hardy, and I have thought the country air might be serviceable on that account. May God overrule in this and all our affairs as shall most consist with his glory, with whom all events must be left.

Sarah Osborn to Joseph Fish, June 4, 1754

Reverend and dear Sir,

I received yours and am much pleased with the prospect of seeing Mr. Fish and both his daughters here. Shall rejoice and think it an honor to me if I may be in any way improved to do them service. As to my journey to Stonington, though I should be exceeding glad to see Madame Fish, I have laid all thoughts of it aside for the present, for I think it would be a very improper time to pretend to it. I shall therefore by permission of Providence steer my coast another way and return again, ready to receive Mr. Fish and daughters.

As to our Negro boy, Sir, when I wrote to you I had a notion that Mr. Fish had a Negro man only, and no small help at all, and therefore thought a boy to do chores might be serviceable. But since I have understood by Mr. Peabody that Mr. Fish has a boy already, I am concerned, really fearing it will rather add to Mr. Fish's difficulties than be of service.[35] For as I intimated before, he loves play and is pretty unlucky [mischievous]. And though I freely own I was selfish in the proposal—that is, I really aimed at the good of the boy, soul and body—yet I cannot desire it at the expense of your comfort. However, Sir, I heartily thank you for entertaining favorable thoughts about taking him, and if Mr. Fish thinks it will be best, that it is an advantage to you to have him, he is still at your service.

But if otherwise, I believe we shall put him to one of my first husband's brothers, at Berkley, near neighbor to the Reverend Mr. Tobey, who wants him. Has no boy at all. The man, I know, has been sober from his youth, and in a judgment of charity, I have thought some years past truly gracious, keeps up the worship of God in his house, &c. The only objection with me there, is he keeps a tavern, but the Reverend Mr. Tobey assures me that the house is so orderly, that he really thinks it will be no disadvantage at all, and advised me by all means to apply to him in case it did not suit Mr. Fish, and told me he would propose it to him, which I found he has, by a letter from my brother [in-law] today, wherein he expresses a desire to have him, or to know my mind as soon as possible because he has the offer of another boy, which he shall take if he has not ours.[36] But I shall not engage him [Bobey] to him till I know your mind, Sir, more fully. I give you this particular account, Sir, that you may be no ways biased in my favor but act freely as God and your prudence shall direct.

I add no more at present but humble and hearty regards to yourself, spouse, and daughters. And thanks for yours and Miss Molly's dear letters. From yours in the strong bonds of friendship and grace, however unworthy,

Sarah Osborn

P. S. Mr. Osborn sends his best regards.

October 5, 1754

The Rev. Mr. Whitefield preached Friday evening from these words: "to know the love of Christ."[37] Saturday evening from these: "Behold the bridegroom cometh." Sabbath forenoon from these: "Blessed and holy is he who has part in the first resurrection." Sabbath evening from these: "I am the way." Monday evening from these: "Awake thou that sleepeth."[38]

O my soul, what a delicious gospel feast hast thou now had. O let it not be lost. Lord, preserve it in my memory. I pray thee, help me to digest it and practice better. Hast thou made me to know the love of Christ as distinguishing, free, expensive love? O, make me to know it yet more. O, may it attract my whole soul! And transform it into the same image. Lord, make me love more than ever, and make me more ready than ever to go forth to meet the bridegroom. Though he come at midnight, let me be looking and watching for him. O blessed savior, how often has thou come at midnight to me. Was it not midnight when I was secure and dead in sins? Has it not oft since been midnight when thou hast appeared—in temptations, violent and strong; in desertions when thy lovely face has been hid? This is midnight indeed, and in outward difficulties, Lord, at midnight thou hast always appeared: strengthened, supported, guided, comforted; yea, wrought deliverance, too. And since, I have this comfortable hope through grace that I have indeed a part in the first resurrection; thou hadst pronounced me blessed and holy.

O Lord, make me more holy for thine honor's sake. Lord, grace is free. It is a great deal, indeed, thou hast already laid out on me. Thou hast purchased me; thou hast by thy Spirit infused the principle of holiness into me. But Lord, of myself I can't improve the stock, nor can I live upon it without fresh supplies. Lord, grant me a great deal of grace, and I'll be content with little else. O, give like thyself; give as great degrees as consists with . . . .

[*The last pages of this diary have been ripped out, either by Osborn or by someone else at a later date. A small part of a page remains with the following words:*]

O, blessed be God, that I have been taught to write, since that is the means that God has made the most effectual of all other to fix my thoughts on eternal things. 'Tis in this way of musing that the fire burns; 'tis in this way I am prepared for the most solemn acts of secret devotion. If I first attempt to read, my thoughts will rove, except in reviewing past experiences. If I try to meditate, they will still flutter as a bird from bow to bow but fix on nothing. If I attempt to pray, 'tis not one time in ten (or scarce I believe) the year throughout that I can get near and wrestle with God, except I am this way prepared—that I seem to lie under (as is already wrote) a necessity to improve my pen if I will be at all lively in religion.[39]

FIVE

The Nature, Certainty, and Evidence of True Christianity, 1755

SARAH OSBORN *became a published author in 1755, when the Reverend Thomas Prince of Boston arranged for a 1753 letter to a female friend to be printed. It is not clear who shared the letter with him, but perhaps someone hoped that he would include it in his periodical,* Christian History, *which published news of revivals around the world.*[1]

We do not know how Osborn initially responded to Prince's request to publish her letter, but she probably never expected to see her name in print. Of almost seventy-four-hundred works published in America between 1640 and 1755, only twenty-six were written by women, and if we eliminate books that were first published in England or France, the number decreases to fourteen. If we also remove books from the list that were published posthumously, the number shrinks to eight. Since many books available for sale in the colonies were imported from England, the number of books written by women in circulation was much higher than these paltry numbers suggest, but as Sarah Osborn must have realized, she was a rare phenomenon: an American female author who was alive when her work appeared in print.[2]

At a time when women were encouraged to be modest and self-effacing, Osborn was identified on the title page only as an anonymous "gentlewoman." As a note explained, "Though this Letter was wrote [in later editions, "written"] in great Privacy from one Friend to another; yet on representing that by allowing it to be printed, it would probably reach to many others in the like afflicted Case, and by the Grace of God be very helpful to them; the Writer was at length prevailed on to suffer it—provided her Name and Place of Abode remain concealed." Whether the Reverend Thomas Prince, who arranged for the letter's publication, or Samuel Kneeland, the publisher, wrote this explanation, readers were encouraged to imagine a humble woman who had "suffered" her words to be published only because of her compassion for others in spiritual distress. As a further frame for her words, the title page included a brief citation to a passage from First Corinthians: "But God hath chosen the foolish things of the world to confound the wise; and God hath chosen the weak things of the world to confound the things which are mighty." Since Osborn never referred to this biblical text in her letter, it is likely that either Kneeland or Prince decided to include it, perhaps as a defense against possible critics. Uneasy about publishing a woman's words, they wanted to emphasize that God could inspire even the weak and the foolish—or in Osborn's case, the female—to spread the gospel.[3]

It is not clear whether Osborn chose the title of her book, but the words "nature," "certainty," and "evidence" connected it to both the rising evangelical movement and the Enlightenment. Her title sounded both scientific and religious, as if she intended to offer indisputable evidence of the truth of Christianity. Writing to a friend who was tormented by doubts about her salvation, Osborn advised her to examine her experiences for evidence of God's grace. "Religion is no imaginary thing," she testified, "but a substantial reality."

July 2, 1753

My very dear, dear Friend!

I have thought much on those few lines you began to write to me; and do not at all wonder that you expect I should improve the opportunity to relieve you,—For surely the strong bonds of friendship, with which we have for some years been bound to each other (was there no bonds of grace at all) demand this; and how much more when *these* are added. And truly, my dear friend, it has not been owing to want of tenderness, and compassion towards you, under your distresses, that my tongue as well as pen have often been silent. No, my bowels yearned, and I longed to speak many times, but your difficulties were such that I dare not open my lips, lest a subtle adversary should turn that against you, which I intended for your comfort, and sink your spirits the lower—as has sometimes, you know, been the case.

And O, that God would now bless the poor weak endeavors of a worthless worm to refresh you. If so, it will rejoice me much, but whether it please him to use a poor, nothing creature as an instrument or no, I am persuaded he

Th Nature, Certainty and Evidence
of TRUE CHRISTIANITY :

IN A

LETTER

FROM A

GENTLEWOMAN

In *Rhode-Island,*

To ANOTHER, her dear Friend, in
great *Darkness, Doubt* and *Concern,* of a
Religious Nature.

---

1 Cor. i. 26—31.

☞ Though this Letter was written in great
Privacy from one Friend to another; yet on
reprefenting that by allowing it to be printed, it
would probably reach to many others in the
like afflicted Cafe, and by the Grace of God be
very helpful to them; the Writer was at length
prevailed on to fuffer it—provided her Name
and Place of Abode remain concealed.

PROVIDENCE: Re-printed by J. CARTER.

The title page of the 1793 edition of *The Nature, Certainty, and Evidence of
True Christianity.* Courtesy of the American Antiquarian Society.

will in his own time revive you, and I rejoice and praise him on your behalf, by grace that he will turn your captivity; and that he will bruise Satan under your feet shortly, and make him gladly quit the field and leave you to enjoy your God. For blessed be God, Christ Jesus is stronger than he and all his combined legions; and he [Satan] can't resist his power, though he has audaciously struck at his honor, and endeavored to impede his blessed work in your soul. Does or has the bold, daring Spirit persuaded to insinuate that all religion, is vain, imaginary, and delusive? Does he pretend that none can know they are right?—Tell him from me, he is a liar, and I am bold to say, I have proved him so, for he has told me the same tale. But blessed be God, I do know that religion is no imaginary thing, but a substantial reality. I do know that there is a God of boundless perfections, truth, and faithfulness that will not deceive. No, nor forsake the soul that puts its trust in him.

But now perhaps you'll say, aye, but how do I know this God is mine, and that I myself am not deceived? I answer, by the evidences of a work of grace wrought in my soul. And now as God shall enable me, my dear friend, I'll tell you truly what God has done for my soul, and what I call evidences of a work of grace. This question I could never verbally answer, when with you, which makes me now attempt to explain myself.

First, then, I do know that God has by his word and Spirit, convinced me of sin, original and actual; that I was by nature a child of wrath, an heir of hell, an enemy to him and his ways, yea, enmity itself; dead in trespasses and sins; and that I was both utterly unable—and unwilling, too—to help myself out of this miserable state, being averse to the gospel way of salvation wrought out by Christ. I plainly see the cause of that complaint, "Ye will not come to me, that ye might have life."[4] God convinced me also that by the deeds of the law, no flesh living should be justified, and that he and his throne would be spotless forever though he should cast me off and condemn me to the hottest hell: Since he owed me nothing nor was any way bound to bestow his grace upon me; and if he did, it would be absolutely free and sovereign. God showed me I was utterly unworthy that he should help me.

Nevertheless, though I had thus destroyed myself, yet in him was my help. Yea, he discovered to me that he had laid help upon ONE who is mighty to save to the utmost all that come to God by him; even a glorious Christ the great Emmanuel God-Man, even one co-equal with himself, the express image of his person; in whom dwells all the fullness of the godhead bodily, one every way complete and suited to all my wants; and that he was not only thus qualified and sealed and sent by the Father, but that he was absolutely willing as well as able to accomplish the great work; and would by no means cast out any that come to him.

Well, upon this discovery of the amiable and lovely Jesus, if I know that I have a being, I do know that God compelled or sweetly constrained me to throw down the weapons of my rebellion and to submit to him as prince and savior, and consent to be saved by him in his own way and upon his own terms; that he should be the Alpha and the Omega, the foundation and the topstone in my salvation. Yea, God caused my heart to go out after him in strong and vehement desires, and to choose him in all his offices, with all his benefits, to be my portion forever. Yea, he appeared to me to be in himself the most lovely and desirable object, the fairest of ten thousand fairs, and God enabled me to give myself—my whole soul and body with all my con-cerns for time and eternity—into his merciful and faithful hands; and had I a thousand precious souls, I would gladly venture them all with him; for I am persuaded he will keep by his mighty power what I have committed to his charge; nor shall all the hosts of hell ever be able to pluck me out of his hands.

But to proceed: upon this choice and surrender to God as Mediator, God the Father manifested himself to me, as my reconciled God and Father; the blessed Spirit took up his abode with me; afforded me his influences and assistance daily; and God made with me an everlasting covenant never to be forgotten, even the sure mercies of David. And I solemnly gave myself up—all I have, am, or can do, both in life and death, in time and for eternity—to God the Father, Son, and Holy Ghost, to be his own in a covenant way, to be disposed of as shall most consist with his glory; and chose the glorious Trinity for my portion forever in opposition to all others, even a God of infinite perfections. O, happy choice; O, happy I, that I lived to see that day wherein God betrothed me to himself in lovingkindness and tender mercy.

Thus I was effectually called and made willing in the day of God's power to receive him; and to as many as received him, to them gave he power to become sons of God, even to those that believe on his name.

And now the foundation of my hopes are laid upon the Rock of Ages.[5] And agreeable to those covenant engagements, a faithful God has ever since dealt with me. And surely I can say: "whereas I was born blind, now I can see"; "old things are done away, all things become new."[6] Now, through grace, I dare appeal to a heart-searching God and say that none of his commands are grievous. I esteem them all holy, right, just, and good; and long to yield a universal obedience to them all. Yea, God does excite in me strong and vehement desires after an entire conformity to his law, as though my whole salvation depended thereon, while at the same time, he will not suffer me to depend on anything but Christ alone, notwithstanding a strong propensity to cleave to the covenant of works, but enables me to account all things as loss and dung and filthy rags, in point of justification. Nor would I for a million worlds appear before God in the best performance I ever did. No, 'tis in that spotless righteousness which Christ has wrought out, imputed to me, and in that only, I dare appear before God. But he gives me to see a beauty in holiness, which far exceeds the luster of all created things. Nor do I know what desire means, after any, or all the enjoyments of time and sense, compared with those ardent longings and pantings which he at some times excites in my soul after the enjoyment of himself, and for sanctifying grace.

And though grace is not always alike in exercise (no, I am sometimes dull and lifeless as to exercise), yet blessed be God it is the habitual and settled bent of my soul, for many years, to choose God, his Christ, and grace for my portion in all conditions, both adverse and prosperous. Blessed be God, my faith has not often been staggered. Sometimes he has bereaved, cut off the streams of earthly comforts, one after another, and then caused me to justify him and fly to him as my all. Sometimes he has hid his face, and caused me to mourn after him, and refuse all comfort till he returned. Sometimes he has permitted Satan to tempt and tyrannize over me for a season, and many a precious jewel has been stolen from me by clouding my evidences and insinuating that all was delusion and hypocrisy. And how many distressing gloomy days I have had, God only knows, but Satan could not keep them, for a faithful God would not suffer me to be tempted above that I was able, but made a way for my escape.

Sometimes he has permitted the remains of indwelling corruption to rally all its force and strive for mastery, but at the same time stirred up an inveterate hatred and abhorrence of it, and myself for it, because 'tis the abominable thing which his soul hates. And sometimes unbelief has so far prevailed, that I have cried out, "I shall one day perish by the hands of these enemies" or "I shall at least fall foully to the dishonor of the dear name by which I am called," if not finally.[7] But for more than sixteen years has God preserved me from open scandalous sins. (Yea, blessed be God, through restraining grace, all my life long), and from ever making a league with sin, since I have through grace proclaimed war with it. And by grace assisting, I am determined never to lay down my arms, but to fight till I die under the banner of the great captain of my salvation. Yea, and truth and veracity itself has said, sin shall not have dominion over you and my grace shall be sufficient for you. And here (my dear), my great strength lies: for all the promises are yea and Amen in Christ Jesus. And since my Lord is mine, *all* is mine, and I shall come off more than a conqueror through him that has loved me and given himself for me, though now I groan under a body of sin and death. And may I never cease to mourn, but daily look on him whom I have pierced. O, it was sin, my sin, that pierced his sacred head and side, that put all the bitter ingredients into the cup, that extorted that heart-piercing cry from him: "My God, my God, why hast thou forsaken me?"[8] And never does it appear more odious, than when I am well-satisfied it never will prove my ruin. God disposes me to choose any affliction, or all the afflictions in the world, rather than sin. I do esteem it the worst of evils. Yea, I would rather have all the furies of hell let loose to perplex me, than to be given over to the tyranny of my own inbred lusts and corruptions. O, thanks be to God, he has said, "it will subdue your iniquities."[9] O, how sweet here to consider Christ as my king, that will ere long set his foot on the necks of these enemies. How sweet to espouse his cause. Bring forth the traitors, and entreat him to stay everyone that says they will not have him to reign over them. O, that Christ would entirely possess his rightful throne in my soul, wholly sway the scepter there, fill every room, that not a lust, a usurper, might ever dare to lift up its venomous head again. O, transporting thought: one everlasting day, this shall be the happy case.

Again, God causes me to love his image wherever I see it: in rich and poor, in bond or free, of what denomination whatsoever. Surely I do esteem the saints, the excellent of the earth, and they are my delight. Again, God enables me to love my enemies, to forgive injuries, and earnestly to pray that God would forgive them also. But I must not enumerate more.

But these, my friend, are what I call evidences of a work of grace, and for my part I had rather be able to read them than to hear a voice from heaven telling me, I am a child of God. If you ask again, if I can always, or of myself, read them to my satisfaction, I answer, without Christ I can do nothing; I am not sufficient for one good thought; all my sufficiency is of God. But God has taught me to live more by faith and less by sense than I used to do, and therefore if he hides his face, I do not raze foundations as formerly, and draw up hard conclusions against myself. But having treasured up the experiences of many years, I repair to them in a dark and cloudy day, and find, thus, and thus, God has done for me, and appeared for my help in times past, and this as an anchor holds me sure, and he will in his own time return and revive me. He has begun that good work in me that he will carry on till the day of Jesus. He was the author, and he will be the finisher of my faith. And so he makes me hang on the faithfulness of a covenant God, who will not deceive nor make any ashamed of their hope, that put their trust in him.

And now my dear, dear friend, I have given you the reason of the hope that is in me. And judge you: are these all the effects of nature, gifts, imagination, or a common work of the Spirit? Will any or all of these latter thus determine the soul for God? Will they enamor the soul with his beauty, because holy, just, faithful, powerful, &c., and make it even break with longings after a conformity to him? Will they cause it to cry out, whom have I in heaven but thee? And make it rejoice because even the brightest Seraph nor all the angelic hosts shall never be able to divert it one moment throughout eternity from God, but he shall be all in all, the heaven of heaven itself? Will nature abhor and dread hypocrisy and always cause the soul, when it has any sense of divine things, to tremble at the very thoughts of it, and earnestly to plead with God to search and try it, if there is any guile or reservation or any false way in it? Yea, will nature lay the soul open and cause it to plead with God that his all-piercing eye may penetrate into the most secret recesses? Yea, and rejoice that it does so? Will nature welcome death, the King of

Terrors, purely because it will deliver the soul from sin and usher it into the immediate presence of God, when no outward difficulties make it desire death, but God in his providence makes things comfortable and easy? Again, will nature cause all things below to appear very vanity, and less than nothing compared with communion with God, even here, and cause it to deprecate and tremble at the thought of any unsanctified prosperity, and absolutely to refuse, accepting of any or all creature comforts, as any part of its portion, or in the room of one degree of sanctifying grace? May not the soul in this case say, there is none on earth I desire besides—ordinances and providences are all empty without thee, and I will not let thee go, I will not be comforted except thou comfort me? Yea, though thou slay me, I will trust in thee, by grace assisting, and leaving the things that are behind, I am determined to press after as great discoveries of Christ, and degrees of sanctification, as 'tis possible for a mortal, finite creature to attain in this imperfect state, since grace is absolutely free and sovereign, and not bestowed for any such worth or worthiness in the object, but for Jesus, his sake alone.

Surely this is a work of almighty power and victorious grace. May God have all the glory. But methinks I see you wondering that I attempt to write in so positive a strain, and withal, your tender heart misgives you, and you fear lest I am influenced by self-confidence, pride, ostentation, or vainglory; and would to God, I dare tell you that I had no remains of these odious sins in me, but doubtless, cleave they will to my best performances as long as I live in this world. However, I trust through grace *that* is not the motive which has constrained me thus freely to communicate my experiences to you. No, but to vindicate the honor and glory of the great God, whom Satan has dared to slander and reproach with his lies; to bear a testimony for God, that I know him to be truth and faithfulness in the abstract, and far to exceed all that ever I could ask or think; and again to declare, that had I a thousand precious souls, I would venture them all on his truth and veracity, and cling to him—I will, in defiance of Satan and all his combined legions, so long as God holds me by the bonds of his Spirit. When God himself rends my hopes from me, I'll let it go, but not till then. And if 'tis the hope of the hypocrite, may it go this moment. And well may I say, so long as God holds me, for I know assuredly, 'tis by grace—and grace only—I stand. For so vile am I of myself, that should I be without it, I should wander from him as far as hell itself, notwithstanding all he has done for me. Whereof, then, have I to boast? O, blessed be God, boasting is forever excluded. O, may the crown be set on Jesus, his head, while I lay my mouth in the dust, and acknowledge I am an unprofitable servant and utterly unworthy of all the mercy he has showed to me.

I entreat you not to conclude from what I have wrote, that I have any desire to establish assurance as the essence of saving grace, or to set up my experiences as a standard.[10] No, no, far be that from me. I know God by his Spirit works variously with his children. But as to the essential and fundamental parts, I trust you will find them agreeable to the scripture. Try them by *that:* to the law and to the testimony. If they agree not with that, reject them immediately as false, delusive, imaginary, and have no light in them. But if you find they are genuine characters of a saving work wrought by almighty power in the soul—discern, I pray thee, whose signet, bracelets, and staff are these. Can you not lay claim to them, and say, surely God has done thus and thus for me also? Or, if you dare not lay claim, dare you deny, dare you say, God has not convinced you of sin and your absolute need of a savior? Has he not determined you for himself? Do you not choose him for your everlasting portion? Do not, for a world, say you do not. I trust you dare not say so. Well, if you ever have chose God for your all, renew your choice, fly to him again, give up yourself and all your vast concerns into his hands through the Mediator; and I doubt not but you will derive strength from the head of all gracious influences. O, say not, you cannot, but try to stretch forth the withered hand, and it will be whole. O, touch but the hem of his garment, and all shall be well. O, lay your impotent, needy soul by the pool, and I trust the angel of the everlasting covenant will ere long descend, and make you whole and restore you to the joys of his salvation. And thus perhaps you'll see, though now they are clouded, that you have the evidences of grace in you; that you do hate sin as sin; that you do love holiness for its own sake, and God because a holy God; that you love his law and long perfectly to obey; that you do prize Christ as a king as well as savior; that you do love his image in his children; that you do love your enemies; and are weaned from this world and all its trifling enjoyments; that you are reaching after greater degrees of sanctifying grace.

I know you will forgive me if I intrude on our patience in this long epistle, and all my freedoms herein, since it proceeds from a heart full of tender concern for you, and wanted vent. O, may God refresh you by it, and lift up the light of his countenance upon you. And I beg you, pray for me that I enter not into temptation. For though I have for some time, through surprising grace, walked up and down in the light of God's countenance, I am yet in my enemies' country: a thousand snares await me from within and without. I have not yet put off the harness, and perhaps comparatively but girding it on; and though the house built upon the rock, Jesus Christ, fall not, yet I have no expectation but that the rain will descend, the floods come, the winds blow and beat upon it. O, pray that I may glorify God in every condition and state of life, and all is well.

This long letter, my dear friend, I commit to your care and prudence as the very secrets of my soul, and as a token of my sincere affection and esteem for you, as my very dear, dear friend: which, pray accept, with hearty regards to you and all dear to you. Pray write to me as soon as you can.

Yours heartily.

SIX

Zion's Troubles, 1756–1758

FRANCE AND GREAT BRITAIN *declared war against each other in 1756, beginning a brutal conflict that spanned seven years and two continents. Much of the fighting happened in Europe, but the theater of war also extended into North America, where both France and England hoped to gain control over the colonies' vast economic resources. Known in Europe as the Seven Years' War and in America as the French and Indian War, the conflict pitted Europe's greatest military powers against one another in a struggle for political and economic dominance.*

For Sarah Osborn, the war was nothing less than a battle between God's chosen people and "Antichrist." Like many other Protestants at the time, she identified the Catholic Church as the "beast" prophesied in the book of Revelation, and she feared that France, a Catholic country, was part of a vast conspiracy to force Protestants to bow down to the authority of the pope. In her eyes, the fact that the French were allied with several Native American tribes was even greater proof of their corruption.

The war led to the deaths of thousands of colonists, including members of Osborn's own family, but she insisted that God was ultimately in control of every detail of the fighting. Because of her belief that God had made a national covenant with New England, his "New Israel," just as he had made an individual covenant with her, she interpreted the war as a crucial chapter in God's providential plan. God was using the war not only to punish the deluded followers of the Catholic Church but also to chastise his own people for their sinfulness. He would pour out his wrath on them until they repented. Often she prayed that God would "glorify his darling attribute"—in other words, show mercy to them—but as always, she insisted that God's punishments were for their own good.

At the beginning of 1756 the war was an abstraction, a far-away conflict that Osborn heard or read about in the Newport Mercury, but by the spring of 1757 it had become frighteningly real. Newport's men enlisted in large numbers, including Henry's two surviving sons—Edward, who enlisted in May, and Johnny, who went to sea as a privateer in August—and the town's economy was devastated by rising prices and food shortages. Sarah and Henry were relatively comfortable at the beginning of the war, but after the French navy blockaded the port, it was impossible for ships to deliver their goods. As the months passed, Sarah became increasingly anxious over how she would pay for food and fuel. Henry had not worked for several years, but as they watched their cash slipping away, he found a job as one of the wardens who kept watch over the harbor, scanning the seas for signs of a French invasion. Yet even with his new contribution to the family's income, they were not able to make ends meet. Sarah occasionally bought tickets in Newport's lottery (which was designed to raise cash for town projects), but she never won, and by spring 1757 she had decided that she had no choice but to raise the price of her school. In 1758, after several students withdrew in protest over the higher fees, she opened a boarding school.

Osborn agonized over these business decisions because of her fear of dishonoring her "profession": in other words, her vocation as a Christian. At a time when the gap between the richest and the poorest in the colonies was widening, especially in cities, she was afraid of appearing covetous or of "grinding the face of the poor."

Sarah Osborn's ethic of self-sacrifice never wavered during the long years of the war. Although she and Henry could barely afford to pay their rent, in 1757 they agreed to take in a poor girl, Almey Greenman, who may have been either an orphan or an apprentice. In return for her help with household chores, they treated her as part of their family, catechizing her in the faith. They also gave money to Henry's son Johnny and his wife, Abigail, who were barely able to support their four children, the oldest not more than nine and the youngest a baby. Sarah hinted in her diary that Johnny had been guilty of "misconduct" in the past, and she clearly disapproved of both him and his wife. Neither of them was a church member. But in 1758, as they became increasingly destitute, she and Henry decided to take in one of their children to feed and clothe as their own. (It is not clear from her diary whether this child was a boy or a girl.) Since Sarah continued to suffer from repeated bouts of illness while running a boarding school and managing the household's finances, it is hard to *imagine how she found the energy to care for yet another child, but she believed that God had called her to a life of service.*

There were many days during the war that Sarah struggled to trust in God's goodness, wondering how long he would allow their enemies to triumph over them. But she consoled herself by reflecting on God's love and mercy in the midst of affliction. When Phillis, an enslaved woman, confided that she had been born again, Osborn celebrated her conversion as yet another sign of God's infinite power. Since Osborn owned Phillis's son, Bobey, the two women had known each other for many years, and Osborn seems to have encouraged her to seek salvation. Phillis became only the third black member of the First Church of Newport and the sole black woman to belong to the women's society.

As Osborn examined her experiences for evidence of God's grace, she found much to be thankful for despite the miseries of poverty, illness, and war. Her ability to pay her rent, Phillis's conversion, Henry's job as a warden, her ability to support her impoverished grandchild—all were proof that God had not abandoned her.

1757

January 9, 1757, Sabbath evening

Blessed be God, a precious Sabbath today. Dear Mr. Vinal preached two lovely sermons from 1 Epistle John 1:15. "Love not the world nor the things of the world. If any man love the world, the love of the father is not in him."[1]

The Lord in mercy wean me and all his children more and more from it. And, O, grant that Christians may no longer act a worse part than even a pharaoh in begrudging to allow thy ministers a comfortable living, when even he assigned the priests a portion and would not suffer them to be impoverished, even though the famine was sore and others were made poor thereby. O, that God will open the hearts of his people that they may cheerfully and thankfully support the gospel.

And as for me, Lord, by thy grace enabling me, I determine I will exert myself to support thy cause, thy gospel. I will, by thy grace strengthening me, gladly exchange interests with thee. I care for thee and leave thee to care for me.

Lord, I again solemnly dedicate my whole soul, body, and interest to thee. O, use me for thyself—all I am, have, or can do—and this shall be my greatest joy, for all is thine, forever thine. O, teach me what is duty, what thou requirest of me, and enable me to do it that thou mayest be glorified in and by me, and 'tis enough, Lord, 'tis enough. O, give me but increase of grace; give me more of thyself. This is my lovely chosen portion, and in this I will rejoice. Give me but this, and give the pleasures, honors, and profits of this world to whom thou pleasest. I will not envy them nor wish to change conditions with them all. No, not with kings and potentates. Thou wilt feed me with food convenient for me, and 'tis enough. Content, Lord—I am content with such things as I have. Yea, I acquiesce: I rejoice in the allotments of thy divine providence.

Thou in infinite wisdom art giving me neither poverty nor riches, and thou hast graciously freed me from anxious cares and perplexing fears about futurities. O, what a mercy. This, Lord, this is thy goodness to thy poor unworthy worm, for didst thou leave me to act myself, I should murmur, I should repine and fret, none would behave worse than I. Therefore, not unto me, not unto me, but to thy name be all the glory.

> From vanity turn off my eyes
> Let no corrupt design
> Nor covetous desires arise
> Within this heart of mine
> Order my footsteps by thy word
> And make my heart sincere
> Let sin have no dominion, Lord
> But keep my conscience clear.[2]

O, let my conversation be ever without covetousness, and make me always content with such things I have, for thee hast said, "I will never leave thee nor forsake thee."[3] Amazing grace, has the great Jehovah promised? Rejoice, my soul, for he will perform. He is not man that he should lie; nor the son of man, that he should repent. What but his own love, pity, and compassion moved him to promise? Was he under any obligation to such a worm? Surely, no. What but love, boundless love, moved him to give thee his pledge—to tell thee, my soul, when the earth was trembling at his presence, that his kindness shall not depart from thee? What but love and tender compassion caused him to say to thee, "be not dismayed; I am thy God" and "it is I; be not afraid"?[4] O, love without a parallel! And was not this designed to beget in thee the strongest love and the strongest, humble confidence? Sure it was.

O my soul, answer the great end: love him more and trust him more than ever; confide safely in him, for truth and faithfulness will never fail thee. He has set his bow in the clouds as a witness of his covenant faithfulness, and so he has given thee his token, his pledge. O, view it and rejoice, and bring forth these bracelets and staff, for he will not disown them, for they were given to thee by his own most blessed Spirit. O astonishing Lord, what is man that thou art thus mindful of him? But what am I, that thou should regard such a dead dog as I am? Lord, did ever absolute sovereignty shine more clear? O rejoice, my soul, for God's grace is sovereign, 'tis free, and therefore he has revealed it to me, a babe. The Lord make me thankful, and again I say: my soul, be thankful.

February 11, 1757

On Wednesday evening, my dear pastor came to visit us, his thoughts greatly exercised under a view of approaching judgments, Zion's troubles, persecutions of the church, the power of Antichrist prevailing, the slaying of the witnesses, fears of his own flinching in times of trial. I was calm and could realize nothing evil compared with the evil of sin, nor nothing too great for us to go through, Christ strengthening us. But I dared not speak before man what I dared think before God. I could not be perplexed.

However, Satan took care I should not wholly escape, for before day, as soon as I awoke, he began to insinuate that I was stupid and none of Zion's friend, for if I loved the cause of Zion, I could not be so easy under a scene of their troubles. But God graciously assisted me and soon enabled me to prove him a liar, and prove that my love to the saints is the same in kind as that I bear to my own precious soul: that my greatest desire is that God may be glorified, that my soul may be purged from its dross and tin. Let it be cast into what furnace infinite wisdom and compassion pleases. "Let him do with me what seemeth good," is my constant language.[5] If he will but accomplish this great end, this shall be all my salvation and all my joy, only let me be conformed to his image and enjoy himself, and all is well.

Thus, blessed be his name, I can, through his grace, commit my precious jewel to his care and rest serene. I can be willing to be purged; yea, and I am willing Christ should purge his church, too, and leave him to do it in his own sovereign way. I know he will not lose one grain of this gold, though there is so much dross mixed therewith that the furnace should be heated seven times hotter than ever it was wont to be heated. And still I cried, "Let him do with Zion what seemeth him good."[6] He has provided glorious chambers of security for his people where they may hide till all these calamities be overpast. His wisdom, his power, his justice, his absolute sovereignty, his mercy, his truth and faithfulness, his care and unchangeableness, which are all infinite and all engaged for the good of his church—into these they may run. The name of the Lord is a strong tower: the righteous run into it and are safe. Zion may enjoy her God more in sufferings than in outward prosperity, and sure I choose anything for her rather than to see her estranged from God as now she is.

Still, Satan urged, I ought to love the bodies as well as the souls of the saints, and 'tis plain I have no tender regard nor love for them, since I can bear to think of their being exposed to prisons, dungeons, racks and tortures, fire and faggots and not be distressed. I answer, by the same rule I love not my own body since, through grace, I am willing God should inflict all these on it rather than suffer sin, the worst of evils, to prevail in me to grieve and dishonor him.

And blessed be God, Satan was forced to quit the field and leave me to acquiesce in the sovereign pleasure of my gracious God, and may his will be forever done on earth as it is in heaven. And I will by grace rejoice in him, for though the mountains depart and hills be removed, his kindness shall not depart from me. No, nor from any one member of Christ's glorious body.

February 11, 1757, Friday evening

I cannot help remarking the gracious dealings of God with me respecting the prospect of approaching calamities. O, that it may indeed be with a truly humble, grateful, thankful soul. About two years ago it pleased God to give me a solemn sense of the danger our sins had exposed us to. Times of persecution and sore distress were brought nigh in my apprehension even at the very door and, realizing it—that many that had professed much love to Christ would flinch, desert his cause, and wound him and their own souls afresh—this made me tremble and earnestly to cry, "Lord is it I?"[7] This made me earnestly to cry for strength that it may not be I, knowing assuredly that should Christ leave me to stand in my own strength, it will be I. This made me cry for help that I may be actually prepared for the worst of times for all events. This caused me to prepare an ark, a strong tower to fly to, my rock, my hiding place. God assured me, "his grace shall be sufficient for me"; "as my day is, so shall my strength be"; and invited me by his word and Spirit to enter into the chambers of security, shut the door behind me, and hide myself till these calamities be overpast.[8]

And enabling me by his Spirit and grace, I sit secure, becalmed, and at rest, while some others' eyes are upon second causes and their fears and perplexities increases. Mine are, through grace, generally fixed on the wisdom, foreknowledge, power, sovereignty, justice, care, unchangeableness, love, and faithfulness of God to his church in the accomplishment of all his promises and in his overruling all events for his own glory and the good of his church. And therefore I have not been scared, terrified, nor afraid of evil tidings, because my heart has thus been fixed, trusting in the Lord.

And O, what a mercy is it that God has given me so deep a sense of the odious nature and bitter evil of sin as has shrunk all other evils or troubles into nothing. The Lord deliver me from this more and more. And O, may I still keep close in the chambers of security and shut the doors behind me, that no unbelieving fears may enter in to disturb my rest in him, since by all the thought I can take, I can't add one cubit; I can do nothing. Though I should wrack my brain, take on me the government of the church, it will only crush me down. I should be my own tormentor, pull on me the evils that may never come.

O, let me still leave all the affairs in the hands of a glorious Christ who has graven Zion on the palms of his hands, who has purchased his church with his own most precious blood, and will not suffer anything to hurt her who is as the apple of his eye. Though God purge every branch in him that it may bring more fruit, surely the wrath of man shall praise him, and the remainder of wrath he shall restrain. Neither men nor devils shall go a hair's breadth further than he permits for his own glory and his church's good. And let him do what him seemeth good. If outward peace and prosperity be most for thy glory and the good of thy children, Lord, grant them. Condescend to use the rod rather than suffer thy dear ones to live at a distance from thee.

I will not dare to prescribe to thy infinite wisdom what methods thou shalt take, only take all thy dear ones nigh thyself. Conform them to thine image that thou mayest be glorified, and all is well, forever well. O, may Zion prosper in his regard; may the kingdom spread far and wide. Lord, take to thyself thy great power, and reign King of Nations as thou art King of Saints. Let the whole earth be full of thy glory. O Lord, pour out thy Spirit for Christ's sake, that thou mayest be loved, adored, and obeyed throughout all the earth.

O, when shall that once be? When shall the Jews be brought in with the fullness of the Gentiles? When wilt thou take the heathen for thine inheritance and the uttermost parts of the earth for thy possession? Lord, when shall Antichrist fall? When shall Babylon sink as a millstone? O, blessed be thy name, in thy own time all these great and good things shall be accomplished; for though heaven and earth shall pass away, one jot or one tittle of thy word shall not pass away till all is fulfilled.

February 18, 1757

Blessed be God, a thousand times more refreshment this morning, and indeed all the day, than I have deserved. Nevertheless, as to sensible comforts the tide has run low, a considerable degree of hysteric disorders, which has pressed down my animal spirits.

Well, the will of the Lord be done. By his grace I will not murmur at that. No, let him do with me what he pleaseth; only preserve me from the evil of evils. O, let me not grieve or dishonor him, and all is well. I have a thousand times more reason to stand astonished that he is ever pleased to take such an unholy soul nigh himself and comfort me, than to wonder or complain when they abate. Who am I, or what am I, that I should expect to be always indulged? O be thankful, my soul, for if God hide his face with lovingkindness, he will return.

Don't distrust him, for he has made with thee an everlasting covenant, ordered in all things and sure. And though thou art deficient and imperfect in a thousand instances, yea in everything, yet in Christ thou art complete, and for his sake God will again look with complacency. He will not suffer his faithfulness to fail. He has said, "though the mountains depart and hills be removed, his kindness shall not depart from me," and it shall not.[9]

I will believe him; I will trust in him. Yea, though he slay me as to comforts, I will trust in him by the help of his Spirit and grace; for he will guide me here, and afterwards bring me to glory, and then I shall be like him, for I shall see him as he is. Then he will smile forever, and I shall adore and praise him forever. O, the riches of redeeming love. God will wipe all tears from my eyes; all sorrow and sighing shall flee away forever.

O my soul, be thankful, be strong and very courageous. A few struggles more with sin, with Satan, with the world and with bodily infirmities, and heaven will make amends for all. Blessed be God for Jesus.[10]

I have this afternoon been to the house of mourning, putting on grave clothes for the dear deceased. Mrs. Mary Allen died today, once Mary Frankling. I hope she is gone to rest.[11]

Will God sanctify this bereavement to the dear relatives, especially her tender mother? O Lord, calm all tumults in her breast and enable her to lay aside all anger, wrath, and every weight—the sin that easily besets her—and enable her to return to thee with all her heart, soul, and mind. Lord, heal her soul of all its maladies for Christ's sake. Heal her backslidings, receive her graciously, and love her freely. O may she be able to say, "It is good for me that I have been afflicted."[12] Now may God be all in all to her precious soul. O, may her corruptions more and more lose of the ground they had before.

O, may her sins be crucified. O, enable her by faith to touch the hem of thy garment and be whole of her plague. Lord, discover to her more and more the fountain from whence all corrupt streams do flow, and help her to plunge into the fountain of Christ's blood that she may be cleansed. O Lord, for Christ's sake, break off her dependence on means. Lord, let her not split upon this rock, I beseech thee.

O, hear for Christ's sake, and magnify the riches of thy grace for Christ's sake. Amen and Amen.

As I have no scruple of conscience about the lawfulness of the thing, we have again adventured to put in a ticket in the lottery.[13] And now, Lord, with submission to thy will and in subordination to thy glory, I come to thee for success, for I know the whole disposal is of the Lord. Not a mite shall go to one or the other without thee.

And thou, Lord, infallibly knowest what shall be for thy glory and my best good. If thou wilt grant me success, and therewith a heart to improve it for thy glory, I am willing to have it, for thou hast made me to know, by happy experience, that thou canst lift up my heart in thy ways by prosperity, as well as bring me back by adversity from declensions.

And I solemnly promise by the assistance of thy Spirit and grace, if thou dost give us anything, I will not only improve it for our own comfort but will also use it for the support of the gospel, the relief of thy poor, or in what way thou in thy providence allotest. Only make the path of duty plain, and by thine assistance I will go in it.

But thou all-wise and heart-searching Jehovah, thou knowest my heart is deceitful, and I dare not trust it, nor do I promise anything further than by thy grace, for shouldst thou leave me to myself, I should grow covetous, worldly-minded. I shall hide my Lord's talent in the earth; I shall set my affections on things below; I shall cast off my trust and reliance on thy providence, and cark and care how to keep and how to add. I shall grow strait-handed to thy dear ambassador and shut up my bowels of compassion to the poor and, in a word, do everything that is dreadful.

Lord, if thou seest these will be the effects, I entreat, I beseech thee, give us nothing. Lord, I deprecate unsanctified prosperity. I cannot, I will not have it. No portion, Lord, for me. Here I humbly tell thee, I solemnly protest, I won't accept it. No, I won't be put off though man wouldst offer me all the world. Lord, give it to whom thou pleasest, but give me thyself, thy Christ, thy Spirit and grace. This—this is my chosen portion. Give me this and I am happy, and without this, I will not be content.

And thou wilt give me my happy choice. It shan't be taken from me, and thou wilt order this and all my affairs in mercy, and I leave them with thee, determining to acquiesce in thy all-wise disposal, whatever it is.

For thou wilt not give me a stone, but the good things I ask, for Christ's sake, to whom be glory forever. Amen and Amen.

March 9, 1757, Wednesday evening

Blessed be God that has in infinite wisdom overruled the affair about which my fancy has been so busy. Drawed a blank [in the lottery] today, in which I rejoice.[14]

The Lord pardon the workings of my idle imagination. Thou knowest I hate these vain thoughts, and 'tis, through thy grace, my settled judgment that thou dost order all things well, and the ardent desire of my soul that thy will may be done on earth as it is in heaven.

And now I know thy will, I do through grace heartily acquiesce; yea, rejoice; yea, bless thee, for thou wilt not give me a stone; thou wilt not give me anything to hurt me, not a portion here, but thou wilt give me the portion I have chosen, and 'tis enough. Thou wilt give me day by day my daily bread.

Some thoughts of getting Peggy Lion to assist me in my business.[15] O Lord, I entreat thee now, let all these rovings of fancy cease. O, sanctify my fancy and take and hold me nigh thyself. O, let me be rather a beggar on a dunghill with a Christ clasped in the arms of my faith, my heart fixed on God, than have my thoughts busied about this and that trifle.

O, I beg thou wilt not suffer vain thoughts to lodge within me. Lord, help me. O, possess me wholly, and forever blessed be thy name for the freedom thou hast granted me at thy throne both yesterday and this day. Lord, hear and answer for Christ's sake.

And O, grant me prudence in my calling. Make me wise and faithful, and direct and overrule in all my affairs. I commit the affair that now lies before me to thee, Lord. Thou knowest what will be best. Incline or disincline as thou seest fit. I am ignorant, Lord. Teach me what is duty, I beseech thee. Make the path of duty plain, and let me not turn to the right hand or the left, nor raise my expectations too high from any creature, for all are vanity and vexation of spirit. Nor suffer me to plunge myself into new difficulties. Thou knowest what thou, by thy providence, will enable me to do and what not. Lord, guide me by thy prudent counsel and overrule for thy own glory in all things for thine honor's sake.

April 3, 1757, Sabbath morning

Our son John's family destitute of the necessities of life.[16]

The Lord in mercy pity the poor and needy. Supply their wants, Lord; thou knowest how to find out ways for their relief. And O, suffer not their misconduct in time past, or now, to shut up the bowels of my compassion, but so far as is in my power, let me cheerfully and thankfully relieve them, for Lord, thou art dealing graciously with us. We feel none of those pinching wants. O, as thou art filling us with food, fill us with gratitude, love, and beneficence also. O, help me to remember thou hast said, "Blessed is he that considereth the poor."[17]

The Lord will deliver him [John] in time of trouble. The Lord will preserve him and keep him alive, and he shall be blessed upon the earth, and thou wilt not deliver him into the will of his enemies.

O, suffer me not to act from selfish principles but from love to God and my fellow creatures. O God, let my heart be fixed on God this day. Give me a deep and solemn sense of eternal things. Lord, permit me to go to thine house, if it be thy blessed will, and suffer me not to mock thee there, but may I worship there in Spirit and truth.

Be with thine ambassador.[18] Lord, touch his lips as with a coal from thine altar. May he come to us this day, and at all times, in the fullness of the blessing of the gospel of peace. And O, purify him more and more, day by day. O, let his dross and tin be purged away. Fill him with the Spirit; grant him a spirit of meekness. O, take him nigh thyself, and for Christ's sake, heal all breaches, remove all prejudices, and let him prosper.

April 5, 1757, Tuesday morning

O blessed be God for any tokens of favor to thy church and people when our enemies are risen up against us, that thou hast at all repulsed them and driven them back.[19] All glory to thy name, for it was thou, Lord, didst it: it was not our own arm saved us, but thine. O, fill my heart with gratitude now; suffer me to pray for Zion's prosperity if I have not prayed as I ought. Let me not always be an idle spectator in Zion's cause while thy other dear children are wrestling and prevailing. Let me adore thee for thy goodness to them and thy church.

Lord, I praise thee for thy goodness, in that thou hast poured out thy Spirit on any of thy dear ones, that thy secrets are with them, that there yet remains in our land, even in these times of awful declensions, some wrestling Jacob and conquering Israels, some like Moses to stand in the gap and turn away thine anger.[20] O, let a spirit of prayer and supplication prevail more and more, and if it may consist with thy blessed will, let me bear my part. O shut me not out as if I had no part or lot in this matter, for surely through thy grace I also am a member of the same glorious body and am united with the same glorious head. Let me then seek the peace and prosperity of Zion.

Lord, go on to prosper her for Christ's sake. Let the enemies of the Lord be driven back more and more till Antichrist be utterly consumed.

April 13, 1757, Wednesday evening

This morning, the body clogged exceedingly. Could make but feeble efforts in devotion. Nevertheless, in reading the charming Hervey, somewhat revived, while Aspasio repeats a song, as he says, "sweeter far than all the melody of the woodland choir, a song that has harmony enough to make the brow of melancholy wear a smile, or to soothe away the sorrows of death itself."[21] Who shall lay anything to the charge of God's elect? It is God that justifieth. Who is it that can condemneth? It is Christ that died, or rather that is risen again, who is even at the right hand of God, who also maketh intercession for us.

Some sweetness from this remained at times all the day, but my disorder brings a gloom I can't quite shake off. Yet blessed be God, my desires are towards him. And some sweet acquiescence in his will I have this day experienced, with earnest longings for direction in everything, that he may be glorified, especially for raising my price for schooling, which at this times seems to be a duty in order to keep us from involvements [debts], as everything of the necessaries of life are so excessively risen.

The Lord search me and try me, and suffer me in no wise to act contrary to his will, but agreeable thereto, for Christ's sake.

April 14, 1757, Thursday morning

O my glorious God, I beseech thee, make the path of duty plain before us. Let the Golden Rule be mine. Preserve me from covetousness, from extortion, from grinding the face of the poor in any wise. Lord, search me and discover to me if it be thy blessed will, if anything of these sins are lurking under cover. If so, O let them not lie hid, nor suffer me to indulge them, but spurn them away in a moment, for I hate them, I abhor them. Lord, thou that knowest all things, knowest I do. From vanity turn off my eyes. Let no corrupt design nor covetous desires arise within this soul of mine. Order my footsteps by thy word and make my heart sincere. Let sin have no dominion, Lord, but keep my conscience clear. And O, having enabled me to act agreeable to thy holy will and the rules of justice and equity, Lord, preserve thine own honor.

Let me not be accused of wounding my profession.[22] Thou knowest I have openly and avowedly professed thee to be my God, and I have a name to live. O, let not thine honor be stained in any wise by me. Lord, I can't bear it. O, if any should be disgusted and throw out any reflections, let them center on worthless me and not on the religion of Jesus. And if thus it is, then grant me that meekness, that patience, that quiet lamblike submission whereby thou mayest be glorified without an overanxious care to vindicate my character to man. Only teach me duty, and I'll leave thee to vindicate my cause and to order all events.

Lord, I commit this case to thee with all my heart and soul, and desire to leave it with thee. O, guide me by thy unerring Spirit; guide me by thine eye.

Teach me duty; enable me to do it and be at rest. Let me not wrong my employers in any shape or form. Thine assistance, Lord God Almighty, I implore, to enable me to be faithful in every branch of duty, or I cannot. O, my precious Christ, without thee I can do nothing. O, let me derive from thee all that wisdom, courage, prudence, patience, and resolution I need to carry me through the difficult but pleasant work thou hast assigned me. O, communicate to me of thine infinite fullness, for thou knowest all my wants and all my weakness. Yea, and thou wilt supply me, for thine own name's sake that thou mayest be glorified, Amen.

Lord, for thy sake I ask, and thou wilt not give me a stone but the grace I need, and all shall be well forever, for I am thine and thou art mine by an union which nothing ever shall or can dissolve, Amen. Hallelujah. Rejoice, my soul, thou art safe, come what will. Though devils rage, they can never rend thee away.

May 2, 1757, Monday morning

O, blessed be God, have had precious seasons in prayer day by day. God has given me the grace I have needed, and thereby filled me with a vehement thirst after greater degrees of grace. The discoveries of a God of spotless purity and matchless holiness has filled me with self-abasement, self-abhorrence, and stripped me of self-dependence: yea, and shrunk me into less than nothing. "Lord, I am vile, unclean, unclean before thee" has been the language of my soul while I am trembling with the sense of it but greatly rejoicing in the imputed righteousness of my dear Redeemer, which is every whit complete. Impartial justice and spotless holiness itself can find no flaw, not the least blemish.

Yesterday my dear pastor preached again. Matthew 14, text: O thou of little faith, wherefore dost thou doubt?[23] The Lord make me thankful that I have again been fed with solid substantial truths, that such comforts, such refreshments, was offered to poor, trembling, doubting Christians. The Lord accompany by his blessed Spirit that their doubts may be removed and they enabled to run the way of his commandments with delight, that thou mayest be glorified in all.

Last evening went with Phillis to talk with Mr. Vinal, and he is so well satisfied with her account of her experiences that he is freely willing to propound her for baptism and full communion.[24] The Lord give her favor in the eyes of her master and mistress, if it be thy blessed will, that she may meet with no obstruction there. And O, may she indeed enjoy sweet and intimate communion with Christ in his ordinances. O, blessed be God for his goodness to that precious soul.

O, may I not humbly hope thou hast for Christ's sake given me my requests for this precious soul? O, adored be thy name, thou glorious hearer and answerer of prayer. Thou alone knows what strong cries thou hast enabled me from time to time to put upon her behalf, and I will rejoice and praise thee that she is thine. Yea, I had rather a thousand times she should be wholly thine than her body mine. This was my servant, but is she now thine? I brought her to thee, and thou hast healed her. O, blessed be thy name forever.

May 2, 1757, Monday evening

O, blessed be God, this has been a comfortable day. Soon after I went down, found all things was likely to be comfortable respecting Phillis. No objection at all.

And though I have feared difficulties respecting raising my price, none has yet arose, but God make all to be at peace with me. O, thanks be to God. 'Tis thou, Lord, dost it; to thee be all the glory.

And with me, Lord, be merciful to the afflicted, tempted soul. (Clark Brown's wife in a distressed condition.)[25] O, let her not be overborne with overmuch sorrow. O, with a discovery of her own heart, give her also a discovery of Christ, her glorious remedy, or she will sink. Lord, heal her backslidings; bruise Satan under her feet; and speak peace and pardon, if it be thy blessed will. Thou knowest all her sorrows and all her maladies. Lord, heal her, and let the riches of thy sovereign grace be magnified if it be thy holy will.

Monday morning, May 9, 1757

On yesterday our son Edward with the rest of our soldiers sailed for Albany.[26] The Lord in mercy go with them; guide, direct, and protect them. O Lord, 'tis thou alone knowest what the event of this attempt will be. O, have mercy on the poor souls, and have mercy on our land for Christ's sake, for we are sinking under the weight of our own guilt. Lord, pardon and save us.

This week I am again called to prepare for the solemn feast.[27] Will God graciously afford me the assistance and influence of his blessed Spirit? For Lord, without thee I can do nothing. Lord, pity me. Thou seest how dull, how lifeless I now am. My soul cleaves to the dust. Quicken thou me, according to thy word.

May 20, 1757, Friday morning

O my God, as a father pities his children, so pity me. Thou seest my frame; thou knowest I am but dust; thou seest the maladies my body now labors under. Father, thy will be done. I don't complain; I don't murmur. Only glorify thyself and all is well. Strengthen me so far, if it be thy will, that I may faithfully discharge my duty in my calling. And O, let not my soul be clogged, but let it either ascend to thee in vigorous acts of devotion or, in profound humility and submission, adore. O, let me be sick or well, what thou wilt, only make thy abode with me.

Strike me, covenant faithful God, as thou pleasest. 'Tis my just deserts, 'tis the effect of sin, but let me kiss the dear, dear hand that strikes. For thy lovingkindness thou wilt not take away, nor suffer thy faithfulness to fail. O, let me not grieve thee, and I fear no other evil.

June 7, 1757, Tuesday morning

Yesterday I found seven or eight at least of my children was gone to other schools on account of price, and do suppose on the same ground almost my whole school totters. And I am so amazed, weak in body, and lifeless that I know no more than a babe how to tend what I have. I seem to be almost laid aside as a useless, broken vessel. Am ready to fear I have done all the good I ever shall do in this world, and now impatience to be gone is rushing upon me.

O, that God will take me into his own hand and mold me into his own image, subdue the peevishness of my spirit and my intolerable unbelief. O Lord, let not my sins against thee be increased. What ever thou hast determined to do with me, I pray thee, for Christ's sake, subdue me to thyself and do with me what thou wilt. But O, give me not up to my own heart's lusts to rebel against thee, to distrust thee, to make thee a liar. O Lord, increase my faith and secure thy honor, and all shall be well by and by, for I am thine forever and ever.

Blessed be God: some relief by prayer at this time.

I mark it for my future encouragement to trust in God, that this week we knew not what to do for food, and our God sent us dainties from day to day: squab, pigeon, sparrowgrass [asparagus], pudding, gingerbread, tarts, gammon &c.[28]

June 23, 1757, Thursday morning

My soul cleaves to the dust: 'tis dry, 'tis barren, every grace and faculty is withering. O, how doleful. At a distance from God and can't get nigh. Lord, draw me and I will run after thee. Quicken thou me, according to thy word, and let not mine enemies triumph over me. Thou knowest how many ways Satan has tried to drive me at a distance from thee, to rob me of communion with thee, envying me my happiness, and shall he gain his end? Shall he insult, and say, where is now your God?

Lord, arise for my help, and take me nigh thyself. I have trusted in thee. Let me not be put to shame. O Lord, some transforming views, some freedom at thy throne, for Christ's sake. I can't live thus. O, pity me.

Blessed be God, after I wrote, had some precious moments in prayer, and again in the afternoon, longings for conformity to God, more near and intimate communion with him here, and full fruition. Longed to get home in the evening. Hysteric disorders came hurrying on and sunk my spirits and damped my desires, and I could not get nigh in any duty. O, when shall these interruptions cease and I be unalterably fixed on God? Lord, preserve me from impatience. Thy will be done.

But O, greater degrees of grace while in this distant land. O, hold me not at a distance from thee, nor suffer me to ramble from thee—my joy, my life, my rock. O, let omnipotence hold me, and I am safe. O, thou faithful, unchangeable Jehovah, I fly to thee, for thou hast said thy kindness shall not depart from me, and it shall not. Though my frame vary, thou changest not.

June 24, 1757, Friday evening

Blessed be God, after I wrote, God, for Christ's sake, condescended to take me nigh himself in prayer. I told him my secret griefs, and he discovered his power and faithfulness, and again assured me he will never leave me nor forsake me. With him all things are possible. And though I am now bowed under a spirit of infirmity, I shall be made straight and glorify God. He will subdue mine iniquities and bruise Satan under my feet shortly. Methought he asked me, "Believest thou I am able to do this?" And I cried, "Lord, I believe. Help thou my unbelief."[29]

I cried for his presence and assistance this day, and he has graciously granted my request, and it has been a pleasant day, a day of rest to my weary soul. Some sweet acquiescing in his infinite wisdom, love, and care in ordering all our affairs in mercy, lessening my school, proportioning my business to my strength, and in the very way I desired, without any anger from anyone, and also in bringing about a way for our help without our forethought, that all is well. O my soul, how canst thou ever distrust this good and faithful God that is always nigh and ready to help in every time of need? Wherefore dost thou care? Wherefore dost thou doubt?

For shame. Forbear. Never distrust this more.

My husband warding.[30] How God has ordered it! I have been able to stand alone some years without his earning anything, and then there was no way that he could earn a shilling to help. But no sooner does God disable me and cause my means to fail, but behold, without my care he immediately finds out another way. Now my husband shall help me, which I never expected as to evenings he would ever do again. Lord, how dost thou triumph over my

unbelief and answer what degree of faith thou findest. Lord, increase my
faith. Thou canst of stones raise up children to believing Abraham; thou
canst turn water into wine; make the meal in the barrel and oil in the cruse
to support in famine; thou canst feed an Elijah even by a greedy raven; yea,
multiply a few loaves and small fishes so as to feed many thousands.[31] And
though miracles are ceased, the Lord's hand is not shortened. Thy wisdom,
power, and carefulness over thine own are still the same as ever they were,
and my God will supply all my need for soul and body. He will heal my
infirmities, too; stanch the issue of my corruption.[32] This overflowing
fountain shall ere long be dried up.

O Lord, when? How long, Lord? How long? O, hasten the time. Dry it
up by swift degrees, or take me home and the work is done in a moment and
done forever. Then I'll never trust thee more. I'll never be slothful more, but
wing as angels do. Yes, yes, I'll fly like a seraph to execute thy commands. I'll
love as I am loved. I'll shout and sing forth the riches of redeeming love to all
eternity. O, blessed be thy name, I shall not then be cramped for want of time,
nor fear one duty interfering with another as now I do.

Lord, teach me while here by thy unerring Spirit. Make every path of
duty plain and ordain to thyself praise out of the mouth of this babe and
suckling, this little child, this dwarf, this worm. Abba, Father, with thee all
things are possible. Glorify thyself. Thou canst do it. O, do, for Christ's sake,
whose I am and will be forever, forever.

Sarah Osborn

June 26, 1757, Sabbath evening

O, thanks be to God. This day my dear Phillis has given herself up to
God in baptism and is taken into full communion with our church.[33] Blessed
be God for the double joy I have in seeing this addition made to the church
of Christ. I trust this is really a member of his mystical body. O Lord, grant
her increase of every grace of thy Spirit.

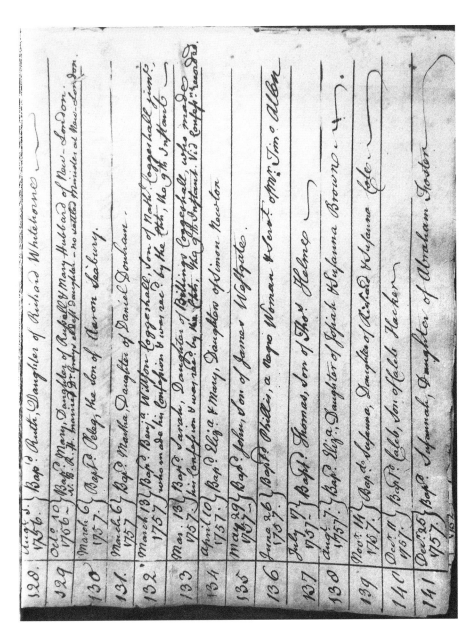

A page from the Records of the First Congregational Church of Newport. On June 26, 1757, "Phillis, a Negro Woman," was baptized into the church. Courtesy of the Newport Historical Society.

July 13, 1757, Wednesday morning

Hitherto a stupid headache. No feeling sense of eternal things, my thoughts taken up about taking one of our son Johnny's children. He is going to sea. (Son Johnny a privateering.)[34]

The Lord in mercy protect and preserve him. O, cover his head in the day of battle, gracious God, and return him in safety, if it be thy blessed will. O Lord, let him not be more and more hardened in sin, but pity him and snatch him as a brand out of the burning. O, make him a monument of thy rich grace, that whether he lives or dies, he may be the Lord's. And O, extend the same mercy to the other [son] also, for Christ's sake, and return them both in thy own time, if it be thy blessed will.

And Lord, direct me what to do about this child. Thou knowest what thou hast determined to do, both for them and for us. O, teach me duty. Suffer me neither to shut up the bowels of compassion nor yet to run myself into trouble, except thou call me to it. I know if 'tis duty, thou wilt provide for me and enable me to go through it, but I know not what is duty. Lord, teach me. Let thy glory be the end of all my actions, and accept me for Christ's sake, whose I am and will forever be.

August 4, 1757, Thursday morning

O, thou great and glorious head of the church, thou Lord of Hosts and God of armies, thou knowest with what power and rage Antichrist is come forth against thy little flock, and thou knowest how to defeat them, if it be thy blessed will, with infinite ease.[35]

True, Lord, we deserve nothing but to be given up to their wills. We have ungratefully requited thee for all past deliverances; we have trampled on thy authority; profaned thy sacred name, thine ordinances, thy Sabbaths, and in a word, done everything that's dreadful. This I would bewail as well as confess.

But thou art God and not man. O then, for Christ's sake, have mercy on us and still be on our side—be on our side no matter how great the difference may be in the number and strength of the fleets and armies. If God be with

ours, though there were a million to one, they should not prevail. And hast
thou not said, "The gates of hell shall not prevail against thy church"?[36] O,
thou that didst divide the Red Sea that thy people might pass through, appear
on our side now.[37] Thou knowest how it is with our fleet and our armies.
Lord, cover their heads in the day of battle and give us Cape Breton if it be
thy blessed will.[38] O, let it not be said by the heathen and followers of Antichrist, God has forsaken us.

But thy will be done on earth as it is in heaven. Glorify thyself, my God,
and if for wise and holy ends thou seest meet to scourge us yet more, let it
be said 'tis our sins has provoked thee. O, mayest thou be justified. Let no
unrighteousness be imputed to thee: *on us forever be the blame.* Let all be
constrained to say, "God is just, God is faithful, 'tis we who have sinned."
This would yield me a satisfaction, amidst bitter reproaches, to hear thee vin-
dicated and we condemned, for we deserve it. *But there is no iniquity in thee.*[39]

Do what thou wilt with us, but O, glorify thy darling attribute and, for
Christ's sake, appear for us, if it may consist with thy determinate counsel,
if it may consist with the predictions of thy written word. Lord, spare us yet
longer and lead us by thy goodness to repentance. Pour out thy Spirit on us
and destroy Antichrist. O, may the gospel yet be established in Cape Breton
on the ruins of Antichrist, on the ruins of idolatry. O Father, glorify thyself,
and do it in thy own way and thy own time. O, when shall the Seventh Angel
proclaim all the sound and great voices be heard in Heaven saying, "All
the kingdoms of this world are become the kingdom of our Lord and his
Christ"?[40] When, Lord God Almighty, when wilt thou take to thyself thy
great power and reign King of Nations? And wilt thou not answer the
prayers of faith excited by thy own Spirit in thy faithful servants long ago,
some of them now with thee, respecting Cape Breton?[41]

Lord, answer them now, if it may consist with thy blessed will, and stir
up all the faithful ministers and dear children now to lay hold on thy strength
by faith, and hold thee on our side. O, be not a departing God but a God nigh
at hand, a God exciting, encouraging, and hearing prayer. Blessed be thy
name that there yet lives some wrestling Jacobs in our nation and land.[42] O,
let these have power with God and prevail for Christ's sake, in whose name
they come. Lord, these come not in their own name; neither do I ask an

answer to their prayers for their own sake, but for Christ's sake. And O, for his sake, hear and answer.

O, be with our fleets and armies if it may be thy blessed will. O Lord, let the solemn prayers of thy people this day ascend as incense perfumed with the blood of the great sacrifice. Spirit thy dear ambassadors and all thy children. Let the prayers of faith ascend today, and O, let me bear my part. Grant me access to thy throne; communicate to me also, vital sap, though but a little branch of the true vine. Though but a babe, yet let me cry to thee for help.

Lord, vain is the help of man. 'Tis thou alone canst help.

August 7, 1757, Sabbath Day

We had the news that our son Edward was shot through the body in a late engagement with the enemy on July 22. The Lord humble us under this frown of thy providence, and if he yet lives, heal his wound, if it be thy blessed will.

But above all—O for Christ's sake—heal the wounds sin has made in his soul. O, sanctify this blow for his awakening and conversion. O, that his soul may yet live. And Lord, have mercy on the rest of thy people and give them the victory. Pity those that are carried away, captive. Heal the wounded and the sick, and do for us according to thy unbounded goodness and not according to our iniquities.

Dear Mr. Vinal preached two more lovely sermons from John 15:4. Lord, grant that I and all his children may abide in Christ and derive vital strength from him at all times. Blessed be God, I did enjoy a blessed Sabbath, refreshed in his house, and this day have had some sweet communion with God. But I want to get nigh in prayer and ease my burdened heart, for my spirits are sunk, notwithstanding many supports. Public affairs now bear with weight, but can't pray.

Sarah Osborn to Joseph Fish, August 7, 1757

My Rev. and worthy friend,

Though I have had no opportunity till now to write to you, I have sympathized with you and bore you with the rest of your dear family almost continually on my heart from the time I heard of dear Miss Becky's sickness till I heard of her recovery.[43] And then rejoiced with you: thanks be to God for sparing her precious life. O, may it be more than ever rooted to God, that he may be glorified in her, and you have double joy.

And now, Sir, we in a peculiar manner stand in need of your pity and prayers. I doubt not but as God enables, we shall have them. This day we heard the heavy news that Mr. Osborn's eldest son [Edward] was (in the late fight of which doubtless you have heard) shot through the body on July 22, of which one of the officers in a letter to his parents, wrote the 25th, gives an account, but says he hopes he will recover. Whether he be yet alive, the Lord knows. O, be earnest, if the Lord will permit, if he be yet in the land of the living that his soul may live. O, for a Christ to be applied to his precious soul. Whatever God has determined concerning his recovery, if it may consist with his sovereign pleasure, may that be granted, but his will be done. O, that God may glorify his darling attribute and snatch him as a brand out of the burning, that whether he lives or dies he may be the Lord's.

I cannot add [admit] I am straitened: I fear he is *not* [the Lord's].

God is just, be it as it will. He has an absolute right to dispose of us and ours as he sees meet; yea, and he is faithful, too, and does all things wisely and well. He gave, and if he has taken, blessed be his name. He himself is a portion that will never fail. The Lord yet lives and reigns; the fountain flows, and there is enough in God to make us happy though every stream were cut off. May we cleave faster to him than ever.

The Lord be with you. My hearty regards to you, dear spouse and children, which concludes these shattered lines from your sincere and affectionate, though unworthy friend,

Sarah Osborn

P.S. Our other son [John] is out in a privateer. I beg prayers for his preservation and salvation. All our friends are well but dear Susa, and she is in a low state of health. Miss Betsy Peabody sends her duty.

August 16, 1757

The Lord make me thankful: on Wednesday morning, I had as large discoveries of the perfections of God perhaps as ever in my life, and I humbly hope I really had communion with him in his holiness. Rejoiced and gave thanks at the remembrance of it, and in his sovereignty, justice, truth and faithfulness, infinite power, wisdom, omnipresence. My faith, love, trust, and confidence drawed forth. Dared appeal to his omnipresence for my sincerity. Felt vile and weak as a babe in myself, but in Christ strong as a Goliath. Could in his strength bid defiance to all the hosts of Sheol.[44] Such a rock, such a shield, such a strong tower did my Christ appear, that all was well. First chapter of Joshua exceeding sweet. Alas, I can't tell how great this feast was, but I know the exercises of my eager, enamored soul were so strong that it wracked my body much.

And when, my God, shall the clay vessel break, the clog fall off, and interrupt no more? O, in thy own time, my gracious sovereign, it will, it will, and I shall drink my fill of those rivers of pleasure that flow from thy right hand forever more. Meantime, O my Christ, keep me from the evil of sin if not from suffering. Thou only knowest what thou hast determined to call me to.

Thy hand is lifted up in a very awful manner against us. Antichrist is prevailing in these parts and laying waste thy heritage—confirmations of the victories, triumphs, cruel murders committed by our bloodthirsty enemies upon our friends and brethren enough to make the ears of all that hear to tingle, and also of their progress to our other stronghold.[45] O God, glorify thyself. Thou art just, do what thou wilt. We have ten thousand times deserved this, yet if it consist with thy glory, Lord, deliver us. But thy will be done on earth as it is in heaven.

Thy name is a strong tower: let the righteous run into it and be safe. Thou wilt keep him in perfect peace whose mind is stayed on thee. He shall not be greatly moved. He shall not be afraid of evil tidings whose heart is fixed, trusting in the Lord, for though the mountains depart and hills be removed, thy kindness shall not depart, nor the covenant of thy peace be removed. Thou wilt bear their joyful souls above destruction and the sword.

Thou wilt keep them alive in famine, and those shall rejoice in thee who are counted worthy to die for thee. Lord, do what thou wilt, for thou wilt do all things wisely and well, and thou hast done all things well. 'Tis only we have done all things ill. The Lord reigns, and blessed be my rock. Did thou not say to me, "Be still and know that I am God"?[46] Lord Jesus, dost thou say, "Peace: be still"?[47] Nothing can raise a storm. Behold, a calm faith lies at anchor in the midst of these waves and believes the accomplishments of the promises.

August 19, 1757

Thanks be to God, some sweet communion with God in prayer after I wrote, renewing my choice and dedications. But in the afternoon, an extreme heaviness seized me, my heart felt ready to burst as a full bottle, yet wanted vent—hoped to get vent—by prayer when I got home. But was prevented from retiring by the news of our son Edward's death.

It appeared to be duty to go to his widow, which I did.[48] May God awaken her to a concern for her soul and enable her to fly to Christ for refuge and find rest.

After I heard this news, God quieted my heart and made it submit to his adorable sovereignty. I realized in some degree his infinite wisdom in ordering all events and was constrained to say he does all things well: the Judge of all the earth has done and will do right.

This remarkable day, the news by an express that Fort William Henry was on Tuesday last taken by the French, and that the communication between Fort Edward and Albany is cut off.[49] Lord, I own thy justice in all that has befallen us. We have deserved this and a thousand times more at thine hand. But Lord, have compassion on us, and upon this mount of difficulty, appear and make the Antichrist and the heathen know that Zion's God has not forsaken her, though he hast scourged her.[50]

Lord, defeat them. Yet if it be thy blessed will, set bounds to their rage and fury. Say to these proud waves, "Hitherto thou shalt come, and no further." O God, defend us and save us for thine own name's sake, and do it in thy own sovereign way, that the glory may be all thy own. Abba, Father, with thee all things are possible. Thy power is infinite—thy mercy, thy truth and faithfulness are unbounded. We have sinned with a high hand and provoked thee.[51] Lord, this I bewail, that thou hast been so awfully dishonored by us. O, humble us and turn us to thyself. Lord, in the midst of wrath remember mercy. Let not thine anger wax hot against us. O, consume us not utterly. Spare thy people, O Lord, and give not thy heritage to reproach, that the heathen should reign over us. Thou art God and not man.[52]

O, for Christ's sake, have compassion for us and sanctify thy rod to my dear consort. Lord, support, quicken, humble, and comfort him. And O, prepare him and me for our great change, which is hastening on. Let us be ready to meet the King of Terrors[53] with joy at what moment thou shalt commission him to seize us. And O, resign us to thy will in all things and at all times. Be our God to and through death, and our unchangeable portion forever, for the dear Mediator's sake.

For whose sake I ask all, to whom be glory forever and ever, Amen.

September 5, 1757

This day, Satan and the other law[54] has been again moving and stirring to interrupt my rest by setting me to scheming at about this world. But through grace I have been enabled to resist and, in some good degree, to stand my ground and not suffer any thoughts to fix.

But just before night I heard the vessel was coming in, in which our son [Johnny] went out, and a panic seized me, fearing he is not. If so, this will try whether I am willing God should be sovereign or not. Lord, thou knowest I do desire to submit to thy will in all things, and by thy grace I can do it. But of myself, I cannot.

O, prepare me for whatever news I am to hear. If thou hast preserved and returned him, let my heart glow with gratitude. If not, still let me bless thy name and be resigned to thy sovereign pleasure.

September 6, 1757

Thanks be to God, he has returned our dear child, and he has enabled me to make some grateful acknowledgments that he is causing us to sing of mercy as well as judgment. O, that God will enlarge our hearts yet more, and O, that he [Johnny] also may by God's goodness be led to repentance.

Blessed be God that what he has got is without shedding of blood. O, thou all-wise sovereign, thou hast done all things well.

September 15, 1757, Thursday evening

O, what shall I render to the Lord for all his benefits towards his poor dust? O, how did he this day appear for me when, beginning to sink for want of access to his throne, he took me nigh himself. His Spirit helped my infirmities and taught me what to pray for. God excited strong cries for conformity to him to be kept from the evil; enabled me solemnly to renew my choice and surrender and, when my heart was eased by faith and prayer, went out satisfied, committing my all to precious Christ. And have had a calm, comfortable day, the Lord be praised.

And now, my God, since in thy providence thou hast brought this poor girl into our family—Almey Greenman, September 15 1757—I beg for Christ's sake thou wilt grant me wisdom to instruct her in a proper manner.[55] And Lord, seal instruction, if it be thy blessed will. O, thou great prophet, open her understanding; convince her of sin—original and actual. Lord, convince her of her danger, of her utter inability to help herself and utter unworthiness that God should help her. And O, thou glorious high priest, though Satan resist, snatch this brand out of the burning. Take away her filthy garments and clothe her with the precious robe of thine own righteousness, that her shame may never appear. O, thou King of Kings, subdue her to thyself. Make her willing in the day of thy power. Lord, thou canst with infinite ease. O, glorify the riches of thy sovereign grace in the conversion of this soul, if it be thy blessed will. The glory will be all thy own, and by thy grace I'll rejoice and praise thee, and all thy saints that know it shall praise thee. The humble shall hear thereof and be glad. Yea, and there shall be joy in heaven: angels shall praise thee if this sinner repenteth, this prodigal returns. True, Lord, you stand in no need of the praises of men or angels, but herein thou art delighted, thou art glorified, and 'tis for the glory of thy sovereign grace that thou hast done all for fallen man, that that might be magnified.

And may it forever be magnified.

September 19, 1757, Monday morning

Thanks be to God, he did pity me and in a measure made me serious and diligent in the duties of the day.

Engaged in instructing the poor girl. Find her extremely ignorant of divine things but, blessed be God, not altogether thoughtless. O, my glorious prophet, thou teacher come from God, thou that teachest as never man taught, I fly to thee. O, take the work into thine own hands, and then she will be effectually taught. Lord, without thee I can do nothing. She is ignorant, and thou knowest I am as a beast before thee. O, grant me wisdom to direct, and may I be willing to spend and be spent for thee. And O, deliver this soul from death, if it may consist with thy blessed will, and do it in thy own sovereign way, that the glory may be all thy own, and I will by grace rejoice and praise thee.

O, adored be thy name for what thou hast done for my poor Phillis. O, thanks be to God that she is going on her way rejoicing.[56] Lord, make her more holy, more and more conformed to thy blessed image. O, blessed be God that this Ethiopian is washed in the blood of Christ, that she is made free indeed. O Lord, what shall I render to thee because thou hast glorified thyself in her and, I trust, will be glorified in her to all eternity?

And now in the arms of faith and prayer I would bring this [Almey Greenman] to thee also, thou Great Physician. Behold, she is sick even unto death: yea, she is really dead in trespasses and sins, but only speak the word, she shall live; she shall stand up and praise thee, too.

September 26, 1757, Monday morning

This day my dear consort with his son going, God willing, over to visit my father and mother.[57] The Lord in mercy protect them from all evils. Preserve their health if it be thy blessed will.

And O, meet with our son [Johnny], even now whilst he is running away from God and from his duty, neglecting the means of grace and committing those things that are abominable in thy sight. O Lord, I bewail it before thee that he appears to be more hardened in sin by this voyage, and if thou does not prevent, sin will prove his ruin. O Lord, convince him thou, God, seest him, and turn him to thyself for Christ's sake. He is not out of the reach of sovereign grace. O, let it be magnified in his conversion and overrule in thy all-wise providence, both for my parents and for him, respecting their affairs. Lord, thou knowest what will be for the best. To thee I would commit this and all their concerns and leave them with thee. Thou needest none of my schemes or anxious cares. Lord, undertake and 'tis enough.

And O, be with my dear consort in a special manner. Grant him thy presence, Lord, I beg of thee. O, except thou go with him, let him not stir from hence, and return him to me, in thy own time, laden with experiences of thy goodness. And O, be with me, thy worthless worm, in his absence, and teach me duty and assist me in it. Make the path of duty plain before me because of my enemies. Lord, thou seest how they stand ready to take an advantage against me every way—either to dissuade me from the duty, lest it should proceed from a vain, hypocritical, ostentatious show, and therefore God will not grant his assistance, or these principles will of a truth prevail and provoke thee to leave me. And thou knowest, without thee I can do nothing. May I become duly sensible of my own wickedness and vileness, depending upon thee for assistance and acceptance. Hide pride from my eyes, and let integrity and uprightness preserve me. For thou, God, seest me.

O, has not this been the practice of godly women in all ages to keep up the worship of God in their families when the head was absent? Whence this struggle now? What a strange change is here: I, that some years ago could open my mouth freely and boldly in presence of many, now afraid of these committed to my immediate care. Lord, search and try me, and discover to me the cause and remove it, if it be thy blessed will. And grant me freedom of access, and by thy grace I will give thee the glory. Accursed self, accursed pride, shall not rob thee if thou wilt grant humility.

O, then give me this grace, and I will not be ashamed or afraid to be singular in this perverse generation. O, lay me in the dust before thee, thou great Jehovah. O, clothe me with humility, and thou wilt hear for Christ's sake a humble and contrite heart. O God, thou wilt not despise. O, my glorious Christ, I fly to thee now. Screen me from evil—the bitter and only evil. Keep me from temptation, or grant me power to resist and overcome. Make a way for my escape, thou faithful God, and I shall praise thee with joyful lips.

September 26, 1757, Monday evening

I have been all this day struggling with discouragements about praying with my family, but resolved, God helping me, I would attempt it, and accordingly have. But thou, Lord, knowest in how poor a manner. O, wash away the sins of the performance in the blood of Christ and, for his sake, accept me and answer my prior petitions.

Thanks to God that thou didst touch the heart of thine handmaid [Almey Greenman]. Lord, awaken her yet more, and teach her to pray for herself. O, begin and carry on a work of grace in her precious soul, and may the child also share in all the blessings of the new and everlasting covenant. And help me to go on steadily in the path of duty, relying on thee for a blessing, for thou hast said thou wilt never leave me nor forsake me.

October 3, 1757, Monday evening

I now record on purpose, that I may give God the glory of providing for us in his providence, that at this time my ways are, as Mr. Eliot expresses it, hedged up with thorns and grow darker and darker daily;[58] for our expense is unavoidably greater than our income, notwithstanding I take every prudential step I can think of to lessen it, the necessaries of life being so vastly risen. A considerable sum (44-odd pounds is no more) is, 'tis probable, lost in bad hands, beside 50 or 60 more that can be had in nothing of eatables or cask, that there is no prospect at present of our being able to provide wood or any one particular for winter.[59]

But the God that has fed me all my life long does know what I need and will supply all my needs, too. Let Satan or unbelief say what they will, he never yet made me ashamed of my hope, nor he never will. He has said he will never leave me nor forsake me.

Sarah Osborn to Joseph Fish, October 5, 1757

Reverend and dear Sir,

I am now at Mr. Peabody's where I have just heard the melancholy news of your indisposition.[60] May God of his infinite mercy bless means for your recovery and fill your precious soul with the incomes of the blessed Spirit, that amidst all your bodily weakness your inward man may be renewed day by day. I am tenderly concerned for you, and beg to hear as soon as possible how you do. Meantime, this is my comfort: that I know you are in the hands of a compassionate and faithful God who will deal graciously with you for his own sake and, I trust, in pity to your dear family, his church, your dear friends, and me, the most unworthy of all, restore you to health again. Fain would I say at all times, "Thy will be done on earth as 'tis in heaven."[61] Yea, and I must say so, for God always has done and ever will do all things well, however he dispose of all things dear to me.

In my last, Sir, I gave you an account of the news that we had, that our son [Edward] on July 22 was wounded. Since, we have heard that on the 25th he died. And we have since sung of mercy as well as judgment, for God has graciously returned our other, our only son [Johnny], from the sea. He went with Tompkins, and it is no small satisfaction to me that the success he has had was without shedding of blood, for privateering does not appear to me like going against our enemies in defense of our King and country in a regular manner, though 'tis not contrary to the laws of man.[62]

But time fails, and I must conclude with telling you Mr. Osborn is well, sends best regards. Deacon Peabody's wife and Betsy also. Mrs. Peabody would have wrote but has not time now. Other friends are well. As to myself, I am, through mercy, able to keep about for the most part but in general in a low state of health. But all is well: God is gracious to me beyond expression. His kindness does not depart; neither is the covenant of his peace removed. All his ways are mercy, truth, and faithfulness. Thanks be to God for Jesus Christ, the foundation of all my hopes. O, how sweet to rest in him, amidst all the threatening storms from within and without, who will surely keep every soul committed to his care. O, what a mercy is it that the Lord reigns, that Christ is king. What a singular comfort this is, in this day of darkness and distress, that infinite wisdom, love, and faithfulness is at the head of all affairs, holds the chain of men and devils in his own hand, and will not suffer them to stir a hair's breadth further than most consists with his own glory and his church's good. And though for our sins he will scourge, yet he will never forsake.

What shall I do? I could talk to you almost all night. But I must forbear and beg your acceptance of this with hearty regards to yourself, dear spouse, and children from your affectionate though unworthy friend,

Sarah Osborn

October 29, 1757

A considerable prospect of the smallpox spreading in this town, and indeed throughout the land. What God has designed I know not. He has oft lifted up his hand, threatened, but kept off the dreaded blow, and if most for the glory of his sacred majesty, he will do so still. And O, if it may be his will to spare in mercy a guilty people, a guilty land sinking under its weight, if he may be glorified in this way, I will by grace rejoice and praise him.

But let God be glorified; let every attribute be glorified. I am, blessed be his name, not distressed. My comfort is the Lord will do right. Infinite wisdom, power, justice, love, mercy, truth, and faithfulness cannot ever, can make no mistake in governing the world. O, I rejoice: all the world and his little flock is in his hands, and he will rule and reign with uncontrollable sway—that he does his will in the armies of heaven and amongst the inhabitants of the earth, and none can stay his hand nor say unto him, "What doest thou?"[63] O my God, I know not what thou art about to do.

But thou knowest, and I cheerfully commit all that can be called dear to me into thy merciful and faithful hands, and determine by his grace to acquiesce in his will, be it what it will, for I have given my all to him. I am not my own, nor is anything belonging to me my own. All is thine by voluntary, free, solemn surrender as well as by absolute right.

And I renew the surrenders and declare, by the assistance of thy grace, I will cheerfully resign whatever thou in thy providence shalt call for, without reserve. Only in exchange, give me thyself; give me thy grace; give me thy Holy Spirit to abide within me, to sanctify me, to make me holy, to conform me to thine image. Resign me to thy will and 'tis enough, Lord; 'tis enough. Do what seemeth thee good.

Lord, here am I, and if it be thy sovereign pleasure to send for me by this messenger, I will, by grace, say "welcome." All this will I embrace, the messenger be it what it will. Or if, by this means, I may be more fitted for usefulness in this world, Lord, I submit. I prescribe not; I determine not. Thy will be done.

I am thine, forever thine, and will be thine forever—forever—and that's enough for me,

Sarah Osborn

December 21, 1757

I think nothing can more resemble my poor soul than a helpless simple sheep in a field, fiercely pursued by a greedy wolf, eager to tear in pieces and swallow up quick. A bear, bereaved of her whelps, espies and pursues the same prey and resolves if possible to possess and destroy it. A roaring lion, also, no less greedy, seeks to devour. They all pursue. And what can the poor creature do? It is helpless. Any one of these, should they overtake, would destroy in a moment. Would even a silly sheep go to meet these enemies or stand still? No, its fears would almost give it wings. How swift would it run to some shelter, to its shepherd. And would its shepherd stand and look on, see it in this distress, and not screen it? Would he give it up to those devourers when it is his particular business to guard it from them, it is committed to his care, he is called its keeper? No, no.

Neither will my glorious Shepherd give me up to sin, which like a ravenous wolf is ever seeking to tear my soul in pieces. Nor shall the world, greedy as a bear, swallow me up. My Christ has bid me, "be of good courage," for he has overcome the world.[64] Nor will the Lion of the tribe of Judah suffer Satan, that roaring lion, to devour me.

O my soul, act only the part that a poor feeble sheep would do, and thou art safe; thy glorious Shepherd will keep thee. Often has he rescued thee; he has kept thee hitherto. Many a time hast thou feared because of the fury of these oppressors, as if they were ready to destroy. But where is the fury of the oppressors? Hitherto the Lord has helped me, and he will not give me up now to these hated, dreaded tyrants. He knows I have not chosen this world for my portion, and he will not put me off with a portion here. He will give me himself, his Spirit, and his grace because he will be faithful. And his kindness will not depart from me though the mountains depart and the hills be removed.

1758

March 3, 1758, Friday evening

Blessed be God, since I wrote last, I have had some sweet seasons at the throne of grace. Vehement strivings after holiness, and that God may be glorified in everything. Glorious discoveries of the fullness and all-sufficiency of my dear Redeemer, and absolute power to heal all my maladies of soul. Under a deep sense of the obstinance of my disease. Renewedly committed my all to him, and have found rest, sweet rest and peace, in believing precious promises applied for my strong consolation, encouragement, and strengthening; and a promising God will prove a performing God.

Refreshed in reading Mr. Erskine's *Upon the Kings Being Heard in the Galleries.*[65] There I have met him, and there my soul vehemently longed to hold him and never let him go. O, that he would make his abode with me, come life, come death, come sickness, come poverty, come what will. If my Lord will but stay with me and sanctify me, resign me to his glorious sovereign will, set me apart for himself, I ask no more, I wish no more. And if he will but give me faith, as a grain of mustard seed, that I may say to the mountains raised by unbelief, "Depart or be removed," I will exert myself in acts of kindness and charity to the poor and needy.[66]

Lord, thou dost know how to find out a way to support me and enable me to do for this poor child.[67] Thou in thy providence art calling me to take it. Is it not hungry? Is it not naked? Is it not neglected, soul and body? Is it not a proper object of charity as any the town produces? Does not charity begin at home? Lord, make me cheerful, make me faithful; let me venture to take it in the name, and relying on the faithfulness, of a promising God who has said, "trust in the Lord and do good; so thou shalt inherit the land, and verily thou shalt be fed."[68]

Lord, bless the little one, and make it a blessing in the world and a comfort to us and its parents. I would dedicate it to thee, and if it be thy will, to permit it solemnly and publicly give it up to thee. (My consort did not see his way clear and so I have been prevented, and none of ours are baptized. This I regret.)[69] Let thy mark and seal be set upon it, and accept the dedicated thing. Let it be engrafted into Christ, washed in his precious blood from its original pollution, sanctified, and entitled to all the blessings of the new and everlasting covenant. And will God establish his covenant with us and with our seed? Grant thy servant, my dear companion, comfort in this branch of his offspring, if it be thy blessed will. Lord, for Christ's sake, grant it, and bless every soul under this roof and all committed to my charge. The Lord pardon all my deficiencies, and for Christ's sake, accept my feeble attempts to instruct. O, seal instruction and let not one soul remain Christless and graceless.

March 6, 1758, Monday

O my God, thou knows our wants in every shape, and thou knows we are in the hands of those that are powerful, subtle, crafty, and resolute and will overreach if thou permit. And I cannot help myself.

Lord, help me, and incline their hearts to deal gently and kindly with me, and order a speedy payment, if it may consist with thy blessed will, that we may render to others their due. Lord, thou canst subdue the stoutest hearts, adored be thy name. Many a time thou hast done it; many a time thou hast withheld such persons from hurting—yea, and made them kind and generous to me. And now, help me. Now I am afraid to put my trust in thee, Lord. Thou, in thy providence, hast put me thus far into their hands.[70]

March 21, 1758, Tuesday morning

My Lord and my God, thou alone knowest what thou art about to do with and for me; I don't know. Thou hast for wise and holy ends hedged up my way so that I know not what to do. No prospect of an house now. Whether this be for the trial of my faith and confidence in thee, or whether thou dost design in this way to stop me in my design of taking boarders, I know not. However, this I do know, blessed be thy name, that thou dost infallibly know what is best for me, and thou wilt order all things well. Light shall spring out of this darkness. I shall see thy hand and rejoice, for thy wilt not scatter darkness in my path. Thou hast always chosen all my changes and all my habitations for me, and do so still. My gracious God, I would have no choice but thine.

This is the first time I was ever plunged in this respect, and was it not best, my good God would not suffer it. So now, Lord, choose for me where thou wilt, or keep me where I am; only go or stay with me. Thou knowest what I need before I ask thee, but thou wilt be inquired of, and I beg for Christ's sake, thou wilt order all things for thy own glory.

This sums up all my petitions in one: Father, glorify thyself. I prescribe not in what way; infinite wisdom knows best. O, let me glorify thee and 'tis enough.

And now, my God, thou hast brought this dear little one under my care.[71] I fly to thee for grace to be faithful to it. And Lord, provide for me that I may provide comfortably for it, if it be thy will. And take possession of it for thy-self; call it thine. To thee, I dedicate it. O, let it be for thee and none other. Slay its natural enmity and contrariety to thee. Wash away its pollutions in thy own most precious blood. Take hold of it by thy almighty power and special grace, and O, keep me still calm and relying on thee. Thanks be to God for the composure of mind thou hast favored me with. Lord, 'tis thy doing, and it is marvelous in my eyes. I could no more attain it myself than I could implant a principle of grace myself. But 'tis but for thee to say, "Peace, be still," and all is well in a moment.[72]

And now renewedly committing myself and all my concerns into thy merciful and faithful hands, my covenant God and Father, I would leave all with thee and care for nothing but how I may please and glorify thee.

March 23, 1758, Thursday morning

May the Lord in mercy overrule in the affairs of this day. Thou knowest my ignorance, Lord; guide and direct.

And O, except thou go with us, let us not stir from hence. Lord, help me; thou knowest I am at the greatest loss, in the utmost consternation. Is not this house of thine own providing? Art thou, by the owners, inviting me thither?[73] O, then go with me; succeed and prosper me. Let me embrace the offer cheer-fully and thankfully and suffer no unbelieving fears to possess my breast. Lord, by thy grace, I'll dedicate it to thee, and there, I will be for thee and none other. Dost thou command me to be strong and of good courage? Dost thou say, "Be not afraid, neither be thou discouraged, for the Lord thy God is with thee whithersoever thou goest"?[74] Lord, this is all. O, as thou hast been with me in this place and in my dear Bethels, so be with me there and let me cheerfully quit this. Here thou hast fed and clothed me and refreshed me by kind and tender neighbors. The Lord reward them for all their benevolence.

And now, my God, I cast myself upon thy immediate care. Thou canst give me wherewith to pay my rent. Thou art not limited; let not unbelief limit thee.[75]

March 25, 1758, Saturday morning

Upon consulting my dear friend, it appeared to be duty to quit the place I had in view when I wrote last, and now another presents, more in the center of my business, but quite different from what I have always chosen. I must have my will crossed in respect of living alone: the person of whom we hire must be under the same roof and her disposition well known to be difficult. But God knows how to moderate her, and how to endow me with prudence to manage suitably, and how to meet with me and bless me in every place, let the conveniencies or ill conveniencies be what they will. And God has said, "his kindness shall not depart from me," and "why should I be afraid?"[76]

O, may I have no will but God's; let it be done on earth as it is in heaven. O Lord, subdue every degree of reluctance; subdue me wholly to thyself, and do with me what thou wilt. Overrule for thy own glory, I beseech thee. And Lord, increase my faith.

April 2, 1758, Sabbath morning

On Friday last we removed, and that very evening the neighbors came in and kindly welcomed a poor, unworthy creature amongst them. Lord, this is thy doing; thou wilt not suffer me to be friendless, go where I will. And now, my only and everlasting friend, I fly to thee for new degrees of grace and strength to glorify thee in this place. Thou hast cast my lot here, and thou canst make it as comfortable to me as ever thou didst any in my life, for it was thou didst sweeten all and teach me how to behave in a prudent, kind, and Christian manner, that I may win her of whom I was afraid, and that thou mayest be glorified by our kind Christian behavior to each other. We stand in a near relation; we profess to be of the same family and sisters in the same church. Let us live as such, that thou may be glorified.

And O God, strengthen me for the business thou callest me to. I pray thee, compose my thoughts and grant me freedom from on high. Lord, I am not sufficient of myself for the business thou callest me to. Thou knowest I

AND

Ames' Almanack,

For the Year 1759.

SARAH OSBORN, Schoolmiſtreſs in Newport,

propoſes to keep a

Boarding School.

ANY Perſon deſirous of ſending Children, may be accommodated, and have them inſtructed in Reading, Writ-ing, Plain Work, Embroidering, Tent Stitch, Samplers, &c. on rea-ſonable Terms.

An advertisement for Sarah Osborn's boarding school in the *Newport Mercury,*
December 19, 1758. Courtesy of the Newport Historical Society.

can do nothing without thee. Lord, help me all my days and be with me on this Sabbath day, both at home and in thy house, if thou permittest me to go there. Lord, go with me, I beseech thee.

August 31, 1758

O, blessed be God, who has provided such help for me that both my family and school are attended to my satisfaction. Lord, keep me diligent both for soul and body, I beseech thee. Suffer me not to waste the precious moments I may now redeem from family cares in idleness, but may I improve them to valuable purposes. Lord, thou dost all things well. I cried to thee and committed this case to thee, and thou hast provided suitable help for me. O, help me to rejoice in thy goodness while I do enjoy, but preserve me from placing happiness on this or any enjoyment, or depending on anything below thyself, my only chosen, happy portion. O, make me rejoice in thee for what thou art in thyself, thou God of infinite perfections, thou God of love, sovereignty, justice, truth, and faithfulness. Yea, I will rejoice in thy goodness to me, too, for thou suppliest all my wants for soul and body, and are bestowing a degree of sweet content.

O Lord, this is thy doing. For this I will bless thee, for had I all the world without this, I should be miserable. And this I can no more attain in myself than I can make all the good things I want. No, it is my God who bestows it. To him be all the glory.

I remark a singular instance wherein God indulged me yesterday. A glazier came to mend our windows, and as he was taking them down, I thought, what shall I do for money to pay for mending them? And immediately, before he had done taking them down, a child came in and brought me money—more than enough to pay him for his work. I received it as coming from the hand of God, who always enables me to pay the laborer, and rejoiced in it. Yea, and he does all things well.

November 1, 1758, Wednesday evening

My glorious, gracious God, I would praise thee with my whole heart. O, how thou dost indulge me. Enable me to provide the comforts of life for myself and also to render to all their due, to do something still for the support of thy gospel.[77] I thank thee for this privilege. Thou knowest I delight in it. And thou art still enabling me to feed the hungry and clothe the naked.

Go on, merciful Father, and for thine own honor's sake, add the mercy of a truly humble, grateful soul. Lord, thou canst make mine such a one. Thou canst preserve me from discontents and murmurings when new straits come on. O, never leave me more to such ingratitude. I dread it; I hate it; I deprecate it. Lord, help me at all times to trust in thee, prospect or no prospect. Thou art worthy to be trusted in the dark as well as in the light. How often hast thou made me ashamed of my vile unbelieving fears.

And I am no more worthy to be called thine because of them. I blush and am ashamed, and yet, my God, I am so vile that I shall surely do it again unless thou, by thy grace, prevent. I fly to thee for protection. O, save me from this bitter evil and do with me what seemeth thee good.

For I am thine own forever,

Sarah Osborn

SEVEN

Open My Hand and Heart, 1759–1760

BY THE SPRING OF 1759, *Sarah and Henry Osborn were so poor that she feared complete destitution. They scraped by on the small income from her boarding school, but there was never enough money to pay all their bills, and Sarah often lay awake wondering how they would pay for food and firewood. With the French and Indian War still raging and basic necessities in short supply, prices in Newport continued to rise. In a poignant letter written to Joseph Fish at one o'clock in the morning, Osborn imagined herself as "a poor, overloaded, weak animal crouching under its burden."*

Despite their poverty, Sarah and Henry continued to give money to Johnny and his wife, Abigail, who were living in squalor, and they offered to care for another one of their children. Sarah was now caring for Almey Greenman, ten boarding students, and two of her grandchildren. When her dear friend Elizabeth Vinal, the minister's wife, died tragically in childbirth in September 1759, Sarah volunteered to bring two of her daughters, Becky and Sally, to board at her school. Characteristically generous, she charged the Reverend Vinal only what they cost "out of pocket." She now had fifteen children under her care.

The closing months of 1759 brought even more hardship and tragedy. In November Sarah and Henry heard the news that Johnny, who had enlisted in the army to support his family, had died at Fort George. Johnny had been Henry's last surviving child, and the loss was deeply painful. Then in December, a brutally cold month, a smallpox epidemic ravaged Newport, leaving many dead. Usually Sarah would have sought solace in her church, but the Reverend Vinal had been so devastated by his wife's death that he was unable to preach. Although Vinal's doctor said that he was suffering from a "nervous fever," it would soon become obvious that he was slipping into alcoholism. Osborn wrote little about her own chronic illness, but she briefly mentioned her "low state" of health to Joseph Fish. In a few of her diary entries in 1759 and 1760 she also complained of "hard rheumatic Pains," "strong pains," and "stupefying" headaches.[1]

Yet despite her own struggles, Osborn devoted herself to helping others in need. "Lord, ever open my hand and heart to the sick, poor, and needy," she pleaded in her diary, "and make me a blessing in my day." One of the hallmarks of the rising evangelical movement was its commitment to benevolence, and Osborn believed that she had a religious duty to serve others. Besides risking her health by visiting those who were ill with smallpox, she asked her friends and neighbors to give charity to Abigail, and she visited two criminals who had been sentenced to death for piracy.

Osborn shared much in common with eighteenth-century reformers who hoped to make the world a better place, but she was convinced that there was no greater act of generosity than to save sinners from damnation. When evangelicals mixed the humanitarian impulses of the Enlightenment with the Christian imperative to preach the gospel, the result was an explosion of missionary zeal. Driven by her desire to save souls, Osborn pleaded with the children in her school, her friends, and her neighbors to repent and seek Christ's mercy.

Osborn also spent many hours in prayer. Usually she prayed alone, but when the women's society began to meet again in 1760 after several years of inactivity, she took turns praying aloud with her friends. Though she wanted to submit patiently to God's will, she saw prayer as a form of action, a way of persuading God to intervene in history. Besides praying for her own individual needs, she often prayed for her students, for the church, for the colonies, and for the defeat of the French.

Despite her commitment to Christian service, Osborn did not hope to earn God's grace by doing good works. Shaped by her Reformed heritage, she believed that humans were helpless to determine their own destinies. Only God had the power to decide who would go to heaven, leaving the rest to damnation. But by visiting the sick and imprisoned, giving money to the poor, telling others about Jesus, and praying for God's help, she hoped to glorify his name.

1759

Sarah Osborn to Joseph Fish, May 3, 1759. One o'clock in the morning

My Reverend and dear friend,

It has been with no less concern on my side than you express on yours that nothing has passed between us respecting the marriage of your dear child [Mary] (I am sure, precious to me), except the letter I wrote to her wherein I congratulated her in the happy prospect, and begged familiarly a line upon the subject, and flattered myself the dear one would redeem a moment before she went away to indulge her unworthy but real friend.[2] But when I found I had none, I checked myself for my freedom, fearing my request was improper, and found excuses enough for her.

As to you, my dear friend, dear Mrs. Fish, and children, be assured if I have not wrote, I have scores of times rejoiced in the goodness of God to you all—may God Almighty bless and prosper the happy pair—and have as often sympathized with you in your sorrow at parting. Forgive, I entreat you, whatever has appeared unfriendly in my silence and inconsistent with the friendship I have professed, which is nevertheless the same as it ever was. But the hindrances that has happened are too many to be enumerated. I could not get time to write my own mother a line all the winter past, though the neglect of the duty lay with great weight upon my spirits, as did my neglect to you.

Exceeding glad I am to hear you had the comfort of seeing your dear child settled in the church before she left you. Thanks be to God for this. Indeed, it revives my heart. I thank you, dear Sir, for your kind invitation of me and mine up to visit you, and never did I come with greater freedom or stronger desire than I should now, if Providence would permit, but it absolutely forbids any attempt. And without there should be any remarkable unexpected turn in our affairs, I fear I never shall be indulged with that privilege again.

O Sir, pray for me that God will strengthen my faith and resign my will, for my trials are great in many respects. As to my health, I am in a low state, and my dear [Henry] in no better for some months past, scarce able to be up half his time. And I fear the consequence: poverty, as an armed man, has been coming on us ever since we was with you last, but this last winter it has made swift progress. For my business—through the sickness of children the

latter part of summer and fall, and bad weather in winter, and measles now—
has failed, so that our income has not been half equivalent to our unavoidable
expense, so that we sink lower and lower day by day. And I can turn no way
either to lessen our charge or increase our income. All, as to means, that
holds up our heads above water at all is a couple of boarders, and provisions
is so excessive dear that 'tis but little we get by them at four pounds a week.
(But at that price, they wash for them and find them beds.)[3]

And our son [John] has, with his family, been in such suffering circumstances that they have daily pulled from me, besides my having two of his
children to maintain. They were hungry, naked, and dragged up as heathen
in a gospel land—real objects of charity—which moved my compassion
towards them. And I can't repent it, nor cast them off, so long as 'tis possible
for me to grapple with them. When I look on them I am most strengthened:
Psalm 41:1 oft supports me.[4] Their father is gone into the army, and there is
a poor slothful wife and two more poor children as wretched as they can be,
but I don't pretend to do for them now. I have given them up to shift for
themselves. I can't hold out any longer to do for them. I am obliged to keep
help, for I haven't strength of body to go through the business of my school,
small as it is, and family affairs, too—that I have five to maintain wholly.[5]

And now, dear Sir, judge: am I a poor, overloaded, weak animal crouching under its burden, or do I only imagine myself so? Besides all the difficulties I have mentioned, I have had five in my family down with the measles,
four at once, so that my business was quite broke up for some weeks. And
since that, one of my boarders has had the pleurisy.

But I'll stop. Pray forgive me this burdening of you with my complaints.
'Tis with a view to your being excited to pray for your afflicted friend. And
O, dear Sir, pray for faith; pray for resignation; pray that my dross and tin
may be purged away. O, that the fruit of all may be to take away my sin. O,
that I may be preserved from murmuring against my gracious God, for he
does me no wrong. 'Tis of his mercy I am not consumed. By grace I am
determined to justify him till I die, and if he will but slay my unbelief, though
he slay me, I will put my trust in him. O, that God may be glorified, come on
me what will, or what seemeth him good. But O, beg that he will lay no more
on me than he will enable me to bear by his glory.

Dear Sir, I hoped to have wrote to dear Mrs. Noyes and Miss Becky, too, but I can't accomplish it. Pray make my hearty regards acceptable to the Reverend Mr. Noyes and spouse and renewedly wish them joy for me.[6] O, how glad I should be to see you all together, but I must submit: it can't be. Pray intercede with both daughters, Sir, for letters for me. Tell them I long to hear them speak to me again, and pray, favor me yourself soon if you possibly can, for your voice does revive me. Give my affectionate regards to Madame Fish. I believe dear Susa writes now.

And I must conclude these shattered lines with wishing you and yours the best of blessings in Christ Jesus. O, I want to get to heaven where I may praise him forever, for he is altogether lovely. My dear [Henry] joins with me in all sincere affection, which pray accept from yours till death,

Sarah Osborn

My compliments to Mr. Eels and spouse. Love to cousin Hewitt.[7]

Sarah Osborn to Joseph Fish, September 5, 1759

Much Honored Reverend and Dear Sir,

When I received the dear letter from Mrs. Noyes, I hastened and redeemed time from sleep to answer it, but unhappily mistook the time of Mr. Fish's return from Sakonnet, and sent my letter an hour or two too late.[8] And as I have heard nothing from you since, I have feared it never came to hand, because in it I earnestly begged a line from you to assure me you forgive everything that looked like a slight or neglect of you and yours.

Pray, Sir, don't be silent to me, for any fears that you are displeased with me is more than I am able to bear. Be assured, my heart is the same to you and yours as ever it was, though the multiplicity of business with which God in his providence has filled my hands, has forbid my so frequent writing as heretofore, together with other impediments too numerous to mention. Pray acquaint me of the welfare of your dear absent child as also of your own and families at home, about all which I am heartily concerned.

And now I must inform you that God has the last week taken to himself, as I make no doubt, our dear friend Mrs. Vinal.[9] She has been poorly some time past and, as I feared, returning to her melancholy distresses, seemed bewildered, but went a little while ago into the country about a week and seemed refreshed and cheered, which made her desirous of going again. And accordingly, on Tuesday last week, having an invitation, she went to Tiverton. She called at our door to bid me farewell, quite cheerful and pleasant, more so than I had seen her for some months. Stayed alert that night and remained cheerful. On Wednesday, the Reverend Mr. Campbell fetched her to his house where she spent the afternoon with him and his wife pleasantly and to all appearance well for one in her circumstances.[10] In the evening she complained of a pain in her stomach, and soon after she appeared to have the hysteric colic. They used proper means, but she remained distressed all night. In the morning about sunrise her colic left her, or rather struck her nerves, and she was convulsed but no ways frighted, and desired they would not, but begged they would hold her hands open and slap them smartly. She had two fits presently, still cheerful between. They asked her if she felt anything like travail. She said no, not at all, but after the third fit they thought they perceived it and sent immediately for help, which came seasonably about eleven o'clock, and no danger appeared as to that. And she remained courageous till her sixth and last fit, which entirely took after her senses. About two she was delivered, but quite insensible, and so remained till sunset, and then expired. The dear babe looked likely to live as any child, cried and sucked heartily, but about eleven at night was taken with a black fit and died in an instant.

All this I had from Mr. Campbell himself, who assured me there was nothing appeared to be the cause of her death but the immediate hand of Providence. She did not look to lie in till the middle of October. Dear Mr. Vinal got there a little before she died, and Mr. Campbell told me he seemed as though he would have died with her. But blessed be God, he seems now to bear up with Christian patience and resignation to the divine will.

And as I may venture to tell you, Sir, God has graciously prepared him for this trial by affording him of late large manifestations of his love and grace; yea, such views of his adorable perfections, such engagedness in wrestling with God, as has even exhausted his strength and broke his outward man, when with sweet freedom he communicated these things to me. "O my friend," says he, "don't think me flighty, 'tis real, 'tis substantial."

Sarah Osborn to Rev. Joseph Fish

Newport Sept 6 1759

Much Honoured
Revd and Dear Sir

When I received the second line from this dear I should have answerd it but
unhappily mistook the date of our Letter
return from seacoast and sent my Letter
an hour or two too Late and as I have
had nothing from you since I have had
to reason came to hand because in it seemed
by this a line from you to assure me you
give every thing that Lookt Like a slight or
neglect of you or yours Pray Sir don't Charge
to me for any thing if you are displeasd with
me is more than I am able to bear to account
my heart is the same to you and yours as ever
it was the multiplicity of business with
which God in His Providence has filld my
hands has forced my so frequent writing as
heretofore together with other impediments
to numerous to mention Pray acquaint
me of the welfare of your Dear... about child
as also of your own and families at Stone
attent all which I am heartily concernd
and since I must inform you if you His the
last week letter to himself as I make no
doubt our Dear friend this visit she has
been Sorely sometime Past and as I saw...
going to New melancholly distresses second remember

[right margin:] I cant loose my charter the Margin must place some pray make
my best respects acceptable to dear Mrs Noel my spouse and Let
ye know if she received my Letter and all about her if you can
for I long to hear — I have two of Dear Mrs visits children with me
which I intend to keep as Long as Providence permits Betsey and Sally

[left column:]
weep with us and Magnifie the Lord with him
but all this must remain a secret I have not
Devulgd it to any other now should I Dare to do it
and oh what benefit has our Dear this Divine
received from Christ as Her Death is the not whole
perfect in Holiness 2d She not immediately pass into her
glory where no sin to near Defile Her more no
hurry Dout that she ever reach Her no more travelling
Doubts and fears however no more Hiding that face
O glorious face the so earnestly sought but could
not find on earth oh how delighted Have transport on her
must she be to behold Her God Looking on Her
with an Everlasting Smile oh what Joy
when so to that Distinct interest and how that Joy
is Joyd what Sickly body but being still united to
Christ is getting up its grace till the resurrection
oh should we not be cruel even while we are
begging for our selves if we do not humbly bless
God for Her release & blessed be God my Dear
friend is not Lost to me methinks I can with
more freedom converse with Her now than
for some years Past I could on earth the Saint
reach Her Exalted strains but how Long I hope
to Join with Her above fully and everlasting grace
accoril with Her am I not forthing an ease
blessed be God I am but oh astonishing grace
Why me worthless worm thus rejoicing in hope
been so father be but I must concealge dear Sir
Let me Love Him more and accept this with your
usual candor and forgive if you can of yours dear Sir
your unworthy but true friend till Death Sarah Osborn

[left edge, rotated:] Wilson Osborn 1759

O Sir, you don't know how it refreshed me to see his elevated soul so flaming with love and praising his (or our) glorious Redeemer.

These things I tell you, Sir, that you may rejoice as well as weep with us, and magnify the Lord with him. But all this must remain a secret. I have not divulged it to any other, nor should I dare to do.

And O, what benefits has our dear Mrs. Vinal received from Christ at her death? Is she not made perfect in holiness? Did she not immediately pass into glory, where no sin shall ever defile her more, no fiery dart shall ever reach her? No more trembling fears and doubts forever, no more hiding that lovely glorious face she so earnestly sought but could not find on earth. O, how delighted, how transported must she be to behold her God looking on her with an everlasting smile. O, what must heaven be to this distressed believer. "Eye hath not seen," &c.[11] And now that clog is dropped, that sickly body, but being still united to Christ, is resting in his grace till the resurrection. O, should we not be cruel, even while we are weeping for ourselves, if we do not humbly bless God for her release? O, blessed be God, my dear friend is not lost to me. Methinks I can with more freedom converse with her now than for some years past I could on earth, though I can't reach her exalted strains. But ere long I hope to join with her more fully and cast down my crown with her. Am I not hastening on apace? Blessed be God, I am, but O, astonishing grace, why me, worthless worm, thus rejoicing in hope? "Even so, Father," &c.[12]

But I must conclude, dear Sir. Let me hear from you, and accept this with vast, sincere, and hearty regards to you and all yours from your unworthy but true friend till death,

Sarah Osborn

I can't lose my charter. The margin must have some. Pray, make my best regards acceptable to dear Mrs. Noyes and spouse, and let me know if she received my letter and all about her that you can, for I long to hear. I have two of dear Mrs. Vinal's children with us, which I intend to keep as long as Providence permits me: Becky and Sally.[13]

(*Opposite*): A letter from Sarah Osborn to Joseph Fish, September 5, 1759.
Courtesy of the American Antiquarian Society.

November 22, 1759, Thursday morning

Blessed God, since I have lived to see this long-wished-for day, a day set apart by our rulers for public thanksgiving, let my whole soul be warm and engaged; for surely I, of all creatures, have cause to be thankful.[14] Let me have some foretaste of the enjoyments and employments of the host above today, whose hearts are ever filled with a sacred glow of gratitude, who are ever offering praise and glorifying God. O, this delightful work of heaven, Lord, let me begin, and carry it on earth.

Let me review with delight the mercies which thou hast been showing to thy church. Notwithstanding all our ill deservings, all our sins and declensions, yet thou hast broken the plots of our enemies, whose merciless jaws were wide open to swallow up quick, to deprive us of all our privileges—sacred and civil—to cut off the very name of Protestantism.

Thanks be to God for the instruments thou hast raised up and preserved to stand for religion and liberty. Thanks be to God for preserving the life of our gracious sovereign, King George, in this difficult and dangerous time.[15] Thanks be to God for raising up that wise and faithful minister, the venerable Mr. Pitt, who under God has done such great things for our nation and for America.[16] Thanks be to God for the noble hero, the king of Prussia.[17] Adored be thy name for the successes thou hast granted him from time to time, and in particular for preserving his precious life again and again when in such imminent danger. O, still preserve him if it be thy holy will, and may he come off victorious. Thanks be to God for our worthy generals, Wolfe and Amherst,[18] who, under God, have done valiantly. Thanks be to God for the reduction of Louisburg, Frontenac, Niagara, Oswego, Ticonderoga, Crown Point, and Quebec. O God, fill our hearts with praise for thou hast done great things for us, whereof we are glad.[19]

Lord, still watch over them and us for good. Thanks be to God for that health and harmony that has subsisted in our armies. Blessed be God, it has not only preserved us from the sword but from the pestilence, from fire, from earthquakes, inundation, and all desolating judgments. Blessed be God, thou hast given us fruitful seasons and a bountiful harvest, that we have food for man and beast, that we have fuel and all the comforts of life still spared to us, a sinful and ungrateful people. Thy mercies are more than I can number. For all, I would bless and adore thy glorious name.

And in special and above all, for Jesus Christ, the mercy of mercies, the greatest blessing the world ever enjoyed, through whom all other blessings flow. I adore thee that we have yet the means of grace and some of us, hopes of glory, for his sake alone. And O my God, shall not my heart burn within me while I realize that I, worthless I, am one of the happy number thou hast chosen and Christ has accepted as a part of his inheritance—redeemed, effectually called, justified, adopted into his family—that I, O rich grace, should be called a child of God, that I should be predestinated to be conformed to the image of thy son. O, thanks be to God that thou hast sanctified me in part, that I am not all enmity now, as I should have been hadst thou left me to myself. O, thanks be to God that I have—at least sometimes—love, resignation, faith, humility, zeal, and holy desires working in my soul.

This is all the Lord's doing. I am not sufficient for a good thought. Thanks be to God, if I have by his grace been enabled to choose him, his Christ, his Spirit, his grace, his word and way, for my portion in time and for eternity; and to give up my whole all, for ought I know, without the least reserve to be forever thine to all intents and purposes. I glory in my happy choice, and surrender this day, and would solemnly renew them: Lord, I am and will be forever thine, and thou art my dear portion, my life, my choice inheritance. O, let me but enjoy thee more and serve thee better, and I am satisfied. Resign my will to thine and I ask no more; I desire no more. Do with me what seemeth thee good. I am thine in solemn covenant; let it stand ratified and confirmed in heaven. Rejoice with me ye saints and angels above. Bear witness that I am the Lord's and he is mine.

Sarah Osborn

November 28, 1759, Wednesday morning

Thanks be to God that on Monday night and yesterday morning, he enabled me to wrestle with him for heart holiness and resignation to his will in all things. O, how does infinite wisdom bring good out of evil; yea, out of the worst of evils. Had not I found the rising of carking cares in my heart, I had not besieged the throne of grace for strength against it, nor had those gracious promises renewed: "I will never leave thee nor forsake thee";[20] "Be not dismayed, I am thy God"[21]; "Have not I commanded thee, be strong and of good cheer? For the Lord thy God is with thee, whithersoever thou goest."[22] Amen, Amen.

The Lord sanctify to us the death of my husband's only son, which yesterday reached our ears. Lord, support thy servant [Henry]; comfort him in thyself, and prepare him and me for all the changes we are to meet with, and especially for our great *and last*. And mercifully take care of the poor widow and orphans in thy kind and tender providence.

November 30, 1759, Friday morning

The Lord in mercy look down in pity on the poor widow and orphans, and teach me duty. Enable me to do all cheerfully thou requirest of me, but not presumptuously to plunge myself in difficulties too great for me to grapple with. Lord, direct and overrule for thy own glory.

December 1, 1759, Saturday evening

I desire to bless God that I have succeeded in part in my attempts to procure relief for our poor distressed widow and orphans. Mrs. Tweedy gave me forty shillings for them.[23]

But as to my endeavors for a reconciliation between husband and wife, they are all in vain. (James Leach and wife.)[24] Found the poor man determined never to be reconciled. The Lord sanctify the affliction to thine handmaid; compose her mind and bring her to a quiet submission. O, may she be enabled to fly to thee, choose thee, and make up all her goods in thee. Lord, help her for Jesus's sake.

As my dear and reverend pastor is not able to go out on the morrow, I propose, God willing, to commune with a neighboring church. The Lord prepare me for thy day and the solemn ordinance. O, there help me, my spouse, and all thy dear people that partake, to renew our solemn covenant with God, and may we derive strength from God to live to thy glory all the days of our lives, Amen, for Jesus's sake.

December 10, 1759, Monday evening

Thanks be to God, this has been a good day to me: God has made me diligent and cheerful.

But the distress threatened by the smallpox calls for consideration and supplication. Ruthie Gibbs carried away last week, Mrs. Gibbs today, and I hear two more of the family poorly, and 'tis in almost all parts of our land: vessels and soldiers daily coming in, whereby we are greatly endangered.[25] The Lord be merciful to us and spare us if it be thy blessed will. But thy will be done. O, prepare me and all thy people for thy sovereign pleasure.

Lord, heal the child I have visited tonight, or prepare that and its parents for thy holy will. (Little Sarah Hacker very sick.)[26] Resign their wills, Lord; grant them submission, I pray thee, for Jesus's sake, that thou mayest be glorified in and by them.

December 11, 1759, Tuesday morning

My thoughts have been much taken up the latter part of the night and this morning about the smallpox. The Lord only knows what he has determined. However, as a scarcity of food will without doubt accompany its spread, I think it must be duty to take every prudential step to procure what we can now, if it to be had, for 'tis in the use, and not in the neglect, of means I am to trust in God; and self-preservation is by God strictly enjoined, and also the providing for my household.

The Lord prosper, and succeed my attempts if it be thy blessed will, and O, deal graciously with thy people. O God, prepare them to meet thee either in a way of mercy or judgment. And as for me and my dear consort, whom I trust thou hast of a truth espoused to thyself, and all thy dear covenant people, let us enter into the glorious chambers of security thou hast provided in thy attributes, promises, and providence and hide ourselves till these calamities be overpast. And if it be thy sovereign pleasure to visit and to take any of us home by the visitation, thy will be done. Happy they that first gets home to rest in thee. Thou knowest the secret joy it would afford. Might I hope it would be my happy lot?

But patience, Lord, I beg for Christ's sake. Answer my cries for grace, faith, and resignation to thy blessed will, and do with me what seemeth thee good. Don't let me sin against and grieve thee, and comparatively, I fear no other evil. What is smallpox or famine or death compared with this? I can glorify thee in all these, if thou wilt, but subdue my sin and grant me grace. I can do all things through Christ strengthening me, but if thou shouldst leave me to myself, O what a monster should I be? I can't bear this; I deprecate this. Lord, anything but this, any affliction rather than sin.

And thou wilt not give me up to this; thou hast said, "Thy grace shall be sufficient for me, and thy strength made perfect in my weakness"; "'Tis enough."[27] I ask no more; I desire no more but to be everything God would have me be, for I am forever thine; thine forever, forever,

Sarah Osborn

December 21, 1759, Friday morning

Cold all this week and snow upon snow.[28]

The Lord in mercy to the lives and healths of thy poor people, moderate this season if it be thy holy will. And O, provide food and fuel for them. Thanks be to God for the wood thou hast provided for our poor widow and orphans.[29] O, let them be the care of thy good providence, and may all my days be spent in admiring thy astonishing goodness to us. We, unworthy as we are, have food to eat, clothes and fires to keep us warm, a comfortable, peaceable habitation.

O my soul, if thou hast a spark of grace, gratitude, love, or ingenuity in thee, rouse up and praise the Lord. Forget not all his benefits, nor dare distrust him for futurity since he is thus triumphing over all thy past unbelieving fears.

December 21, 1759, Friday evening

O my God, what reason have I to stand amazed and astonished at the goodness of my gracious God. Thirty pounds again received today (by Mr. Thurston), and now we have wherewith to purchase flour, meat, and meal.[30]

The Lord make me thankful; yea, I do now rejoice in thee, and O, may thy unexpected, unmerited, yea undefiled goodness strengthen my faith as long as I live, for 'tis in covenant love and faithfulness thou art thus giving me success. I know it is, because thou art also filling me with hungerings and thirstings after thyself, thy grace, heart holiness. No temporal good can satisfy me as my portion, or in lieu of sanctifying grace. O, thanks be to God for the sweet communion I this day enjoyed with God in pouring out my soul before him. O God, thou only knowest how nigh thou dist take me to thyself, how thou didst indulge me. O, truth and faithfulness in the abstract, thy kindness dost not depart from me.

I have been reading the life of Janeway.[31] As thou was with Moses, as thou was with Joshua, as thou was with Janeway, so thou art with me, and thou wilt never fail me all the days of my life, never leave nor forsake me, because from everlasting to everlasting thou art the same unchangeable faithful God, the same as at the beginning: the same yesterday, today, and forever.

And I am, in Christ Jesus, forever thine. Amen, Hallelujah, Hallelujah. Thine forever,
Sarah Osborn

1760

January 2, 1760, Wednesday morning

My headache was very stupefying yesterday morning so that I could not do as I hoped I should, and indeed, remains so still.

I think I foolishly affronted a poor creature last night, and I can't help being sorry. Though by too frequent feeding him, it encourages his visits, which are not desirable, yet I wish I had asked him to eat. Perhaps some time or other I might have prevailed with him to listen to something serious, but if I have his ill will, my opportunities are all gone. 'Tis true my hopes have died long ago, for nothing can send him away sooner than any attempts that way. The Lord in mercy have compassion on him, for he is evidently running full speed to destruction. The enmity of his nature is not concealed. He plainly declares he hates the ways of holiness. Lord, pity him, and snatch him as a brand out of the burning, if it be thy holy will.

And let me not be perplexed with very trifles but fix my heart on thy glorious self. O thou unchangeable God, though my frames vary, thou art still the same as ever thou were. And thou wilt quicken me and revive me again in thy own time. Thy will be done. Lord, anything but sin, anything but resisting thy will. O, let me have no will this year but thine. Heavenly Father, with thee all things are possible. I would choose nothing but that everything should be just as thou seest fit. I would choose neither life nor death, poverty nor riches, health nor sickness, but to be resigned and glorify God in all he allots me.

My God, wilt thou, for Christ's sake, grant me my petition, and enable me by thy grace to live securely on thy wisdom, power, love, care, and faithfulness this year? Forgive what of self-love is at the bottom of this request. 'Tis a most happy frame. But adored be thy name. Thy glory is closely connected with it; yea, so closely that it can't be separated. Then delight to glorify thyself in making me happy in this life by doing and submitting to thy will as well as in heaven.

Lord, bear with my importunity. This petition has lain long before thee, and by thy grace it ever shall, till for Christ's sake 'tis granted. I will not let thee go without this blessing. I will hold thee by the arms of my faith, Christ strengthening me, till I pull down power from on high to enable me to acquiesce in all thy will. Lord, only say, "be it unto thee as thou wilt," and 'tis done: my will rebels no more, Amen.[32] Grant me this, and give crowns and kingdoms to whom thou pleasest. I covet none of them, Lord; send me not away without the blessing I come in the name of, and for the sake of Jesus.

I am utterly unworthy. I have no merit, but he has merited enough for me; yea, and for his sake, thou wilt be gracious to worthless me.

January 4, 1760, Friday morning

I bless thee, my gracious God, for sweet access to thy throne. In the day when I cried, thou answered me and didst strengthen me with strength in my soul. I bless thee for that calm reliance on thy all-sufficiency I now feel, without knowing how or in which way thou wilt provide for us to pay our debts. Lord, increase my dependence on thee, for the earth is the Lord's and the fullness thereof.

And hide pride from my eyes while thou dost enable me to exert myself in procuring relief for our poor widow and orphans. (The doctor's lady gave me 20s and meat, sauce, sugar, tea, and cheese. Capt. Moore gave me 40s for her.)[33] Let me not as the hypocrite sound a trumpet before me while I am telling one and another the methods I have taken and the success I have had, but grant my aims may be right. Thanks be to God that others has been excited, lively to extend their charity. The Lord reward them a thousandfold, and grant the town may now do her justice and relieve her, since they have taken all she had to depend on for bread out of her hands.[34] And make her content with the allotments of thy providence. Restore her health, gracious God, if it be thy holy will, or prepare her for death.

February 3, 1760, Sabbath morning

Since I wrote last I have been engaged in reading past experiences. O how much of the faithfulness of God I find.

And may I not venture to say without boasting, as I thought some time ago that I might almost have known that this would be a hard winter by the ample provision God made for me, for he never failed, especially in the article of wood. I am always a spectator but never feel the pinching want. Now it is four and twenty pounds for charred, green, oak wood. The Lord pity the poor and needy and supply their wants and strengthen my faith for Jesus's sake.

Sarah Osborn to Joseph Fish, February 14, 1760

Much Honored and Reverend Sir,

I received your kind engaging letter wrote the night before you went on your journey to New Haven, and return my most hearty thanks there, for I have wanted to write ever since your return but could by no means hear a word how things was circumstanced, whether Mrs. Noyes and child were well or otherwise, that I was altogether at a loss whether to condole or congratulate, till the fourth instant, the Reverend Mr. Stiles informed me upon my inquiry that Mrs. Noyes was delivered of a daughter and both were well, which caused my heart to rejoice in the goodness of God to you all.[35]

And now, Sir, I do most heartily wish you and your dear spouse all the joy that can result from this tender branch God has added to your family. May the dear babe live and grow up to be a comfort to its parents and all it is dear unto, a blessing in the world and to the church of Christ. Blessed be God that spared both root and branch to you, [the God who] appeared on the mount of difficulty and commanded deliverance. O, how great is his goodness in preserving comforts and lending more, and O, how sweet our mercies when we enjoy God in all here. Dear Sir, your happiness exceeds what worldly parents know.

Dear Sir, I have almost a thousand things to say to you had I opportunity but must at present waive particulars and only tell you in general that God is gracious beyond expression to the most unworthy creature that treads on this earth or breathes in this air, because he is a sovereign, merciful God, ever self-moved. I verily believe goodness and mercy shall follow me all my days, and I shall dwell in the house of the Lord forever. O, pray, dear Sir, pray for me, that I may render to the Lord all his benefits, and there I must be wholly for him, and none other, for he engages me a thousand ways besides his absolute right: by creation, preservation, redemption, effectual calling, and self-dedication. He feeds me, clothes me, chooses all my changes in mercy, comforts me and subdues the tyranny of my obstinate will, heals the wounds unbelief and carking cares had made on my soul, and brings me to rely on his faithfulness in some degree—prospect or no prospect as to means.

And O, Sir, this is better than thousands of gold and silver; 'tis better to trust in the Lord than to put confidence in princes. For whoever trusted in God and was put to shame? I had rather have my unbelief slain than to possess crowns and kingdoms. When shall it be entirely so? O, not till death, but then it shall, and I'll rejoice in every victory my dear Redeemer gives me in the way, for my glorious King will go on from conquering to conquer till he has finally subdued. Amen. May the crown forever rest and flourish on his sacred head.

I thought two sides of my letter must have done this time, but I find it can't be. Dear Sir, perhaps you have heard that Mr. Osborn has lost his only son in the army. He died last September at Fort George.[36] Has left a poor helpless widow and four orphans, two of which I have wholly taken, and I am almost confident God will uphold me in doing for them. (Excuse me saying I and not we.)[37] My dear could not, 'tis true, say this was a stream of comfort cut off, but rather a living sorrow buried. But yet the bonds of nature are strong. It was his all, and many sorrows attend such a loss. But blessed be God that enables him to bear up with Christian patience and resignation to the divine will. I have reason to think God has sanctified all his dispensations, and by everything is bringing him higher and higher to himself. Great is my comfort in him. O, may I also reap benefit from the rod.

And in a special way may God sanctify to us, all of our church and congregation, the rebukes of his providence in taking off our dear pastor from his labors. We have been for many months frequently scattered, as sheep without a shepherd, and ever since thanksgiving in November he has been wholly laid by. We have sometimes been favored with Mr. Maxson's assistance, minister of the Seventh Day Baptist church, a gracious good man who feeds us with wholesome food: sincere milk, and strong meat, too.[38] And blessed be God, I have sometimes been comforted in attending on the ministry of Mr. Stiles, though some things remain not quite to my satisfaction.[39] Yet I am greatly encouraged to hope he will prove a great blessing to the church of Christ. He is vastly come off from the Arminian scheme and sometimes seems full in the doctrines of grace. He is a pleasant, affable, desirable gentleman, and thanks be to God, through the entire friendship betwixt our dear pastor and him, there is the most harmony betwixt the two societies that ever I knew. May God increase it.

But to return to our dear pastor.[40] His disorder is, the doctor says, a nervous fever. He keeps about house and is better but can't bear the air. O, pray for him and for us, for there is greater difficulties attends him and us than I dare mention. The Lord in mercy preserve his own glory and prevent, if it be his holy will, all things running into confusion. There is great disaffection and dissatisfactions on all sides. His people do everything wrong, so that instead of longing for, I almost dread his going into the pulpit again, for fear his resentment should rise too high. He does also everything wrong. His most innocent actions are as great crimes as any: for instance, though they are assured his two children's boarding with me costs him no more than they cost me out of pocket or must cost him at home, for I have but half price for them, yet it is such a crime it can't be borne with. If I beg I may be allowed to do it for dear Susa's sake—who has herself to maintain the care of the family, and five to mend and make for, only for her victuals, which her parents would gladly give her for her company—this won't do: there is no need of her, neither.[41] She is in the utmost perplexity. Her tenderness to the dear children binds her, and fears that things will go to destruction if she leaves him, and [fears] his importunity. For he will by no means consent to her going, and yet on many accounts she thinks 'tis best she should. The path of duty is yet hid. The Lord direct her.

All this, Sir, is only to excite your earnest cries to God for us all and to go no farther, as I am confident it will not. Unreasonable prejudices on both sides is the foundation of all these difficulties. O, that the love of God will yet unite us. I don't know that he [Vinal] ever heard a word of the clamor either about Susa or me, for we endeavor to conceal everything from him that we think would either grieve or vex him. I am oft faulted for this and told I am not his friend because I don't tell him, &c., but this don't much affect me. Would to God I could always keep his mind composed. However, this I suppose occasioned the enclosed dream.

He is much behindhand in the world and must of necessity have his salary raised. The Lord overrule and spirit his people to relieve him, or I believe he will leave us. Things seem to be come to an extremity. O, may the event be for God's glory.

And now, as 'tis high time, with my most hearty regards to you, Sir,

Madame Fish, and dear Miss Becky, I conclude, and subscribe myself your sincere though unworthy friend,

Sarah Osborn

P.S. Pray send my best respects to the Reverend Mr. Noyes and spouse and wish them joy for me. And pray, Sir, favor me with a line as soon as you can.

[*Osborn enclosed the following account of her dream in this letter. It is dated November 7, 1759.*]

As on my bed I lay, perhaps I dreamed I see a number of poor fatigued travelers passing through a howling wilderness and just famished for thirst. Anon they come to a spring of water provided on purpose for the refreshment of travelers. "Come," says one, "let us sit down, rest, and drink."

"No," says the other. "We can't, for there is dirt at the bottom, and a great deal, too; we are sure there is, and you know it."

"I grant it," says the other, "and I know of no springs without it. Yet see: here's clear water; 'tis sweet and wholesome; 'tis of a refreshing cleansing nature. I have been revived by it many a time. I know 'tis good. I scarce ever drank better. Pray, drink, and let the dirt at bottom lie still. The spring is purging every day and there is nothing there that will hurt you. Only let it alone; don't disturb it, and drink your fill."

"No," say they. "We won't. We are sure 'tis best to stir it up that we may know what there is. We want it cleaned, and you, if you were wise, would do so, too. However, we'll take but a little twig just to reach the bottom."

Well, 'tis done, and the dirt arises; the water is thick; the poor pilgrims can't drink at all, nor indeed can any take the pleasure in drinking they might have done. And now they lament and mourn: "O, that we had but some sweet clear water such as we used to have in this place, but those springs are dry, and this is so muddy we can't drink and we are ready to die for thirst. What shall we do?"

"Why, let it alone," said the other. "Pray be persuaded it will settle again by and by and be as clear as ever, and then you may drink as much as you please."

"No, we won't," said they. "We will stir it again and let you see how much filth there is in your beloved spring."

"And can you cleanse it," said he, "when you have done all?"

"No," said they. "We have not strength enough for that."

"Well then, pray let it alone. Let it settle. It will be clear and good if you will only be persuaded."

"No," said they. "If you are so foolish, we won't. We are sure 'tis best to know what is there."

And along came another and another of the same mind, and in short, kept the water so continually roiled that it was hard to find a time that it could be settled enough to be clear and sweet, and so every traveler suffered by it. Some would not drink at all, and others were forced to strain it before they could be refreshed.

Now, where the fault lay most, whether in the spring itself; in him that would gladly keep it undisturbed, that himself and all around him might be refreshed by it; or in those that thought it best and would disturb it, I leave it to the judicious reader.

March 21, 1760, Friday

I have thoughts of this day purchasing, with leave of Providence, the half of a ticket in the granary lottery for Abigail Osborn with some money given me last evening for her.[42] If it proves a blank, I determine to bear the loss myself, and will faithfully say to her what was given me for her in the necessaries she wants. If it proves a prize, I will improve it for the comfort of her and her children. The other half of the ticket I purpose to own myself with hope of getting something thereby to pay our just debts, if it may consist with the divine will. With God I desire to leave it. If it please him thus to relieve the widow and fatherless, and thus to enable me to render others their due and support those under my care, I will by grace rejoice in him and receive it as his bounty, for I know the whole disposing is of the Lord. And if it is his sovereign pleasure to deny success, I determine also by grace to acquiesce. May his will be done. I will be glad that he has put it in my power to contribute to so good a thing as a granary, which will I hope be of lasting use to the poor. The Lord direct me in all my ways and take all my affairs in his own hand for Christ's sake, while in the morning I sow thy seed. And in the evening withhold not thy hand, since I know not what shall prosper, this or that, or whether they shall both be alike good.

I would always say, if the Lord will, I shall do this or that and rejoice in his will, and I know all shall be well.

March 23, 1760, Sabbath morning

I have been now three days running abroad, yesterday partly on business for our poor widow and partly on friendly visits in business. I did not succeed. And in my visits was not satisfied. O, how little of God have I heard or said. The Lord forgive for Christ's sake.

And now my poor fatigued body and barren heart join to rob me of all sensible communion with my God, and except the blessed Spirit does interpose, this will be a lost Sabbath. Glorious God, thou art just if thou dost leave me to grope in darkness and tug in my own strength, for I forfeit thy assistance every moment. But Lord, what shall I do? What work shall I make without thee? I shall do nothing; I can do nothing.

But come, blessed Spirit, condescend to come in and warm my heart, and I shall be in a moment as a roe or a young hart, spritely and active in thy service; or as a dove, I should bemoan thy absence and bemoan my sins that grieve thee. But without thee I can be no other than a senseless block. Lord, leave me not to stupidity, I beg, for Christ's sake. Pity my needy soul and weary body, and let me have a Sabbath Day's rest in God. O, come forth with thine ambassadors; let them come in the fullness of the blessing of the gospel of peace and reach the hearts of saints and sinners. And O, send forth more laborers into thy harvest and revive thy own work.

And pity the poor distressed people of Boston, whom thou hast permitted the flames of fire so awfully to prevail against.[43] The Lord compassionate their case, support and succor them, and enable them by grace to fly from everlasting burnings. O, sanctify this awful dispensation of providence to our whole nation and land. 'Tis sin has procured this punishment. Thou art showing thy just resentment. Though thou hast not suffered our enemies to overrun, yet thou wilt not leave room for any to think thou art altogether such a one as ourselves. No, thou wilt show thyself a sin-hating God, for we are a guilty people. Lord, help us now to lay our mouths in the dust and be humbled before thee, and to realize it that here we have no continuing city; riches make to themselves wings and flee away. O teach us all the vanity of the creature, the vanity of all things under the sun. For Jesus Christ's sake, say Amen.

April 15, 1760, Tuesday evening

I have this day had opportunity to inform myself what was my lot [lottery ticket] and find it is nothing at all. And now, my gracious God, I would fly to thee and beg, for Christ's sake, thou wilt bow my will and forbid I should harbor one hard thought, since I am sure it was all overruled by thy all-wise providence, and hadst thou seen it best for me, I should have had a share.

Why should I reluct at this? For 'tis not owing to want of knowledge in my affairs (for my heavenly Father knows what I want better than I do and before I ask him), nor to want of wisdom or power to direct. He has seen it for my good. All things are ordered by counsel concerning me, and the widow and fatherless, too. And if 'tis the decree of heaven that we shall all be poor, that I shall not have it in my power to do for them as I thought I would, it is for the best. He knows the pride of my heart. Sure, 'tis best. I would renewedly cast them on God to take care of them in his own power. Sure, 'tis best of all.

What he doth, I know not now, but I shall know hereafter. Wait, my soul, with patience. God gives no account of his matters here. Secret things belong to God, but when I come to heaven these secrets will be unfolded; then I shall know why God has denied success. Meantime, be satisfied, because infinite wisdom, love, and faithfulness cannot ever and will never fail. Lord, grant me an entire acquiescence in thy will.

O, suffer me not to reluct, I pray thee, but rejoice in thee and all thy will. I would have no will but thine. O, when shall it once be? I had rather have my will resigned to thine than to possess thousands.

April 17, 1760, Thursday morning

Blessed be God that yesterday he again triumphed over my unbelief and sent me relief—twenty pounds—and now I have paid part of one debt and have wherewith to pay for wood, meal, digging garden, &c. How easy is my mind relieved in the ordinary course of God's providence, and what need of any extraordinary way. Bless the Lord, O my soul, and forget not these benefits, nor any of his benefits. Rejoice in God, my soul, more than in any earthly good, for he is a God of infinite love and faithfulness.

Blessed be his name, I had a sweet refreshing evening with my dear friends (Mrs. Mason, Mrs. Short, Mrs. Haggar, and Miss Kitty King).[44]

Blessed be God for assistance. Two more added to the society. Lord, increase our graces for Christ's sake. O, how much better is this hitherto than I expected. O, may it be a nursery for piety. And O, may my school also be a school wherein children shall be trained up for Christ, and to that end, O my God, give me a spirit of government, I beseech thee. Meekness and courage, Lord: let these join with prudence, and by thy assistance I can do great things for my generation. But without thy help, all will be confusion; I can do nothing.

Lord, help me. O, help me for thine honor's sake, and dispose of me this afternoon as most consists with thy glory.

April 22, 1760, Tuesday morning

O my precious Savior, grant me a cleansing, healing touch this morning, for if I may but touch the hem of thy garment I also shall be made whole as well as she.[45] My issue shall be stanched, too. Amen.

Lord, stanch it, I pray thee, for thou seest to what in excess it runs: as soon as one stream seems a little stopped, it gushes out in another, and none but Christ can stanch the effusion. Lord Jesus, apply thy precious blood that cleanseth from all sin without exception. Are thou not called the Lamb of God that taketh away the sins of the world? O, as for my transgressions, take them away, Lord—not only pardon, but take them away. Sweet Lord, except thou prevent, they will be as Jordan overflowing all its banks and will cause a perfect inundation. I can't prevent. I turn from the right to the left and endeavor to bank up here, and guard there, but all in vain. The torrent is so strong it will burst through all. Here I murmur and complain; there I am puffed up with pride; there groan under the weight and sorrows of the world, and there get so glued to it that it infatuates my heart, yea, calls for even my affections and delights that ought all to center in thee.

Lord, I can't bear this. O, rectify these disorders in my precious soul. I bless thee for all the pleasant accommodations thou hast granted me in the world. But with submission I humbly tell thee, I won't have these for my portion. Thou hast given me thyself, and by grace I will be satisfied with nothing less. I can't—I won't—have the world for my portion. If I am pleased with the beauties of creation—trees, flowers, and gardens—let all lead me to the Creator. Let all my delights center in God.

Thou hast said, "Son, give me thy heart."[46] Lord, take it wholly and forever. Suffer it not to be divided. It is all thy own. O, keep it to thyself and shout aloud for joy. O, keep me by thy almighty power so that nothing upon earth may wear off my heart from God. Let me enjoy and possess all things below as though I possess not. O, keep me as the apple of thine eye, for I am the purchase of Christ's precious blood. O, view the price that was paid to redeem me, and I shall be precious in thy sight. See the best robe thou didst put on thy returning prodigal, and my nakedness shall disappear.[47] This precious robe is full; 'tis long; it will cover from the crown of the head to the sole of the foot. Let me lift up my head and plead it, for 'tis white as snow as no fuller on earth can whiten. 'Tis without one spot or stain. 'Tis thy delight; yea, thy justice delights in it, and it is mine. I fling away all my rags and, in this, appear boldly in thy majesty's presence with humble reverence.

And now let me go in peace, depending on thy protection, for thou wilt keep me for Jesus's sake.

April 25, 1760, Friday morning

O, I lament it: my business was all confused yesterday. It was altogether out of my power to do anything in my school to purpose. Lord, help me, or I can do nothing. I can't, Lord; thou seest I can't. O, help, for Christ's sake;

help in mercy to the poor children. Lord, incline their hearts to receive instruction and submit to discipline. O, subdue them, Lord; help in pity to thy poor fatigued worm. Thou seest my weakness in body as well as in mind and how my vital strength fails.

And I am sinking under the weight of business, and yet the necessities of my family oblige me to covet it. Lord, help, and lay no more on me than thou wilt enable me with grace and patience to bear to thy glory. O, grant me so much business, so much sickness, so much health, so much poverty, and so much prosperity as will bring me nearest to thyself and most advance thy declarative glory. And no more of either, Lord, no more of anything than thou wilt sanctify, I beg for Jesus's sake.

For, except thou sanctify, business will hurry, fatigue, fret, and carry off my heart from God. Sickness will clog and utterly unfit for duty, secret and social, and nothing will be attended to but an impatient complaining of aches and weakness—an impatient, Jonah-like spirit, wishing rather to die than live.[48] Health will be wantonly squandered away in the delights of sense. I shall sacrilegiously waste that precious enjoyment and rove from God among the creatures. Ah, woeful depravity. Ah, bitter remains of enmity and contrariety to God that will abuse every mercy.

Poverty, unsanctified, will make me murmur and complain, and care and cark, and quarrel with the dispensations of thy all-wise providence. O, cutting thought. Thou knowest I shall murmur in my tent, and distrust thee in everything, and impudently charge God foolishly, and hang down my hands, and unbelievingly cry, "It will never be better than now."[49] I shall bury all my mercies; they will all be lost in vile ingratitude, and I shall dishonor God all the day long. O, can I bear it? Lord, canst thou, wilt thou, bear it? For Jesus's sake, forbid.

Prosperity will puff me up; pride will rear up its venomous head; and I shall be glued to this world and take up contentment in it, instead of laying up all my good in God.

But Lord, sanctify, and all these shall work together for good, and bring me nearer thyself. For business, I'll rejoice and bless thee, diligently attend, and rely on thee for a blessing, strength, and success. In sickness, I'll submit and kiss the dear hand that strikes the blow. I'll lie down, and adore, and praise, and cry, "thy will be done" when I cannot kneel and wrestle.[50] In health, I'll arise and with joy run the ways of thy commandments. I can do all things, Christ strengthening me. In poverty I will trust thee, and cling to thee, and rejoice in thee as my only portion; yea, though thou slay me, I will trust in thee. I'll acknowledge every morsel more than I deserve, and in prosperity my heart shall be still lifted up in the way of the Lord.

Therefore, O my covenant God, sanctify all to me and do with me what seemeth thee good. I have no choice to make but that by which thou wilt be most glorified. Lord, anything, only possess my whole soul, suffer no rivals, and it is enough. O, keep me, keep me from the evil, for I am thine, forever thine. My strong tower, I fly to thee for protection this day and all my days. O, let me be safe.

June 25, 1760, Wednesday morning

Thanks be to God that did help me yesterday and brought me comfortably through the day. I was diligent myself and brought the business of the day through to my satisfaction. O, my poor foolish faint heart. When wilt thou cease to sink and droop at every petty difficulty, and give up hope, and cry, "'tis all over with me, I shall never do no better," &c.? Strange thou canst not at all hope in the mercy of God at such times, who has said, "I will never leave thee nor forsake thee."[51]

O, this obstinate unbelief. When will it be slain? Lord, when? How prone to a cowardly fear am I when any the least danger appears, and how often has God made me ashamed, and yet I go at it again and again. Lord, go on still to triumph over all my fears by affording thy help. I stand in infinite need. Thou knowest without thee I can do nothing. Suffer me never to go forth alone, but go with me into my business day by day. O, let me not stir from hence.

O God, how thou art still triumphing over our fears with respect to public affairs. Thanks be to God for the certain news that the siege of Quebec is raised. Lord, how evidently dost thou make it appear the battle is the Lord's, that thou art Zion's God and canst save by few as well as by many. What a disproportion was there: they fifteen thousand strong, and we but three thousand, and yet they first to flee and leave the spoil—all their warlike stores—

to us.[52] O gracious God, how art thou avenging the blood of thy dear saints that have been carried and butchered there. O, go on to subdue for Christ's sake, but have compassion on the souls of our enemies, if it be thy holy will, and turn them to thyself as well as to us.

Thanks be to God for the arrival of our fleet and that thou hast enabled them to do such great exploits in destroying the shipping. Thanks be to God that has now supplied our people with stores and provisions for their refreshment. O, let us now, upon receiving this great and good news, rejoice as Christians and not as heathen and madmen. Lord, restrain vice for thy own glory as thou hast restrained the wrath of man for thy own glory, and draw forth the hearts of thy own children in cheerful thanksgivings for all mercies. O, let us offer up our cheerful praise to thee. Let us enter thy courts with praise, and praise thee with humble hearts and joyful lips; and for Christ's sake, smell a sweet savor and accept us and our offerings.

July 25, 1760, Friday morning

I have been every opportunity this week casting up accounts to see how affairs stand betwixt us and the world, and find for want of thus searching, I have been deceived, for I thought we was upon full as good ground now as at this time twelve month, but upon examination see we are at least an hundred and twenty-odd pounds poorer than we was then.

This, with a considerable degree of hysteric disorders, has damped my spirits and cast a melancholy gloom on all my enjoyments, and what is worst of all, God holds me at a distance. I can't get nigh to pour out my complaints into his bosom against sin and Satan that seems in every shape to be rallying their forces against me to cast me down, frequently causing that scripture to occur to my mind, "God has forsaken him; persecute and take him."[53]

But rejoice not against me, O mine enemy: though I fall, I shall arise. God has said he will never leave me nor forsake me. My soul, thou hast the same merits now to plead as ever thou hadst. Let thy sins be as much more aggravated as thy will, Christ is the same—all glorious Redeemer—as ever he was, and for his sake, God will appear for both soul and body. Stand still and see the salvation of God.

No date, written between July 27 and August 3, 1760

I remained in but a poor frame on Sabbath day, Sabbath evening, Monday and Tuesday nights. Spent all the time I could redeem in writing to two poor distressed criminals (Parks and Hawkins).[54]

Determining whether God would condescend to comfort me or no, I will by grace lay myself out every way I can for his glory and the conversion or support of others. Thanks be to God, on Tuesday and Wednesday mornings I had some precious moments in prayer, was strengthened and encouraged. While the messenger was gone with the letter, heard it was thankfully accepted. The Lord command a blessing for Jesus's sake.

And O God, look down on me while I am mourning and sympathizing with others in their sorrows. Let not my own spirits be overborne, nor let me be so far the keepers of others' vineyards as to neglect my own. O my precious Christ, into whose merciful and faithful hands my jewel is committed, keep me from the evil. Lord, pity me. Remember, dear Savior, that I am in my enemy's country surrounded with sins and sorrows, and 'tis thou alone canst prevent my falling a prey. Lord, while on the one hand thou guardest me from spiritual sloth, which at present I most dread, I entreat thee, grant me resignation to thy will in all things.

Is thy hand upon me by bodily indisposition? Have my disorders again took a turn so as to require more sleep than for a year or two past? O, suffer me not to murmur but be thankful for the release I have had from such sleepy disorders, and that thou didst enable me by grace to improve my precious mornings. And now make me thankful that thou givest me sleep to fit my poor crazy body for the duties of the day.

And Lord, make me thankful that the time is hastening on when my dear body may sleep on and take its rest in the silent grave, while I shall be all activity and all reverence and love in the realms above. Hail, happy day, when will it dawn? Lord, when shall I see thee as thou art, be like thee, and ever do the things that please thee without the abominable taint of sin, this dead fly that now spoils all the ointment? O God, when shall it be that I shall never more have one selfish view, but be nothing, and God all in all, when thy glory shall be all my delight, my joy and transport? O let it be more so in time, for Christ's sake. I rejoice that I know it will be so in eternity.

But now, Lord, strip me of selfish views and let it be all my life and joy to glorify thee here upon earth, for I am thine to all intents and purposes. Every faculty of my soul and every member of body, O let them be all used for thee and grant me sweet content since thou art my portion. O my soul, what, cast down when the Lord is thine? O, cheer up and go on thy way rejoicing in Christ Jesus.

August 3, 1760, Sabbath morning

I have been reading from John 14 to the end of the book in hopes of meeting with something in those dear chapters to revive or affect me, but I am just the same. I am with Peter, continually crying, "Lord, and what shall this man do?" and do not follow hard after Christ myself.[55] I lose sight of him while poring on the distressed circumstances of others, making everyone's burden my own, and thinking I am bound in duty to exert myself to do something for the relief of everyone that I know to be distressed.

And yet am so deficient in all; don't satisfy neither the world nor conscience. The distressed have reason to think themselves neglected, and I don't know what to do, nor which way is the path of duty many times. My children and family require my time at home; my friends, abroad; and my poor soul is languishing for want of more secret communication with God.

Lord, for Christ's sake, appear for my help and make every path of duty plain before my face, because of mine enemies (spiritual, I mean) who are perpetually watching for my halting, because the accuser of the brethren is perpetually breaking my peace.[56] Lord, guide me with thine eye; grant me greater degrees of grace and prudence that I may diligently and orderly pursue all the work thou guidest me to. O, let me cheerfully and faithfully do all the Lord my God requires of me, and not distress myself by moving above my sphere in anywise, and pulling on myself more cares than God requires of me; nor yet be so distressed on account of my deficiencies in every duty. Lord, show me that thou art not looking for perfection in me, nor marking iniquity against me. O, let me not look on thee as an angry austere judge, looking for perfection[57] where thou knowest it is not to be found. Lord, thou knowest I am, and always shall be in this life, a poor imperfect creature. Look not on my sins but turn thine eye on the face of thine anointed and see perfection of beauty and holiness. There, Lord, 'tis complete.

And O, turn my eyes off from my filthy scanty rags and fix them on the perfect righteousness of my all glorious Redeemer. And let me be joyful in my King and my God. O Father, my heavenly Father, since thou didst clothe this prodigal in the best robe in the day she returned to thee, let me now with joy lift up my head and plead it and rejoice in it amidst all my imperfections, while I am not willfully departing from my God nor casting his laws behind my back, but esteeming them all holy, just, and good and only wanting conformity to them. While to will is present with me, though how to perform I find not. O, let me not be discouraged at this other law in my members warring against the law of my mind.[58] O God, thou knowest what I would, I do not; and what I hate, that I do. O God, do I not hate sin with cruel hatred? Lord, I do; thou knowest I do, and yet sin against thee every day. Do not I love thy law? Sure I do, and yet break it every day. But precious Christ never breaks it; he has fulfilled it.

O, then be not angry with me, nor hide thy face from me, but return, thou God of love, return, and for Christ's sake, look on me with complacency. Say not, "I have no pleasure in thee."[59] Lord, I can't bear this. O, conform me more and more to thy lovely image and delight to dwell with me. O, come glorious Trinity and make thy abode with me; sweet Jesus, thou hast said, "We will come and make our abode with him."[60] Amen. Lord, come take up thy residence; I am forever thine. O, hold every room, every faculty, every member, in possession by almighty power, and I will exceedingly rejoice. O, seize me only for thyself and I wish no more. Ah! How long, Lord? How long? How long ere I be wholly for thee and none other? When thou shalt have all my love, soul, and strength? And I shall praise thee in exalted strains and bow before thy majestic throne.

Lord, if it be thy will I go to thy house and table, I pray, meet me there, draweth forth every sacramental grace, and communicate vital strength and nourishment to me, to me and all thy church there, and cleanse me by thy precious blood. Thy will be done whether I stay or go. Lord, be with me.

Thanks be to God, it rains hard. The earth is refreshed, and so is my poor weary soul.

August 10, 1760, Sabbath eve

I have been engaged in writing to the poor distressed creatures. The Lord accompany with thy blessing to their poor souls.

I was last evening obliged to correct a child from a sense of duty with some degree of severity in hope of preventing her running to utter destruction. The Lord sanctify the rod, for Christ's sake, and secure thine own honor. Thou knowest this was not the effect of passion but was done in obedience to thy injunction, "Correct thy son while there is hope, and let not thy soul spare for his crying."[61] The rod was small and tender and in no respect an unreasonable weapon; nevertheless, those who suffer children to do as they list thought me cruel and immediately reflected on my profession.

O my God, so overrule it to be thy blessed will that I may not be obliged to do anything to open the mouths of thine enemies. O, give me the wisdom of the serpent and the innocence of the dove, and make me everything thou wouldst have me to be, for I am thine, forever thine.

I thank thee for all the assurance thou hast granted me this day. Compose me to sleep, and fit me for death or the duties of the ensuing week if I live, and especially for the solemn ordinance of the Lord's Supper. O, prepare me for and grant me sweet communion with thee in that feast of love. Lord, let my soul be refreshed and strengthened: some comfort, Lord, I pray thee, in this vale of tears to bear me up under all the trials of life, some increase of grace, faith, and resignation to thy will that thou mayest be glorified by me on earth. O, hear and answer for Christ's sake, in whose worthy name I plead, and for whose sake I hope for a gracious answer.

August 14, 1760, Thursday morning

A stupid headache now, fit for no duty at all. O this body, how oft it clogs. But let me not complain. There is no sin in being sick, though 'tis the effect of sin, but there is sin in complaining. Why should a living man complain?

Lord, keep me from sin, and make me holy, and accept me for Christ's sake, and all is well. Resign my will and 'tis enough. And will God teach me duty?

Shall I write again, and if so, will God accompany and strip me of all selfish views? O, I pray thee, rend self away and use me for thyself. Lord, I bless thee for the refreshments of yesterday morning and last evening. And O, be with me this day for Christ's sake.

I did write again by way of a close examination to a change of heart and closure with Christ. Heard it was thankfully accepted, but the poor creature thought it was not possible for him to write again. I have heard he said on Sabbath evening that he had more peace than ever, and that Christ had manifested himself to his soul. If so, all shall be well with him forever.

August 21, 1760, Thursday morning

The decisive day is now come: the poor men are to be executed.

We concluded in our dear society to spend last evening in successive prayer for the poor criminals. We did so, and God assisted us, and blessed be his name, heard and answered us.[62]

The Lord in mercy overrule for thy glory this day. Prevent any insurrection. O, let not the poor creatures be disturbed at the last nor suffer any mischief to be done this day. Lord, give not sinners up to their own hearts' lusts this day to seek revenge, nor suffer thy people to get enraged with the rulers of thy people. But may we all realize it, that as justice first followed them and brought them out, so the law condemned them. And enable us to consider thy overruling hand, that 'tis thou wouldst not suffer them to have a reprieve, though so many hearts have been set upon it.

And now, gracious God, into thy merciful and faithful hands I commit them. Lord Jesus, receive thy departing spirits to thyself.

August 23, 1760

Blessed and adored be thy name, most gracious God, that thou didst appear for the poor soul on the morning of that day on which he was executed, and so compose his mind and reconcile him to his death and that he could then tell me, "I think myself dead in sin, but alive through the alone merits of Jesus Christ."[63] My God, 'tis enough. I bless and adore thy name for the room I have to hope that where sin had abounded, grace did much more abound. O, the riches of free sovereign grace, boundless depth. Lord, I rejoice; I bless thee that as I have sowed in tears, I now reap that thou hast glorified thy darling attribute in the salvation of this soul.

As to the other, I know the judge of all the earth has done right and am therefore satisfied.

My thoughts have been so engaged on this account that I have had no time to remark the dealings of God with my own soul, but blessed be his name, they have been very gracious. Sweet, sweet communion with Christ at his table, renewing choice, surrenders, earnest petitions for pardon and cleansing, strengthening grace that God might be glorified in me. Pleaded Christ's righteousness, blood, and intercession. Renouncing all my own rags and pleading hope of a gracious answer, was bid to go in peace, and promise upon promise applied. And blessed be God, I have found my soul sensibly strengthened again and again, a precious season at the throne of grace last night, and I shall go from strength to strength, from ordinance to ordinance, and from one degree of grace to another, till I appear before God in Zion, because Christ obeyed, died, arose, and ascended for me, and ever lives to make intercession for me. Because he lives, I shall live also. Amen. Thanks be to God for Jesus Christ, my life, my joy, my crown, my all.

October 23, 1760, Thursday evening

Thanks be to God, we did get one half a pound of tea, one half a quarter of sugar, and a barrel of flour from those where I little expected it would come—and without going to law, too.[64]

O my God, how kindly dost thou deal with me. How dost thee in unexpected ways supply my wants. O, never suffer me to suspect thee more. Lord increase my faith. O God, strengthen my faith of reliance on thee for all supplies for soul and body, thou full, overflowing, never-failing fountain of all goodness. Wilt thou graciously provide for my family this winter also? O God, then let me be all for thee.

I have been to Mr. Chesebrough's today, and Miss Nabby gave me a present of eight pounds.[65] Thanks be to God for this. Lord, bless all my bene-factors.[66] Reward them a thousand fold in their own bosom, and especially thine handmaid, whom thou hast this day inclined to open heart and hand to me. Lord, accept it as done to thine, though to the most unworthy of all thine, and bless her Lord. Bless her, I beseech thee, in her soul and in the grand affair before thee.[67] I trust thou hast espoused her to thyself. O Lord, espouse him also who is dear to her. And if it be thy will that they are come together, I pray thee, enable them to live as heirs of the grace of life.

And bless all that family. Let the smiles of heaven be upon them.

November 5, 1760, Wednesday morning

Thanks be to God, I had in the main a comfortable Sabbath; was, through grace, diligent. Worthy Mr. Maxson preached for us upon repen-tance from Job 42:6: "Wherefore I abhor myself and repent in dust and ashes."[68]

O my God, the more thou goest on to discover thy perfections to me or any other creature, the more we shall do thus. Lord, only unveil thy beauty and 'tis done. O, let the awakened be helped on their way by these precious sermons. Lord, carry on thy own work in each of their souls for Christ's sake. O, espouse them to thyself, I pray thee, and awaken others.

O Lord, when shall the glorious day dawn when the Jews, the seed of Abraham, thine ancient friend, shall be brought in with the fullness of the Gentiles? Thou hast made glorious promises concerning the latter days. O, let them be speedily accomplished, if it be thy holy will. I bless God for the remnant yet preserved amidst so many attempts to destroy.

I thank God for the miraculous preservation of his church on the fifth of November.[69] O, that the hearts of all might be warmed with gratitude and praise to God. Lord, restrain revelings this night and be glorified in the thanksgivings of thy children the world throughout. Let all that love Zion rejoice in thee, who art Zion's God.

I thank God for sweet freedom at his throne the last two evenings, and for Christ's sake, I will expect a gracious answer to my prayers. I am still pursuing my Bible night and day and extracting food for my soul by marginal notes.

And may I not, warrantable, sing repentance to my soul and say, "Soul, take thine ease; thou hast much goods laid up in store for many years"?[70] O, this treasure is better than ten thousands of gold and silver. 'Tis sweeter than honey and the honeycomb.

November 11, 1760

I would now record the various prospects of supplies I have had this fall. And yet, hitherto all seems failing. Early in September, Providence provided money to procure four cords of wood, which we paid for and was promised we should receive in a few days, but have had but two cords yet and can't get the other.

Fourth of October, we received wherewith to buy two cords more, was promised by another we should have that in a few days, but that fails yet. Three or four cords by another, but the boat leaks, and that is like to fail.

Thought we should have apples, pork, potatoes, and meal the same way, but at present all ways seems hedged up. Thought we had been provided with flour; that proved naught, and none in the room of it. Yet perhaps Providence has ordered the door thus to open and shut, to break off my dependence on creatures that I may look to him alone. Maybe 'tis his pleasure I shall believe for my mercies before I receive them, and then see more clearly how immediately they come from his hand, that I may taste adorable sweetness when I receive them. O my God, then grant me faith and I'll wait thy time. I'll look at thee and all my expectations shall be from thee. I'll depend on thy providence to overrule all my affairs with men. Every heart is in thy hand, and every circumstance is ordered by thee. Lord, I believe; help thou my unbelief.

I believe thou wilt deal kindly with me. I would only act the rational part and leave all my cares with thee—leave thee to work in thy own way and time. I would only stand still in the use of means and see the salvation of God. O, only make me just what thou wouldst have me to be, and do with me what thou wilt. Only make me submissive, holy, and heavenly that thou mayest be glorified in me, and I have my most vehement desires. Thou, God, seest me. O give me the desires of my heart, excited by thy Spirit and grace, though thou deny me every other desire.

And dear Lord, I beseech thee, do deny me everything that will not bring me nigher to thyself. Let me not have one unsanctified enjoyment. O, I deprecate it; let nothing entice away my affections from Jesus Christ, but kindle them to a mighty flame which many waters cannot quench, neither can the floods drown. O, that I could love thee more, thou altogether lovely one. Lord, when shall I? When wilt thou enflame my love, kindle my zeal for God according to knowledge? When shall I be holy as thou art holy? O speedy conformity, Lord God almighty. Behold thy Christ and my Christ and give, for his sake, all the grace I need. Let none of my sins bar me, nor debar me. View me with complacency because I am Christ's, and Christ is God's; yea, is God over all, blessed forever. Behold his perfect obedience when in my stead he perfectly fulfilled thy law, and be pleased with me for his sake. Blot out my sins. Speak peace and pardon, establish thy word on which thou didst cause me to hope, when the earth was trembling at thy majesty's presence, that though the mountains should depart and the hills be removed, yet thy kindness should not depart from me; neither should the covenant of thy peace be removed. O thou faithful, covenant, faithful God, help me by faith to view, as I view the bow in the clouds, this token of thy covenant with me, for thy kindness shall not depart from me, because thou art a faithful God.

O, let me trust thee and rely on thee while I have a being, and bless thee, live to thee. For I am, and will be, thine forever as thou art mine,

Sarah Osborn

November 12, 1760, Wednesday morning

Thanks be to God for assistance of his Spirit yesterday morning and for favors throughout the day, for Providence smiled in bringing our Negro boy home to see us, who has been from hence six years, and by him a present from his master of some pounds value, in sauce, &c.[71] I find him quite contented and desire to be thankful he is so.

And now will God direct me and overrule in the affair before me. Lord, thou infallibly knowest what is best for me, and what thou wilt enable me to do. Make the path of duty plain, I beseech thee; suffer me not to plunge myself into unnecessary change, but if it be most for thy glory and my good as well as the child's, I pray thee, bring it to pass. Let me neither decline it through distrust of thy providence nor yet unwarrantably presume on providence. To thee I would commit it; with thee, I would leave it. Lord, make the path of duty plain to me.

November 13, 1760, Thursday morning

It was a terrible storm last night. No more here last evening but Miss Davis and Miss Susa, it was so tempestuous. Lord, smile on us again if it be thy holy will.[72]

Fear our poor servant went away just before it come up, and how it was with them, God knows. I attempted to pray for his preservation but could not persist. Endeavored to commit him, with myself and all I have, to God. And if 'tis most for God's glory and my good, he is and will be preserved.

But I find as his time draws nearer being out with his master, my dependence begins more and more to fix on him, and expectations from this withering gourd are raised, as if this would shadow me from the heat. O, when shall I cease from man, whose breath is in his nostrils?[73] When shall I cease to catch at and build upon every prospect of prosperity, and when shall I cease to fear and droop at every fear of disappointment? Do I not know that all things below are changeable, and God above, unchangeable? Do I know that all things shall terminate according to the counsel of his own will?

Who ordered me that boarder [boarding student] at first, whereby I have been so relieved and supported? Was it not God? And if it 'tis his pleasure to suffer her remove, shall I repine? Is the Lord's hand shortened? O, for a Habakkuk's faith instead of a Jonah-like spirit.[74] And O, let the Lord do with me what seemeth good. O God, still choose all my changes for me. I would choose neither this nor that, but a heart made holy, and a will resigned to thine in all things without exception, that God may be glorified in me. O, when shall it once be? Lord, delay not; make haste to help me in this regard. O, give me but faith, and 'tis enough. Temporal mercies won't cause these disorders of my soul, though thou heap one upon the back of another. As long as this Mordecai, this unbelief, sits at the gate, there will be murmurings, fears, and discontents.[75] I shall dishonor God in thought, word, and deed. But slay this enemy, and I shall glorify God and enjoy thee, and be thankful, too, for all mercies, spiritual and temporal. O, will God help me to overcome this enemy for Christ's sake? Help, I fly to thee, thou faithful God; I fly to thee, for thou hast said, "I will help thee; I will strengthen thee; I will uphold thee by the right hand of my righteousness."[76] Amen, Amen. O, let thy grace be sufficient for me, and thy strength made perfect in my weakness, and I ask no more. Dear Lord, give me my petition and my request. O, deny me not in this. I come not in my own name. If so, thou mightest justly send me empty away, but I come in the name who has said, "Whatsoever I ask in his name, thou wilt give."[77] Shall I go away strong in faith, giving glory to God? Lord, shall I say, I *shall* say, "Go in peace, for thy faith hath made thee whole"?[78] Say, "Thy sins are forgiven."[79] Say, "Woman, thou art loosed; I shall be straight and glorify God."[80] And glory shall redound to Father, Son, and Holy Ghost.

Lord, wilt thou help me? I cannot let thee go. I have no strength to stand before any temptation: the least will be too hard for me. I shall fall except thou hold me up. O, help me to believe thou art able and willing to do this, that thy kindness shall not depart from me, unworthy as I am, for thou art my God and I am and will be thine forever. Yea, I will, I will,

Sarah Osborn

November 25, 1760, Tuesday morning

In casting up accounts last night, I find we are in debt to several persons: Mrs. Cary over an hundred and thirty pounds, and to the butcher, near forty, besides other debts.

And now we are contracting, for wood and provision, more and more. O Lord, help, and in thy all-wise providence overrule, that these just debts may be honestly and timely paid. It is not to consume on our lusts, but for the comfortable subsistence of our family, that we are thus involving. Lord, help, and enable others to render us our due, and yet send us business, and make us thankful for it and faithful in it.

Business is now failing every day. Grant me a Habakkuk's faith, that although all should be cut off, yet I may trust and rejoice in thee. O, still glorify thyself, and grant that all may have their just due. Thou knowest how to bring all things to pass for thine own glory. O, help me to believe thou wilt do so in all things concerning me, and let my heart be at rest in God as to carking cares. And yet, my God, preserve me from a careless indolent frame of spirit. Lord, keep me awake, I beseech thee. O my God, preserve me from a carnally secure, slothful frame. O, pour out a spirit of prayer, and help me to pray and watch, and watch and pray, lest I enter into temptations. Dear Jesus, keep me, O, keep me by thy almighty power. My soul is committed to thy keeping.

Lord, I humbly expect preservation from thee. I fly to thee, O my shield. Defend me; ward off every blow that sin will strike and every fiery dart that Satan will throw. Thou canst defeat the world in all its snares, whether to elevate and puff up or to frown and cast down. Lord, all is alike to thee, nothing too hard for thee, though all too hard for me alone. I can overcome all through Christ strengthening me. O, thou art my sun to enlighten me, my shield to defend me. Help me to rest in thy faithful word and suck at this full breast of consolation. For the Lord God is a sun and a shield. The Lord will give grace and glory, and "no good thing will be withheld from them that walk uprightly."[81] In this blessed text, all is comprehended my heart can wish. O, thanks be to God for the promise of grace as well as glory—grace to enable to walk uprightly, and that no good thing shall be withholden. O, let me seize the promise of grace now and cheerfully trust for the rest. Lord, give me this part now, and I can trust for glory and all good things. Faith can cheerfully wait thy time.

Hast thou not said thou wilt withhold no good thing?[82] Then withhold not grace. Give me this in hand now, Lord, this moment, greater degrees for Jesus's sake. Communicate from the full fountain, the head of all gracious influences. It will never be exhausted. Fill me to the brim. There is an infinite fullness, a fullness[83] for needy creatures. Am I not a needy creature? Lord, thou knowest I am; indeed, I am. O, withhold not grace. Let me bear away the blessing now, if it may be thy holy will. O, let me have no will but thine, and is not this thy will, even my sanctification? O, then let me be lean no longer, but fat and flourishing for Christ's sake.

Lord, say Amen and 'tis done: thou shalt be glorified in and by me. Glory shall be ascribed to Father, Son, and Holy Ghost, and I will be thine now and forever,

Sarah Osborn

November 27, 1760, Thursday morning

Blessed be God, a precious morning again yesterday. A deep sense while I wrote, and God helped me to wrestle for the blessings. A comfortable day and evening; God smiled in his providence. We received [payment] here and there. Thanks be to God, we have good success in gathering in our harvest, and God will supply all our need. Does the husbandman expect another crop in winter? No more can I. Thanks be to God who enabled me, with the ant, to improve the summer. And as in the use of means, as to the world, I have done and do all I can. What remains but that I now wholly depend on God, and believe he will withhold no good thing from me. O God, enable me to keep up high and honorable thoughts of God, believing thou wilt be kind and gracious; believing thou wilt give grace; also believing, as far as the heavens are above the earth, so far are thy thoughts above my thoughts, and thy ways above my ways. Lord, preserve me from low, mean, and unworthy thoughts of God. Suffer me not to limit thee in anywise, for soul or body, for thy compassion has no bounds.

And O, will God, in infinite mercy, look on thy dear child again buffeted by Satan. (Poor Miss Betty Seabury again exercised with violent temptations to blaspheme, O God, so that she has bit her lip almost through to keep from speaking.)[84] O God, thou knows how great her trials are, how Satan is again injecting his hellish blasphemies. Lord Jesus, shorten his chain if it be thy will; deliver her again out of the paw of this roaring lion, or succor and support her. Lord Jesus, thou knows what it is to be tempted. True, Satan found nothing in thee, but thy dear child has a body of sin and death, and except thou prevent, her heart will join and lips utter, too. O God, preserve her as a chaste virgin. O, suffer not Satan to commit a rape upon her.

Is not this a brand thou hast plucked out of the burning? Lord, is she not thy own? Thou infallibly knowest. I trust she is indeed so. O, keep her as the apple of thy eye. Lord, call off Satan if it be thy holy will. Only say, "Come out of her."[85] He can't resist thee. He shall flee before thee. O Lord, help her in faith to resist him that he may flee from her. O, help her to draw nigh to God, and do thou draw nigh to her. O, enable her to take the shield of faith whereby she *shall* be able to quench the fiery darts of the devil. O sweet Jesus, be thou her sun and shield; thou, her great captain. Do thou make the powers of hell to tremble and give her the victory in thy own time. Lord, pity and succor her, for thy own name's sake.

December 12, 1760, Friday morning

Blessed be God I have enjoyed almost a steady calm ever since I wrote last. I trust real actings of faith and acquiescence in the divine will. A prospect last week of three boarders being added to my family, this but all fell through. No matter for that. That is set in God's way. He knows what I want, and that's enough.

How graciously did God overrule an innocent jest, on Saturday last, to supply my need. I begged in jest without the least thought of receiving wood. God inclined the good lady to open heart and hand in earnest. (Dear Mrs. Coggeshall.)[86]

The Lord reward her a thousandfold. Lord, I think this was given for thy sake. Let not thine handmaid lose her reward, but bless her, Lord, with the best of spiritual blessings in Christ Jesus, the same that I covet for my own sake, and at last take her to thyself to behold thy glory.

I have been all my leisure moments engaged in reading past experiences, whereby God has strengthened me more and more. Thanks be to God, his mercy endureth forever.

EIGHT

Glorify Thyself in Me, 1761–1763

SARAH OSBORN BELIEVED *that the purpose of her life was to glorify God. From reading the Bible, she knew that great things were expected of her, and she wanted to demonstrate her faith in all of her words and actions, no matter how small. In her diary in 1762 she longed "to have a single eye to his glory, to be nothing that Christ may be all."*

Yet in practice, Osborn often struggled to determine what this meant. Between 1761 and 1763, the year that the French and Indian War finally ended, she implored God to help her understand her obligations to herself and to others. What exactly did God want her to do? Her questions ranged from whether she, as a woman, could lead family prayer to how she should treat Christians outside of her own denomination, especially those with a reputation for radicalism.

As the end of Bobey's apprenticeship drew near, Osborn was especially concerned about her responsibilities as a slave owner. She had reared Bobey from infancy as a Christian, and she had always prayed for his conversion. But she also assumed that slavery had been ordained by God, and she viewed Bobey as her property. At a time when she and Henry were so poor that they were forced to rely on charity to pay for food and fuel, Bobey was the most valuable thing that she owned. In good conscience, could she sell him?

Osborn's health continued to deteriorate during these years. In a letter that she wrote to Joseph Fish in 1762, she mentioned that she was no longer able to walk significant distances, and she no longer attended church or visited friends unless she was offered a ride in a chaise. Her illness was slowly robbing her of both her eyesight and her ability to walk.

Despite her fears about the future, Osborn continued to search for ways to glo-

rify God. When she received an unexpected bequest in 1762 from her Uncle Guyse, she and Henry decided to bring Johnny, the youngest of their grandchildren, to live with them. They were now the guardians of three of John and Abigail's impoverished children. (The fourth child, Nancy, seems to have been apprenticed out as a servant.)

1761

January 11, 1761

O Lord, who can stand before thy cold? O, pity the poor and needy; provide for them out of thine infinite stores. Spirit those on whom thou hast bestowed this world's good to relieve their wants, as thou dost spirit such to relieve the wants of thy poor unworthy creature, for which I bless thee, and pray thee to reward my benefactors. I trust they do indeed give for Jesus's sake. O, let them not lose a reward of grace. Of thy free, rich grace, Lord, reward them.

And as it is thy sovereign pleasure that my circumstances rather call me to receive than give, I would cheerfully submit and believe it is best of all. Lord, anything, any circumstance in life thou seest best, so thou wilt but make me strong in faith, lead me to and hold me near thyself, and all is well. If my hands may not relieve the poor, pour out on me a spirit of prayer for them. O, permit me to bring them to thee in the arms of faith and prayer, to thy full stores, day by day, that these their wants may be supplied.

And yet, as opportunities offer, and God gives leave, let me cheerfully cast in my mites for their support. O, never let me be unmindful of the poor, the sick and languishing, the prisoner and captive, the aged, and the tempted soul. O my God, since thou hast done so great things for me, I pray thee, fill me with bowels of compassion, and let the widow and fatherless still be the objects of my tender concern and care. And may my zeal for the support of the gospel never die. Let me still cheerfully do all I can, and when I can do no more, Lord, help me to pray continually that thy gospel may be supported and for the prosperity of Zion. And O God, hear and answer for Jesus's sake.

Let God glorify himself, and let him do as seemeth good to him. I have no other choice to make this new year but that God may be glorified in me and mine, and all affairs and things. And yet, while I am thus anxiously careful for nothing, I would daily, in everything, by prayer and thanksgiving, make known my requests to God. I would pray more than ever from the exalted views and earnest longings that God may be glorified. O, are not these motives as strong to make me thirst and long and wrestle, as anxious, distressing cares? O God, let me not be freed from them in vain, but now may I get up and run, with more vigor and cheerfulness than ever, the ways of thy commandments, rejoicing in God, and in all the great and glorious events of his providence.

February 19, 1761

Yesterday I was comfortable some part of the day and came through the whole as well as usual. In the evening, serious and engaged when telling my friends of the society, when met, of the dealings of God with the soul of Mr. ———.[1] And when I came to pray for him, my whole soul was engaged. He appeared to me, as indeed he was, hovering just on the brink of eternity and ready to launch into it in a moment. And God gave me a deep sense of the worth of his precious soul, of his utter inability to help himself, of his utter unworthiness to receive mercy (and mine, or ours), earnestly to apply to the throne of grace in his behalf. But pleaded encouragements from our being jointly engaged for mercy for him, and I trust we really were so throughout the room.

I bless God, who gave such a number of us opportunity to unite and implore mercy for him, and commit him into the hands of a glorious Christ, to be clothed with all the glorious and spotless robe of his righteousness, in which he might lift up his head before strict and impartial justice before the bar of a holy God. I could heartily plead the glory of God in the salvation of this soul, and had a lively view of the joy in heaven in the presence of the blessed angels over this sinner repenting and arriving there and, I humbly trust, a sensible view both of the worth of his soul, his undone state without Christ, his unworthiness to receive or mine to implore mercy, the fullness and sufficiency of Christ for him as well as for Jerusalem sinners who had imbrued their hands in his own precious blood.[2]

And [I saw that] the glory that would redound to both, in heaven and on earth, in the salvation of this soul was from God, that those discoveries were from him, and the desires were excited by his own Spirit. It was he who emboldened me, who am but dust and ashes, thus to draw near and plead with a righteous God. And I hope he has answered the desires of his own exciting.

It was between seven and eight o'clock when we were thus united at the throne of grace, more than ten in number. And a little before nine, dear Susa (Miss Anthony) was our mouth, and spread his case before God with earnestness and importunity.

And before we broke up we heard the bell toll for his death. And I believe it was Satan who suggested to me that my desires were not excited by the Spirit of God. For he was not then the subject of prayer, and therefore my prayer was lost, for God never assisted any to pray for the dead.[3] It gave my spirits a considerable damp, for I verily thought that God by his Spirit had held me up to wrestle with him, and given me such boldness and freedom of access and even strong confidence that God would hear and answer for Christ's sake. And if he was dead at that very time, I knew not what to make of it! Still I could not help thinking God was with me of a truth in that prayer. I therefore went down to the house, and inquired at what time he died. And his sister told me, just at nine.

And God did help me. And he shall have all the glory, while I rejoice in hope that he is glorified in heaven, for the salvation of that soul.

And now, my God, lay me in the dust, and comfort the near and dear relations, and all to whom he was dear. And sanctify it to all this town and to all who may hear of it.

April 2, 1761

Thanks be to God for increasing the number of our dear society. We are now thirty-five in number. Twenty here last evening. O that God will, for Christ's sake, increase our graces. Dear Lord, quicken thy dear children and strengthen them, encourage and comfort them. O, build us up; smile upon us, Lord. We meet together to speak to one another of the Lord. Hearken and hear, and let us be thine in the day when thou makest up thy jewels. O let this society be a nursery for piety.

Sarah Osborn to Joseph Fish, May 10, 1761

My honored and Reverend friend,

With joy I received your last epistle and have wanted an opportunity to congratulate you, as I most sincerely do, on account of God's merciful dealings with you and your dear child, and indeed with you all, in restoring and granting such a measure of health and comfort. Thanks be to God, he has again appeared for Mrs. Noyes and made her the living mother of a living perfect child.[4] O, that none may be suffered to lose this dear babe hence but may it live and grow up a rich blessing, if it be God's holy will. Pray, Sir, send my most hearty regards when you write to New Haven.

I had, dear Sir, upon reflecting on my repeatedly troubling you with my anxiety on account of the trials of dear friends, concluded in my own mind that you would think me fully ripe for another reproof and kindly administer one to me. I cut out several ways in which it was to come: sometimes as to a busybody in other men's matters, &c. But all failed, except silence in the affair was intended as such. I don't know but I have had as hard a struggle to give up that dear name [Susa] to reproach as ever I had to give up my own. However, I trust in some degree God has made me willing to give her up to reproach, as well as to sickness and death if God see meet, which I trust I was enabled to do long ago, if God see it best for her and most for his glory. And now I verily believe it was for both his glory and her good. She has had a sharp trial, but in the scuffle with the world, as she expresses it, she has somehow lost almost all her reserve. Seems to be rising out of the furnace more bright and clear than ever—strong and free and communicative, which has endeared her to many—that you may see, Sir, how graciously God has dealt with her.[5] I have sent you the copy of the letter she wrote to the person who sought her hurt. I borrowed it to peruse myself. Be pleased to return it by the bearer.[6]

I desire, Sir, to bless God and you as long as I live for that dear letter you feared would be offensive to me. By that sweet, gentle reproof, I was convinced of my folly in being too anxious about the opinion or judgment or anger of others and, through mercy, have ever since been set at liberty in that point as to myself. And while I seem to beg, indulge me in tenderly loving this dear creature because she bears the image of my glorious Redeemer in an eminent degree, yet spare me not wherein you think I have erred. I trust it shall be as excellent oil, &c., if you faithfully smite.[7]

I know not, Sir, whether I have ever given you an account of the revival of our society, which for many years had been dropped, partly through some marrying, others falling away, and partly for want of conveniency, which difficulty was removed last January. It was twelvemonth when God graciously gave me a retired convenient room, and my dear Susa and I, with two other Christian friends, concluded to attempt the revival of a society on Wednesday evenings. But O, what a mountain it did appear. Yet God graciously encouraged us and condescended to afford us tokens of the divine presence from time to time, and more so, and we are now twenty-six in number. Several of the most serious that did formerly belong are returned, dear Mrs. Peabody for one, and we have the mothers and their children—three mothers with their daughters.[8] Blessed be God, we find it a sweet bond of union and do with much more freedom than formerly converse on vital and experimental religion. And all things are carried on in an orderly, secret way: we have none that divulges to the world what passes amongst us that I ever heard of, so that we enjoy the sweetest freedom with each other. I have reason, in a judgment of charity, to think there is not one amongst us but what is either espoused already or is seeking Jesus, sorrowing. Some wonderfully assisted in the duty of prayer.

And O, could you, Sir, but be in a corner and hear our dear Susa, when wrestling for the outpourings of God's Spirit for the conversion of sinners, for strengthening, sanctifying grace, that God may be glorified in his children and for gospel ministers, I believe you would, with me, be constrained to say you never heard anything to exceed if even to equal.[9] Such a Jacob is she that it often brings to my mind what I heard Mr. Byram say of Mr. Brainerd, when telling of praying in the wilderness for the conversion of the

Indians. "I verily thought," said he, "the dear man would have died on the spot."[10]

I have no small hope that God is about to revive his own work. This dear society was set up when almost all seemed fast asleep, if not dead, and it gradually increases. The other was set up in the height of fervor and zeal, and as that abated, the society dropped. Our dear pastor has promised to meet with and encourage us as soon as his strength will allow, and I have often wished you nigh us, dear Sir, that we might have your company sometimes. It would be very sweet to enjoy the helps of dear, faithful, regular ministers. These my doors and heart should be open to receive, but I have, from the first, declared they should be shut against all intruders into the ministerial office, and against all such as run wild, make rents in churches, etc.[11] We have not one such member amongst us, and I hope we never shall.

Dear Sir, on behalf of all, I beg your prayers and counsels, too. O, that our society may indeed be a nursery of piety. Ten Sabbaths, now, our dear Mr. Vinal has preached to us, and verily he does exceed himself. I trust God has of a truth done his servant good by all the trials he has exercised him with.

But I must conclude now with most humble and hearty regards to you, Sir, your dear spouse, and Miss Becca, from your sincere though unworthy friend and humble servant,

Sarah Osborn

All friends are through mercy able to keep about, though 'tis a general time of colds with us. Mr. Osborn sends his best regards. Pray for me, Sir, with respect to my family and school that I may have grace to be faithful. Great is the charge God has entrusted me with.

Sarah Osborn to Joseph Fish, July 20, 1761

Honored and Reverend Sir,

As I have this good opportunity by dear Mrs. Eels, I cheerfully embrace it to return to you my most hearty thanks for your last speedy answer to mine, as for all other favors.[12] I rejoice in all the goodness of God towards you and yours, and mourn with you all that is afflictive so far as I am acquainted therewith. A mixture of joy and sorrow seems to be our constant lot here, where every sweet has its bitters.

Few parents, dear Sir, are as happy as you in dear, delightful dutiful children. The Lord continue so rich blessings to you, but here must not be happiness complete. For wise and holy ends, Providence forbids the constant enjoyment of their company. Thanks be to God that the day is hastening on when all partings shall cease forever.

I long, dear Sir, for the leisure hour to come in which you will kindly answer my letter more particularly and, as God shall enable you, advise, caution, strengthen, and encourage us of the dear society. And I would give you some hints, Sir, about what in particular I want your counsel to strengthen me, as I am pretty well satisfied you will approve of my opinion in this point.

The case is this: we have one amongst us, one who did formerly belong to our society who is a Baptist, but one that is a regular member of Mr. Thurston's church, of a generous catholic spirit, clear and sound in fundamental doctrines, one of great gifts and, I believe, great grace. She has a happy way of conveying her ideas for the edification of others; exemplary in her life and conversation.[13] In a word, I look upon her an ornament to our society, and I would be tender of her as of the apple of my eye. We have always avoided disputable points, and no difficulty has ever arose on her account, till now that very thing lays me under one.

Thus, one of our members—a serious good woman, I believe—is intimate with two persons, of whose piety she has a high opinion, that are entangled with the disorderly people called New Lights: they have refused to be baptized by Mr. Thurston and drawn off from him because he could not tolerate their following those preachers who run before they are sent, and such they will have liberty to hear and encourage.[14] These persons, we hear, have a mind to join with us, and I objected because I fear it's opening a door to disorders and confusions. Doubtless the excellent sermons heard would be frequently spoke of, and I fear it might cause our young ones, at least, to have itching ears and to be drawed away.[15]

And I can't find a freedom to admit them. Here, perhaps, I am thought a little partial, as we have one, 'tis pleaded, of another society already: why not more? My friends' opinion of these persons' piety makes it a tender point, and maybe I appear somewhat rigid and uncharitable that I can't freely join with such. I would be tender of my friend, but I can't see my way clear to admit such persons. Sir, as you have suffered so much this way, a word of caution from you, without taking notice that you know the particular or circumstance, might be of great service, or perhaps of more still if they do know that I have wrote for your advice, for I am persuaded they will be pleased therewith more than for me to act from my own judgment.[16] I leave it with your prudence. I would carefully avoid doing anything that looks as though I thought I have power or authority more than the rest, and would gladly leave it to be determined by the major part of us whether to admit or not. But I am afraid, for I am not sure there is any more than dear Susa that would be of my mind, 'tis so generally believed that these persons are real Christians, and I dare not say they are not so. To their own Master they stand or fall. But my plea is: if they are real Christians they are fallen into errors, and we ought not to fall in with or encourage the errors of real Christians.

Dear Sir, if I am right, be pleased to screen me and strengthen me by your counsel, which has always been blessed to me. If I am wrong, show it to me, for I would not be self-opinionated or indulge the hateful remains of pride. O, God forbid that cursed principle in me should ever mar or prevent the blessing of the Lord from resting upon us. When I read your dear letter to Susa I could not help crying: "Lord, is it I puffed up with pride?" etc. And a subtle adversary that knows how to take advantage everywhere, and of everything, would fain have carried things to such an extreme as to force us both to shut up our mouths in conversation and prayer also, lest all should proceed from pride.[17]

For some weeks those evenings which before we delighted in became our dread, and indeed I cannot say I have ever enjoyed myself in them as before, because I always think my heart is the most deeply fraught with that sin (as you once beautifully expressed it), of anyone where it does not reign. For blessed be God, I trust it does not reign, and after all, it is my support that God alone infallibly does know all the secret workings of my heart.

And I think upon the most close and critical examinations I have ever been capable of making into my views, motives, aims, and principles, I have found that if ever I knew what it was to be divested of self, to shrink into nothing under a view of the perfections of Jehovah; if ever I knew what it was to have a single eye to his glory, to be nothing that Christ may be all; if ever I knew what it was to be constrained by the love of Christ, to declare what he has done for my soul with hope that he alone would be glorified thereby and a tribute of praise redound to his great name, and a thanksgiving of his saints on my behalf; if ever I longed that King Jesus should be adored and the crown set on his royal head, while I esteemed myself less than the least of all saints, unworthy of all his mercies, and lay prostrate at his feet—it has been at those very seasons when I have been [sure that sin does not reign in my heart].

[*This letter is not signed.*]

October 15, 1761, Thursday morning

Thanks be to God for the refreshments of last evening; and that I did lie down with God and my sleep was savored with divine things; that I awoke with God, renewedly committing my precious jewel into the faithful hands of precious Christ and dedicating myself to him, into whose hands is given all power in heaven and in earth. Keep, dear Jesus, what I have committed to thy charge. Keep me this day from the only and bitter evil. Lord, thou knowest the strength and power of sin yet in my soul, and the wiles of Satan and the world, and 'tis none but thy power alone can oppose them. Lord, thou seest I can't. One moment they will break in upon me, even now in thy majesty's presence. I look to thee for victory, glorious Lord. Say, "No sin or temptation shall be too hard for me."[18]

O, assist me in my calling today, Lord: undertake for me there. Thou seest how I am fairly outdone. I can do nothing, nor never shall, to any purpose thou dost not undertake for me. Lord, thou must be on both sides— mine and the children's, all in all—or all I can do will be in vain. 'Tis thou who must inspire me with wisdom from on high, prudence, courage, and resolution. 'Tis thou who must give me strength to overcome that, in my natural temper, of which they take so much advantage, whether a foolish fondness or a weakness in judgment, yielding too much to their own notions, overlooking and passing by their failings till they run to great lengths. Lord, thou canst overcome.

And give me strength to overcome these follies. O do it, that thou mayest be glorified by me in my calling. I am sick and ashamed of the confusions that attend it and yet can do nothing to prevent it. I have wrote and read good rules to them for the regulating their behavior, for soul and body, but except thou command a blessing, they never will be minded or do any good at all. Lord, undertake for the dear children. They are in thy hand. Incline their hearts to hearken to instruction and reproof and to submit to discipline. Bow their wills, Lord. Do it for thine own honor's sake and for their own sake as well as for my sake, and suffer me in this case to plead that "as a father pities his children, so the Lord pities those that fear him."[19]

Thou knowest my frame. Remember I am but dust, and say, "Thy grace shall be sufficient for me"; say, "Thy strength shall be made perfect in my weakness."[20] I am thine, forever thine. O, glorify thyself in me. O, do, dear Lord; do go forth with me from day to day or let me not stir from hence.

And dispose of me this afternoon as shall most consist with thy glory, whether at home or abroad.

October 19, 1761, Monday morning

Blessed be God, I had a sweet morning yesterday. I trust God was with me of a truth. Thanks be to God for returning his servant Vinal and assisting him to deliver precious truths. All the day was comfortable except some good things breaking upon me in a wrong season.

In the evening I was again refreshed in talking with Miss Molly Allen, Phillis, and Gosper.[21] A lively hope that our glorious Lord will soon return to revive the church. Some freedom for dear sick friends in prayer. A comfortable night.

Awoke with God and have been employed for my generation this morning. And now, my God, go with me, take care of me, and keep me from the only and bitter evil this day.

And bless me even more in my calling this day. Lord, command a blessing on me and on my children, for Jesus Christ's sake, whose I am and will be forever,

S.O.

October 21, 1761, Wednesday morning

The 21st of October, thirty years ago, I first entered the marriage state. O, that I could be sure I had been then espoused to Jesus Christ, but I cannot, though at some times hoped I was. The Lord infallibly knows. O adored be his name that, I trust, he knows I am now his. The foundation of God standeth sure, having this seal. The Lord knows who are his.

And if I am his now, let me evidence it to all the world that knows me by keeping his dear commandments, doing justice, loving mercy, and walking humbly with my God.

Now let me frequently appear amongst the Lord's people. Now others are crowding together, running all risks to attend the devil's entertainments. Let love to Jesus Christ and each other excite us to meet and visit each other. Let us that fear the Lord speak often one to another. And in all humility give him the glory of his sovereign grace, declare what he has done and is doing for our souls. Let us show forth his faithfulness and encourage each other to put our own trust in him, for he is a faithful God and none ever trusted in him and was put to shame. O may the whole of our conversation be to speak honorably of God; exalt God and Christ and the operations of his blessed Spirit and grace and lay self in the dust. O let self be debased. Let us never forget: "O not I, not unto me, not unto me but to God be glory."[22]

Thus let us communicate to each other and provoke to emulation; thus let us scatter and yet increase; thus let us blow up all the coals till we are all a flame of love to Jesus Christ and each other. Lord, thus bless our dear society; thus let us love as Christians: yes, as primitive Christians who were dear to each other as their own lives. Let us begin to live and love as we shall do in heaven. Let us while here on earth abound in piety towards God and charity to men, especially the household of faith, Christ's dear sick and poor, Christ's precious ambassadors.

O let us build upon the dear, the sure foundation Christ Jesus all the good works we can. O, let this be ever as oil to our wheels to make them run swift. Inasmuch as ye did it unto them ye did it unto me. O, may God reward every kind benefactor he has raised to me in every time of distress. O, may they never lose their reward, though they did it to the least of thine. Let them hear thee say, dear Lord, to their precious souls, even here, "Inasmuch as ye did it, ye did it unto me."[23] O reward them a thousandfold into their own bosoms, and may gratitude ever glow in my breasts to God and them.

And as I have freely received in times of my distress, so let me freely give as God enables and occasion offers. Lord, ever open my hand and heart to the sick, poor, and needy and make me a blessing in my day. O make me extensively useful in my family, in my school, in the dear, dear society, to all around me. O let the Lord God almighty delight to own me, to use me, to set me apart for himself—in secret, in private, and in every way my proper station admits.

Why do I still lie below if I may not glorify God upon earth? Why not permitted to glorify him in heaven? O God, glorify thyself in me somewhere, I beseech thee. I know thou standest in no need of me, but say me not, "Nay."[24] I am thine.

October 23, 1761

Yesterday afternoon I went to Deacon Coggeshall's house. Had a pleasant afternoon and I trust a profitable one, too. Read a good deal in *Family Instructor*, second volume.[25]

Met with one stroke in it, that gave me a shock, about the woman praying with her children herself as though her husband was not worthy. O Lord, teach me duty; never suffer me to behave insolently towards my dear companion in praying with my dear children myself, that I may evidence my tender regard for them by letting them see and know that I do bring them in the arms of prayer to Jesus.

O, grant I may encourage thy servant [Henry] in every path of duty. O, may we be mutual helps to each other. Lord, assist him in the duty of prayer, and may the worship of God be ever carried on in our family with all decency and reverence. O God, grant a sweet harmony betwixt us may ever appear;

may we walk before our house with a perfect heart, commanding our household after us to keep the way of the Lord. With Joshua, constantly determining that, let others do what they will, as for us and our house, we will serve the Lord.[26]

And O, gracious God, be with us both under our frequent indispositions. Lord, sanctify them to us, and let us be quickened by them to improve every moment for the glory of God either by active or passive obedience. Go forth with me this day, my gracious God, and help me in my calling. O, let decency and order attend my school for thine honor's sake.

Lord, help me.

Sarah Osborn to Joseph Fish, November 2, 1761

Reverend and dear Sir,

The double and treble obligations you have laid me under by your gen-erous, kind, convincing, endearing letters constrains me to attempt some-thing by way of answer, but I fear it will be quite unworthy your acceptance, however lengthy it may prove, for my head is extremely shattered, so that it looks next to impossible to gather in my thoughts at all, or fix them on any-thing particular. You, dear Sir, will candidly accept them as they rove just as a token of gratitude, for I am sensible I am so deep in arrears, I dare not plead, "have patience with me, and I pay you all," as I am sure I never can.[27]

I thank you, dear Sir, a thousand times for the account you gave me of how your precious time is swallowed up. I desire to bless God from my inmost soul that he is exciting here and there one of his dear ambassadors to set forward a work of reformation in this dark and dismal day. It is matter of great encouragement to me, and at some times gives me a strong hope, that the nights of darkness are almost expired, that our glorious Lord will ere long return and fulfill his glorious promises concerning the latter days. He will revive his own work to the inexpressible joy of those faithful servants who are now working while our Lord is withdrawn, girding up their loins and trimming their lamps, setting his house in order, ready to receive or go in with the glorious bridegroom.[28] May the Lord God almighty bless you, my dear and reverend friend, and by his secret power, strengthen and encourage your precious soul in this way and work; yea, I am almost ready to say you shall see the work of the Lord prosper in your hands, that you shall see good according to the days wherein you have seen evil.

But however God has determined as to that, in this I have no doubt, but you shall at last receive a reward of grace that shall make ample amends for all your toil. O, how ravishing will it be to hear your great Lord and Master say, "Well done, good and faithful servant, &c. Enter then into the joy of your Lord."[29] Would to God every dear minister, and every private Christian in their proper sphere, might follow your example and put their hand to the blessed work of reformation. And sure, if Christians have one spark of zeal, love, and gratitude left, now is the time to shew it, especially in poor Rhode Island. Now unrighteousness is running down our streets as a stream, and iniquity as an overflowing flood. Now multitudes are flocking to the theater of iniquity (as my dear pastor yesterday styled it—I bless God he is neither afraid nor ashamed to bear his testimony against it).[30] O, dear Sir, this has been the most cutting, humbling thing for me that perhaps I ever met with, that poor Rhode Island should still be suffered to be the very sink of sin and to fill up its measure by such swift degrees. O, woe to us, except God pour out a spirit of repentance upon us.

But nothing has cut me to the heart, nor hardened sinners in their practice, like professors of Christianity following the multitude to do evil. O God, convince and pardon for Jesus's sake. Is it not a most melancholy thing to think of: that those that by profession have sworn to be the Lord's, for him and no other, can go and see the Majesty of heaven affronted by vile wretches feignedly lifting up their impious eyes and hands to heaven, imploring the divine help while mimicking the agonies of death, &c.? How can they bear to see him thus mocked, and at other times hear his dreadful name swore by and blasphemed? What virtuous eye and ear can help being either wounded or defiled by hearing and seeing their lewd, filthy, amorous stuff and behavior? Sure grace must be at a low ebb when all this can be brooked, and they can dare to cast such contempt on the institutions of Christ, which we enjoy at the expense of his own most precious blood, as to say there is as much good to be got there as at a sermon, and account all stupid, those mortals that have no taste for their husks.[31]

God, grant me a taste for and the enjoyment of sublimer pleasures, and I am content to be called low-lived, &c., &c. 'Tis pleaded in defense that great and good men have attended the play. O, how will one slip of a great and good man harden multitudes in sin while all their holy and pious practices are forgot to be imitated. But 'tis the opinion of great and good men, too, that the stage has been one of the greatest corrupters of our nation, one of the great weights under which our guilty nation is sinking. Would to God all the advocates for it had it in their hand, and would duly weigh, what is said by *Britain's Remembrancer,* and in Pike or Hayward on that *Case of Conscience.*[32]

Forgive me, dear Sir, if I detain you too long here. I am heartsick for these follies. I mourn before the Lord for them, and 'tis some relief to make my moan to you. As to me, I humbly hope God has brought some good out of this evil to me. Perhaps nothing has ever more roused my zeal for the honor and glory of God, or made me more resolutely determined by his grace and help. Let others do what they will. As for me and my house, we will serve the Lord. Thanks be to God, he has made me neither ashamed nor afraid to appear on the Lord's side and bear my testimony against the vices of the times. It appears to me a loud call to Christians to arise. This is no time, surely, for us to hide our heads and sneak into a corner, when our Lord's honor and interest lies at stake—is trampled underfoot by bold transgressors. If our Lord is withdrawn as to his comforting cheering presence, now is the time to evidence to God, to our own souls, and to the world that we have chosen him for himself, for his own perfections and his word and ways, for the beauty and excellency there is in them, and that in keeping them there is great reward. God forbid that Christians should leave room for any to think that stage players can exhibit a pleasure equal to theirs. But I have done with them at this time. Thanks be to God, their performances are ended for the present time. They are going from us. O, but the evil contracted lies upon. O, for pardon and cleansing by the blood of Christ.

Surely now, my soul, 'tis time to turn inward. Methinks my venerable friend begins to nauseate and grow heartsick of me, as I have been of others, while what I have wrote savors so much of vain boasting: a Pharisaical, "God, I thank thee I am not as others," &c. O God, search and try me, and discover to me, for Jesus's sake, if I am influenced by the zeal of a Jehu; if espying the mote in my brother's eye and neglecting the beam in my own; if despising others and saying, "Stand by thyself, for I am holier than thou"; if thinking, "I stand; O may I take heed lest I fall." Has God preserved me from turning after Absalom? No thanks to my vile heart; not unto me, not unto me, but to my glorious Jesus who has kept me by his almighty power, be all the praise. Perhaps Adonijah may be more suited to my cast of mind, and if so, nothing but all-conquering grace will prevent my turning after him.[33] O, may I ever remember all my security lies in those gracious promises: "My grace is or shall be sufficient for thee"; "I will never fail thee all the days of thy life."[34] Amen.

Here let me humbly hang and rest while I view the sink of sin in me, the seeds of every abomination, enemies of every kind and size lying in ambush, or like coming forth against me from time to time, or I shall cry out, "I shall one day fall or perish by the hand of Saul."[35] Methinks I always sail as betwixt two great rocks: discouragement from view of the plague of my own heart, on the one hand, and spiritual pride, on the other, ever in danger of being sunk by the one or dashed all to pieces by the other. O, what should I do if the blessed Spirit had not engaged to pilot, protect, and conduct me safe to the desired haven?

But O, he will, for his own honor's sake, he will preserve me; he will keep me. A glorious Trinity engaged on my side cannot fail to conquer all this and my enemies, and to enable me to surmount all difficulties. God will not leave this work unfinished. The blood—the precious blood of Jesus—will cleanse my polluted soul for his sake. God will still forgive. Rejoice, my soul, for there is forgiveness with him (even for such sins as thine) that he may be feared, loved, and adored. O, what God like my God, forgiving iniquity, transgression, and sin? May I ever lie low before him and adore his pardoning grace and redeeming love. Lord, why me the object of it? Why not the object of revenging justice? O, my friend, does not divine sovereignty here dazzle your sight? Sure it shines gloriously.

I have often since been refreshed in reflecting on a sentence in the excellent Mr. Gano's sermon, when endeavoring to convince sinners how unreasonable it is to spurn at the sovereignty of God or to account that an uncomfortable terrible doctrine, when, says he, "I do aver there is more sovereignty in the salvation of one soul than there had been in the condemnation of the whole, for that had been an act of pure justice, but this of absolute sovereignty, because he will have mercy on whom he will have mercy,"[36] &c.

But 'tis now high time I ask pardon for my neglecting to answer your precious letters. The reasons are too many to give. I rejoice, dear Sir, in all the goodness of God towards *you* and *yours,* especially that your dear spouse's life was preserved when in imminent danger. O, may all your lives and health be still precious in God's sight.

Your dear letters have been blessed to clear, relieve, and strengthen my mind every way. Heartily approve of all you have said relating to Separates and our not admitting, &c. But for some reasons I have not yet shewed your dear letters to anyone of the society but my dear Susa, but keep them against a time of need. At present the thing seems to be entirely dropped among us. Before I received yours, dear Sir, I had lent or read to my friends the copies of those letters you know of (wrote to a Separate friend), which plainly convinced them I could not in conscience join with such, and for ought I know, was further satisfactory.[37] They said they approved, &c. And I have some advantage by the meeting being at our house beyond what I should if we met elsewhere. And dear Susa and I concluded to let it rest as long as our members seem satisfied and steady, lest any controversy should arise amongst us. If they should ever move it again, I have your opinion to produce, and the word of God on which 'tis grounded. If we can but keep clear of that sort of people, I am willing to avoid all controversy amongst ourselves, and I really believe nothing strengthens them, or any inclining to them, like being strenuously opposed. Indeed, they value themselves upon the least degree of opposition and count themselves persecuted at once. But I assure you, Sir, I am far from thinking you have shewn the least degree of untenderness more than the case absolutely requires.

Through divine goodness I have at some times lately been refreshed in our meetings, and in the sanctuary, and in secret duties, after the sharpest conflict with temptations to atheism I have endured some years. O, I know the Lord, he is God, and a covenant-keeping, faithful God, too. And his honor and interest has since been dearer to me than life. I humbly trust Satan got no ground in the end, but rather, against his will, hastened my flight to Christ my King for protection. And did he appear and bruise him under my feet? And ere long, I trust he will make me more than a conqueror through his grace. Dear Sir, pray for me that no temptation may ever be too hard for me.

I would acquaint you, Sir, for your refreshment that Providence unexpectedly cast my lot over to Tiverton when my dear Mr. Vinal was gone to Boston. I kept Sabbath at the Reverend Mr. Campbell's.[38] Find he is stirring also to set forward a reformation. To that intent, a private meeting of men is set up, two of which, who are bright as to natural powers, are, 'tis believed, savingly brought home *since*. They walk very circumspectly. Several others under concern. A lecture also once a fortnight set up. I have also intelligence from the women's society in Boston, with whom Mr. Campbell meets when he goes down, that they have set seasons apart to pray for the outpourings of the Spirit.[39] There seems, as my dear Susa expressed it, to be a feeling after God in the dark, for perhaps, after all, a darker time was never known. O, that these days may be shortened lest the righteous put forth their hand to iniquity and draw near to apostasy.

Pray, have patience, Sir. I don't know how to leave off talking. I am greatly obliged and much refreshed by dear Mrs. Noyes's letters you sent me, and by one since by the Reverend Mr. Stiles, all which I hope to answer the first opportunity. The grace of God shines sweetly in her. I rejoice with her and with you. Pray send my hearty regards when you write. My kind love to Miss Becca, most affectionate regards to yourself and spouse, which pray accept from your unworthy friend,

S.O.

My dear pastor has preached four solemn sweet sermons from those words, "If the righteous scarcely be saved, where shall the wicked," &c.[40]

As oft as you can spare time, Sir, I beg to hear from you. When I begin to charge myself with cruelty in urging letters when I know you have so much on your hands, I think again, it all goes in your day's work, it's all for the glory of God and good of precious souls, and then I ask with courage. Forgive my freedoms, dear Sir. My hearty regards to the Reverend Mr. Eels and spouse. I determine to write to her the first opportunity. I am yours sincerely,

S. O.

December 1, 1761

An affair of importance now lies before us. I would fain commit it to God and, in a way of prudent conduct, rely on thy all-wise providence, thou great and good disposer of all events.[41] Grant us discretion, Lord, if it be thy holy will, in the ordering of this affair and let my heart be set upon nothing but what thy will determines: whether to keep[42] Bobey or to dispose of him. I believe my heart has been too much set on keeping him, and now I fear if we keep him he will be rather an encumbrance than a comfort, as neither his master nor I can manage him.[43]

If this be thy will, Lord, make the path of duty plain before us and bring it to pass in thy own way and time. If not, I pray thee, let me have no will. I pray thee, Lord, let me not be entangled with this world.[44] O, let it not eat out my duties and estrange my heart from God. If my wretched heart must and will cling to earthly enjoyments, Lord, take all away rather, I beseech thee, than suffer it. But O, thou that givest more grace to some of thine own, give to me, for Jesus's sake, grace to overcome the world, to possess as though I possessed not, and to enjoy God in all, or else let me possess nothing but my God alone. I hate and detest servants or anything else if it will stand in competition with thee. I would shake them all off as the dust off my feet.

Lord thou knowest I would leave all and follow thee. I would renew my solemn covenant through grace to leave, lose, and deny all that is dear to me when it stands in contrariety to thee or in competition with thee, even life itself. Lord, search and try me, and see if there is any guile conversation.[45] Is there any darling sin or dear enjoyment that I can't or don't give up? Lord, discover it to me and help me, and I will not hold or endeavor to hold it. I will let these go and follow thee, but leave me not to myself, for if thou durst I shall, contrary to the settled bent of my heart, break through all bonds, vows, and resolutions. O, then hold me by the same almighty power that made me at first willing to be the Lord's, and then I will be wholly for thee forever.

December 4, 1761

Thanks be to God, I had a cheerful, pleasant thanksgiving in the morning, my whole soul engaged when writing, comfortable in the house of God. Text, Psalm 101: "I will sing of mercy and judgment."[46] A pleasant afternoon with dear friends of the society. God assisted in prayer.

And all was well till I asked the opinion of Phillis about our selling of Bobey, which, contrary to my expectations, vexed her. I really expected as we have not business for him and he must be let out from place to place, and run to risk of being made unsteady or quite spoiled, or of going to sea, she would have rather chosen to have him settled under a steady master whom he loves, where he has lived more than seven years, the whole family fond of him and he of them, where he has and will enjoy the privileges of God's house, the worship of God in the family, instructions for his soul, and all the comforts of this life necessary for him.

But it was quite otherwise. Her reason seems at present to be laid aside and a fondness to take place—or rather, anger. The Lord calm her spirits and compose her mind. I am now grieved I mentioned it this week lest it should unfit her for preparations for the Lord's table. O God, appear for us both, I pray thee, and overrule in this affair as shall be most for thy own glory, and let my and her thoughts be fixed on God and eternal things.

December 5, 1761

O, that God would enable me to leave thinking of this affair and to leave it with God. O, let not me, nor his mother, have any will but thine. And thou, that knowest all things, knowest what is best. O, let integrity and uprightness preserve me. O my God, enable me to act from right principles, sincere aims at thy glory, and the boy's good. Lord, overrule in thy all-wise providence. Not a sparrow falls without thee. O, help me to leave it and have no will but thine. Lord, help me. All this morning is gone and I can't get nigh thee in anywise. O, prepare me for the solemn feast. Shall I go there with a roving heart, cold affections, worldly thoughts? O, for Christ's sake, appear for me, and call forth sacramental graces into exercise.

Awake! repentance, faith, and love. Awake! O every grace. Come, come attend your glorious King—and bow before his face. O, for increase of grace this time. I am weary of this sinning again and again; I am weary of this worldly roving heart. Lord, help.

December 7, 1761

A most terrible tempest since Saturday night. The Lord in mercy sanctify it to thy people. O God, let not sinners remain secure, taking no notice of the signs of thy coming or ascribing them all to natural causes till thou come on them as a thief in the night, unlooked for.[47]

And O God, while thy judgments are abroad in the earth, let all the inhabitants learn righteousness. And O, thou who camest from Edom, with dyed garments from Bozrah, thou that was glorious in thy apparel, traveling in the greatness of his strength, thou that speakest in righteousness, mighty to save, look down on me and save me from my sins and from this world.[48]

O Lord, forgive. Thou knowest the tempest in my breasts. Lord, shall I never get the world under my feet? Thou that knowest all things, knowest my conflicts ever since Thursday night—at first with tenderness to Phillis and Bobey both, my heart clinging to them, so loathe to grieve her or part with him that I was ready on that account to give up what appeared to be duty and for the boy's good, both soul and body.

But ever since Friday night, my struggle has been of another kind. I have from resentment been ready to give him up to his father's and mother's will since they can't believe that either his master or I have honesty enough to speak the truth, or at all to aim at his good.[49] O, how hard it has been to me to be thus mistrusted by Phillis, to whom I think I have never been unfaithful, by her who I always thought had a better opinion of me.

O, let this teach me to my dying day how ungrateful, how ungenerous and cruel it is for me to disbelieve my gracious, faithful God who never deceived me. The Lord give me grace to overcome my anger and grief and to do that, that I can answer to God and conscience, either in life or at death and judgment, let who will be pleased or displeased. O, let me not be willing to give the child up to be exposed to hardships and ruin to gratify them, nor yet to encumber myself with cares, distresses, and perplexities at home and abroad that God, in his providence, seems at present kindly to offer to free me from.

My God, thou knowest I am a poor short-sighted creature and can't know what is best. I pray thee, take this affair in thy own hands. Pardon all our sins and deal with us in covenant faithfulness. Resign our wills to thine, whatever it is. Thou hast said, "Thy kindness shall not depart from me."[50] Lord, I believe; help thou my unbelief.

December 8, 1761

Lord, help me. Though I had through his mercy a comfortable day as to my health and business, yet Satan or my own corruptions kept crowding this affair upon me so that I can think of nothing else, Lord.

I beseech thee, O Lord, calm my spirits and help me to leave all and follow thee. O Lord, shall I go from ordinance to ordinance, and even to thy holy table, and yet derive no strength from thee to overcome the world? Shall every new thing of what kind soever—whether temptations to tenderness and grief for others, or to anger and to plotting and contriving this or that— shall all take off my heart from God and eternal things?

Lord, deliver me from these cruel tyrants. O King Jesus, thou who camest from Edom with dyed garments from Bozrah, thou that was and are glorious in thy apparel, traveling in the greatness of thy strength, thou that speakest in righteousness, mighty to save, wilt thou not save me now? Remember, Lord, what thou hast done for me. Thy garments has been dyed for me and thou hast come traveling in the greatness of thy strength for me. Thou hast spoken in righteousness and said, "I will never leave thee nor forsake thee."[51] Thou hast saved me, and saved me many a time when earth, self, and hell has combined against me, and thou art now as mighty to save as ever thou was. Thy glorious hand is not shortened. O then, for thy own name's sake, save me now and glorify thyself in me, for I am forever thine,

Sarah Osborn

December 9, 1761

O my God, for Christ's sake, have mercy on me and attract my heart to thyself. O what? No strength derived from Christ in this sacrament? O, I am weary of this unholy heart. O God, strengthen me in grace and enable me to overcome all temptations. Make a way for my escape, thou faithful God, and especially guard me against all temptations to anger. I see how every one thing will aggravate if once I give way, and I will not.

I will rather pity and make much of the poor creature and endeavor, if we do sell him, to make up to her the disappointment as far as in me lies. I will not humor Satan, who has a design against us both, but will love her still for Jesus's sake, O Lord.

And be thou her support and comfort. O, do thou refresh her precious soul and be better to her than ten sons, and overrule in this affair.[52] Thou dost absolutely know what is best for us all. Help us all to act as rational creatures and leave the event with God. Let us have no wills [of our own]. Thou hast always done all things well for us, even when we have cried out, "All these things are against me."[53]

December 12, 1761

I am still at a distance from God—dull, dry, barren, wandering. I am tugging at the oars continually. I carry self-loathing about me.[54] What I hate, that do I. I hate these forehand contrivances, these effects of unbelief, but I am carried away with them as down a mighty torrent. I beat against the wind and tide all day long. I want to cast off all, and leave all with God by venturesome believing, but I can't. Though I am not distressed with tormenting fears, yet I am so amused with this affair and at such a loss to know what is duty that I can bend to nothing else.[55] Lord, help me. Offer a breath of the Spirit to waft me heavenward.

O, precious Christ, espouse thy own cause against the world, the flesh, and the devil. See me, Lord, dragged away from thee by them all. Wilt thou bear it? O, be jealous for thy own right. My heart is forever thine; I have freely given it to thee. Lord, hold it. I have committed it to thee to keep; I can't keep it. O, my faithful Savior, keep what I have committed to thy charge, not only against that day but from the pollution of sin. O thou that hast overcome the world, overcome for me and let this conflict end in thy glory. Let this work together for my good, for thou that knowest all things, knowest all this. While I love thee and would fain be all for thee, O, let the world, sin, and Satan all lose ground.

My glorious captain, bring me out of the field of battle victorious. Make me more than a conqueror through thy grace, for I am thine forever,

S. Osborn

December 13, 1761

O, Lord Jesus, thou hast said, "I will never leave thee nor forsake thee"; "I will never fail thee all the days of my life."[56] Help me to devote this Sabbath to thee. O Lord, take my thoughts off from this subject and turn them to thyself. O, that I could leave off thinking and fall to praying, and leave all with God to determine just as he sees best. I am wearied out, and heartsick of thinking and weighing one thing with another, and after all, can't tell what is best.

Lord, help, and make the path of duty plain. The good man orders his affairs with discretion, but that discretion must come from thee. The steps of a good man are ordered by the Lord. O, order mine also, and let me have communion with thee in thy providences. Lord, bring me to stand still and see the salvation of God. All things will then come to rights. Thou doest all things well.

Order this affair as shall be most for thy glory. Teach me duty. Thou knowest the scruples of my conscience about hiding a talent in a napkin, and also about usury.[57] Thou seest my covetousness, or reluctance to spending more than the income. Thou seest how wavering I am about parting with the child when fears take place about his proving bad, taking to bad courses, going to sea. Then I am fond of settling him with a steady master, but, on the other hand, I have no lease of his master's life no more than of his. Nor can his master or I convey grace to his soul. All must be done by God alone if ever it is done at all, and should his master die and leave him, I can't conclude how it might be as to religious privileges or other comforts he now enjoys.

Then I turn and think, and why should we part with him? Why can't I still trust him in the hands of that gracious God that at first gave him to me, and believe that he will take care of both him and me—believe he was given to me in mercy when I was cheerfully giving up all at the call of divine providence? Then God gave him to me, and was it not in a covenant way? Was it not in mercy? And is not it ungrateful in me to think it was for a scourge? Had I not better hope in the mercy of God and commit him to him [God] to keep for me, who has preserved him so long and preserved him from falling into gross sins, too? He is honest and averse to drink and is—as his master says—more and more faithful, and he shall do us all the service God sees best for us. He shan't, nor he can't, go to sea except God pleases. He can control him if we can't, and his life, his health, his living is in God's hands. The whole disposing is of the Lord's, and I think I had rather commit him to him [God] to keep for me than to commit him to the care of any man.[58]

This is my present frame, and now Lord, help me to leave him with thee, and turn from him to thee. Now, Lord, unveil thy glorious perfections and attract my heart this day. For Jesus's sake, I beg it.

December 18, 1761, Tuesday morning

I humbly trust I have been in some degree in the exercise of faith since I wrote last, especially as to the disposals of divine providence. Inclined to leave all with God, and when once I can fully do this, I know all shall be well. I need take no further care, for I now solemnly protest I never did commit any one affair to God in my life and leave it with him believingly—hoping and trusting in his mercy—but he brought me to acquiesce and rejoice in him in the event, let things appear as they would to the eye of reason, or in the judgment of my judicious friends at the beginning. O, let this be the case now.

Most gracious God, let me have no will but thine. Let me not ungratefully despise thy gift to me in my distress, and be willing to part with it without thy call. (It was the gift of a faithful; it was the gift of many good earthly friends. Also it was to me as something saved from shipwreck when all the rest was cast over.)[59] Nor yet endeavor to hold him a moment when thou dost call me in thy providence, either by poverty, or his death, or any way thou callest. Only let me see thy call clear and by grace I'll resign at once. O, teach me that precious lesson: to see a need of everything God gives me, and to need nothing he denies me, and all shall be well. And O my God, permit me to bring my dear servant's soul to thee day by day in the arms of faith and prayer; that is sick if his body is well.[60] I pray thee, come and heal him.

O, to whomsoever he belongs in this world, I pray thee, let him belong to thee by regeneration and adoption.[61] O let him be thy child, thy servant. He has been cast upon thee from the womb.[62] He was brought forth through thy overruling providence in a land of gospel light; he has been instructed in those things that belong to his everlasting peace; he has sat under the droppings of the sanctuary.[63] He has been taught to read and to pray, and learned the principles of our holy religion. Lord, only command a blessing upon the means, and the work is done: he is made a new creature, too. I adore thee that his heart is in thy hand, thou glorious, faithful Savior to whom all power is given both in heaven and in earth. Thou glorious sovereign potter, make this a vessel of honor. Mold this soul into thine own image. Thou art the way, blessed Spirit; show him the way, the truth, and the life. Cause Ethiopia to stretch forth his hands to thee, and though he cannot change his skin, nor his heart, thou canst change his heart in a moment.[64]

I bless thee, God, from my very soul for his mother. She, I trust, is thine. Thou hast appeared for her. O, appear for her offspring, both of them, if it may be thy blessed will, and turn them to thyself.[65] Glorify thy darling attribute in them, if it may be thy holy will. Lord, hear me.

December 25, 1761, Christmas Day[66]

I have been this morning reviewing the experiences of the past year and beginning of this, and find God was in a peculiar manner disposing me to leave all my affairs with him and, blessed be his name, has inclined me more than usual so to do throughout the year, and he has done all things well.

I was laid by last Christmas with headache, and am this day exercised the same way. Awoke with it before day and can bend to no duty at all. O, that I could rejoice in that glorious Christ that was born for me. When shall I be wholly devoted to him? When shall the days of darkness end?

I was last evening engaged in writing to a choice friend to remove some disgust I think is taken at some of my conduct.[67] Will God compose my friend and convince I designed no slight at all, but to improve all means for my establishment in the path of duty? And will God help me to leave the affair with him? Suffer me not to be overanxious but, in patience, possess my soul and quietly wait the return of temper. Suffer not a breach, I beseech thee, Lord.

Blessed be thy name that we are both in covenant with a faithful unchangeable God who will make all things work together for good to those that love thee. I pray thee, Lord, let Satan have no hand in this affair, either on one side or the other, for he will blow up the spark to a flame if possible.

December 30, 1761, Wednesday morning

Thanks be to God, I humbly hope the fire of anger is, or will be, quite quenched out, and the fire of love to Christ and each other as his disciples kindled afresh.

Blessed be God, I was permitted to go out on Lord's Day, though extremely cold, and hear our dear pastor preach two lovely sermons from Psalm 119:32: "I will run the way of thy commandments, when thou shalt enlarge my heart." Lord, thus I determine by grace. O help me, for Christ's sake, and so overrule in thy providence that we may have this new year's day to set apart for solemn fasting and prayer. And O, may it be such a fast as our God requires of us, the children of the bridechamber, for now our glorious bridegroom is absent.[68]

1762

January 2, 1762, Saturday morning

Bless the Lord, O my soul, and forget not all his benefits. God graciously indulged our endeavors and favored our designs of setting apart yesterday for solemn fasting and spirited all that could attend to come: 1. Mrs. Daves, 2. Mrs. Fairbanks, 3. Mrs. Glading, 4. Mrs. James, 5. Mrs. Hannah Lamb, 6. Mrs. Creapman, 7. Mrs. Barret, 8. Mrs. Henshaw, 9. Mrs. Emmes, 10. Mrs. Hacker, 11. Mrs. Peabody, 12. Mrs. Ross, 13. Mrs. Anthony, 14. Mrs. Mary Anthony, 15. Mrs. Susa, 16. Miss Molly Donnely, 17. Miss Mary Allen, 18. Mrs. Nancy Rosom, 19. Phillis, 20. myself.[69]

God mercifully assisted in prayer: first, poor unworthy me, then Mrs. Daves, then Mrs. Susa, then Mrs. Henshaw, then Susa again, and last, myself. Thanks be to God we were not left dry, confused, and wandering. No, God did pour out a spirit of supplication, helped our infirmities.

And now, my glorious God, give us faith to look out for answers of peace for Jesus Christ's sake alone, and not for anything we ever have or can do. O, be with us this year. Now, my God, accept my sincere desires to be devoted to thy service; now, Lord, take a full, a free possession. Accept an entire surrender of my whole self, soul, and body to thee this year, for I am thine forever.

Sarah Osborn

February 21, 1762, Sabbath morning

Yesterday afternoon I heard that my Reverend uncle Doctor Guise has given me 20 pounds sterling, which is 640 pounds our currency, 125 of which I devote to support the gospel, buy books to lend or give away to children, and to relieve the needy.[70]

Lord, for Christ's sake, take away all thoughts of the world and everything in it this day any further than it will lead me to thyself. O my God, while I admire thy goodness, thy bounty to me, I pray thee, let not my heart center on the gift but on the glorious giver. O, let thy grace be sufficient for me now to keep the world under my feet. Let me use it and not abuse it; let me possess as though I possess not.

And now, Lord, a part I devote to thy service. If thou permit me to receive it, Lord, accept it as a freewill and a thanks offering. I beseech thee, for Christ's sake, accept it at my hands and let the rest be cheerfully and comfortably and thankfully used for the comfort of myself and whole family as need requires, without one grudging thought or unbelieving fear, and to relieve any necessitous, distressed poor as God gives leave and opportunity. Lord, let this little fund be as the widow's cause.[71]

Lord, I deprecate these ever taking place again in my soul. O, let me live by faith all the days of my life, and believe thee kind in all thy dealings with me—believe thou dost design to draw me nigher to thyself by all the temporal mercies. O, let me harbor no ungenerous suspicions that thou wilt put me off with this world instead of thyself or thy grace. Lord, permit a worm to humbly and yet boldly to tell thee I cannot, I will not, be put off with this world as my portion. No, in this sense I would despise it and disdain it in my very heart. I will have nothing as my portion but Father, Son, and Holy Ghost. This portion thou hast given me—this I have chosen, and to this by grace I will cling, and thou wilt not take it away. Mary has chosen that better part that shall not be taken away from her.[72] Lord, I will believe thy designs are altogether love and faithfulness towards me for body and soul.

And O, look down on thy dear, distressed child, thou faithful God, and manifest thyself to her. (My dear Susa deserted.)[73] O, give her not up to the will of her enemies. Let not Satan or unbelief gain ground while thou hidest thy face from her. Lord, appear for her help.

March 6, 1762, Saturday morning

My dear husband very poorly, Mrs. Leach also, and myself.[74] I have been discontented these three mornings, obliged to rise, and I have lost the sweetness of a spiritual frame.

I have also to do with a vile heart and a cruel devil that would fain stir up all the combustible matter lodged there, and embitter every sweet God bestows on me. Before I had tidings of my legacy, all was well; I had enough; I declared myself satisfied. And upon the first receiving the news, I was moved by gratitude to my great benefactor to determine a fifth part to his service and to use the rest cheerfully as need requires without grudging or reserves.[75]

But now Satan has taken me in hand and lays wait every way. I am advised by dear friends, and was inclined myself, to take this opportunity of getting for myself a handsome suit of black silk that is taffeta, and a Prussian cloak, both very decent for persons in years. It is given, and gratitude seems to oblige to acknowledge the giver by appearing in decent mourning for his sake, who was worthy of the most honorable respect. Thus far I am inclined. But on the other hand, I am perplexed lest pride and a conformity to the world should be the motive. These things appear too grand for me; there is no need of them; I can be comfortable without them; and why should I indulge pride? But on the other hand, I find unbelief is at the bottom. There is a fear that when that is gone, all is gone, and what shall I do in future straits if I am extravagant in spending what God bestows? I have no warrant to expect he will further provide for me. Thus I am tossed and can't find a way to mortify one lust without gratifying another. The Lord in mercy direct me. My very sleep has been perplexed these two nights past. I find upon calculation the suit and cloak will cost upwards of 300 pounds, 125 pounds set apart before, that a very little will be left for other helps. 22 pounds, 17 shillings already to two poor widows.[76]

And what if there is not a farthing? There is the same providence as before, but here unbelief or the devil suggests (for I don't know which it is) that 'tis a shame to squander away the gift of divine providence, and no matter what straits I endure if I do so, willful waste makes woeful want. When that's gone, all is gone. I can expect no more from England, be sure. No, nor I did not expect this. No matter from whence it comes, when faith can lift up its head, it says I shall have enough. The word of God says, "Take no thought for the morrow, the morrow shall take thought for the things of itself."[77]

And shall this cursed unbelief gain ground again? I am ready to determine to spend every farthing rather than have a mite to depend on. Lord, let the world say what they will, for being condemned by the worldly wise I find is a great thing with me. Who will pity me if I am reduced, if I don't improve when I have it? The Lord help me for Christ's sake; help me to glorify thee in prosperity and adversity and still to order my affairs with discretion, and in a prudent way to leave all events with thee.

March 18, 1762, Thursday morning

Mrs. Wanscoat wants to take our little Nancy, and I have offered to take Johnny, the youngest, and set his mother at liberty to work for herself.[78]

My God, now permit me by solemn prayer to commit the case to thee I am attempting, and entirely leave it with thee to the conduct of thy all-wise providence. Let me have no will in it but eye [see] thy hand. If the child's mother relucts and is not willing I should have it, enable me to leave it with thee to provide for them, or do with them as seemeth thee good. If it is thy pleasure that they, through her obstinacy, as a just punishment for sloth and other sins, shall remain miserable, who am I that I should oppose it? Lord, I submit.

But if it be thy sovereign pleasure, thou father of the fatherless, in thy providence to commit this child also to my care, I pray thee, confirm my confidence and reliance on thee. Lord, let me do it with the utmost cheerfulness, fixed dependence on thee, and single eye to thy glory, and not to be seen of men. Suffer me not to consult with flesh and blood as to regarding either applause or blame. Thou hast graciously upheld me and enabled me to provide for the other two dear lambs. These I took in straitened circumstances when I knew not which way to turn, but blessed be thy name, thou hast now relieved me from my straits, and surely I may now venture cheerfully on thy bounty and rely on thy assistance. No greater objects [of pity] are to be found in this place than these.

The Lord provide for the little girl [Nancy], also, one that shall care for her soul and body; and spirit their mother, if it be thy will to take care of her own soul and body, too. O, let her not be miserable through time and to eternity through laziness. But I leave her in thy wise, just, and faithful hands.

Lord, go forth with me this day for Christ's sake.

March 26, 1762, Friday morning

Thanks be to God that indulged fifteen of us with an opportunity to unite yesterday, in the afternoon, in crying for the outpouring of the Spirit upon the whole world: upon our nation and land, this town, every minister and congregation in it, for ministers in general everywhere, for our dear pastor in particular, and for a revival in that church and congregation in particular, for criminals, for our dear society, for relatives, for my family, for absent members, and school.

And God did assist, and for Christ's sake will answer. O now, for his sake alone, I would look out for a gracious answer. Thanks be to God that appeared for my help all day, was with me in the morning, brought me through my school with composure, and bore me up, that I was no ways unfitted for duty for want of food till after sunset. This, to me, evidently appears to be the Lord strengthening me, for in general I am exercised with such a raving, craving, disordered appetite that I am hardly ever easy but when eating, my stomach is so pained. But God showed me by his word how my dear Redeemer forgot his food when engaged for the good of souls and pressed that scripture upon me: "this kind goeth not out but by fasting and prayer," and "that I and my maidens will fast also, and so will I go into the king."[79] I know 'tis the Lord's doing, for I have made many an attempt, and by noon have been utterly unfit for duty. Let this confirm me that with God all things are possible, and all things are possible to them that believe, too.

And now, Lord, help us all to cast off all dependence on our prayers as ours, and yet look out for a gracious acceptance of those of his own electing, for Christ's sake alone. He will answer in mercy, for he never said to the seed of Jacob, seek me in vain.[80] And now, Lord, go forth with me and teach me how to apply myself faithfully and skillfully to the duties of my calling. And O, appear for me, my Lord and my God, and help me rule the children for me: they are in thy hand, and thou canst incline them to submit to discipline and receive instruction, and thou canst remove the follies of and weaknesses of my natural temper, of which they take advantage from time to time.

Lord, thou canst strengthen my memory and resolutions, and do all in me and for me and them. O, do everything that will be for thy own glory. I commit myself and dear lambs into thy merciful and faithful hands. O, let me now go forth in the strength of the Lord and fear no evil.

Sarah Osborn to Joseph Fish, May 16, 1762, Sabbath evening

Reverend and Dear Sir,

As I have so good an opportunity by that good, that truly pious lady, worthy Mrs. Chesebrough, who has condescended to honor me with her acquaintance, I could not omit a line (though I must not now enlarge) just to let you know that through divine goodness we are able to keep about.[81] A great mercy this, and ten thousand more a gracious God for his own sake bestows on the most unworthy of all his creatures. O may laws of gratitude be written on my heart.[82]

The dear person I gave you an account of, Sir, that I trusted had experienced a remarkable change, has since been brought to the gates of the grave by convulsion, fits. But by this dispensation I trust God has glorified himself. Thus she has had an opportunity to declare the love of God to her soul when to all appearances she was just launching into eternity. The joy of the Lord carried her quite above the fears of death and all her pains, though extreme. She has been a very pattern of patience and resignation to the divine will. She, when a little lost as to reason, would still be pleading with [her soul] to return to God, answering all objections that could be made, showing the fullness and sufficiency of Christ and his willingness to save to the uttermost, pleading that none might despair since she, the chief of sinners, had found mercy. It would have revived your heart, dear Sir, to have heard dear Susa. She was daily there. And dear Mr. Vinal's heart has been quite refreshed: he was with her almost every day. Her relatives and acquaintances seem to be much affected and desirous that God will sanctify it to them. Oh, that it may be so, that glory may redound to his great name.

I have seen her but once when Deacon Coggeshall's lady was kind enough to come and take me in her chaise. I can go nowhere but where my friends take that trouble with me. I have had some fears of late that I shall soon be shut out of the house of the Lord. Oh, if it may be his will to continue that privilege, I cheerfully forego civil visits. But if not, he will be a little sanctuary to me. I think I have not attempted more than once this twelvemonth on foot, and I am now come to a conclusion it is downright presumption to walk, though to visit the afflicted, because it overwhelms me to such a degree. My friends are exceeding good about helping me to meet-ing. Blessed be God for such favors, and may his will be done. Only grace sufficient. Here am I, &c.[83]

But to return to my dear Rhoda Wilcox, God is now, we trust, saying to her, "return." Her comforts remain and she seems desirous of devoting her whole life to God. She has been propounded for special ordinances today, though not yet able to come out.[84] Dear Sir, God seems to deal much with us in spirituals as in great droughts: many shows of rain, and here and there a little refreshing shower. Oh let us with faith and patience wait and cry, for there shall be a plentiful effusion in his own time. Not a tittle of his word shall fail.

Dear Sir, 'tis never worthwhile to believe me if I tell you in the begin-ning of a line I can't enlarge—for thus it is and will be when I write to you. I beg that what hint I gave you might be no manner of grief to you or back-ward in your writing to me, for all is quite cheerful and well. All I aimed at was to be quite at liberty whether to show or conceal, just as I thought it would or would not bear.[85] God forbid I should act in the character of a backbiter or mischief maker. Believe me, Sir, there is a most hearty regard for you *there*.

You will forgive my using scraps of paper.[86] It was because no epistles should be embarrassed. If I have any hint on those things I shall be glad of it the same way, for Susa knows nothing of my giving you any hint. If I am worthy of reproof for hinting at all, don't spare me. Let the righteous smite.

1763

October 27, 1763, Thursday

The last Thursday in the month is come.

And now will God graciously bring his handmaids here this afternoon, and meet with us, and excite in us vehement longings and strong cries for thy Holy Spirit.[87] O, let us so ask that we may receive for ourselves and others. Give the Holy Spirit to those who ask him this day. This comprehends all other blessings. O, come blessed Spirit; come and make thy abode with us, and it is enough. We shall be holy then. Then we shall pray and praise; we shall run and strive; we shall submit and love; we shall believe and rejoice, acquiesce and adore. Thy will shall be our will; thy cause and interest, ours. And we shall grow strong in all the grace there is in Christ Jesus. Blessed Spirit, O come. It is by thy help alone, we can ask.

O, come this day and make intercession within us, with groanings which cannot be uttered. O, come and revive our dear society. Lord, come in the midst today and revive our drooping souls. O, let us find it is good for us to be here, and let us receive lasting benefits, even the abode of the blessed Spirit with us. O, come as on the day of Pentecost, and fill this room with thy glory and our hearts with thy praise.[88]

NINE

Revive Thy Work, 1764–1768

SARAH OSBORN *had often prayed for a revival in Newport. "Come as on the day of Pentecost," she implored God in 1763. During the spring of 1764, when large numbers of people began meeting at her house to seek Christ, she rejoiced that her prayer had been answered.*

Osborn's meetings seem to have begun with a slave named Quaum (also known as Quamenee Church and later John Quamine), who had been kidnapped from Africa and sold into slavery in Newport in 1754 or 1755. Although it is not clear when Sarah and Quaum first met, she seems to have encouraged him to become a Christian, and after he experienced conversion in 1764, many other slaves and free blacks—as many as 100—began coming to her house on Sunday evenings to pray with her. Intrigued by Quaum's story, a group of white boys also began knocking at her door, and by 1765 Osborn was holding different meetings virtually every night of the week for blacks, children, young women, and adult men. She also continued to hold prayer meetings with the women's society. Warm, earnest, and charismatic, she seemed to have had a gift for touching people's hearts, and the crowds flocking to her house grew larger during 1765 and 1766. Astonished by the hundreds of people who came through her doors every week, Osborn worried that the throng "would indeed be as the river Jordan overflowing all the banks," but she was convinced that the revival was the work of God, a glorious outpouring of his grace. By 1767 as many as 525 people gathered at her house each week.

Osborn's prayer meetings were controversial. Influenced by the words of Saint Paul, many Christians in Newport believed that women should "keep silence in the churches," and they were fearful that Osborn was not just praying with the men at her meetings but also preaching to them. Often she was accused of pretending to be a minister or usurping men's religious authority. Even her close friend Joseph Fish worried that she had stepped "beyond her line."

Anxious about appearing presumptuous, Osborn tried to convince local ministers—including her own pastor, the Reverend Vinal—to lead her meetings. But Vinal, struggling with alcoholism, often failed to preach on Sunday mornings, and in the religious vacuum created by his absence, she felt called to save as many souls as possible. Though she feared causing a scandal, she could not believe that God wanted her to be silent. "Would you advise me to shut up my mouth and doors and creep into obscurity?" she asked Joseph Fish. "Will this be most for God's glory and the good of souls? Sometimes I am tempted thus to do, but hitherto I dare not."[1]

The people of Newport were particularly alarmed by Osborn's meetings because of the crowds of slaves who assembled at her house on Sunday evenings. As Sons of Liberty protested against the Sugar and Stamp Acts during the 1760s by burning effigies of stamp collectors and tarring and feathering Loyalists and attacking their houses, slave owners feared that the spirit of liberty might be contagious. Osborn insisted that Christianity would make slaves more obedient, and she herself does not seem to have questioned the morality of slavery until later in her life. But many people in Newport seemed to have feared that the Bible, with its story of Moses leading the captive Israelites to freedom in the Promised Land, could be a dangerous book in the hands of slaves.

To add to the controversy swirling around her, Osborn welcomed Christians of all denominations to her meetings, including Baptists, Seventh-Day Baptists, and Anglicans. She longed to unite Christians across the boundaries that separated them, certain that God wanted a single church. Yet her ecumenical vision proved too radical for her time. Faced with accusations that she was exposing her fellow Congregationalists to "false" doctrine, especially the Baptists' rejection of infant baptism, she eventually limited her meetings to Christians in her own denomination.

Osborn's diaries during the 1760s reflect both her elation and her anxiety about the extraordinary revival at her house. Buffeted by criticism, she often feared that she would dishonor God's "glorious name," and she tried to quench any feelings of pride by denigrating herself as weak and unworthy. Yet when she prayed for humility, she always came to the same conclusion. "Let me but please God," she wrote in her diary, "and 'tis enough."[2] She was certain that she had been called to serve him.

1764

June 7, 1764, Tuesday morning

Lord, overrule for thy own glory, both as to servants and children. Let me not take one step, but what shall indeed be for thy glory and their good. Incline still further or disincline, open a door or shut it, as to the means as thou seest best. As to the heart, it is thou who openest, and no man can shut it. Lord, suffer not Satan to shut it by his insinuations that I am about to train up a company of pharisaical hypocrites like myself. O, make the path of duty plain because of my enemies. Let me not take one wrong step.

O, guide me by thine unerring Spirit, and enable me to devote all the strength thou wilt give me to thy service. Come forth and show myself on the Lord's side, neither afraid of man nor ashamed to own Christ and his ways before the world. O God, be with me. I know I am unworthy to be employed for thee, unworthy to be owned and blessed. And if thou dealest with me according to my deserts, thou wilt fling back all my endeavors as dung in my face, with a "Who hath required these things at thy hands?"[3]

But I ask not acceptance or success in my own name or for my own sake, but for thy glory and for Christ's sake. Revive thy work here: Rhode Island sinners are capable of salvation.

July 19, 1764, Tuesday morning

What a very fool I am. I can tell servants they are free from cares because it is their masters' part to provide and theirs only to do their duty, and is this not the very case with me? Am I not a servant to a better master than any earthly one? A child to a better Father than the world affords, let them be as indulgent as they will? And yet I am caring and fearing. Poor, silly mortal.

Lord, forgive, and give me more grace for Christ's sake.

Sarah Osborn to Joseph Fish, September 3, 1764

Reverend Sir,

Since God in infinite mercy has preserved your invaluable life, permit your broken worthless friend once more to speak to you by a line, though I assure you, Sir, nothing worth your acceptance can come from her barren heart. O, pray for a time of refreshing from the Lord for restoring mercy, recovering grace. And may God visit Zion and unite his ministers and people in this day of his power and grace. O, that this may prove a cementing work and that your broken heart may be bound up. And may all the ministers of the Lord be aroused, come forth and declare on the Lord's side, and help to build up the broken walls of Jerusalem. May Satan be bound in chains and not suffered to impede this blessed work till all the glorious promises concerning the latter day have their full accomplishment.

O, pray for poor Rhode Island—for our churches and societies, for my family and school. If I know what joy means nowadays, I rejoice in the hope of a revival of religion. And in all the mercy of God to you and yours in recoveries from sickness, safe deliveries, etc., etc.

But I am in haste, with best regards to all, sincerely yours,

Sarah Osborn

P.S. I hope, Sir, our next meeting will be in a better world than this. Thanks be to God, this hope is not quite cut off because Jesus Christ is the same yesterday, today, and forever.

Sarah Osborn to Joseph Fish, December 1764

My dear Reverend and worthy friend,

Forgive that your much desired and refreshing favor of Sept. 15, 1764, has never till now been actually answered. My purposes to do it have been many, but my barren heart would not bring forth matter. I could not compose a letter, nor will you now have anything worth your acceptance. I have, however, indeed sympathized with you in all your trials both as to sickness and other affairs. May the great head of the church appear for your help and for his own cause, his own glory and Zion's good.

I am sorry to hear of further separations.[4] O, that God will graciously rectify all that is amiss and unite his people in peace and love, and indeed cause this land to become Emmanuel's. Blessed be his name, I do hope he has begun and carried on a work of meritorious grace in the year past. However

Satan may have in some things presented himself *also*, God shall overcome at the last.

Thus far I wrote perhaps three months ago, but my barren heart could get no farther, though I frequently purposed to finish. But as God has now in his righteous providence added to my experiences of his adorable sovereignty, boundless love, and faithfulness in visiting my transgressions with a rod and my iniquity with stripes, but his lovingkindness he has not taken away, &c.[5] By his leave and help I'll proceed and tell you, Sir, what God has been doing with and for me.

On February 19, a special messenger came from Little Rest for me.[6] My aged and honored mother then lying, as was supposed, at the point of death, was thought to be expiring the night before. My infirmities and the badness of riding absolutely forbid my going. Close trial, *this*. My *dear* [Henry] went over, and in a few days our servant, &c., &c. And from a kind neighborhood *there* I had letters and intelligence as often as possible.[7] But no hope of life. The illness was a consumption; she was thought to be dying almost every day and then would revive a little. The trembling fears of these anxious days, my worthy friend, I must leave you to guess at while I imagined her almost every minute to be in the agonies of death. And expecting everyone that knocked at the door was come to bring me the decisive news.

Thus I labored till March 21st, and then it reached my ears she died the night before about sunset, and withal that she desired to be brought over to me, which she was on Friday the 22nd, and buried on Saturday from our house. Laid her by my honored father. I hope ere long to lie down by her and sleep in peace (for the worms shan't disturb me) till the morning of a glorious resurrection.

I bless God I am not left to mourn without hope. But, forever blessed be my glorious God, I find there is a something more noble and satisfying to an acquiescence in the divine will, and that the righteous judge of all the earth has done exactly right, and is and will be glorified to eternal ages, than even that hope can give, considered as only standing in relation to me or what I once called mine. But when I hope pardoning grace and mercy is magnified in and through a dear Redeemer's blood, and righteousness and justice equally so, it does indeed add to the consolation. O, the beautiful plan of salvation by Christ. Forever blessed be God that he still permits the vilest of worms to be a witness of this truth and faithfulness: that he does not leave or forsake but is a present help in trouble.

As to outward circumstances, perhaps I was never in a closer hedge than *now*, for greatly through a secret method (as we hope) we found out one that lived with me, who seemed as much attached to my interest and almost as strong as in affection as a mother or sister could be for more than five years, yet by her was consumed, day by day, want of all the comforts we provided for our own family, secretly conveyed away for the support of another: as meat, flour, sugar, butter, cheese, meal, &c., &c., &c., that the demands of the family for about two years and a half were as the house Leach.[8] And how to account for it, I knew not, for I was sure everything was frugally used; however, we sunk three hundred pounds year before last and four hundred pounds last year. And in a word, at the end of harvest as to business last October, before we had anything provided at all for winter, we was one hundred pounds worse than nothing as to debts due to and from us, and no cash at all.

And yet God has brought me cheerfully and comfortably through the winter, and we have not wanted a day. I am still called to stand still and see the salvation of God. But through God's grace *alone* scarce ever in a more comfortable situation, because as Mr. Eliot says, "When God helps, he sees reason hath to work upon more freely when it casts itself upon the faithfulness of God."[9] No thanks to me if I have a moment's rest in God, *I know*. For did he permit, [I in justice would be] my own tormenter.[10] Though I know not for an hour what is before me, I can pull on me the evils of months and years, both as to myself and church of Christ, in one day to the very breaking of my heart. May the praise for every moment's comfort be his own, and for all the hopes I yet have that I shall at last get to heaven by the way of a free pardon through the blood and righteousness of precious, precious Christ. O, shall I yet be a monumental pillar there, to go no more out with multiplied pardons inscribed? Shall I stand a monument of the victories of Christ over sin and Satan?[11] Amen, hallelujah.

1765

Sarah Osborn to Joseph Fish, April 21, 1765[12]

Pray, my candid worthy friend, forgive the badness of ink and everything else in the enclosed poor blotted scrawl. I would have transcribed, but indeed I had not time, and I found if I attempted it I should lose the opportunity of sending. Both ways I was shamed of putting you off so, but you'll forgive.

May the Lord God almighty be with you and all yours and comfort you till he take you with open face to behold his glory. O, my dear friend, let us take courage, and in the strength of Christ march or wade boldly on, since through boundless grace these light afflictions, &c., will work out for us a far more enduring and eternal weight of glory. And let Zion's King and Zion's God do his will in the armies of heaven and amongst us poor inhabitants on his earth. Blessed be his name, his will is holy, and he will glorify himself. Let him overturn and overturn and overturn till he shall reign whose right it is.[13] O, for an acquiescence in all his will. O, pray for me that I may have no will but God's.

In Mr. Thurston's church there is some considerable ingathering, and I hope of such as shall be saved, and if any part of the vineyard flourishes 'tis matter of joy and thanksgiving.[14] We are all one in Christ Jesus. O, that we may be one in the bonds of love. We remain, for ought I know, in our congregation and others, much as we were. Our dear Mr. Vinal is still complaining he labors in vain, &c. But I do hope our dear society is a little quickened and encouraged, waiting upon God.

There is several Ethiopians, thoughtful, who having their liberty to go where they list on Lord's day evenings, have asked liberty to repair to our house for the benefit of family prayer, reading, &c., and I have thought it a duty to encourage them, only charging them never to disobey their masters, &c. The experience of one of them I have sent you, Sir, in his own broken language. I have altered nothing. Please to return it the first opportunity.[15]

Mr. Osborn sends best regards, is somewhat better than he has been, and I am accounted so far as to walk to meeting half the day last Sabbath and was not laid up, but today too lame to walk even about the house much.

Pray, Sir, make my best regards acceptable to your dear spouse and to

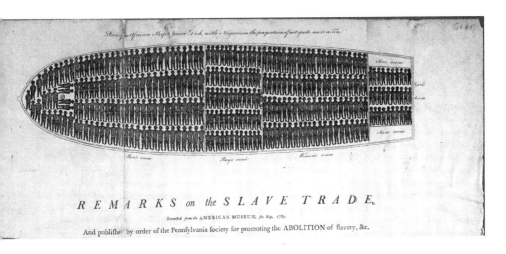

A diagram of the lower deck of a slave ship. Some of the enslaved men and women who attended Osborn's prayer meetings were kidnapped Africans who had endured the Middle Passage. Courtesy of the American Antiquarian Society.

your children when you write. I hope dear Susa will finish her letter now. She also begun long ago. She bears you continually on her heart more than ever since she left you. I thank you, Sir and Madame, for all kindness shewed to her when with you, whom I esteem as mine own life. But she is a naughty girl about writing. But alas, we can no more write when we will than we can pray when we will, and it seems, I might add, nor leave off when we will. I find I am constrained again to beg your patience or forgiveness while I tire it.

And conclude with sincere regards from your affectionate though unworthy friend,

Sarah Osborn

Our deacon Peabody's family well, and all our dear friends except Mr. Vinal. He has some threatening of his fever, but preached today. When you can spare time, Sir, pray write me.

1766

Sarah Osborn to Joseph Fish, June 29, 1766

Dear Sir,

The circumstances of neighbors' daughters pressing in, mentioned in the enclosed, gave me some uneasiness lest at last it should give some occasion of offense.[16] I knew not how to forbid them without proposing something else in the room of it, so I proposed their giving up the Sabbath evening to the black people and I would devote Thursday evening, by God's leave and help, to read to them, &c. O, that God will overrule for his own glory.

I am at present greatly fearing convictions dying away, notwithstanding increasing numbers. O, that God will send by whom he will send. Will it be amiss if my worthy friend, concealing the woman's name, should give the Reverend Mr. Eells, Mr. Hart, or any other of like stamp engaged in the Lord's work, some idea of our circumstances?[17] God does wholly work by instruments, though he is confined to none; the event must be left with him. But methinks when the ear does begin to be open, no stone should be left unturned.

Sabbaths are become melancholy seasons to our church. We are scattered today by our dear pastor's indisposition and expect to be so soon by a journey, and we know not what to do with ourselves between *this* and *that*. O, I hope God will graciously prosper your way towards us. I do long to hear the sound of the gospel from your mouth.[18] The Lord be with you at home and abroad and crown your labors with success.

Dear Sir, you have long waited for a line, but you see I am as unreasonable a talker as I ever was and, as surely, your sincere though unworthy friend,

Sarah Osborn

Sarah Osborn to Joseph Fish, August 9, 1766

My honored, compassionate, and reverend friend,

I thank you for your endearing, strengthening, faithful epistle. O, may God hear and answer you, and for Christ's sake, keep me humble that I sully not all his glory. I sometimes can thank God for the ballast cast into this little vessel to keep it from being puffed over by pride, but I sometimes fear it will sink with the weight.

I know not how to convey to you my trials at this day better than by the enclosed copy, which I beg you, dear Sir, to conceal at present.[19] Keep it safe till Providence calls for it. Maybe it will one day be a vindication of God's honor and glory, or a witness for his worthless worm when she shall be charged as the ringleader of rents or separations, which from the very soul she abhors, but surely stands liable to be charged with, to the lasting reproach of Zion's cause, if she cannot be favored with assistance from the standing ministry and our own denomination. For thus the hearts of poor creatures will cling to those that are ready to appear for their help, and 'tis probable they will follow them. I think I am fully determined not to run this plague by inviting Baptist ministers, nor will I grieve my dear pastor since he tells me he disapproves. The Lord look upon my affliction and . . . .[20]

Look with pity upon poor Uriah in the forefront of the battle all withdrawing from—but a pleasing thought stops me for a moment: we trust God received Uriah's soul when the archers had done their worst—yea, see your weakling friend stand trembling for the ark and dreading the giving a presumptuous touch, dreading to desert the cause of Zion's King.[21] Sure none but such as knows what such labyrinths mean, can know how to pity. The pressure is so great that I have lost six whole nights' sleep out of eleven without so much as one wink, a seventh slept but one hour, and the last but from two, till between four and five o'clock. Fever increases and flesh begins to waste. And except God appears for my help, I fear reason will go next.

O, pray for me and for us all, for it is more than midnight with our church and congregation. Our dear pastor's indisposition increases, and we are scattered—a killing alienation of affection on both sides. The distinguishing badge is awfully lost, a stupefaction and insensibility of our critical melancholy situation has seized us.[22] We doze, just wake enough to fret and lull again. And 'tis dark enough now to be near the dawn of day, but a righteous, sovereign God will be just forever if he never suffer it to dawn.

Yet let me hope in his mercy, and may we be enabled to follow on to know the Lord, till we do see him going forth prepared as the morning, one of dear Mr. Buell's texts.[23] God is preparing his way by giving the listening ear; here is work enough for ministers now. O, that God will spirit his servant to come forth. Mr. Buell was so pressed: we gave him no rest night or day. He preached twelve sermons in our meetinghouse, twice at Deacon Coggeshall's, twice at our house to our society.[24] Prayed with and talked to my dear children that came to catechizing. I called them together on purpose. And once with the poor blacks who also came together on purpose. We were always thronged wherever he was. I dined with him and spouse abroad once and again. But we are only as poor impotents waiting for divine influence.[25] I can't say I think we are not in good earnest engaged, and yet there is a pressing after means. O, that God will take the work in own hand. My soul, wait thou only upon God; he will in his own time. O, that all my expectations may be from him. I have had two precious letters from Mr. Buell, which I have not yet answered. He condescends to ask a correspondence and promises to be honest enough to tell me when he is weary of my pen—and maybe he will.

Dear Sir, I wrote the paragraph in your letter relating to the Reverend Mr. Vinal and sent it to him, but as my dear Susa observed, I fear Stonington and Newport will be almost as soon brought together in one mainland as that scheme to be followed.[26] There is so much indisposition and he is so much dispirited, yet I trust God will bring you here: indeed, it would be a deed of charity to the distressed to visit at this time if your own affairs will admit.

My dear Sir, you desire me to give your compliments to Mr. —— and spouse, and say you hope the good lady is with us.[27] Indeed, I believe her heart is sincerely with us, but she is not allowed to be with us in person. Mrs. Hutcherson and the other holy sisters have long been a great eyesore, and now all intercourse is as much as possible cut off: perhaps the reproachful sound of keeping a Negro house is too intolerable to be borne.[28] If you should come here and a favorable word can be safely spoken of your unworthy friend, perhaps it won't be amiss *there*. But the truth is that such a one is not allowed to have one intimate friend in the world. O, the bitters that lurk under the most splendid appearances in this world. The daughter is alike drawed off, but I fear partly through the gaieties of life. Though the same difficulties in part reach her, I still hope the root of the matter is hers.[29]

I think you will not be able to tell me, Sir, that I refreshed you by this letter, but I congratulate you on account of God's goodness to you and my dear Mrs. Noyes. The Lord still go on to bless you and all dear to you. May you, with good old Jacob, rejoice over your Joseph for many years. May he be as a faithful bough, &c.[30] My dear Mr. Osborn is gone in the country for his health. O, bear me upon your heart, for I never needed pity and prayer more than now. Forgive everything amiss; cover all failings with the mantle of love; but O, not so as to withhold reproof if 'tis needful in any instance.

Pray, Sir, write me and accept this from your most obliged and affectionate friend,

Sarah Osborn

My most hearty regards to yourself and dear spouse.

Sarah Osborn to Joseph Fish, August 1766[31]

Dear Sir,

Since I finished my letter I received this answer from my dear Mr. [Vinal]. Verbatim: Dear Madame, I received your letter but am not able to write a proper answer. Your proposal of having proselytizing ministers to assist in carrying on your religion I do by no means approve of: that has a worse tendency than you think, for your zeal for God, if you are not on your guard, will carry you astray. Yours, W. V.[32]

Now, my reverend faithful tried friend, you still see my situation. I assure you there never has been any breach of friendship, and at present I don't purpose to grieve by inviting the disapproved ones. My end in proposing as I did was to bring him, if possible, to propose what method I should take, for I well knew to insist, or desire him constantly to assist, would be an intolerable burden and esteemed as downright cruelty. O, could I but be favored at home I should never ramble abroad. But I have for more than four years entreated such a one, as often as I dared, only to come once and pray with our dear society, and never could obtain by night or by day: only on one season that was set apart by us to implore mercy for a poor creature, delirious and then present with us. He came and made one prayer. And the one I mentioned in my last is all.[33] I say not this to accuse but give it as a reason for my proposal. But I am only barred up and left.

However, my mind is more relieved than it was. When human help fails it is God's time to appear, and I trust he will look upon my affliction, pardon all my sin, and O, may he deal graciously with his servant, and yet refresh his precious soul with renewed communications from himself. "May a view of the endearing glories of Jehovah," as Mr. Buell beautifully expresses, "make his soul all alive for God."[34] And may my zeal for God be ever according to knowledge, and may it never be quenched. O how little have I; how little do I do for my gracious God.

I am once more constrained, my dear Sir, to beg that you don't desire me to deliver any message to Mr. [Vinal], for though there is a peculiar regard for you in his own breast, yet I must have a great regard for but *one*. Jealousy is cruel as the grave, and for that reason I conceal all correspondence with other ministers for some years past as much as I can, for fear of grieving, &c. All these things, dear Sir, I commit to your wisdom and prudence, for if I know myself, I would be tender of him as the apple of my eye. No one here so fully knows my trials but my dear, dear sweet Susa, though all can't be concealed.

Dear Sir, do not decline writing to me, for you see I more than ever need your assistance, and I am persuaded you will pity me though I am unworthy of your regard. Believe me, Sir, I do reluct exceedingly at thus divulging the infirmities of ——, but I want your sympathy and prayer for the shepherd and the sheep.[35] And how can it be except you know our case?

August 11, 1766, Monday morning[36]

I have dismissed the two last Sabbath evenings without prayer and determine to do so till the path of duty appears plain.[37] Thus far it is plain: I read to them, sing with them, talk with them, and request their going to God by secret prayer for converting grace, &c. And thus I determine to go on, God helping me, without turning to the right hand or left, till God appear for his own cause.

Our dear pastor and his eldest daughter quite poorly. No meeting yesterday. The Lord be merciful to us. But forgive your wearisome S. O. for thus intruding upon your time and patience.

August 14, 1766[38]

I have another burden added that is heavier than all the rest, but that I dare not mention just now. The Lord appear for his own cause.

September 13, 1766[39]

Under this pressure, poor Jonah fled, as not knowing how to subsist. The waves, indeed, threatened to swallow up, but blessed be God, the soul was not then dismayed. A watery grave, if God see it best, was no error. That the sea should give up its dead, a sweet support. And Zion's cause could then be left with Zion's God, who stood in no need of me. However, for wise and holy ends, God commanded the wind and the sea and they obeyed, and a gourd was prepared to shelter from the heat: it indeed sprung up in a night but, blessed be God, is not yet withered away but still affords refreshment.[40]

Great kindness from friends, &c., but more substantial joys refreshed the poor pilgrim in a strange land, where God determined the soul to take up with nothing short of himself, and the Comforter came down and caused faith to look above the tops of the mountains and they flowed down at his presence.[41]

O grace, forever to be adored. The Lord yet reigneth. O may my poor soul rejoice and forever be devoted to him.

I am yours,

S. O.

1767

January 11, 1767, Sunday

Thanks be to God that has now granted a whole week's moderate pleasant weather in mercy to the poor and needy, and this day given me an opportunity to wait on him in his house again. Blessed be God for bringing his servant, our pastor, forth and indulging us with such precious truths from John's Second Epistle, first verse: "I rejoiced greatly that I found of thy children walking in truth, as we received a commandment from the Father."[42]

Lord, in mercy grant there may be many such children found in our day. Stir up parents to parental instruction and seal it for Christ's sake. And O, bless the instructions of thy poor worm to this end, and hear prayer, and let there be a godly seed to serve thee. O, let there be a godly seed to serve thee when we, that now live, are sleeping in the dust.

And O my God, direct me how I shall conduct with respect to the poor blacks. O, take this work into thine own hand or it will all come to naught. Some will turn back with the dog to his vomit and become more hardened and profane than ever. Some will run into wild enthusiasm and start out of their proper places to the dishonor of thy great name. O, for divine influence. O come, blessed Spirit, and lead into all truth. I cannot go forth to the work without thee; I don't know what to do; I can do nothing without thee. O, leave me not to my own weakness and folly; I can't do anything without thee. O, permit me to tell thee, I dare not go forth to the work without thee. How can I? Only say, "I will be with thee," and here am I, ready to work till I die, if thou permit.[43]

But O, leave me not. What shall I be myself but a formal, cold, hypocritical wretch if thou dost not warm my heart? Lord, all our pretenses to give or receive instruction will be but a mocking thee, except thou engage our hearts. Then will others say (as one already has, and a professor, too), "It's all a joke; there is no religion in these things."[44]

The Lord vindicate his own cause, and guide and direct all that are engaged in it. O, succeed the deacon's endeavors, if it be thy holy will.[45]

January 12, 1767, Monday

My dear pastor preached from these words, "Whatsoever thy hand finds to do, do it with thy might, for there is no work, nor device, nor knowledge in the grave whither thou goest."[46] The Lord thus enable me to do, for Christ's sake.

And guide me by unerring counsel at all times. O my God, my God, thou seest my plunges. I know not what in the world to do. The blacks decline going to the deacon's. Will cling here except those that draw off to Mr. B., all of which was last night perplexing.[47] Some black boys I sent down to the deacon's, but was afraid they rather went to play. And to add to my perplexity, I was deceived an hour by the glass, which made it after nine before I dismissed.[48] The Lord preserve the honor of his name. I was all faintings and drawing back, till by reading what I wrote from June 9 to 22 last, I revived a little. The Lord strengthen my resolution to serve him and enable me to leave my name and all events with him. O, may I cast my burden upon the Lord.

And do thou sustain me, O thou guide of my youth, that didst prevent a thousand mischiefs my folly would have run into. Now be the staff of my age; now let me lean upon thee for support; now guide all my doubtful ways. O, guide me by thy eye and teach me in the way I should go. Guide me by counsel till thou receive me to glory. Permit me to plead thy promise, and rely on thy promise for this, for Christ's sake, unworthy as I am.[49]

And bow the heart of the Jew at this time, that thine handmaid may receive.[50] Lord, I ask that justice may be done. Hear and answer, if it be thy will.

January 20, 1767, Tuesday morning

Blessed be God that is still gathering precious souls together to hear something serious. Thirty-four young girls together here last evening from the age of eight or nine to twenty. O, that the hand of the Lord might be not only with his dear ministers but with his worthless nothing also, and all his dear children that are engaged in reformation work. O, that God may excite many, as Abner, to arise and endeavor to bring about this whole people to the King of Kings.[51] O, that they may believe and turn to the Lord. O, that the hand of the Lord may be with all who are willing, through grace, to strike in with the motions of the blessed Spirit. Accept our feeble attempts for Jesus's sake; accept us in the Beloved, and protect us from every wile of Satan. O, secure us from the fowler's snare. Blessed be God that he himself has been thus far my protection, my safeguard from error and enthusiasm.

Blessed be God for the impressions he has made on my spirits to keep me in my proper place, and for every regulation he has brought about. The Lord go on to bless and suppress every degree of levity in young ones when going from hence, that none may be offended nor every serious thought quenched in them. O Lord, forgive all thy pure eyes sees amiss for Christ's sake, for we are all pollution.

January 21, 1767, Wednesday morning

Fourteen boys here last evening. The Lord command a blessing. O be not angry and withhold. Withhold not thy blessed Spirit, O God, because of my unworthiness. O, I pray thee for Christ's sake, pardon my iniquity, for it is very great. Lord, in everything I offend, and in all come short of the glory of God. O, let me lay in the dust and bewail it without discouragement. O, clothe me with humility; let me own thy sovereignty and justice. Do what thou wilt with them or with me, but withhold Satan from discouraging me, and help me to fly to the pardoning cleansing blood and perfect, complete righteousness of Christ, and there look up and hope in a triumphing mercy and boundless grace, and rejoice that God is the sovereign—that the Lord God omnipotent reigns and will accomplish all his own purposes after all. The wiles of Satan and my own traitorous lusts shall bow at the presence of Jehovah. O, that thou wouldst rend the heavens and come down and cause every mountain to flow down at thy presence. O come, O come. Let the hand of the Lord be with thy dear ministers and with all that are engaged in reformation work. And O, may many believe of a truth and be turned to the Lord.[52]

I have heard there is three of the little lads that meets privately to pray with each other. The Lord in mercy engage these of a truth for thyself. O, hear their little lispings in prayer. Pour out thy Spirit upon them, a spirit of prayer and supplication.

January 26, 1767, Monday morning

Snow yesterday, and I was poorly and slothful and confused and could not attain to any sweet communion with God in duty all the day, yet in the evening was strong and lively, and I trust God did help me to converse to the edification of the poor dear souls. O Lord, seal instruction. Own thy worthless nothing and the glory shall—it will—be thine, Father, Son, and Holy Ghost forever.

The house was full, no weathers stops them. The Lord bless them.

Lord, teach me what thou wilt have me do. Let me be influenced by divine teaching alone and not by Satan or indwelling corruption. I want none of their influence or teaching. Make me quick to discern what is from thee and what not. And O my God, I pray thee, make this path of duty straight and plain in this matter, and either spirit me to the work and enable me to do it judiciously in such a manner as will stand the test, or else to lay it aside and do nothing at all. O, let it not eat out every duty by night and by day at this rate. I beseech thee, Lord, call off Satan. This must be he that will never let me have rest in thee, if he can any way prevent. I pray thee, let me not please him in this matter, but please thee in all I do. O, I want to please thee, to approve myself to thee, and to have a conscience void of offense towards God and man.

Lord, help me; Lord, help me; be my sure defense now against evil. O, I commit this cause to thee. I would be influenced by thy word. I have chosen it as my rule to walk by. Does it say, "Touch not my anointed and do my prophets no harm"? Amen, Lord, withhold me, by his word, from all Satan's wiles to draw me into a snare on this hand and on the other way. May this word—"if any love father and mother more than me, he is not worthy of me"—deter me from conniving at sin in the nearest and dearest upon earth, and especially in myself.[53] O, may I ever hate myself while I bemoan the sins of others; pursue mine with vengeance and indignation while I pity and pray for others. O Lord, give both them and me the victory through Jesus Christ our Lord.

January 27, 1767, Tuesday morning

O my Lord and my God, appear for my help now as thou hast appeared for my help heretofore. Fain would I raise a tribute of humble praise and thanksgiving for thy condescension and grace to me in the year past, for the Lord himself has vouchsafed to be my safeguard, my protection from error and confusions, amidst the throng he has gathered around me. To thee be all the glory forever.

In July last, the number had amounted to 300 souls, and now the Lord has increased it to 525 that has statedly resorted here, and yet no evil has yet followed. Though my fears and dreads has often been alarmed with respect to Lord's Day evenings, yet all is quiet, and every company more seriously composed and settled in steadily pursuing after knowledge. Blessed be God that indulges me with frequent tidings of blacks and little ones being more concerned and getting alone to pray (Sammy Thurston, Tommy [Pea]body, Billy Gardner, Polly Cahoon).[54]

O, that the Lord in his infinite wisdom will carry on his glorious work in this own gradual way, which he has chosen, and confound all the wisdom of the wise. We have been allotting upon great and extraordinary impressions upon souls here, and by great and extraordinary means, but God will take his own way, and use what clay and spittle he pleases to open blind eyes, and cause the walls to fall by what ram's horns he pleases. Amen. Let the most despised worm upon earth yet be employed for God, that the glory may evidently be his own. O Lord, let not such a crawling creature as this rob thee of thy glory if souls are awakened, brought home, or established in grace. O, God forbid; O, lay me at thy foot ascribing all glory to thee with a "not I, not I," as constant as I breathe: that it is not I, if I labor, but the grace of God in me.[55] And to him be all the glory.

And O, in mercy take every eye from me and fix them on thy glorious self. O, let none sin against thee by robbing thee of thy glory. I can't be a robber of God. O, I hate it; thou knowest I hate it. Lord, crush my pride to death. O, let me never aspire, never be influenced by self-confidence or vainglory, but clothe me with the garments of humility from the crown of my head to the sole of my foot. I fly to the blood of Christ to make atonement for all the pollutions of my holy things. Thou knowest how they are all tainted, though mortals do not. O, freely pardon for Christ's sake alone. I humbly plead a free pardon.

'Tis by this I hope to get to heaven. I have no righteousness to plead. I fly from my scanty polluted rags. I own in everything I offend and, in all, come short of thy glory. I don't plead nothing but a pardon. I fly to the complete righteousness of Christ, and there I will hang and plead for acceptance with God. Lord, this is perfect; this is complete; thy law and justice will own it so. And this is mine: thou didst clothe me with his best robe in the day I returned. Let me wear it day by day and appear lovely in thy sight.

View me, Lord, from head to foot, and see me complete in Christ; view me and smile, my Father; show me thy reconciled face, thy love tokens, thou God of love. Though in myself, I am no more worthy to be called thine, yet by the grace of God I am what I am: thine own adopted child, thy devoted and sworn servant, thy dedicated thing. O, secure thyself of me; love me still against my froward will; subdue me wholly to thyself; make me holy and abide with me forever.

January 28, 1767, Wednesday morning

Blessed be God for the easy circumstances in life he has again brought me into, for my God does supply all my need, blessed be his name, and still enables me to render to others their due. Mr. Breuley paid me twenty pounds.[56]

I thank thee, my God, for this delightful indulgence in thy gracious, all-wise, overruling providence. I will, by the help of thy Spirit and grace, still trust thee and believe the Jew can't resist thee, and thou wilt indulge me, since I come to thee not to gratify my lusts but to help me do justice in return for the comforts of life thine handmaid supplies me with Lord, by grace.[57] Thou knowest I do delight to do justice as well as love and mercy and to walk humbly with my God. O, enlarge my heart to lay myself out for God every way. Let me be upon the stretch now, since I am in the decline of life, finishing the work my God has given me to do. Let my last days be my best days. I bless thee that I shall surely die.

And now I would labor day and night to set my house in order. O, let me have nothing to do but to die when death comes, yet let my locks be growing more and more.[58] And then, if it be thy will, may I do more with my dying breath than in all my life before. My time is in thy hand. I commit it with my precious soul to thee, and bless thee for thy amazing love to me in Christ Jesus.

And I am thine and thou art mine forever,

Sarah Osborn

Thanks be to God, twenty-six boys here last night. The Lord seal instruction and grant them converting grace for Jesus's sake.

January 31, 1767, Saturday morning

O my compassionate, faithful God, now appear for my help, and again repel the fiery darts, red hot from the anvil of hell, that Satan is perpetually throwing in to distress and worry me. O, remember thy gracious promise that no weapon formed against me shall prosper. Thou knowest his malice; thou knowest his hellish policy to prevent any suitable preparation for my holy ordinances. Lord, stop these thieves from robbing of jewels and throwing in rubbish in the room thereof. Stop them from taking my spiritual life away. I have been boasting in thee as my safeguard, my protection. I have said thou wilt be so to my last breath, and now let me not be ashamed of my hope and trust in thee.

But now of thy infinite mercy and unmerited grace, appear and prevent Satan's reviving my grief and embittering my spirit because thy servant refused to protect me.[59] The Lord graciously forgive him, and from my inmost soul enable me to do it. And O, do thou graciously convince him, thy own self, wherein he has failed in part of duty, care, and watchfulness, and furnish him with every ministerial gift and qualification. Lord, defend him against all the wiles of Satan. Lord, defend him against all the efforts of indwelling corruption, natural temper, or whatever may molest him or impede thy own work. Grant him evangelical repentance, strong and lively faith, love, joy and zeal, heart holiness, speedy sanctification, Lord God Almighty, yea, more. A double portion of thy blessed Spirit I humbly beg may rest upon him, and by grace, I will rejoice, and praise thee, and adore thy name, if the work of the Lord may yet prosper in thy servant's hands. And O God, send by whom thou wilt send, and still vouchsafe to be my sure defense from every error, every delusion, every false step. O God, defend me, thy helpless babe, thy weakling. I still humbly possess my name, thou faithful God, that art with every temptation making a way for my escape that I may be able to bear it. Blessed be God for Jesus Christ. Many are the afflictions of the righteous, but for his sake the Lord delivers them out of them all.

But, my soul, dare I assume that character? Yes, through the righteousness of Christ imputed to me, I dare, and will look up and see the salvation of God.

February 3, 1767, Tuesday morning

In reading an abridgement of Dr. Cotton Mather's *Life*, I met with an instructive passage for me, which I record for my reproof, correction, and imitation.[60] The Lord enable me to improve it so, from this moment to the end of my life. O my God, humble me for my sinful practice in all I do. O my defects, O my taints and pollutions, that like dead flies spoils all my ointment.[61]

'Tis said he never corrected any of his children with blows, and never but in case of obstinacy or for something highly criminal. For he looked upon that slavish way of education, which is so commonly practiced in schools and families, by raving at children and beating them for every fault, to be a dreadful judgment of God upon the world and a very abominable practice.[62]

O how long, O God, how long before I obtain wisdom from on high to guide and direct me in this point? O, and be my safeguard. Thou knowest my folly and hastiness of spirit. O protect me, Lord; protect me. I am ashamed of my conduct, Lord; forgive me for Christ's sake.[63] Secure thy own honor, which I have this way exposed, and strengthen me for time to come. O blessed God, with thee all things are possible. Though I have labored many years to overcome this in my natural temper to little purpose, yet thou canst help me. Lord, help me, and let not my conduct be a dreadful judgment upon the world. O, go forth with me this day, or day by day I shall fall.

February 5, 1767, Thursday morning

Twenty-four boys here on Tuesday evening.

Wednesday morning so cold, ink froze. I could not write. A little moderated now, and some snow. The Lord knows what is best. May his name be praised.

And O, may I be stirred up to greater diligence in improving precious time. In reading the life of Dr. Mather, I appear to myself, as indeed I am, a very snail or drone compared with him. Here in the records of one year it appears that he had preached seventy-two public sermons, besides many private ones; in one year, that not a day had passed without some contrivance to do good, nor in which some of his reserves had been dealt out to charitable and pious uses; that in that one year, he had composed and published fourteen books; and that he had kept sixty fasts and twenty-two vigils. And yet notwithstanding his amazing diligence in improving his time, he humbly has filled his diary with continual censures upon himself and his defects. For instance, at the end of one year he writes, "time so misspent as to render it unfit to be called life"; another year he calls, "a year of a forfeited life." On the review of another year, he says, "another year of my sinning against my precious Redeemer; alas, my unfruitfulness." Another year he calls, "a year whiled away in sin and sloth."[64]

O my soul, if this holy man could thus reflect, how ought I to lie in dust and bemoan my unfruitfulness. The Lord pardon me for Christ's sake, and suffer not Satan to take me by the throat; I owe him nothing. And Lord, let him not crush me down by aggravating my deficiencies. I own in everything I offend, and in all come short of the glory of God. I can't fulfill the law, but Jesus has, to a tittle. O, I fly to him; thou hast accepted him. Lord, pardon me; let me escape to heaven by the way of a free pardon, but yet make me holy, too.

February 20, 1767, morning

Blessed be God, thirty-nine children to catechizing, and one person come to talk with me who is under concern for her poor soul.

The Lord grant me wisdom to say the things that are right concerning thee, and O Lord, carry on thy own work in this precious soul. Lord, give her an effectual call now, at the eleventh hour. Blessed God, thou art causing thoughtfulness in old and young, sick and poor, bond and free. O, let it not die away, but perfect thy own work and magnify the riches of thy free distinguishing grace. O, that there may be great admirers of free, rich distinguishing grace here amongst us, the chief of sinners. O thou sovereign God, work and none shall let revive the things that are ready to die in those whom thou hast awakened.

Lord, have mercy in particular on my dear nephew, N. C., and [Sammy] Gibbins, about whom thou didst encourage my poor heart.[65] O Lord, pardon their resisting and quenching thy Holy Spirit, and try them yet again. And O, thou Dove of Heaven, come with irresistible power and make them willing to submit to King Jesus. They never will except thou sweetly constrain them. O, let them be of that happy number that shall be made willing in the day of thy power. O, forever blessed be thy name. Stout as they are, they can't resist thee, nor can my poor Ishmael or grandchild.[66] O, let them yet live before thee, and refresh my dear consort. Lord, pardon and comfort him, and revive my own poor soul for thy mercies' sake, and all that have ever asked a remembrance with me. My dear, dear Susa, Lord, succor, support, and comfort her under all trials and conflicts. Thou knowest her precious soul in adversity. O, bind up her broken heart and give us yet to rejoice together as we have mourned together.

And O Lord, appear for thy church mystical everywhere, and for our own dear church in particular. O, let these dry bones live, and revive the shepherd and the sheep. Bless thy dear servant. Is he not thine, Lord? Thou knowest. I trust he is. O then, dear compassionate Redeemer, turn and look him into an evangelical flow of repentance that shall never be repented of, and arouse him to his work. O, that he might lay himself out with might and main in his great Lord and Master's work. And O, let it yet prosper in his hands, and souls be gathered by him into the fold of Christ. O, yet cause that vine to flourish for thy mercy's sake.

February 21, 1767, Saturday morning

The Lord in mercy bless thy servant and handmaid, and if thou dost admit them into the church, I pray thee, let them be of that number that shall be saved and shall walk circumspectly all their days to the honor and glory of thy sovereign grace.[67] Thou, Lord, dost infallibly know what thou hast done for their souls. O, let them not be deceived, and may thy own children glorify thee in them and rejoice when they see the grace of God in them. Lord, guide me this day.

February 24, 1767, Tuesday morning

Lord provide us wood if it be thy holy will, and command a blessing on my poor endeavors to serve thee. O Lord, overrule for good the numbers that resort here: eighty-four below last Sabbath evening besides our own family, more than a hundred above and below; thirty-three young girls here last night. O my God, appear for my help. Make my heart sincere; make me upright; make me fervent in spirit, serving the Lord and my generation according to his will, and make every path of duty plain before me because of my enemies. O, guide me by thine eye, and let me neither sin against thee nor be distressed with Satan's lies. Lord, O, overrule all I do for thy own glory.

Mr. Elisha Gibbs and wife, and Mrs. Sarah Rossey, stand now propounded for full communion. O, that they may indeed be of such as shall be saved and let such be daily added to thy church. O, yet cause that vine to flourish.

February 25, 1767, Wednesday morning

The Lord in mercy be with our dear society. O, bless every member of it and meet us this evening and engage our prayers for thine own cause. Lord, support and resign thine handmaid; thy sovereign will is now done, and be the widow's God. Lord, comfort her.[68] O, comfort her.

Numbers are still daily increasing: thirty-two boys here last evening and behaved with decency. O God, take the work to thy own hand. My waiting eyes are unto thee. O, command a blessing on my feeble attempts for thine own name's sake, because thou art a sovereign God and will have mercy on whom thou wilt have mercy. Pardon all my sins and suffer them not to stand as a bar to the blessing. O God, be merciful to me a sinner, and bow thy eternal heavens and come down with divine influence upon us all, and upon all this town. O Lord, bow us as one to the scepter of thy grace, and glory shall redound to Father, Son, and Holy Ghost.

Sarah Osborn to Joseph Fish, February 28, 1767

Reverend and worthy Sir,

I hope mine by post to the care of the Reverend Mr. Cole came to hand. Indeed, my dear friends, my heart is very much with you. The Lord support and comfort you. O, blessed be his name that he is a present help in time of trouble. O, may you be able to say, "'Tis good for us that we have been afflicted."[69] O, blessed be God, heaven will make amends for all your sorrows. These are those that come out of great tribulations, and the cup that our heavenly Father gives us, shall we not drink it? Yes, by the help of his Spirit and grace we can do this, but resignation is his gift, and a blessed gift it is, which I hope my worthy friends are in sweet possession of, blessing the God that gave and the God that has taken away. Into his merciful and faithful hands, with my own precious soul I commit you, who loves you a thousand times better than I do or can, and he will comfort you who are as the apple of his eye, who are graven on the palms of his hands.[70]

And now, believing Zion's cause is as dear as ever to my venerable friend, permit me to set myself as a child in the presence of her father to give you the most satisfactory account of my conduct as to religious affairs I am capable. I will begin with the great one respecting the poor blacks on Lord's Day evenings, which above all the rest has been exercising to my mind. And first let me assure you, Sir, it would be the joy of my heart to commit it into superior hands did any arise for their help. My Reverend pastor and brethren are my witnesses that I have earnestly sought—yea, in bitterness of soul—for their assistance and protection. Would gladly be under inspection of a pastor and church, and turn things into a safe channel. O, forever blessed be my gracious God that has himself vouchsafed to be my protection hitherto, by putting his fear into my heart and thereby moving me as far as possible, in this surprising day, to avoid moving beyond my line.[71]

While I was anxiously desirous the poor creatures should be found with some suitable one to pray with them, I was greatly distressed, but as I could not obtain, I have given it up. And they have not had above one made with them, I believe, Sir, since you was here. I only read to them, talk to them, and sing a psalm or hymns with them, and then at eight o'clock dismiss all by name as upon list. They call it school, and I should rather it be called almost anything that is good than meeting, I reluct so much at being thought head of anything that bears that name. Pray, my dear Sir, don't look upon it as a rejecting of your counsel that I have not yet dismissed. It is such a tender point with me while the poor creatures attend with so much decency and quietness. You might almost hear, as we say, the shaking of a leaf when there is more than an hundred under the roof at once. (I mean with the young men's society in the chamber.) For all there was so many, "yet the net was not broken." This has sometimes been a refreshing thought.[72] They cling and beg for the privilege, and no weather this winter stops them from enjoying it. Nor have I been once prevented from attending them.

I know of no one in the town now who is against me. My dear Mrs. Chesebrough and Mrs. Grant have both been to see me and thanked me for persisting steadily in the path of duty against their discouragements. Owned they were at first uneasy but now rejoiced, &c. Wished a blessing. Mr. C[hesebrough] is quite silent.[73] Every intimate brother and friend entreats, and charges me not to dismiss so long as things rest as they are, telling me it would be the worst day's work that ever I did if I should, for God himself has thus employed me. If any disturbance or disorder should arise, either to the breaking of public or family peace, that would immediately make the path of duty plain for dismissing *at once*. But on the contrary, ministers and magistrates send their servants and approve, and masters and mistresses frequently send me presents as tokens of gratitude, express their thanks, speaking of the good effects that, through the blessing of the Lord, it has had upon their servants. And my dear Sir, what shall I do? Did not a Onesimus, a servant, and once a vile one, too, supply the want of a Philemon? Were Philemon present, Onesimus would soon give way.[74]

As to some of the marks of reformation, I am informed are these: from unwillingness to know or learn anything good, they are now intent on learning to read, &c., at home and abroad; some that were unwilling to serve and saucy are become diligent and condescending; some that were guilty of drinking, gaming, swearing, Sabbath breaking, and uncleanness are at present reformed; several couples lately married who had lived together without but could not bear to live in the sin any longer. Two of the women wept night and day. One being asked after marriage if she was easy now, replied: "I am so far easy that I don't live in the sin, but I have a weight of sins upon me that none but the blood of Christ can take away." Some I hear of, that by the families are discovered to be constant in secret prayer.

And these are to me encouraging tokens that bear my spirits up against discouragements that sometimes arise. In December I was affrighted at the

throng and greatly feared that it would indeed be as the river Jordan overflowing all the banks, and was upon the point of dismissing on that account,
and I told Deacon Coggeshall so. He still insisted I ought not to do it. Then
I told him he must help me some way: he must take the overflowings. I would
send them down to him. He consented, and said I might send him some white
boys, too, for they pressed in likewise. The next Lord's Day evening I told
them of it, that the Deacon was as willing to do them good as I, and I would
have all go that could not find comfortable room here. I spoke to the boys, in
particular, and begged them to go once and again, but they kept their places
and would not stir. There was thirty-eight of them, I think. At last I told
them if they would consent to give way to the poor black folk *then,* as they
could come no other night, if they had rather come and see me than go to
play on Tuesday evening, I would devote that to them. Then twenty-six of
them and ten blacks rise cheerfully and went down to the Deacon's, and his
house usually full ever since, but I have seldom less than sixteen or seventeen boys. Still they will come, and on Tuesday evenings upwards of thirty,
almost all weathers, from eight or nine years old to fifteen or sixteen. I don't
pray with these because of those big ones, but Mr. Osborn does. I have heard
of two or three of these meeting privately together to read, pray, and converse, and now I heard last week they are drawing up a little society for
prayer at one of their houses on Thursday night. They don't know I know
anything about it. May God overrule it for good. It is at the house of *church
folks, too.*[75]

As to the young men that did in summer visit us on Tuesday evenings,
and spend the evening in religious exercises, praying in turn, &c., but as soon
as time came to work on evenings in September, that ceased. The boys fills
that vacancy now, and the young men have only the privilege of resting in
our chamber on Sabbath evenings. I have nothing to do with them, only have
the pleasure of getting my candlestick and stool.[76] This convenient, retired
habitation, God gave me in answer to prayer, and as soon as I removed to it,
I solemnly dedicated it with all its conveniencies to his service. And I can't
help rejoicing an opportunity to improve it, so I dare not desire the young
men to remove from hence, as I know not that any one of them has conveniency, and our female society was broke up many years on that very account.

And as they will not invite ministers disapproved, hope their meeting here will be no ways offensive to any.

There is usually thirty-odd young girls every Monday evening, except the weather be excessive bad, and indeed it is surprising to see their constancy through almost all weathers. Yet I know of no extraordinary effects, but *here* they behave quite serious, and passions are sometimes touched, I think. My companies are all volunteers. Our society on Wednesday evenings is, I hope, not on the decline but rather growing.

The children for catechizing on Thursday afternoon hold on with surprising cheerfulness and steadiness, though not so numerous as before winter set in, and for that reason boys and girls come together for the winter on one day only in the week, either Thursday or Saturday as the weather suits. The room is usually full, consisting of all denominations. I have hope that God has awakened some few of the little girls to a concern about their precious souls: some their parents cultivate and are the more careful to send them, too, but I think I did hear the parents of one complained I had spoiled their child, for she did nothing but get alone and read and pray and cry, and they could not divert her all they could do. O, may God perfect this work and preserve the dear lamb from falling back. I don't know who it is, only heard it was among the church folk.[77] Deacon Coggeshall told me this.

As to Friday evening friends, my dear Sir, I by no means set up for their instructor. They come indeed for mutual edification, and sometimes condescend to direct part of conversation to me, and so far I bear a part as to answer, etc., but no other way. They consist of the brethren of our own church or congregation and members of societies either that meet at the Deacon's or our young men—all, I think, except my only one according to the flesh, viz., my own brother's son, Mr. Haggar, who sits under Dr. Stiles—so that these gatherings at our house, Sir, I imagine no way tend to separations, rents, or divisions, but are rather a sweet cementing bond of union that hold us together in this critical day.[78] My dear Mr. Osborn, through infirmity, is unable to go often to the Deacon's on Thursday evenings and is very fond of this Friday night visit.

And they are sweet refreshing evenings, my resting reaping times, and as God has gathered I dare not scatter in anywise. I trust my reasons for encouraging, rather than dispersing, will prevent your thinking me obstinate in a bad sense. I don't reject counsel. Don't let my honored father think I do. The exercises of the evening consist in singing, reading God's word, annotations, other good books, prayer in turn twice, and seven or eight of them are most excellent men in prayer. I believe few private Christians exceed them. O, I trust our God is in the midst of us, does pour out on us a spirit of prayer and supplication. Some of our female society went frequently to the other female society on Friday evenings, and as a means gradually to draw them off without objecting against their going (because they are Baptist), I have invited such here with consent of the brethren, and we were twenty in number last evening.[79]

March 4, 1767, Wednesday morning

On Monday evening, there were here thirty-three young girls. Polly Evans was amongst them, which caused me to speak to her and other fatherless ones in particular, and bring them in prayer, and their passions were moved in general, even to sobbing.[80] The Lord seal instruction, though from the most unworthy in the world, and all the glory shall be thine forever.

Last evening, thirty-four boys. O Lord, thou hast surely given the hearing ear; I pray thee, give the understanding heart, that these may rise and close with Christ on his own terms, and do worthily for God when I am dead and gone. O, let all those shoals which thou hast gathered be caught in the gospel net. O, direct thy ministers on which side the ship to put down the net for a draught. O, let there be an ingathering of souls here and all over this land. Let it all become Emmanuel's.

March 6, 1767, Friday morning

My treacherous memory let slip yesterday morning that it was my birthday, but O my God, since thou hast brought me to end my fifty-third year in peace, let my fifty-fourth, if I live, be devoted to thee. Blessed be thy name for covenant love and for thy fullness to this very day, that hitherto the Lord has helped me. O, pardon the millions of sins of three and fifty years. I fly to the blood of Christ to wash them all away. Let them be done away and now purified by that blood that cleanseth from all sin. O God, make me holy now; engage my soul all for thee now. Now make me love thee more and love thee better.

And appear for thy servant [Joseph] Clark and make the path of duty plain to him. (A supposition that he was inclined to the Baptist; caused neglect and coldness.)[81] O, that he may be tenderly treated, that God would subdue that corrupt nature—that prejudice that is the undoing of everything in ministerial work—that thy servant [Vinal] may be disposed to see him kindly, to bear with the infirmities of the weak and comfort the feebleminded. O Lord, make the path of duty plain because of his enemies.

Sarah Osborn to Joseph Fish, March 7, 1767

One branch of my exercise with children, servants, and other young ones, I observe, Sir, you are silent about, viz., singing. And lest you should fear I now assumed that as part of divine worship, permit me how to tell you how it came to pass. When the Reverend Mr. Fish was in town the time before this last, many years ago, I heard him reasoning with Deacon Peabody in a beautiful, striking, convincing manner on the duty of singing in families in family worship, and among other arguments, showed how it took off that natural bashfulness and backwardness that usually attend young ones in congregations, and by this means they were trained up for public praise.

With this view in part, we have ever since practiced singing in our family, in school, and I always did with my boarders night and morning, at times of their particular instruction. And with the same views, Sir, I have continued the practice that I may, by the blessing of God on my weak endeavors, train up all for public praise with whom I am concerned. Am I right, or do I err at this day? Because there is so many, the servants appear to me no otherwise now than children, though for stature men and women.

But I come now to answer your tender, important enquiry after approving of part of my work, viz., have you strength, ability, and time consistent with other duties to fill a larger sphere by attending the various exercises of other meetings, in close succession, too? A Moses may undertake more (from a tender concern of the people, too) than his shoulders was able to bear. Jethro's advice was seasonable, &c.[82]

As to strength, Sir, it is evident I gain by spending. God will in no wise suffer me to be a loser by his service. I am much confirmed in my belief of that word, "He that will lose his life for thy sake shall save it," as I used to lie by, unable to sit up, usually one day in the week for years together.[83] I have lain by but one this winter and comparatively know nothing about weariness to what I did when I had so great a school and ten or more children in family to attend. I always feel stronger when my companies break up than when they come in. And blessed be God, I have a good appetite and sleep well, except any great pressure is on my spirits.

As to my ability, I can only say I trust Christ's strength is made perfect in my weakness, and at some times I am made to glory even in my infirmities, that the power of Christ may rest upon me, and rejoice that I am nothing and can do nothing without him. And yet, though I was born as the wild ass's colt and fit for nothing till brought to by sovereign grace, as Mr. Henry notes, yet he can serve himself of me and glorify himself in me and in his own way, too, however mysterious to me and all around me.[84] He has chosen the weak things of this world, &c.[85]

As to time consistent with other duties, it is most true, dear Sir, that I am called by the providence of God as well as by his word to be a redeemer of time, precious time, and I'll tell my worthy friend how I do. My waking time, except unwell or weary with exercise, generally presents the dawning of the day. Mr. Osborn rises while it is still dark, can just see to dress, &c., from which time I am alone as to any interruption. For driven by infirmity and want of conveniency, I was about a dozen years ago constrained to make my bed my closet, curtains drawn except just to let in light. And have ever since found it, of all other places, most convenient for me. I do not lie there but turn upon my knees, my stomach supported with bolster and pillows, and I am thus secured from the inclemency of all seasons and from all interruptions from family affairs. There I read and write almost everything of a religious nature: thus I redeem an hour or two without which I must *starve*.

And this privilege, blessed be God, I have been enabled to hold through all my schemes of business, sickness in family only excepted. I never go down till breakfast is near ready. After breakfast, family worship, then giving some orders as to family affairs, I apply to my school, to which you know.

Sir, a kind Providence has limited my earning time for support of my family and, if in this time I educate the children of poor neighbors who gladly pay me in washing, ironing, mending, and making, I imagine it is the same thing as if I did it with my own hands. I think my family does not suffer through my neglect, though doubtless if I had a full purse and nothing to do but look after them, some things might be done with more exactness than now. But every dear friend is ready to set a stitch or help me in anywise, and all is well here. My fragments in the intervals, I pick up for keeping and drawing out accounts, &c., or whatever my hand finds to do besides refreshing the body.

Thursday afternoon and evening after catechizing, except the last Thursday in every month on which our society meets, is reserved for transient visitors, business, or whatever Providence allots. Saturday afternoon is my dear Miss Susa's particular time to visit me. Saturday evening is reserved to ourselves. Now, Sir, if my evenings were not thus improved, I could not spend them to such advantage that I know of any other way. For indeed I am not so capable, after the exercises of the day, of working at my needle. That overpowers me vastly more than the duties I am engaged in. I could not retire the evening, as I could not endure cold, &c. Nor can I long attain to close, fixed meditation or any clearness of thought, though I labor ever so much for it. I am at that season much more capable of social duties than any other. These seem then to refresh, recruit, and enliven my exhausted spirits. And companies, most of them, are dismissed at nine o'clock, that I have some time left for other duties. My family has the advantage of all these seasons except the Wednesday evenings *only*. Mr. Osborn withdraws a little while before they break up, I mean from the young ones. And if my evenings were not thus filled up, they doubtless would be with transient visitors, and some chat less to edification, especially in this *critical day*, would break in, which by this means is *shut out*, that at present I do acquiesce in my time thus being taken up.

Thus, Sir, I have given you the best account of my time I am capable of, but after all, while others are wondering, I find cause daily to bemoan before

God the misspence of precious time and often appear to myself a very loiterer, a very snail, a lump of deformity. I fly with haste from all my poor, narrow, scanty performances, and bless God I have a perfect righteousness to plead, and hope to escape to heaven after all by the way of a free pardon.

I would now humbly beg leave just to speak a word as to Jethro's advice, which I own to be very good. But here, my dear Sir, lies the difference: Moses was head of the people, and so had it in his power to comply with Jethro's advice by appointing elders, &c., to take part with him. But I am rather as a sergeant that has a great work assigned him, and however unworthy and unequal he may think himself, and others may think him, and however ardently he may wish it was in superior hands or that his master would at least help him, yet if he declines, he dares not tell him, "Well, if you won't do it yourself, it shall go undone, for I will not." But rather, tries to do what he can till God, in his providence, point out a way for it to be better done. And God did uphold Moses till he pointed out that way of relief he could comply with.[86]

Don't think me obstinate, Sir, if I don't know how to let go these shoals of fish, to which my dear Susa compares them, that we hope God has gathered, ready to be caught in the gospel net, whenever it shall please him to shew his dear ministers on which side the ship to let it down for a draught.[87] The harvest truly appears to be plenteous, but the laborers are few. O, that the Lord of the harvest may send forth laborers into his harvest and crown their labors with success.

Last summer all things were new and astonishing to me, and I appeared to myself upon the very brink of ruin, except I had speedy help. But infinite wisdom has hitherto prevented all the mischiefs I feared and brought things into so regular a way, that I am quietly waiting his time and trust he will glorify himself in his own way and time.

But O, forgive me—forgive me for thus intruding upon your patience, first in writing and now by my prolixity. Cover my failings with the mantle of love. Please to let me know by post, if no other way presents, whether all comes safe to hand. I have dealings with the Mumfords. Don't be afraid of the charge, Sir. Mr. Mumford is always handsome to me, and indeed, never charges me anything. But if he does, all is well.[88]

Make my sincere regards acceptable to dear Mrs. Fish, Mrs. Noyes, and all other enquiring friends, in which Mr. Osborn and Mrs. Susa joins me, too. Pray, Sir, accept yourself from your sincere though unworthy friend,

S. Osborn

P. S. I long to hear how you all do.

March 10, 1767, Tuesday morning

I yesterday wrote in behalf of poor Joseph Clark to move one to compassionate him, and withal to signify how I had conducted by resolving not to invite the disapproved.[89] What distressing scenes I passed through for want of help, signified the bitterness my soul was in when I wrote. I blessed God, who himself had vouchsafed to be my protection and hitherto prevented all the evils. I feared standing alone, afraid of being unestablishment in principles, yet not one had attempted to shake so much as by a single word. And rejoiced from my inmost soul I was dedicated to God an infant to own and stand by my baptismal covenant, and determine, God helping me, to walk orderly and inoffensively towards that pastor and church to which I have given myself by the will of God. And verily believed the young man was no ways biased by the Baptist: that 'tis a settled point amongst our youth not to meddle with those things in conversation, and I never heard they did, &c. The Lord accompany this with his blessing and convince of the necessity of compassionating the distressed.

And will God in mercy bless thy dear young handmaids here last evening, thirty-seven in number. O Lord, pour out grace and increase their graces. O, my waiting eyes are unto thee. Thou knowest without thee, I can do nothing. O Lord, take the work into thine own hand, for Christ's sake. Do, or we shall be ashamed and confounded at the last. O, thou triumphant, sovereign God that will have mercy because thou wilt have mercy, let my unworthiness be no bar.

March 17, 1767, Tuesday morning

Yesterday produced things variable in the morning. Engaged in writing to strengthen one against whom Satan is raging. The Lord build him up in defiance of Satan's rage.

In the day I heard of efforts of Satan to break up my evening exercise, which has been so refreshing to me. The Lord put his hook in his nose and turn him back by the way he came.[90] Thou knowest his rage and blasphemy against thee. O Lord, defeat him; suffer him not to gain his point, I pray thee.

And now, Lord, give me the wisdom of the serpent with the innocency of the dove.[91] This is a critical affair. I need thy protection or I shall offend or grieve some of thine. And protect me, keep me within the bounds of moderation, I pray thee. Subdue my temper; suffer that not to rise while I am bemoaning the bitterness of others. O God, calm my own [bitterness], and let a spirit of meekness and humility run through all my conduct towards every individual soul in this and all other affairs.

I went with Mrs. Anthony to see Mrs. Champlin yesterday. The Deacon, his spouse, and Mrs. Challenor there. It was in the main a pleasant afternoon, only the above affair pestered me when I came home. No less than forty-three young girls came in the evening, an unusual solemnity amongst them. I read Mr. Buell's narrative about the surprising week of God's marvelous work in Easthampton.[92] God granted me assistance, I trust, in talking to them and praying with them, but I felt not that humbling sense I wanted. O, let me not mock thee, my gracious God; let me not mock thee, but pour out on us a spirit of prayer and supplication.[93]

March 18, 1767, Wednesday morning

This is the memorable day on which our sovereign, King George the Third, gave his royal assent to the repeal of the Stamp Act.[94] O, that liberty —precious liberty—were used for the glory of God. Let not this day be remembered only by way of reveling instead of thanksgiving. Lord, bring me and others of thy children to rejoice in the liberty wherewith Christ has made us free, and let us not be again entangled with the yoke of bondage. Lord, free us yet more from the bondage of sin. And Satan, relieve my mind of the tossings thou knowest.

O, that thou wouldst grant me all the resolution I need in every point, O thou glorious God. Thou seest the snares that Satan is laying to entangle me on every side. I pray, I beseech thee, deliver my soul. Grant me integrity and uprightness of soul. Grant me wisdom from on high, freedom from all covetousness and hypocrisy. O, grant me engagement of heart, and overrule in all the affairs thou knowest, and let my mourning yet be turned into joy and good be brought out of all the evils that have perplexed me, for the honor of thy own glorious name.

Lord, I would not be anxious about anything that can befall me or any dear to me. Personally considered, I would not fear my character, or fear those that can only kill the body, and after that have no more that they can do. But I fear in anywise to dishonor thy glorious names.

March 25, 1767, Wednesday morning

O my Lord, O my Lord, my sun and shield, enlighten and defend me. O, see thy helpless babe surrounded by snares on the right hand and left. Fain would I go straight, but alas, standest the triple alliance between the world, the flesh, and the devil. How can I stand except thou art on my side? Are not plots devised in hell and weapons stored there? Are not snares perpetually laid at my feet? Thou knowest I would be all for thee and aim at thy glory in all I do.

And I pray, God, dash everything I touch that does not tend to thy glory and the advancement of thy kingdom and its precious souls. O, let none of Satan's devices or weapons prosper. Make him know I have an almighty friend, a reconciled God and Father who will not leave me to the dreaded sin of bringing dishonor to his glorious name. O my strength, my rock, my sure defense, let me come up out of the wilderness leaning on thee. I have no might nor strength; I fly to thee for protection. Thou hast brought me to hoary hairs and hast said, "I will never leave thee nor forsake thee."[95] Help me to rest secure in thee and believe thou wilt grant me wisdom to direct in all my affairs. O pray, do. For Christ's sake, do. Thou see my weakness and folly, how I may be betrayed by the very least trifle; yea, for a copper I may risk thy glory. O, prevent my doing it though I should gain the world or, on the contrary, starve for want. O, raise me above the world and its petty trifles. O, thou that hast upheld me on the verge of ruin all my days, guard every step I take now, that I may not at last plunge to the dishonor of thy name. O, either glorify thyself in me or hide me in the grave. Let me not live to see the dreaded day when thou, and thy ways, shall be reproved on my account, because of my sin and folly. Look upon the affliction of thine handmaid, and let thy grace be sufficient for me. And here I am then. Will I be devoted to thee all the days of life, devoid of selfish views?

And as to what has now offended, I determine *as things now appear* not to run any more in this matter. (I sold so many cookies on Tuesday evenings after the exercise was over.)[96] I have, to the taking, ten tuppence one evening; three[97] the next; and four the last, the profit of which is three. But I will venture no further, lest a suspicion that I invite for worldly gain should mar the whole.[98] My God, thou knowest all my wants; supply them to the honor of thy name, and I will by grace rejoice and bless thee. And O, stop those in their mad career who dare swear, quarrel, and blaspheme thy name.

And, in mercy, grant true grace and humility to the poor child puffed up with self-conceit. O, let him not think himself something, when indeed he is nothing. O, show him the plague of his own heart, and seal instruction to the whole, for Jesus Christ's sake alone. Own and bless my poor endeavors, and bless the youth, and bless the poor blacks, and be with thy dear handmaids this night. Lord, sanctify.

March 27, 1767, Friday morning

Eternal praises to thee, thy best of beings, for thy goodness and mercy to me yesterday. Thou didst grant me kind access in the morning; thou didst draw my faith and confidence, and enable me by prayer to make known my requests for the supplies thou knowest we wanted; was enabled to cast care upon God and rest and trust in him. Blessed be God that makes me believe for my mercies before I had them, and that makes them as Isaac's when they come, as I see them coming from the hand of a prayer-hearing God that delights in filling the mouth of faith with a blessing.[99]

Thanks be to God as to temporals. We received cash to complete the payment of our rent, had a supply of sugar and tea from our landlord beside, and a present of a pistareen from Mrs. Champlain to purchase sugar for the society.[100]

And God granted me sweet access to the throne of grace; and all his dear handmaids that attempted to pray, and it was a precious season. Bless the Lord, O my soul, and forget not all his benefits.

March 28, 1767, Saturday

Blessed be God that again excited a patient reliance on him for wood under prospect of delay or disappointment from man. And God sent us an ample supply and caused me to rejoice in his goodness.

And O, that my harp might not be again unstrung. Lord, teach me to praise thee with all my heart and soul and strength and mind.

O blessed God, let not Satan gain his end by damping or discouraging those who meet on Friday evenings. Lord, enlarge our hearts; O enlarge our hearts and make us willing to be extensively useful, to encourage, to strengthen the feebleminded, to cheer the dejected, to bear with the bashful and help inquiring souls. O my God, defeat Satan in his attempt to break us, and prevent his taking advantage and discouraging any by what was read on predestination and reprobation.[101]

Lord, thou art infinitely just in choosing whom thou wilt, and infinitely just in withholding that grace thou art no ways bound to give. O, convince dear inquiring souls of thy justice, adorable sovereignty, and fullness of thy love and grace in Christ Jesus, and let them be encouraged thereby to cast themselves at the foot of divine sovereignty, and there plead for mercy for Christ's sake alone, and rejoice that God is absolutely free and sovereign.

O, defeat Satan; defeat Satan and calm my fears, I pray thee, and raise

my soul to thee this day. Bring my dear Susa, if it be thy will, and give us a
favorable opportunity, and let it be for our mutual edification.

April 1, 1767, Wednesday morning

O most glorious God, thou seest my discouragements now. And sure I
am, all my hopes will be dashed and come to nothing at all, and every soul of
those who meet at my house, will be yet more hardened through the deceit-
fulness of sin, except thou dost in infinite mercy take hold of their hearts by
thy Spirit. I am but adding to their condemnation by all that I am doing,
making hard hearts harder and blind eyes blinder. O Lord, thou knowest
they will, through the malice of Satan, dishonor thee more than ever; be
more averse to the ways and people of God than ever, except thou dost turn
them about by thy almighty power.

Lord, is thy hand shortened that it cannot save? Are even the children of
Rhode Island out of the reach of sovereign grace? Shall goodly appearances
all wear off and come to naught? O, that thou wouldst rend the heavens and
come down, and cause all mountains to flow down at thy presence. Thou
canst stop these poor young creatures in their mad career. Thou canst rescue
them out of the paw of the lion of hell. O my Lord, O thou self-sufficient
being, I know thou standest in need of none of us. Thou canst be forever
happy, and thy throne forever spotless, though all Rhode Island should
perish. And I will, by grace, justify thee till I die, though no one soul should
ever be profited by me, though I should labor in vain all my days, as even thy
ministers have done.[102]

But O my God, if it may consist with thy sovereign pleasure, triumph over
all my unworthiness and make me an instrument for good to these precious
souls. O my God, will not glory redound to Father, Son, and Holy Ghost if
they are created anew in Christ Jesus? If thine image is restored, will they not
be precious in thy sight? O thou who was ever self-moved to pity man, pity
Rhode Island now. I have nothing to plead but our misery, our poverty, our
undone state without thy sovereign grace and mercy. O, thou who spared not
thine own son but freely delivered him up for sinners, have mercy on us—

mercy, Lord; free mercy—and for Christ's sake alone. For 'tis a faithful saying, and worthy of all acceptation, that Christ Jesus died to save sinners, of whom we are chief: hardened sinners, gospel despisers, gospel impenitents, old and young, rich and poor, bond and free, Sabbath breakers, and whatnot. Lord, what not.

O, let pure mercy plead on our behalf. Justice is satisfied in the death of thy only beloved Son, for the chief of sinners. Now let mercy plead, because of the full atonement. O, because of the full atonement, let me lift up my guilty head and plead for sovereign mercy and boundless grace. O, why should we go on hardened? Why should we go on impenitent and unreclaimed? O my God, I would humbly bless thee that some are, I trust, brought home. O, let it be as an earnest of a plentiful harvest. O, get to thyself a great name here. Angels will rejoice and adore, and saints will bless thee.

And thou hast said, "Whoso offereth praise, glorifieth me."[103]

April 7, 1767, Tuesday morning

Lord, help me; help me to do thy will with cheerfulness and delight, and to wait thy will with cheerfulness and delight, too. He that believes, makes not haste. Lord, increase my faith, my hope, my trust and confidence in thee. Let me not be thus all diffidence and distrust, nor let me dare to limit the Holy One. Who am I that I should sit down discouraged because I have read and talked a little, and yet don't see poor souls earnestly inquiring what shall they do to be saved? Have worthy, faithful, painful, and laborious ministers toiled all the night and caught nothing?[104] Shall I murmur and hang down my hands?[105]

No, no. Let me, God helping me, go steadily on in the path of duty, and rejoice that the Lord reigns and the world is in his hands forever, and be thankful for that consideration many are brought to, that listening ear and hope in God, that in his own time he will give the understanding heart.[106]

Blessed be God for that solemnity that evidently appeared both on Sabbath night and last evening; also on the first. We were so crowded there was scarce room to stir hand or foot. And last evening, forty-five young ones. O, that God will help them to choose whom they will serve; O, that God will graciously inspire them with a Joshua's resolution.[107] O, that they may make their happy, their early choice of Father, Son, and Holy Ghost now. O, help them to hold on their way now, if it be thy sovereign pleasure.

And come with the lads this evening. O, overrule all for thine own honor and glory.

April 8, 1767, Wednesday morning

Thanks be to God for good news from a far country, that I am informed by the Reverend Mr. Buell of the rise and progress of the Lord's work in many places. O, that it may be genuine and sincere. Last evening, Deacon Coggeshall, Mr. Isaacs, and Mr. Hix of Long Island was here. The young men came down out of the chamber, the black people out of the kitchen, and the room was filled. Deacon Coggeshall prayed twice and conversed. We sung twice.

O, that it may not be all lip service. O Lord, reach our hearts or glory will never redound to thee but all will perish with a lie in their right hand.

> O, for one powerful glance,
> Dear savior, from thy face
> These rebel hearts no more withstands
> But sinks beneath thy grace (Watts).[108]

O let dear Easthampton, Stonington, New York, Rhode Island—yea, all our land—become Emmanuel's. O, when shall it once be? O God, our waiting, longing eyes are unto thee. Let not our expectations fail; accomplish thy own promises concerning the latter-day glory when Zion shall be for a name and a praise in all the earth; when the Redeemer shall see of the travail of his soul, and be satisfied; when saints and angels shall rejoice, bow, and adore because sinners repent and turn to the Lord. O, turn thou us, and we shall be turned for thou.[109]

Is not the Lord our God? Assist us this day. Bring thy handmaids this evening and prepare us all for the public fast we are called to on the morrow. O, let it be a day of deep humiliation, deep confession and contrition, evangelical repentance, O Christ. Thy servant, Lord, strengthen him to wrestle and cause us all to unite, and hear our united cries for the outpourings of thy

Spirit. O, for a plentiful effusion. O, thou glorious intercessor at the Father's right hand, present our cause; undertake for us; let *everlasting* unmerited love and mercy move towards us. *O Holy God—Father, Son, and Spirit—say,* "Let us make these creatures anew in Christ Jesus."[110] It is done: we shall bear thy image and glorify thee forever, and the cries of all thy worshipping assemblies.[111]

April 10, 1767, Friday morning

Blessed be God, after lying down to rest awhile, God graciously re-cruited my strength and spirits, and kindly carried me to his house and in a degree engaged me there.

Brought twenty-four of us together in the afternoon, and graciously engaged my whole soul in prayer, and my dear Susa, Mrs. Henshaw, and Mrs. Peabody.[112] Our grand plea was for heart holiness, the subduing of our lusts and corruptions, for strength from heaven to be and do what God would have us be and do, and for the outpourings of God's Spirit upon all the world, especially about our isle, our town, our churches, our ministers, our minister, church, and congregation, our society, all dear to us by the bonds of nature, grace, and friendship.

The Lord hear and answer for the Redeemer's sake. Blessed be thy name that when thou comest to build up Zion, thou regardest prayer.

April 11, 1767, Saturday morning

The Lord be praised, yesterday in the forenoon I was in a degree in possession of my dear Redeemer's legacy: that peace, peace, which the world cannot give; neither can it take away. But in the afternoon, more tossed; in the evening, there was the number, if I mistake not, of thirty-five men, women, and children.

There was some strangers, and some other little circumstances took off the sweetness of the evening. The Lord forbid Satan should ever gain his point to disconcert, discourage, and break up that exercise that has been so sweet and refreshing to our poor souls.

April 14, 1767, Tuesday morning

Lord God Almighty, I pray thee, teach me duty. O, be my safeguard on my right hand and on my left. Lord, as ever didst thou teach me duty, I pray teach me now.

Shall I pray with the company of young women now that there is, I know not who, strangers continually, and the number so great, forty-nine last evening? Is it not a work of supererogation more than the Lord my God requires of me in my private capacity? Does it not savor so much of a Pharisaical, ostentatious show as to be offensive to thee and to thy servants and children? Will it not cause the enemy to blaspheme and many to stumble? Dost thou withhold freedom of access to convince me of duty, to convince me that I ought not to pray in so public a manner, as it were, in the corner of the street to be seen, &c.?[113]

Then thy will be done. Determine me for thine own honor and glory, and I ask no more. O, bring down the balance for thy own honor and glory, and I will, by grace, go in that path of duty thou shalt make straight and plain to me, be it what it will. O thou guide of my youth, thou staff of my age, thou determiner of my doubtful ways, thou that hast upheld me upon a precipice all my days—keep me from falling on the right hand or left. Thou seest the pit is continually opened by Satan for me, by some means, to plunge into; the snares are spread for my feet; plots are designed in hell to accomplish my overthrow, and weapons are formed against me whether I proceed or withdraw. And what can I do except thou appear and make every path of duty plain to my own soul?

Man can't determine *me*. Man's opinion *alone* shan't content me for or against. 'Tis thy approbation I want. Let me but please God, and 'tis enough. Only let me know, by thy Spirit accompanying thy word, that I do so, and it is enough. Here I am; let not Satan tyrannize over me with his taunts and lies that I want to draw back from thy work, for by grace I will pursue it till I die. Only show me what thou wilt have me to do; set home some good word of thine to clear my way. I pray thee, thou knowest my weakness and folly and everything in me that opposeth thee and thy ways. Let omnipotence subdue; let infinite grace triumph over all; and say, with the power of a God, "*I will* this soul shall be *all, all* for me and none other, *now* and forever."[114] Amen, Amen, Hallelujah.

Let *all, all* that opposes, *all, all* that loves thee not, be anathema Maranatha. O, let it be accursed with a bitter curse; let the curse of Meroz light on all in me that opposes my coming forth to the work and help of the Lord, so far as he requires by his word and providence, and will by his Spirit and grace assist.[115] Lord, here I am; serve thyself of me to my latest breath. Let this poor wild ass's colt, this ram's horn, this clay and spittle, be improved for thy honor and glory as long as she lives.[116] Behold the dedicated thing, and accept me in the Beloved amidst all my imperfections that taint and pollute thy holy things. I fly to the full atonement.

And I am thine forever,

Sarah Osborn

April 23, 1767, Thursday

It has pleased a righteous, holy, and good God to lay his hand on me from Saturday afternoon so that I have been unable to attend on either the black people, young women, lads, or school. Have kept my chamber from Lord's Day, attended with an ague in my face, much swollen, a fever, &c.

And blessed be God, a sweet content, a resigned will, some little glimpse of hope that I might possibly go home. A sweet satisfaction in a settled belief, that, however poor, short-sighted, ignorant mortals may, through frailty, have set their eyes too much on a worthless worm, God stands in no need of me. Whatever infinite love and wisdom has devised, infinite power will effect. I cannot cause a single word to do good to anyone, but God can do his own work by whom he will. Blessed be his name that it does not depend on so slender a thing as my poor, feeble frame. Though that were dissolved, the Lord yet lives. Let this comfort me and all my dear friends, and resign us all to thy holy will.

But, Lord, if it be thy pleasure to continue me in life, thy will be done. Then, even here, do what thou wilt with me. Only glorify thyself in me; only make the path of duty plain to me, and I will by grace go into it. Whether thou dost call me to active or passive obedience, thy will be done. If the Lord hath no more for me to do, who am I that I should contend? If it be his pleasure, I should yet serve him and my generation, according to his will. He will bring me back, restore health of body and fortitude of mind *against Satan's wiles*. He will kindle my love to him and his cause afresh. He will, of his own sovereign grace, grant me warmer zeal to run the heavenly road. For he is a faithful God, and he will clothe me with that humility that shall, of his infinite grace, prevent his work being marred in my worthless hands. And glory shall redound to Father, Son, and Holy Ghost, through the thanksgivings of many, on my behalf.

And now I determine, by grace, cheerfully to go forth to the work God shall call me to this day and evening, so far as God, with strength of body and assistance of his Spirit, permit. Thou knowest that without thee I can do nothing. Only help me, Lord, and I will never flinch nor fear but work till I die.

Blessed be God for sweet renewals of covenants yesterday. And I am thine forever,

Sarah Osborn

April 23, 1767, Wednesday[117]

Blessed be God for preserving the life of dear little Albro Anthony on Friday last, when their heavy oxcart wheel, as I am told, went over his bowels.[118] A surprising providence. Did omnipotence itself strengthen the feeble frame to bear the weighty crush? Or was its guardian angel employed to bear up the wheel that, with its weight and grind, it might not force its bowels out?—which, reason tells us, it must have done had not almighty power been engaged for its preservation.

O, may its spared life be devoted to God, and laws of gratitude be written on its dear parents' hearts. O, may they and all theirs be forever thine.

April 24, 1767, Friday morning

Yesterday Mr. Anthony brought the dear preserved lamb to school.

When I see it [him], it overcame me with joy and thankfulness, which I constrained to vent by tears before I could speak.

Mr. Anthony assured me he was just by the cart himself, and see the wheel bring down the child flat on its back with the head under the cart and feet out, and the wheel went over its belly. And yet there is not the least sign of a bruise nor a bit of skin broke, only at first looked red and a little mark of the wheel.

Many are ready to think that in his fright he was mistaken, that it was impossible for the child to have remained so little hurt if the wheel had gone over it thus. When his little daughter Nabby heard the doctor thus scrupling, she said to her father afterward, "Why won't the doctor believe, Daddy? Is anything impossible with God? Could not God as easily kept *that* wheel from hurting Albro as he could keep the fire from hurting the three men that were cast into the furnace?"

The Lord be praised for what he is doing for that dear creature's soul; and complete his own work, for Jesus's sake.

God mercifully supported me yesterday and through the evening. I dared not omit praying. Deacon Coggeshall had bid me omit it if I dared, and I dared not.[119]

God granted me utterance, yet not that deep humble sense I wanted. O my Christ, crush my pride to death. Is anything too hard for God? Shall this monster live—live to rob thee of thy glory, live to puff up a worm? O, let me die rather than that should live, and do slay it for the honor of thy glorious name. 'Tis thine enemy; it strikes at thy crown and dignity; it robs thee of all thy glory as far as in its power. Here's the traitor, Lord, that says it will not have thee to reign; would not have thee to be all, and I, nothing at all. [Satan] usurps the throne and would sway the scepter in my soul, but thou art my king. Come forth in terrible majesty and flaming vengeance; come, justice, come slay this foe. Wilt thou suffer it to live? O, be jealous for thy own honor and glory, thy own crown and dignity. Wilt thou give up thy right and thy glory to this cursed foe? Shall this rise when anything is done by thee alone, and cry, "It is I"? O come omnipotence, come truth and faithfulness, and espouse thine own cause and secure the poor soul that delights to be nothing, that God may be all.

My dear Redeemer, I renewedly commit my precious jewel to thee; keep it from the ravages of this cruel monster; keep it also a chaste virgin whom thou hast espoused in lovingkindness and tender mercy. O thou, under whose wings I am come to trust, be my protection. Is anything too hard for God? Thou canst subdue my pride, and clothe me with humility as with a garment. O, do it; O, do it. Say me not, "nay." Give me my petition and my request. Consider what I ask and for whose end I ask—'tis thy own glory—and in whose name I ask. It is in thy own son's name I come. Permit me to plead the promise, "Ask, &c., it shall be given you; seek and ye shall find."[120] And wilt thou not give me the good things I ask? Say to me, "Go in peace"; "The Lord hath heard thy voice, thy supplication."[121]

And for this I will call upon thee as long as I live, and I will be for thee and none other as long as I live, for I am thine forever. And humility shall be improved for God as long as I live, and in humility I will adore to all eternity the glorious Three One. There I will fall prostrate, cast down my crown, and cry, "Not unto me, not unto me, but to thee be glory forever and ever."[122]

O grace! grace! that did from eternity choose me. Lord, why me? Why am I here?

May 12, 1767, Tuesday morning

Last evening forty-four young women here; the evening to me was solemn. I humbly hope God assisted me of a truth in reading and conversing, and God gave me the most engagedness of soul in prayer that I have yet had. Was enabled in some degree, as Abraham, to draw nigh and plead again and again.[123] O, that God will answer for Christ's sake alone.

I had given my word to offer [charity], and it appeared duty to fulfill when God, by an unexpected providence, had put it in my hands to do it. And also to pay my friend something when I could, appeared an act of gratitude and justice, and I believed God would provide for my necessities, and so he will.[124]

Though now thou art so rescuing me in withdrawing folly, had I not done it, thou wouldst have fastened covetousness and injustice upon me with a bitterness not to have been borne. O, my unwearied foe. Blessed be God, the time is drawing on when the accuser of the brethren shall be cast down forever, that now accuses day and night, whether I turn to the right hand or the left. The Lord rebuke thee, Satan.

Saturday, May 16, 1767

O thou glorious God, that know the secret turnings and windings of the heart and the secret malice and subtlety of Satan and sin, his accursed spawn. Appear for the help of thy servants and protect them.[125] Lord, preserve them, for thy own honor's sake, from turning back to the world. O, either spirit them to go on as they did before, or else, I pray thee, point out to them something more for thine honor and their eternal good.

And as for me, I go whither I may, only be with me thyself, whether in company or alone, and I ask no more. I am indeed unworthy of the privilege thou didst grant me. I would humbly bless thee for what I have enjoyed, and submit to be deprived if that is the most agreeable to thy will. But O, glorify thyself in us all, I beseech thee.

Sarah Osborn to Joseph Fish, May 26, 1767

My most sincerely honored and venerable friend,

Permit me once more to speak to you by my dear Mrs. Champlain, though utterly unworthy your regard, and accept ten thousand thanks for your care and tender regard for me, from the first day you honored me with your friendship to this day.

And permit me to beg you will not cast me off, however you may think my conduct, in any respect, has rendered me yet more unworthy of further notice. But in imitation of your great Lord and Master, let your goodness triumph over all my provocations. Forever blessed be his name.

I do long for a word from you to know how you do, and your dear family, since a holy and faithful covenant-keeping God has laid his afflicting hand on you.[126] I trust you have received my poor scrawls on that subject, once and again. O, may God be ever your support and comfort. Through divine goodness, we are all as usual, and religious affairs in much the same situation as mentioned in the packet that accompanies this.[127] I add no more but sincere regards to you and spouse and all dear to you, in which Mr. Osborn and our dear Susa joins me. I am yours in simplicity,

Sarah Osborn

P.S. I hope dear Mrs. Champlain is serious by inquiring what she shall do to be saved. I would just add, Sir, that what you wrote me was blessed to clear my way for communion, and a transcript of some passages has cleared the way for other dear friends alike perplexed, and that I believe none that you conversed with has gone to the Baptists on Lord's days since you was here. By this, Sir, you may know our ears are open to affectionate spiritual reasonings, and we are not bent upon rents, &c. From November last, those things that caused our Sabbath day's conflicts has been withheld, and we have been fed with sweet wholesome delicious food.[128] Have gone in and out and have found pastors. The Lord be praised.

Agreeable to your request, Sir, I have invited [the Reverend Vinal] again and again and assure you, that as I know not of any anger on either side, I had no backwardness to *that*, but what proceeded from fear of his taking it hard, being urged.[129] I also [presumed] he would not comply, and thought other requests as in temporals, etc.[130] I have since had several obliging friendly tokens of regard. I have not had the pleasure of speaking one single word to him, since I see you, anywhere but at meeting. While I had my feet and could go to him, these things made no difficulty with me, nor would they now if I could go to him: 'tis that that makes it differ from former times, together with my situation as to religious affairs.

But I accuse not; I condemn not. All mysteries will be unfolded in God's time.

I am yours as before,

S.O.

Sarah Osborn to Joseph Fish, September 15, 1767

Reverend and Dear Sir,

Yours of June 17 is before me, for which I am greatly obliged, and should have answered sooner but have been late various ways. And now my dull sight, confused head, and barren heart forbids your having anything worth your acceptance or reading. I think sometimes it is but wasting my dear friend's precious time to crowd my epistles upon him. But I say no more on this head, as my worthy friend has often assured me they are welcome to him, poor as they are.

O, that God will enable me to write as a Christian, and not always in a complaining strain. 'Tis a mercy I am out of hell and not entirely given up to restless sin and raging hell, my constant combatants as I go from stage to stage and from scene to scene.[131] I have sometimes a little space to breathe, stand, and wonder and adore the grace that has hitherto protected me from direful plunges to the dishonor of God and wounding my profession. For sure there never was any creature upheld upon precipices as I have been all my days: a mere babe, a weakling, a foolish presumptuous creature that would rush as the horse into battle at any time, did not God prevent.[132] "But I withheld thee," says God.[133]

O, blessed be his name for restraints. Sure this one thing I have desired: viz., that he will keep me from the evil to the honor of his glorious name. And who can tell but I shall yet be preserved from falling? Jesus is able to keep me from falling here, as well as to present me faultless at last through his own blood and righteousness imputed to me. After all the insults of my cruel foes that my turn is coming, and I shall yet fall, O, that the Lord himself will still vouchsafe to be my protection, and let me stand a witness to his truth and faithfulness to my latest breath. I know the Lord hath no need of me and can vindicate his own honor though I should fall.

O, yet may I stand, and never harden sinners against him and his ways, nor make the hearts of the righteous sad. Let me not add to the many wounds Christ has received in the house of his friends. The Lord knows I choose anything rather than this. O, pray for me that God will uphold me by his grace till he take me beyond the reach of sin and Satan to the full enjoyment of himself, to all eternity.

My fears are alarmed, for I perceive waxing cold in myself and others more than in months past. The quickening, convincing influences of God's Spirit are more withdrawn. And he is just, though he should cease to strive anymore. I hear few inquiring the way to Zion with solicitude—the poor little ones for catechizing are most of them tired, and what few does come, seem to be rather burdened than pleased. There is no gaining their attention as heretofore. The lads for Tuesday evenings dropped off, all to three or four, and as they fail, so my bodily strength and spirits fail, too. Some attend on Sabbath evenings still, here and at the deacon's, too. As to black people, I think they hold out much the same: there is usually about seventy and they esteem it a privilege, and I am spirited and gain strength in trying to instruct them. And likewise on Monday evenings there is generally upwards of fifty young girls. They also attend with decency, but I hear of no effect. Yet I feel disposed to go steadily on and leave accounts with God. Wednesday evening and Friday evening are still attended, and are through mercy sometimes refreshing.

Our dear Mr. Vinal has for many months preached in a most lovely, engaging strain and, I am informed, is more excellent in conversation than ever, but I am unable to visit him and so lack the benefit as to myself. But I submit: God knows what is best for me. I rejoice that others reap it. I sent your message, dear Sir, and heard Mr. Vinal wrote you.

Don't let my worthy and highly esteemed friend think it was out of a slight to him that I did not subscribe, for I could not, after many reasonings with myself, [believe it to be] consistent with that serious declaration I had often made in conversation with Mr. Thurston and his people, that I did wish from the bottom of my heart that the controversy betwixt us might cease, and we ministers and people might join heart and hand in the great work of winning souls to Jesus Christ.[134] As Deacon Peabody has subscribed, I hope to read them. I believe, Sir, this was the case with other dear friends as well as myself, or Newport would have had more.

Our connections with Mr. Thurston and his people are much broken off, and I have never heard him or any other Baptist since I see you, Sir, because I would neither grieve nor offend. But as to their inoffensive behavior towards us, they have a testimony in my conscience as well as many others that none but themselves can erase. I speak in point of proselytizing, for they have generously avoided the least attempt to shake my principles so much as by a single word. And I do believe those that declare the same things to me, though for other reasons they have drawn off from us to them. It was not their seeking.

Forgive me, Sir, for enlarging on this head. I mean not to grieve you, but knowing those same have been so much suspected, raised in me a generous pity while I wrote and made me say more than I designed. May the Lord command a blessing on all your labors. This I sincerely wish, and hope to gain light by the present performance.

Pray, Sir, favor me with a line when you have leisure. Make my best regards acceptable to spouse and children. My dear Susa joins me. Mr. Osborn is in the country for his health or would be kindly remembered. I add no more but the most sincere, cordial, sympathizing love.

And wishing the best of blessings and comforts may rest on you, I am, dear Sir, your unworthy friend,

S. Osborn

Sarah Osborn to Joseph Fish, December 7, 1767

My Reverend and Honored friend,

This comes to return my grateful thanks for your last as for all other favors. O, may I be led by it to trust in God, in whom alone is protection and safety.

Things wear a very different aspect from what they did this time twelve-month. Then there was such pressing after anything that would speak a serious word that I feared Jordan overflowing, &c. But now not, so there is evidently a decline in every shape. The young lads and children for catechizing is almost done. All is a weariness, a task and burden, rather than delight to them, a few excepted. The young women *almost* [full] on Monday nights, and black people on Lord's day evening pretty full yet, and some, I hope, steady. Societies yet kept up, but alas, our coldness.

O, that God will appear for his honor's sake, and through all these waxings and wanings, keep us by his almighty power through faith unto salvation.

Dear Sir, I had wrote you sooner but have diverse ways been led, and indeed, at first was big with hopes of seeing you. But man appoints and God disappoints. O, may you be enabled to kiss the dear hand that has struck repeated blows. Blessed be God that all things shall work together for good to those that love him. Is not God answering prayer when he is weaning us from all the world, taking by degrees one thing after another on which our affections and dependence for comfort was placed, that all may center freely on himself alone? The Lord Almighty comfort you, and all yours, in himself, and enable you and your dear child to drink of the cup he has given you, to drink and to see 'tis the cup his own infinite wisdom and goodness has mixed, and there is not a drop of poison in it or anything to hurt you, since the Lord yet lives to make up in himself, his Christ, and his grace, the loss of all these things here below.

My dear Sir, forgive my freedom. You know these things better than I do, yet while I long to comfort you, I know not how any other way but by turning your eye on that God who is above, a present help in time of trouble. He wounds, and he heals the wounds he has in love and faithfulness made. O, may it be his sovereign pleasure, for the dear Redeemer's sake, to take you and yours nigh himself now, lay you in his bosom where you may rest your weary heads and drink large draughts of that fountain of consolation opened in Christ Jesus.[135] As the streams of earthly comfort are cut off or dry away, blessed be God for past comfort in the streams. While many parents have been called to sorrow in life on account of their children's vicious lives, and to sorrow at death without hope (a bitter sorrow this, except God graciously condescends to bow his will to his adorable sovereignty and justice, and quiet the soul in himself), you have enjoyed the greatest blessings in life, and have hope in death, too. O, blessed be God that goodness and mercy has thus followed you and is still following you in the surviving streams, that through surprising grace you and yours may sing in the midst of judgment and say, "surely goodness and mercy has and shall follow us all our days, and we shall all dwell together in the house of the Lord forever" when our earthly tabernacle is dissolved.[136] For blessed be God, we must die, too. And we have a house not made with hands, eternal in the heavens, *eternal in the heavens*. O death, where is thy sting? O grave, where is thy victory? Thanks be to God who giveth us the victory through our Lord Jesus Christ.

The repeat was undesigned, but I would not erase it. The Lord comfort you, my dear, dear friend.

I must now conclude with a thousand loves to the whole family. I am, dear Sir, your sincere though unworthy friend,

Sarah Osborn

P.S. I can hear of no one of your books in town, Sir, and shall be obliged if you please to favor me with the reading of one. All friends are well and desire proper regards that know of my writing, Mr. Osborn in particular. I hope our dear Susa will write herself: if she does not, it is not want of love, but want of time, that will prevent.

1768

Sarah Osborn to Joseph Fish, April 28, 1768

Reverend and Dear Sir,

As to the state of religious affairs, it is a time of killing deadness, sore trials, temptations, and conflicts. There seems to be no standing for our feet, a snare on every side. Yet when we say they slip, God's mercy holds them up. O, that we may take your sweet refreshing counsel in your last to me, Sir, since God has hitherto preserved us (bless him), and take courage.

Our dear Susa extremely, extremely exercised with trials, yet she shines steadily against all opposition from earth or hell. As for me, the Lord only knows what I am. I somehow trudge on in what appears to be the path of duty, yet strangely stupid, almost a fool, and I don't know that I do any good. Yet dare not draw back, however weak, till I am convinced 'tis duty to do so. For amidst all our seeming and real insensibility, by some secret power astonishing to me, the companies God in his providence has gathered are held together with seriousness and decency while together. And I know of no bad behavior coming or going, or scandalous outbreakings at any time.

There is seldom less than sixty or seventy odd blacks on Lord's day evening, three of which now stand propounded for baptism and full communion: one in the sister church and two in ours. And a desirable member of our female society, a white person, is also propounded in *ours*.[137] These, I trust, are subjects of sovereign grace, but that God alone infallibly knows. Yet the ground of hope is matter of thoughtfulness. On Monday evenings, thirty, forty, or fifty are frequently the number of young girls that seriously attend to reading, &c. On Tuesday evenings, some lads, and they stick close to the deacon's on Sabbath evenings. Our society holds steadily on, and I hope not quite without some tokens of the divine presence. Friday evenings, conference prayers, &c., still refreshing sometimes. I trust we can say, "did not our hearts burn," &c.[138] Catechizing remains, though not so full, but to my

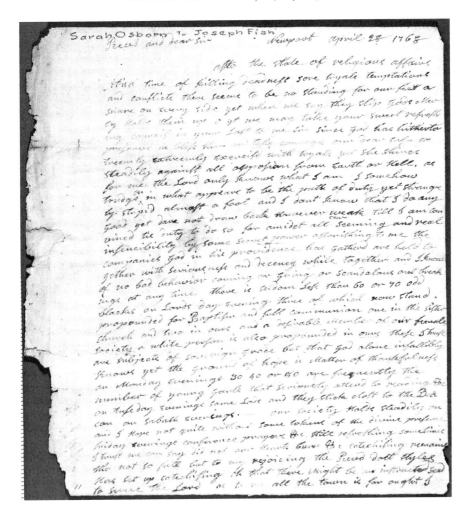

A letter from Sarah Osborn to Joseph Fish, April 28, 1768.
Courtesy of the American Antiquarian Society.

rejoicing, the Reverend Dr. Stiles has set up catechizing. O, that there might
be an instructor sent to serve the Lord.

As to me, all the town is, for ought I know, hushed as to any objections.
What the event of my poor endeavors will finally be is with God alone to
determine. But O, that I could be thankful as I ought for his protection
hitherto in such a critical situation, while I am left to stand *alone* or fall as
I will: *one* seeming not to care for my soul.[139] Lord, lay not this sin to the

charge of him whom I have besought in anguish of soul, but forgive for
Christ's sake.

I add no more but sincere regards to your whole self, dear Mrs. Noyes
and all there, the Reverend Mr. Eels, his spouse and family. And beg to hear
from you, dear Sir, as soon as you can, for it is a great comfort to me. And I
am in simplicity, however unworthy, your affectionate, sympathizing friend.
I hope you received mine on the last sore bereavement, or you must think I
disregard you. Mr. Osborn is poorly but joins me in due regards to all,

Sarah Osborn

Wednesday morning, July 27, 1768

I have been very poorly and unfit for every duty. The disorder by which
I first lost my strength followed me closely yesterday, and I began to be
cheered with hopes of taking my farewell to life. But may the will of God
be done. If I cannot be active, then let me be passive. Passive obedience will
be accepted through Jesus Christ my Lord. And if I cannot do his will, let me
suffer it patiently and, all the days of my appointed time, wait till my great
change come.

Only, my Lord and my God, keep me from the evil and sanctify me
through the truth. Thy word is true. This petition is, and has been, upon file.
It is put up in the name of Jesus. It is before thee. It is put in, and was put in
when kind access was granted, when the golden scepter was held out. I drew
nigh and touched the top, and thou didst tell me, "Whatsoever I ask in Jesus's
name shall be granted."[140] I cannot withdraw this petition, Lord. Encourage
me to renew it and believe that, as sure as the enemies of Esther and her
people were slain and caused to perish, so sure will Jesus yet triumph over
my cruel foes: over my pride, which, as Haman, would bear down all before
it; over my unbelief, sloth, sullen ill nature, ingratitude, covetousness; and all
that now press me down and vaunt over me, as a poor, despicable outcast, for
whom, against the prevalency of these daring lusts, there is no help in God
while I live in this world.[141]

O God, confound their rage; turn Satan back by the way he came; put a
bridle in his nose. Thou knowest his blasphemy and rage against thee. Let

him not prevail against me. I have trusted in thee, and thou hast said, "I shall never be confounded."[142] Overrule for thine own glory all that concerns me and mine, and all thine. Make sin and Satan know we have an almighty friend who will not deliver us up to the will of our enemies, but as he has glorified his name in us, he will yet glorify it.

TEN

Great Influence, 1769–1774

SARAH OSBORN'S RELIGIOUS MEETINGS *dwindled during the late 1760s, but slaves and free blacks continued to gather with her on Sunday evenings, and the members of her church often came to her house seeking spiritual guidance. As the Reverend Vinal slipped further into alcoholism, her house became the spiritual center of the congregation, an alternate church.*

In 1768 the First Church of Christ Committee (the governing body of the church) voted to dismiss Vinal on the grounds of his "excessive use of spirituous liquors." Frustrated by his drunkenness, his combativeness, and his frequent absences from the pulpit on Sundays, they began searching for a new pastor. Vinal offered a contrite confession, but after the church refused to reinstate him, he retaliated by falsely accusing several members of the church—including Osborn, Susanna Anthony, and Deacon Coggeshall—of drunkenness, telling lies, and other "immoralities." Although a church council made up of local ministers finally cleared the First Church of any wrongdoing in 1774, Osborn was profoundly hurt by Vinal's betrayal.

A parade of ministerial candidates visited Newport in 1769 and 1770, often preaching at Osborn's house. Impressed by the Reverend Samuel Hopkins, Osborn fervently urged the men of the First Church to support his candidacy, and when they initially voted against him, she insisted that they reconsider. Though she could not vote because of her gender, she was a power to be reckoned with in her church—and she knew it. According to the Reverend Ezra Stiles, Hopkins owed his 1770 election to her and the "Sorority" (the women's society), who were "violently engaged and had great Influence."[1]

Osborn's close friendship with Hopkins was one of the greatest joys of her later life. They had tea together every Saturday afternoon, and as her health declined he became the leader of her meetings for slaves and free blacks. Until moving to Newport he seems to have assumed that slavery was God's will, but after meeting large numbers of slaves at Osborn's house and listening to their tragic stories of captivity, he became an antislavery activist. Though the timing is unclear, Osborn, too, eventually became convinced that slavery should be abolished. In a poem that she composed sometime during the last twenty or twenty-five years of her life, she denounced slavery as a "horrid sin."[2] In 1784, her church voted that "the slave trade, and the slavery of the Africans, as it has taken place among us, is a gross violation of the righteousness and benevolence which are so much inculcated in the Gospel. And therefore we will not tolerate it in this church."[3]

1769

Sarah Osborn to Mary Noyes, July 9, 1769

My most worthy, esteemed, and dearly beloved friend,

I received your dear letter per Major Otis, and as a friend was born for the day of adversity, it is no wonder at all you are at a loss to know the reason of my silence.[4] In the first place, suffer me to assure my dear friend, it was not owing to want of sympathy with you. I have indeed bore you on my heart, and purposed writing from week to week almost ever since I received yours, though I have never known of one direct opportunity till it was passed, except Mrs. Hubbard, I heard of the night before she went, but then omitted, partly because I had heard you was *then* at Stonington (which I now suppose was a mistake).[5] And indeed, a severe headache prevented me . . . when I first received yours last September.[6] Indeed, my spirits was so overborne, thoughts and time swallowed up, on account of the grievous affair relating to our poor Mr. Vinal and church—the particulars of which I can't revive, it cuts too close—that I could not attend to anything else hardly at all, except the other constant engagements that are daily upon me. And the pain in my eyes and loss of sight has more unfitted me for corresponding with my friends than all the other infirmities I have had to grapple with all my life.

It's now impossible with me to be, as usual, a redeemer of time. In the evening I can neither see to read or write at all. I am entirely cut off, and if I presume and venture to strain my sight a little, the pain is so great in my eyes, and my head so amazed and confused that I am utterly unfitted for all duties, secret and social, perhaps for a week or two. These, my dear, with the constant engagements I am under, which fill up almost every moment, are the true reasons of my omitting to write to so dear a friend. You will be satisfied with them, since 'tis the Lord's will that it should be.

Cease not to write to me, and as God gives leave, I'll gladly answer you. If you are forced to wait long, exercise a generous candor, as I know you do, and believe me still your *own*. Give my kind leave to your dear sister, darling though unknown, and tell her I hope for an everlasting acquaintance with her.[7] And through the all-atoning blood and righteousness of Christ, I hope to be the first of you all that shall arrive in heaven. O, for an actual as well as habitual preparation for the great and solemn change, when I shall pass out of time into eternity: see our Emmanuel in all his glory, in all his mediatorial fullness; yes, one God in three persons. And while God is all and all, thoughts of an interview with dear departed friends who are sleeping in Jesus— thoughts of bidding you that survive me a hearty welcome to our Father's house, where there is rich entertainments, fullness of joy, rivers of pleasure, no sinning or sorrowing, no more parting to all eternity—'tis sometimes refreshing to me. O my dear soul, though God for wise and holy ends has seen meet to strip you of such near and dear enjoyments, he will not strip you of himself. He hath said, "He will never leave you nor forsake thee."[8] He will be better than them all, and though you miss the prudent counsel of your honored and dear mother Noyes, God has promised to guide you by his counsel and afterward receive you to glory.[9] My friend, there is no repairing these breaches but God himself.

But I must cease. The Lord himself comfort you.

As to us, God has dealt very mercifully with us in affording us the pious and faithful labors of Mr. Judson and Austin.[10] O, that God will give the increase. I have abundant reason to be thankful, for they have both indulged us with their presence and assistance. The Lord reward them. They have preached repeatedly at our house to our private praying societies, male and female, and to the black people and the children. I hope and trust they will both be burning and shining lights wherever God is pleased to place them. Who God has chosen for us is yet amongst the secrets of his will. O, that it may be a man after his own heart.[11]

Accept this with a thousand thanks from your affectionate,

Sarah Osborn

Dear friends desire kind love and are well. Only our dear Susa is in a low state of health and is now at Stonington. Mr. Osborn desires his kind love to you. Kiss your dear babes for me. I long to see both you and them.

Sarah Osborn to Samuel Hopkins, July 29, 1769

Reverend Sir,

I have observed you are tenderly concerned about the education of children and imagine it will be agreeable to you, Sir, to visit them, instruct and pray with them. This day will not admit, but if you are disposed, God willing, on Saturday next in the afternoon at 2 or 3 o'clock to bestow your labor upon them, or on Thursday, if that will suit you best, I will give them notice what time you appoint.

God has also providentially gathered a number of black people, servants and free, that have usually attended on reading, catechizing, &c., on Sabbath evenings at our house who will also be glad of your instructions. Sir, if you incline to visit them on Sunday evening next, please to let us know your pleasure and, if God permit, I will give them notice tomorrow night.

Be assured, Sir, your coming to our house as oft as you are disposed and have leisure, with company or without, will be esteemed a favor and privilege by me. However, the perplexities of my mind may at some times shut up my mouth. It is sweet to me to roll the work of instruction into the hands of the ministry and set down and be instructed myself, who need it as much as any that come about me. O, that God will teach us all to profit. I could gladly have borne a part in conversation last evening if I had not feared being immodestly forward.

The question proposed gave a spring to my spirits and some degree of joy that the riches of sovereign grace shall be magnified, and the triumphs of the great Redeemer shown, in the great day when all the secret sins that now break the poor believer's heart shall be laid open before men and angels.

But time and paper fails. I am yours, &c.,

S. O.

Since I mentioned Thursday, I bethought myself that I believe that will interfere with Doctor Stiles's catechizings, for all sorts and sects, almost promiscuously, come to our house.[12] They all have a welcome there. If Friday evenings is consistent with your circumstances, Sir, I shall rejoice in your constant visits at that time especially, perhaps so the meeting will be upheld.

Pray, Sir, continue to pray for me that I may be strengthened and directed so to conduct the little while I have to live, that God may be glorified in and by me. And may you have many for your crown of rejoicing in the great day.[13]

Sarah Osborn to Samuel Hopkins, August 26, 1769

Reverend and dear Sir,

As I think the general run of my discourse with you has been in the discouraging line, as I have been no way desirous you should be deceived or think of us as better than we are, &c., I begin to think it is time to be a little on my guard on the other hand, lest I should be instrumental of giving you a meaner opinion of the dear people God in his providence is now calling you to settle with than *they, as to Man,* deserve.

I know Rhode Island has long been a stench in the nostrils of the serious in the other colonies, and I always esteemed it a great unhappiness that our dear Mr. ——— was prepossessed with the thought that we were some of the most abandoned of the human race, from whom nothing but the vilest treatment was to be expected, &c.[14] And as to the general run, the prejudice was so deeply fixed that no kindness shown could remove it to the last. It was *not* the case with me, for I was favored: endearing things passed between us. But still it was matter of grief that many others, who I thought would be indeed kind and friendly to a minister if only a candid, prudent condescension was shown (without giving up *one jot or tittle of truth*), they might be won and perhaps brought to receive truth in the love of it, too, if corruption was not irritated by needless reflections arising from the prejudices at first imbibed, which too oft made things uncomfortable. (What I have said relating to Mr. ——, Sir, you will wisely conceal. The bonds of friendship ever did constrain me to be close-mouthed, and I choose it still.)[15]

In a word, Sir, I do hope and believe you will meet with nothing worse in this people than what the dear and faithful ministers of Jesus Christ are to expect in what part of the vineyard soever they settle. The unregenerate part will fret against the truth and the ministers that faithfully preach it. There is no doubt of that, be it where it will. They can't love it and delight in it till God change the heart. We know, therefore, this is to be expected, and in this no new thing will happen to you, Sir. And if in this way ye suffer for Christ's sake, happy are ye. As to those that in a judgment of charity we suppose to be real Christians, 'tis probable there is no church and congregation on earth that everyone in it can see eye to eye on all points. Neither can they in ours.

As to the plan on which you settle, in which I greatly rejoice (relating to infants' discipline, &c.), it's no wonder if the alteration makes some restless at first, that by calm reasoning will be won by and by.[16] Indeed, by what I can learn, the compliance is far beyond expectation, and as to what little brunt has been, it's better now than hereafter. Again, it is not at all unlikely that through misunderstanding, things said either in public or private (as in the instance the other day) may be misinterpreted, and yet without any mischievous design, but quite the reverse.

All these things, I suppose, is the common lot of every dear minister of the gospel. And without doubt, Sir, you will find some less candid, generous, and ministerial than others, but there is a considerable number that do delight in showing kindness to their ministers according to their ability. Our dear Mr. Clap and Helyer freely acknowledged this.[17] Upon the whole, I do hope and believe you will find the people as kind as any elsewhere. The briars and thorns are not to be escaped in this life.

As to Christian friends, I hope you will have comfort in them who are already here as well as those that may come to or with you, who I hope we shall receive with pleasure among us. I think I know of none that will stand in more need of your candor and forbearance, a covering of imperfections with the mantle of love, &c., than the unworthy one now writing, who in everything offends and in all comes short of the glory of God, and is a very lump of deficiency towards her friends. Yet by the grace of God is what she is, and don't designedly offend or grieve.

But I must intrude no further on your patience. May God in mercy comfort you and glorify the riches of sovereign grace in making you a blessing to us and we to you, and grant you many seals of your ministry *here*, if it be his holy will for your crown of rejoicing in the great day.

Pray, Sir, make my kind regards acceptable to your dear spouse, family, and friends though unknown. I wish you a prosperous journey and safe return to us by the will of God, and O, may you come in the fullness of the blessing of the gospel of peace.

I am, Sir, yours in simplicity,

Sarah Osborn

P.S. Pray, pray for me and for us.

Sarah Osborn to Samuel Hopkins, October 26, 1769

This, with hearty regards, comes to welcome you home and your daughter to Newport.[18] I have indeed longed to see and hear you again; knew not that you was come till Wednesday evening; had invited you here yesterday but concluded you was engaged with the company that came with you; shall be glad to wait on you this evening or tomorrow afternoon if it suits your conveniency, and on Monday evening, Tuesday evening, Wednesday evening, Thursday afternoon or evening, Friday evening, Saturday afternoon, just as often as you please, Sir, *every week*, whether in a private or public way as you think proper to appoint, with particular companies or promiscuous. Our house is open and, God helping us, our hearts shall be open and rejoice to receive you and the word of God spoken by you, whether public or private.

Do, my dear Sir, accept this general invitation and conduct according to it *every week* with the *greatest freedom*, just as the path of duty opens to you from time to time. Only as to what is public, or requires others knowing it, please to let me have timely notice to acquaint, prepare, &c. This can be done perhaps at any time by a line per little Isaac.[19] Now do, Sir, let this general invitation be so accepted as to excuse all my want of presence of mind, quickness of thought, or any damps I may have on my spirits (but I have a thousand), lest I should be too *bold, forward,* and encroaching in particular invitations, which oft prevent my cheerfully inviting, &c. And if you are disposed to visit my poor little school and pray with me, and that (talk &c.) at ten o'clock on any day whenever it suits you, I shall rejoice in it as a favor, as that is the hour appointed for prayer &c. It will not interfere with the teaching part, Sir.

And now permit me with submission to ask how you do—I mean as to particular trials. Has your gracious, faithful God made the path of duty plain, or are you for wise and holy ends still shut up? Excuse my freedom, Sir. I must be tenderly concerned or amazingly stupid in this important affair. O, that our God will appear for you and us, guide and direct both you and my dear brethren. The thoughts of parting does indeed cut deeper and deeper. But O, that I might have no will but God's. He does infallibly know what he has determined, and if it 'tis his will to give you to us, you *shall* stay, and none can let. If not his will, you cannot stay; I know this. O, that the wheel within the wheel may be our support in this trying time.[20]

Farewell, dear Sir. The Lord almighty be with you and comfort you. Cease not to pray for us and me and believe me yours in simplicity with great affection.

Yours, I trust, in the dear Lord Jesus,

S. Osborn

P.S. I shall be glad to wait on your daughter at our house as soon as may be, tomorrow if it suits her.

Sarah Osborn to Deacon ———, 1769[21]

Yours of March 29, 1769, came not to hand till June 24th. I now write to return to you a thousand unfeigned thanks for your kind, endearing, friendly, and Christian caution. Blessed be thou of the Lord, and blessed be thine advice. The Lord sanctify it to me as a preservative against the sin of devils, that monster of monsters, spiritual pride—that sin which would rob God of all his glory and even *dethrone* the Majesty of heaven, if in its power, and set up the idol, self, in his room.

Can the jealous eye of Jehovah bear this without the utmost indignation and abhorrence? What can provoke this sacred majesty more than the prevalency of this sin? Or cause him to leave the soul, influenced by it, to fall into scandalous sins for its humiliation? Pride goes before destruction, and a haughty spirit, before a fall."[22] "God resisteth the proud."[23]

O, Sir, I have lived more than fifty-five years, and more than thirty-two of them have been fighting, watching, praying, weeping, and groaning for deliverance from this monster with a thousand heads, and yet must lay my hand upon my breast and say, "The traitor is there still to the breaking of my heart." I find it intermixing itself with every attempt I make to glorify God. And O, how does it cut the soul to the quick to find the most solemn, ardent, and vigorous duties tainted with pride and self.

O, Sir, very sore have been my trials and conflicts, on account of my character and correspondence with my superiors. By these things, I have sometimes appeared to myself as a mark, set up for Satan to level all his darts against. I have wanted to hide or creep into some secret corner to avoid the rage of sin and hell. But still, Providence has forbid, and without my seeking, correspondents have increased upon me from time to time, and great good hath God brought to my weary soul hereby. Blessed be God, he favors me with the counsel of the judicious, the faithful, and the wise. This is a privilege God has indulged me with, and why should I cast it away, merely because God hath made me, and my poor performances, acceptable to my friends? If he will display his divine sovereignty in such a babe, ought I not to say, "Even so, Father, for so it seemeth good in thy sight."[24]

My pen, as well as myself, have long, I trust, been solemnly given up to God, to be used by him and for no other. And when, through sore conflicts, I am tempted to lay it aside, the sin of the slothful servant stares me in the face, and I dare not.[25] Besides, every friend, as you have now done, Sir, lays me under an obligation to answer them. Was I not to answer you, what could you conclude but that I was offended at your endearing faithfulness? And I cannot bear the thought. Had you applauded me, I had nauseated your epistle and perhaps never answered it; but now, though I at first relucted at writing, yet I am constrained to beg a continuance not only of your kind caution but of your reproofs, too, if you find it needful. Let the righteous smite me; it shall, I trust, be an excellent oil that shall not break my head.[26] As to the charitable opinions, which you and others entertain, of my having grace in truth, I trust, through adorable sovereignty, which hath triumphed over the chief of sinners, that you are not mistaken.

I dare not say I have no grace, or that I do not know the Lord Jesus Christ. But as to the opinion of any that I am an eminent Christian, &c., it avails but little with me so long as I daily find sin, worse than a Mordecai, sitting at the gate and refusing to bow.[27] The opinion of others, so far as I know it, I conclude proceeds from their own humility or their ignorance of me: so to myself, I appear to fall awfully short in every peculiar excellency I see in them. And all the peculiar imperfections that I may see in one and another, which I might wish were otherwise, I turn inward and find them *all* centering in me. So that I am constrained to inscribe on myself, when compared with other Christians, less than the least of all saints, and when compared with the law of God, no more worthy to be called his. Thus God preserves me from being puffed up by keeping me, in a degree, in sight of myself.

But if pride is, in a degree, suppressed this way, I run into another extreme no less provoking in the sight of God: viz., sinful discouragement, distrust of his grace, and forget the Lord, my maker. And when I feel myself thus forlorn and am filled with self-loathing, seeing sin in every corner, I fear continually every day because of the fury of the oppressor, as if he were ready to destroy.

Perhaps I have never heard of the fall of any Christian, for many years, but it is almost incessantly suggested, it is my turn next. And when I wrote to you last fall, Sir, I was under distressing fears of this. My own sins appeared so provoking in the sight of God that I seemed to stand upon a precipice, ready for a plunge every moment. I am often constrained to say, in the bitterness of my soul, "As the Lord liveth, I have no hope of standing but in himself alone, for I am every way exposed." But O, since omnipotence and faithfulness itself hath hitherto upheld me, is not my dear Redeemer still able to keep me from falling now, as to present me faultless at last? Is not his grace sufficient for me, vile as I am? And though God stands in no need of me to uphold his honor and glory, yet since he hath condescended to say to mortals, "ye are my witnesses," cease not to pray, dear Sir, that I may stand to my latest breath, a witness to his truth and faithfulness, that he will make sin and Satan know that I have an almighty friend: he who will not deliver me up nor suffer any to pluck me out of his hands, who hath said, "Because I live, ye shall live also," "With me, thou shalt be in safeguard."[28]

May I not yet lift up my drooping head and take courage from union to Christ, by faith; from the tenor of the new and everlasting covenant; the intercession of my glorious Advocate in heaven; and the promises of God that he will never leave me nor forsake me? O, that I may look to Jesus, who was the author and shall be the finisher of my faith. Will not God, for his sake, go on to forgive me as he hath done from Egypt, even until now, blot out my transgressions as a cloud and speak peace and pardon to my soul?

Thanks be to God for some spring to my hope at this time, that after all my trials, the great captain of my salvation will bring me out of the field of battle more than a conqueror through his grace. Blessed be God, who hath raised me up a praying friend, here and there, for this purpose.

But it is time to beg you will forgive any intrusion on your patience. You have opened such a door of freedom, Sir, and I found the field I was in so large, I could not speedily get out.

May the Lord go on to enrich your precious soul. May you mount up as on eagle's wings towards heaven; run, and not be weary; walk, and not faint. That the joy of the Lord may be your strength, till you arrive in glory, is the heavenly desire of your much obliged, unworthy friend,

S. O.

1770

Sarah Osborn to Samuel Hopkins, January 4, 1770

My dear Sir,

I am ashamed I have not answered your grateful, endearing letter before now, but the perplexities of the last week prevented me. I had such a severe pain in my head and eyes on Friday (as is usual, after reading or going abroad) that I could do nothing at all in that affair, so have sent nothing. I regret that I took up your precious time in it, Sir, but I had sweet satisfaction afterward in hearing you converse, and I hope it was a strengthening visit to me and my friend, too.

I tendered your thanks to the dear society at your request, but sure we are a thousand times more under obligations to you. The Lord of his infinite grace reward you! And fill your precious soul up to the brim with communications from himself. O, that the joy of the Lord may be your strength this new year; yea, and all your days may he stand by you and enable you to defend his truths to your latest breath, and may precious truth, either delivered in preaching or conversation, or written by you, be owned and blessed of God to convince many in your day and to the latest posterity.

However ashamed you were of the last Sabbath day's exercises, Sir, I desire to bless God that I heard the clear, striking, convincing truths then delivered, and to bless God, too, that they were accompanied with a degree of convincing and establishing power on the souls of others as well as my *own*, for I have heard several speak of those sermons with satisfaction. And in particular, Mr. *Clark*, he told me he never see so into your drift as he did last Sabbath, viz., to strip man of everything, &c.[29] He is full in the doctrine of man's depravity and is, I really believe, a precious child of God that longs he *alone* should be exalted.[30]

You will take no notice of any hint from me, Sir, but if you please visit him as soon as you can, I believe his ear is now open to receive instruction from you. I have lately heard him earnestly pray for you and yours *and* that you might be made a rich and lasting blessing to *us*. This was quite in a different line from his former manner of praying, and was rejoicing to me. One remark he made was pleasing to me: said he, "If these things be so, how amazingly have we sunk down into legality in urging anything short of repentance and faith."[31]

It is my constant request that God will appear for his own cause and truth and fix you *here*, and *here* strengthen and support you and uphold you in all he calls you to, whether doing or suffering for his sake. And this was more than ever the general tenor of the petitions put up for you in the dear society on New Year's Day, though we pleaded against an obstinate will and desired to commit it to infinite wisdom.

Thanks be to God and you, Sir, for the clear truths you yesterday delivered. There is no flying from them, I think, but by flying from the Bible.

Oh! Cease not to pray for your worthless friend now writing, that God will thus glorify himself in *her,* for the glory *will* forever redound to Father, Son, and Holy Ghost. If this barren, barren *Sarah* is enabled to bring forth fruits of holiness even to old age, if she lives, it will show that the Lord is upright, that he is *her* rock, and there is no unrighteousness in him.[32] For I have trusted in him.

Sarah Osborn to Samuel Hopkins, January 22, 1770

Much honored, heartily esteemed, and Reverend Sir,

I am so ashamed in reading your dear letter that I know not how to lift up my head to hear you expressing your obligations to *me,* when they indeed all lie on my side. And the bare recognition of my poor scrawl ought to be acknowledged with the warmest gratitude and thanks to God and you. But has *God* in very deed made worthless me instrumental to refresh your precious soul, and draw forth your graces into exercise that *he* has received a revenue of praise and thanksgiving? Then let me fall prostrate and adore! And with grateful thanks give him all the glory. Not unto me, not unto me, 'tis the Lord's doing, and marvelous in my eyes. But he has and will choose weak things, &c., and in this I rejoice: that the glory may be all his own.[33]

My dear Sir, I reflected on myself afterward for mentioning *some* outwriting you, lest it should appear as a complaining of you, but I meant no such thing. I was rather faulting my too forward and intruding pen. Be assured, Sir, that while I always rejoice in the favor of receiving, I would not press you above measure. Never be afraid of my thinking you wanting to me if I stand by a little for affairs of more consequence to take place. But use me with greatest freedom, Sir, and this will oblige me. I know you will answer when you *can.* I have no doubt of *that,* except when I think mine are such shocking things that you cannot answer them. Sometimes, indeed, I am exercised this way, but then all the blame centers in myself.

It affects me to hear you say, Sir, you are really afraid of being the means of damping, &c., and even driving all religion out of Newport. I know what such exercises *mean*, but Satan was a liar from the beginning and ever will be so, in all his suggestions to distress the servants of the most high. *No, no*, Sir, you have not damped the hearts of dear Christian friends. If they have at any time been damped, it is through the remains of corruption and subtlety of Satan, and you have been made an instrument, either in preaching, writing, or conversation, to recover them from those damps, and strengthening them with strength in their souls. And your unworthy friends are still hoping and praying that God will give you to them for their furtherance and joy of faith, and turn the hearts of his own people to you as one man.

As to your visits, Sir, being an interruption at our house, I can't think of it but with grief that such a thought should be thrown into your mind. I entreat you, Sir, give it *no* harbor, but assure yourself you are always welcome; and your friends do indeed think it a great privilege, while the one now writing knows she is unworthy that you or any of the dear ministers of Christ should come under our roof.[34] All, in *this matter,* that *we* your friends are longing for, is for more uninterrupted freedom in conversing with you, and perhaps God will favor us ere long. And pray, Sir, come with freedom when you *can*, and as oft as you can, and we shall be the more obliged. Our dear Molly has wanted in particular to converse with you, Sir; has been in every way prevented by other engagements and from writing, too, for which she begs your excuse.[35]

I have sent you the dear little script from my precious Susa, that you may the more ardently carry her in the arms of faith and prayer to God, her only refuge. And if the Lord will that you speak a word to her for her support, Sir, I shall rejoice. And O, may he own and bless you to revive her drooping heart. I know and feel her burdens and, amidst a thousand other things, bear her on my heart night and day. But I want to engage wrestling Jacobs in her behalf: for what they ask for God's glory and her good in Christ's name, he will give, and he will yet receive her and glorify himself in her. I trust she has an advocate also with the Father, whom he hears always.

Thus I cut you out work, Sir, in every way I can, and look to God to reward *you*. I know we never can. O! May he enrich your precious soul with communications from himself till it is filled to the brim from the boundless ocean and can hold no more!

But I must cease now, only begging that you cease not to pray for your worthless friend, for I am almost confident I feel the effects of Zion's prayers, and yours in particular, and God will yet strengthen me with strength in my soul, and I shall yet praise him, &c.

And I am, Sir, I trust, as Mr. Buell expresses, yours in the Lord of love.[36] Or as you sweetly express: yours, I hope, forever,

Sarah Osborn

Sarah Osborn to Susanna Anthony, May 19, 1770

My dear,

I find by your manner of answering me yesterday that you think my troubles not much to be regarded. As to my own omissions, &c., they may not be very dreadful, as no evil was intended.

But I can't think my trouble on the other account is trifling for these reasons. You know my aversion to controversy was ever grounded on the bitterness that usually attends them, and *that part* of my aversion will, I believe, ever remain unconquerable, as I can never see that it tends to promote the glory of God or the good of souls but, so far as God permits, mars both.

It does appear to me that all attempts to make each other perhaps look ridiculous and odious ought to be out of the question, and truth and error only be set in opposition to each other. Could this be ever attained, I imagine aversion to controversy would cease in a great degree, and precious truth, by calm scriptural reasonings, would make its way into the understanding and gain its gradual conquest, establish the people of God and, perhaps, thus of a truth, the happy millennium may be ushered in.

My hopes of this has been raised of late, and now finding Mr. Hart so bitter, and seeming to resolve to provoke and aggravate and turn it all into a personal quarrel, has given me very distressing apprehensions, or fears, that the vindication of precious truth will in some sense drop in the vindication of characters. And people will either lay the disputes aside and have nothing to do with them, or else be engaged *each one* for *his friend* instead of being engaged for truth and searching for truth.[37] I know our dear, dear pastor is a man of like passions with others and not above the reach of provocation except victorious grace triumph! Even a Moses spake unadvisedly with his lips when provoked, and if he should be provoked to do so now, so far the glorious cause in which he is engaged suffers and is perhaps marred in his hands.

I know indeed God has carried him above resentment in this place, and how beautiful in this very thing did he appear, how great and truly godlike. And in this, I am persuaded God was pleased with him, and made some of his enemies to be at peace with him, and in this way if he persists, I doubt not but God will own and bless him still, and make him an instrument of great good to the souls of many. But if he should be drawed forth to espouse his own cause instead of God's, my hopes fail. I view him as standing upon a precipice. O, may God uphold him for his own name's sake and vindicate his own cause by him.

When I see dear Mr. West so struck, and when I heard what Mr. Brown wrote, read, I did not think I should have been so cut to the heart by Mr. Hart's ungenerous treatment as I find I am.[38] I own I don't know how to bear it, and perhaps 'tis the struggle I have with my own corruptions that fills me with such fears with respect to my dear, dear Mr. Hopkins.

O, that I might be enabled to pray for him night and day as well as for myself and others.

If you still think me foolish in my concern, do bear with me and don't banter me. Speak serious to me, for my mind is perplexed and I can't help it. If Satan has engaged to perplex me, perhaps God will go on to bless you, my dear, as an instrument to break his snares.

Pray for your weak and unworthy yet affectionate friend,

SO

1771

Sarah Osborn to William Vinal, circa 1771–1774[39]

Reverend Sir,

I received yours and return you thanks for all favors; am obliged by your letter in what you say of the great and glorious Redeemer. They are precious truths, and I assure you that as to any kindness it was in my power to show to you or *yours*, either for soul or body, you was welcome. As you was my *own* pastor, and I esteemed you as a minister of Jesus Christ, I esteemed it my honor and privilege to relieve you, as far as I could, of both care and charge. You and yours were and are dear to me, and I could gladly relieve you still. In all your comforts I rejoiced and in all your sorrows I mourned, so far as I knew them, and it is a comfort to me now that conscience bear me witness. I hope that through the whole course of your ministry with us, I never offended or grieved you. Nor can I now grieve you without sensible *pain*. Could I conscientiously do it, I should rather delight in comforting you.

But I am indeed distressed, Sir, exceedingly so from time to time, with the inconsistences that attend your writings, while you speak of such precious experiences of consolations and of waiting patiently on God, &c., and at the same time persist in such bitter exclamations against the Church of Christ in Newport, which I trust he has purchased with his own precious blood. And if so, it is *dear* to him and its character not to be set at naught. He has warned against offending such. Surely Christ regards his little ones as well as those in more eminent stations.

And as for me, Sir, I can have no greater assurance than I have (without an infallible knowledge of the heart, which I don't pretend into) that the Church of Christ in Newport has treated you with all the forbearance, kindness, and tenderness the case would bear, and even to the exposing themselves to reproach from others for being close-mouthed so long, which is enough for them to bear without your unwearied endeavors to render them odious, malicious, cruel, unmerciful, &c. I believe, Sir, it is no small consolation to them that the great searcher of hearts, who knows perfectly all aims, views, and designs, will in his own time *reveal theirs*, especially at the *great* day.

As to Deacon Coggeshall and Mr. Baltch, with whom I am the most intimate, I was witness to their sighs, tears, and prayers for you, and for direction for themselves. I bore the burden with them and so *fulfilled* the law of Christ, and God was witness to the heartbreaking sorrows of our hearts in that distressing day.[40] We were ready to think no sorrow like our sorrow while our poor hearts were even bleeding for you and yours as well as ourselves.

As for me, the pressure was so great when the affair was first told to me in August that I thought my very life must go, as it was a confirmation of all the fears my *own* senses had given an alarm to once and again at times for years before, but I had been striving with all my might to disbelieve. I then compared myself to one that had had a dear relative sick, and through earnest desire of life, hoped against hope and flattered themselves with every favorable symptom they could catch at, till death gave the fatal blow. And then all hope was cut off at once.

Indeed, Sir, with grief of heart I speak it: it is no manner of doubt with me but that I myself have seen in you the effects of spirituous liquor more than once or twice while I was able to walk to your house.[41] And have come home with a heavy heart on the account, and many a sorrowful hour I had when my sleep departed, in conflicting and sighing and weeping, when I dared not lisp it even to my own husband. O, how I longed to act the part of a faithful friend by you, and tell you my fears and plead with you to deny yourself, &c., but I had no reason to think it would bear, and my only relief was in God alone. To him I carried you with my own soul and cried for strength that both you and I might be enabled to overcome temptation. I pitied you from my inmost soul. I knew by experience what great infirmities of body, pressures of spirits, and strong temptations to take a little for relishment. I knew how the duty of self-preservation—yes, through the subtlety of Satan—the glory of God itself could be urged in this case, and my heart was all tenderness and sympathy towards you.

And when, in the spring of *1766*, I sent you those writings which concerned things of that nature, respecting others with whom I was laboring, with my own letter giving an account of my own trials and victory thus far through Jesus Christ my Lord, and my pleadings with them also to deny themselves, it was with a secret hope, accompanied with cries to God, that the duty of self-denial might then be open to you, and that God would bless that seemingly undesigned thing for good to your precious soul.

All this, Sir, God was witness to, of my concern for you in this matter before I ever heard any one of my dear brethren open their lips about you in that affair. You know that was in August, and sure I am I was a stranger to prejudice or malice against you. On the contrary, you was dear to me as my very life, and had you been so happy as to have stood by your own confession and let the church had rest, you had ever been dear to me and to your other faithful friends at Newport. We had never known anything but tender sympathy, love, and compassion towards you. Your character had been reestablished and 'tis very probable you, before this, employed in the ministry.

But dear Sir, as long as you will persist in laying heavy charges against the church and rendering them that treated with you as the vilest of men, nothing can be more just and equal than that they show the reasons and grounds of their conduct. And as soon as any one sees *that*, their judgments are convinced, and they are astonished at your *own* conduct and can do no other in conscience but espouse the church's cause.

And so, Sir, 'tis yourself that pull on you the troubles that ensue, and I do believe you will find the more you try to extricate yourself by flying from your own *solemn* confession and casting all the blame and shame upon the church, the deeper you will plunge. For God has said it and never will revoke it: "He that covereth his sin shall not prosper."[42] And if you are resolute, Sir, after all the entreaties of your most faithful and affectionate friends, that you will persist in this way, no friend that knows the affair can justify you in it.

Dear Sir, is this not the same as refusing to hear the church while you labored to make your confession null and void and repent of all your repentance? This cuts me to the heart; it even tears me all to pieces; it stumbles; it grieves me almost to death; it gives my cruel foe such an advantage against me that I don't know if ever I shall get over it to my last breath. It is a thousand times worse to me than the thing itself, as it takes off all my comfort in you, cuts in two the very sinews of my hope that your repentance is genuine.

I can't join you, Sir, in that part, viz., contradicting your confession; nor can I in conscience side with you in casting the blame on the church and accuse them with malice, &c. I cannot do it. If you were my own father I could not do it. On the contrary, I think myself bound in duty to declare to every serious enquirer after truth that I do believe in my heart that the church's proceedings with you were *conscientious* and not malicious. And your heavy charges against them, Sir, has endeared them to me exceedingly.

May God of his infinite mercy open your eyes and give you a repentance *never, never* to be repented of, and a full and free pardon through the blood of Christ. This is and shall be, God helping me, my constant plea at the throne of grace for you.

And I am,

your afflicted friend

ELEVEN

All That Hath Befallen Us, 1779–1780

DURING THE 1760S AND 1770S *Sarah Osborn rallied behind the Patriot cause. For years she had prayed that the millennium might be imminent, and as colonists clashed with the British over imperial policies, she prayed that the struggle for freedom might have a deeper religious significance.*

In December 1776, British troops occupied Newport. Terrorizing the residents, they looted stores, tore down houses for firewood, and desecrated the churches that were identified with the Patriot cause, including the First Church, which they turned into a hospital and a barracks. More than half of the population fled the city, but Henry, now ninety-two years old, was frail, and he and Sarah were too poor to leave. He died in 1778, and soon afterward, Sally, Sarah's beloved granddaughter, left with her husband and young child. As Samuel Hopkins remembered later, their departure meant that Sarah, ill and "destitute," was "left alone."[1]

Yet even in the midst of poverty and illness, Sarah remained hopeful that the war was part of God's plan. In two letters that she sent to Joseph Fish in the late 1770s, she wondered whether the Revolution heralded the beginning of the "latter days," the second coming of Christ. Clinging to her faith in the goodness of God, she asked Joseph Fish, "May not all that hath befallen us, both in church and state, serve rather to strengthen than stagger our faith?"

Osborn was forced to dictate her later letters to Fish because she had almost completely lost her eyesight. When she had been younger her illness had alternated with periods of remission, but as she grew older she became progressively more impaired. Unable to walk and nearly blind, she rarely left her house.

1779

Sarah Osborn to Joseph Fish, December 28, 1779

My very dear and venerable friend,

I received your favor. I heartily thank you for it, and now am attempting by the favor of a friend to fulfill your request, by giving you some account of the dealings of God with me.[2] Blessed be his name, I'm called to sing of mercy in the midst of judgment.

I have been stripped of my dearest enjoyments on earth, attendance on public worship, reading, writing, my dear and worthy pastor, Christian friends, grandchildren, my dear aged companion, yet have upheld under all, and in every apparent danger throughout the captivity, God mercifully granted me renewed strength and courage.[3] I have the privilege without molestation of uniting with worthy Deacon Coggeshall, Mr. Brown, and some others of our church in prayer on every Wednesday.[4] As to my health, it is much as it has been for years past. I live easy and content with my lot, have a kind neighbor in the house with me who reads to me in the Bible every night and prevents my being exposed or going beyond my strength in anything.[5]

As to support, my dear friends are unwearied in their kindnesses amidst all their own difficulties. Blessed be God, I have lacked for nothing. O what a display of divine faithfulness have I seen. Grace abounds to the chief of sinners. God's little remnant were safe as Noah when the Lord shut him in, the three children in the fiery furnace when the son of God was in the midst, Daniel in the den when God shut the mouth of the lions.[6]

Many distressing things passed before us, as the destruction of the house of the Lord's—the enemy profanely roaring therein—yet God suffered them not utterly to destroy.[7] As for me, I was preserved from hearing the hateful din or profane swearing while many more righteous than I were vexed from day to day by the filthy conversation of the wicked. When they were about to evacuate, we frequently heard we were to be left in devouring flames, but instead of that, they went as gentle as lambs. This was the Lord's doing and marvelous in our eyes. Thus ends the captivity.

Now a new scene opens. For the first fortnight or three weeks upon the return of Christian friends to visit me, my elevation of spirits and alternate sinkings at hearing what they have undergone and other sad tidings, were almost too much for my feeble frame, and indeed, the abounding of iniquity I daily hear of among those who professed to be on the side of religion and liberty, but vastly deeper than what I hear of those who professedly say, "who is the Lord that we should obey him?"[8] While we remain as people thus hardened and impenitent, the words of Jehu often occurs to my mind: "What have we to do with peace so long," &c.[9] I know God will be infinitely just should he say, "let those that are filthy be filthy still," and go on to vindicate his injured honor till he utterly consumes us.[10] Yet I hope in his mercy that for the great Redeemer's sake, who came to destroy the works of the devil, and whose kingdom shall rise and flourish, that he will in his own time grant repentance and maintain his own right in America.

Deacon Coggeshall has gone to spend the winter at Middleborough. Be pleased to make my kind regards acceptable to your dear spouse and daughter; hope God will command deliverance for her dear companion in his own way and time. I tenderly sympathize with her in her affliction. Also my regards to . . . Mr. Eels, Mr. Chesebrough, and all inquiring friends.[11]

Deacon Peabody has been here twice but not removed.[12] I have not an individual friend but who . . . by losses, depreciation and extortions . . . .[13] The . . . wants of many here often deprives me of my comforts of food and fuel. For the want of the latter our dear pastor was constrained to leave us, which is very trying to me.

But I must not add anymore but that I am with all due respect, your sincere and affectionate friend,

S. Osborn

Mrs. S. Anthony is still at Voluntown. Mrs. Mary Anthony is here.

Sarah Osborn to Joseph Fish, undated[14]

Reverend and dear Sir,

When a friend providentially brought me your letter, I rejoiced much to hear of your welfare and anxiously desired to speak to my worthy friend.

The bearer kindly offered to write for me. We had but little time; my thoughts were as the swellings of Jordan; language failed; and doubtless conveyed ideas different from my meaning. I have been much dissatisfied with some parts of my letter, especially my omissions, as I did not tell my dear friend how much I had borne him on my heart; nor so much as to ask the continuance of his prayers for me, though I doubt not the mercies with which I have been indulged, both spiritual and temporal, as also the preservations and deliverance of Newport, are in answer to yours, and others of God's people's prayers. And sure I am, I had rather had an interest in the prayers of the people of God than to possess millions of gold and silver.

And now, Sir, I earnestly pray you will not cease to pray for me. O, pray that I may be a widow indeed—solemnly devoted to God, to my latest breath, and may the best of blessings rest on you and yours forever.

Forgive, dear Sir, if you think my affections were too bold, respecting the safety of God's little remnant. I had at that time such a view of the adorable attributes of the infinitely glorious, unchangeable, faithful, covenant-keeping Jehovah, and the safety of all those who trusted in him, that I could not find language to express my ideas.

Verily, though miracles have ceased, God is the only refuge of his people. The name of the Lord is a strong tower. He is an all-sufficient good in the absence of the dearest enjoyments on earth. Happy people, whose God is the Lord.

The strength and courage I mentioned, which God graciously granted me in times of danger, was not the result of any confident persuasion, that I should not be slain. No, when the bullets were whizzing around me, I realized the *next* might have a commission to reach *me;* and if this was the way infinite wisdom had chosen, I had no objection to make. I chose neither life nor death, only that God might glorify himself in me, and that, whether I lived or died, I might be the Lord's. I know every shot was directed by unerring wisdom; and every heart of the enemy, as *much* at his control, who hath said to the restless ocean, "Hitherto shalt thou come, and no further; and here shall thy proud waves be stayed."[15]

Thus I rested on God. O boundless grace, adorable sovereignty, why was I not rather called to drink the very dregs of the cup of his displeasure?

Why was I not made even a terror to myself and all around me—I, who have had so great a hand in drawing down the judgments of God upon us. O, my friend, adore with me, and let me be reckoned among the chief of sinners.

Through the goodness of that God who hath said, "I will never leave thee nor forsake thee," I am again called to set up my Ebenezer, for hitherto the Lord hath helped me.[16] I have been unwell, but through mercy have been better. I have known no sufferings this hard winter but what hath been the effect of sympathy: for while many others have been ready to perish, I have had a constant supply of food and fuel.

Touching Zion's cause: my dear Sir, since I wrote you, while thinking on the sad things we bemoan, I have been much refreshed with the thought that when Elijah complained that true religion was lost, God had reserved to himself seven thousand.[17] And who can say, that God has not many more in this dark time than we are aware of. I rest in this truth, "The foundation of God standeth sure: having this seal, the Lord knoweth who are his."[18] And though the prevalence of error and delusion are matter of sore lamentation, yet may not mourners in Zion be comforted in this, that the chosen of God shall never be finally deceived, though such should arise as would, if possible, deceive the very elect. We know that the gates of hell shall never prevail against that church which Christ hath purchased with his own most precious blood.

Blessed be God, the great head of the church, in whom dwells all the fullness of the Godhead bodily, is equal to all the work assigned him, able to protect and defend his own as well as to redeem them. May not all that hath befallen us, both in church and state, serve rather to strengthen than stagger our faith, since our divine Redeemer faithfully warned us of the coming of such things in the latter days? We see that not one jot or tittle of his word fails, in this part; and shall not latter-day *promises* be as truly fulfilled? May we not lift up our heads because redemption draweth nigh?

O, Sir, when I get fast hold of that foundation truth, spoken by precious Christ himself, "All that the Father hath given me *shall* come unto me; and him that cometh, I will in no wise cast out,"[19] then, as saith Mr. Elliott, "Faith lies at anchor in the midst of waves and billows, and believes the accomplishment of the promises."[20] Then I can travel not only over this vast continent but over all the globe, and be assured that every soul born, or yet unborn, who were given to Christ in the covenant of redemption shall come to him; and of those whom the Father hath given him, he will lose none. No, not one. Even in this dark day, none shall pluck them out of his hands.

And when the set time to favor Zion is come, then Christ will be avenged on Satan for all the mischief he hath done. The old serpent shall be bound, that he deceive the nations no more. God shall pour out his Spirit in plentiful effusions. The knowledge of God shall cover the earth as the waters fill the sea. Then Christ Jesus will reign triumphant, King of Nations, as he is now King of Saints. Amen. Hallelujah! So come Lord Jesus.

Whether you or I shall live to see the dawn of that blessed day is not known to us. But if we are so happy as to arrive safe in heaven before it commence—where there is joy among the angels over one sinner that repenteth—what transports of joy shall we behold when *millions* repent, when a *nation*, is born in a day. Shall we not then be partakers of that joy which is unspeakable and full of glory? Shall not our souls exult in seeing the glory of the once crucified, but now risen, ascended, enthroned Redeemer? Thanks be to him, that he hath said: "Father, I will that those, whom thou hast given me, be with me where I am, to behold my glory."[21] O, pray that I may be prepared for this. These are the comforts on which I live.

Pray, Sir, pardon the length of my letter. I could not stop; my heart was full; and it is probable this is the last time I shall be permitted to speak to you in this world, as every attempt to indite is an overthrow to my feeble frame. I thank you, Sir, for all your past indulgence and for all the helps you have afforded me in my various trials. The Lord reward you. May a double portion of his Spirit rest upon you. May you ever taste the sweetness of the, "Lo, I am with you always," till, having turned many to righteousness, you finish your course and enter into the joy of your Lord.[22]

Farewell, my dear friend, farewell. Please to give my tender love to your spouse and daughter, and accept the same yourself, from yours, in the delightful bonds of love, gratitude, and friendship,

S. O.

TWELVE

Visions of Heaven

SARAH OSBORN *died on August 2, 1796, at the age of eighty-two. Her friends had been keeping watch over her during an illness, but after leaving for a few minutes to let her sleep, they returned to find that her breathing had stopped. As Samuel Hopkins commented, it was the kind of death she had always wanted: "calm and serene, without the least perceivable struggle or groan."*[1]

We know little about the last twenty years of Osborn's life because she was no longer able to keep a diary or to write letters, but it is clear that her world grew smaller with each passing year as her illness deprived her of both sight and strength. Many of her closest friends had died, including Joseph Fish in 1781 and Susanna Anthony in 1791. During her last years, according to Hopkins, she was no longer able to read, attend church, or meet with the women's society, and she spent most of her days in prayer. Though she knew large parts of the Bible by heart, she often asked her friends to read the scripture aloud to her, treasuring the familiar stories of Job, Jacob, Esther, Hannah, and most of all, Jesus. She also composed poems in her head, some of which she managed to write down, and others which were transcribed by her friends.

The two selections below are taken from Osborn's many writings about death. In the first, a poem that she composed during the last twenty years of her life, she imagined what her life would be like in heaven. In the second, a diary entry from 1753, she tried to imagine the overpowering joy of hearing God speak to her. After a lifetime of pouring out her heart to him in prayer, she longed to see him face to face and to hear his voice in return.

The Employment and Society of Heaven[2]

What goodness this, which God extends
To us, who once were not his friends!
Compassion had on whom he would
Though we did evil as we could.

Infinite love. 'Tis all divine;
God's wisdom formed the vast design;
His power has kept and brought us in,
Through all the assaults of hell and sin.

And now we shall forever gaze
On God, and his perfections praise;
We shall be like him more and more;
The Incomprehensible adore

No hateful sin, or weariness,
Shall cause us any more distress.
To do God's will with Seraph's joy,
Shall ever be our sweet employ.

Ye dear companions here at rest,
With love sincere in every breast,
We now will cordially embrace,
Without a blush in any face.

No more misunderstandings here;
No misconstruction now we fear;
No censures hard, those bitter roots,
Which cast out love and blast its fruits.

No envy now, or selfishness,
Will e'er again our souls possess;
Benevolence shall sweetly flow:
We felt too little when below.

No prejudice shall make us stand
Aloof, as in that foreign land;
Because when there we could not see,
We in essentials did agree.

We surely did, since we are here,
Where none but friends to Christ appear;
And now our God hath brought us home,
We ever will rejoice as one.

O here's no trace of discontent;
Not one who murmurs in his tent:
Nor are there any fiery darts,
Ever to break or vex our hearts.

O precious blood, that once was spilt,
To cleanse our souls from all their guilt;
By which we are indeed made free
Our souls from sin at liberty.

O this gives joy its fullest tide,
That our Redeemer glorified;
With satisfaction views the whole,
The fruitful travail of his soul.

Ye who are now before our eyes,
Who were on earth our enemies,
We bless the Lord that you're forgiven.
And are arrived safe in heaven.

For this we gave the Lord no rest,
And he has answered our request;
For which we magnify his grace,
And join with you to sing his praise.

Ye worthy friends, who did relieve
Our pinching wants, ye now receive

The great reward Christ promised you;
Ten thousand thanks to God most true.

Now grateful love our souls doth cheer,
That we enjoy your presence here:
You did it for King Jesus's sake,
And of his joy you do partake.

Ye sweet acquaintance, Christian friends,
Partakers of our joys and pains,
How oft by you did God afford
Relief to us from his own word!

Your tender sympathy and love
Did oft to us as cordials prove;
By sweet reproofs, and fervent prayer,
Ye kindly did our burdens bear.

In sore temptations, sharp and long,
You faithful held the Lord, and strong
The great atonement all complete,
The promises most sure and sweet.

Ten thousand welcomes to this state,
Each other we congratulate,
And now our work shall be all praise
Through an eternity of days.

Though bonds of nature now do cease,
Our happiness it does increase,
To see our godly parents here,
And relatives to Christ most dear.

Can we review God's providence,
And yet retain no grateful sense
Of all your love and tender care,
Us for this heaven to prepare?

Do we not know you? Yes, we do,
No ignorance hides you from our view:
The leaks in memory are all stopped
Since we our imperfections dropped.

What multitudes are these which rise
To fill our souls with sweet surprise?
It is the charming infant race,
Brought here through rich and sovereign grace.

These little ones were born again
And did believe in Christ, 'tis plain:
God's Spirit wrought the work; but how
On earth we could not fully know.

Glory to God that now we see
Nothing's too hard for Deity:
These were the lambs, whom Christ caressed,
Took in his holy arms and blessed.

Thanks be to him his word was given
"Of such the kingdom is of heaven,"[3]
Now they behold his glory too:
Sweet babes we do rejoice with you.

New wonders still! Lo, here are they,
Unjustly brought from Africa!
They've heard the gospel's joyful sound,
Though lost indeed they are now found.

Those we see here who once have been
Made slaves to man by horrid sin,
Now through rich grace in Christ are free,
Forever set at liberty.

Thanks be to God, though not to man,
'Twas he who laid this glorious plan

From evil great, this good to bring
All glory to our God and King.

Hail Ministers of Jesus's name,
Who this salvation did proclaim;
Our very souls do live anew
That we in heaven do meet with you.

You have received the sweet, "Well done": [4]
And your eternal joy's begun;
Rich and complete is your reward,
And we forever bless the Lord.

What saints are these with crowns we see
Of joy and immortality?
Gladly we find they are the same
Who out of tribulation came.

The holy prophets who did die
Because they truth did prophesy.
Apostles blessed, and Martyrs, slain
Because Christ's truth they did maintain.

We know that these the world did hate;
But Christ has made them rich and great.
He promised them this great reward
And we adore the faithful Lord.

New scenes arise. Let us attend:
Here's Abraham's seed, God's ancient friend.
We see God's covenant was sure,
And did from age to age endure.

All these have had repentance given,
The true Messiah owned from heaven.
His promises they did embrace,
And now behold his glorious face.

That very blood by them was spilt,
Which truly washed away their guilt,
Glory to God! We see the Jew:
We, Gentiles, do rejoice with you.

Transporting scene! All is delight!
Throngs numberless are in our sight,
Of every kindred, tongue, and size,
To overwhelm us with surprise.

When Christ a thousand years did reign,
Ten thousands then were born again;
Who now, through rich and sovereign grace,
Are here to fill this holy place.

Language is pure and refined;
Quickly we know each other's mind.
All here is concord; all at peace;
And happiness doth still increase.

These holy angels all have skill
To know and do Jehovah's will:
They joyed at our Redeemer's birth,
And ministered to him on earth.

The Angels, who excel in strength:
Who were our guardians all the length,
Of the afflictive, tiresome road,
And bear us safe to this abode.

Is this the heaven of which we heard!
Are these the mansions Christ prepared?
How low have our conceptions been,
In a blind world of night and sin.

O come, yet lower let us fall,
Before our God, our all in all.

Sing praises to the worthy Lamb:
Ever adore the great I AM.
Amen, Hallelujah.

May 15, 1753, Tuesday morning

On Saturday evening, Sabbath morning and evening, and yesterday morning, I have been much refreshed in writing on death and judgment. I find, by examination, still good ground to hope, through riches of grace, that the great judge of quick and dead is, in very deed, my everlasting friend and therefore never will disown me. Never will say, "I know you not: depart from me."[5] But, on the contrary, will say, "Come ye blessed of my Father, inherit the kingdom prepared for you before the foundation of the world."[6] For I have paid the ransom for you: I have redeemed you with the price of my precious blood. I effectually called you in time and enabled you by faith to embrace me on my own terms. I made you sincere, from the day I called you, though you were then very imperfect.

You was then sanctified but in part. You groaned under a body of sin and death, which caused you to wander from me, wound your own soul, and grieve my blessed Spirit. But I kept thee by the bonds of the everlasting covenant, and by my mighty power, through faith unto salvation. And for my sake, all thy poor, imperfect performances and sincere endeavors to serve me were accepted. I pitied and succored thee then. I had a feeling of thy infirmities. I remembered thy frame, that thou was but dust. I heard thy groanings because of thy spiritual enemies, thy inbred lusts and corruptions, as well as Satan and the world, which held thee at a distance from me when thou was in that vale of tears. I beheld all thy thirstings and longings after me and my grace, universal obedience and perfection in holiness. It was I that excited and strengthened them. I encouraged and strengthened thy faith, when thou didst cleave to me and would not let me go. I caused thee to delight in me above all other objects. I discovered something of my excellencies to thee then, which caused thee to be enamored with my beauty. But thou sawest only through a glass darkly.

But now, behold, the veil is rent from top to bottom. I will never any more hide my face me from thee. Come, all thy desires are fulfilled; all thy imperfections are done away; and, according to thy wish, thou art made perfect in holiness. Thou shalt never find any more weariness in my service. And thou mayest now with open face behold me, constantly look on my perfections, see my glory, and the luster of it shall not confound thee. Come, here is the open vision, the full fruition thou didst long for. Come, drink in as much of God now as thy finite capacity can hold, and I will still enlarge thy capacity. Thou shalt pass from glory to glory and be more and more transformed into the same image. Come, drink and swim, and drink again of those rivers of pleasure, which flow from the right hand of God forevermore. Here is the boundless ocean, in which thee mayest dive throughout the endless ages of eternity, and thy delights shall be forever new.

Come, search into the wonders of redeeming love and grace, which has brought so many of the apostate sons and daughters of Adam to glory. And now, in this everlasting *now,* give to God the glory of his sovereign grace. Come, tune thy harp, and sound upon the highest string. Shout aloud for joy, for he has given grace, and glory too. Here is no danger of ostentation or spiritual pride, or of grieving any of the inhabitants of this world. No, they will all join with thee, and each for himself, and on thy behalf, give glory to God in the highest strains. Didst thou long to be thus employed? Well, go on forever to praise and adore the glorious Three in One. Didst thou delight to commune with me in providences as well as in ordinances? Well, thou mayest now learn the mysteries of them: they shall be unfolded. Unbelief shall no more molest thee. Now thou shalt see how by the watchful eye of my providence, I preserved thee from every danger. How I swayed the scepter in righteousness and caused all things to work together for thy good—even when thou saidst, "All these things are against me!"[7] I never took my eye from thee, nor turned away from doing thee good. Now, thou mayest adore forever on this account also, and see what thou didst, when thou didst commit all thy concerns to me for time and eternity.

Didst thou delight in the company and communion of my ambassadors [ministers] and dear children? Did they appear the most lovely and agreeable of all the inhabitants of the lower world? Especially, when thou didst discern, through their imperfections, as the sun through a cloud, my image, drawn in an eminent degree upon their souls? Didst thou love them for my sake, wherever thou sawest them? Were they, in thy esteem, indeed the excellent of the earth? Well, here thou shalt forever enjoy the communion of saints: these shall be thy companions forever. All their imperfections, as well as thine, are done away. They are now perfect and shall never ensnare thee, as even *they* were wont to do. They shall never turn off thy eyes from me. No, not the brightest seraph in all the heavenly regions shall ever be able to do it, nor all the glittering robes of glorified saints and angels. But thou shalt enjoy me in all these. I will forever feast my soul with communications from myself. And if I, who am God all-sufficient, can make thee happy, thou shalt be so, for I will be thy portion to eternity.

And didst thou in time, by faith, commit the keeping of thy soul and body into my merciful and faithful hands against this great day? I excited and enabled thee to do it, and now thou seest the effect. Thy expectations from me shall never be disappointed; neither shalt thou ever be ashamed of thy hope. I kept thee by my power while on earth. I kept thee in the hour of death, when Satan would gladly have hurled thy soul into the infernal regions, but he could not pluck thee out of my hands. I sent thy guardian angels to conduct thy precious soul to Abraham's bosom. And I still took care of thy moldering dust while in the grave. Not an atom of it is lost. And now, behold! I have raised it a glorious body, fashioned like my own. And now the union between soul and body shall never be dissolved, but the dear partner shall forever reap together as they sowed together. Behold, according to thy faith and hope, I now present them spotless and blameless before the throne of God. I have redeemed them by my blood. By my obedience and death I have satisfied justice and have purchased reconciliation with God. Mercy and truth have met together; righteousness and peace have kissed each other. I have washed away all thy pollutions. And now, I give thee joy, and all the host of heaven give thee joy; therefore, enter thou into the joy of thy Lord. I gave thee joy in the day of thy espousals, and in frequent after manifestations, as an earnest of this. Thou hast had a taste of the same in kind, when I revealed myself to thee on earth, but the degree shall now be greater than thou could then ask or think.

THIRTEEN

Sarah Osborn's Will and Inventory

TWO YEARS BEFORE SHE DIED, *Sarah Osborn wrote a will giving almost all of her possessions to the First Church. Though she mentioned that she had "reserved" a few items, presumably for her friends, she wanted the value of her estate to be used to support the pastor and the poor of her church.*

According to Samuel Hopkins, Osborn bequeathed her diaries and other manuscripts to him with instructions to use them as he wished.[1] Her writings were far more valuable to her than any of her material goods.

After Osborn's death in 1796, an inventory revealed the extent of her poverty. Almost everything that she owned was described as "old," and the total value of her estate was only forty-four dollars and sixty-one cents. An "old gown," "old pewter," "two old combs," an "old maple desk," "a parcel of old trumpery"—this was the sum of Sarah Osborn's earthly life, a life that she had always insisted was only a dim reflection of the glory to come.

Sarah Osborn's Will

Be it known to all men, by these presents, that I, Sarah Osborn of Newport in the county of Newport and state of Rhode Island, etc., widow, having lived to old age, and as I know not the day of my death, or how soon my reason may fail, which through mercy I enjoy in a good degree at present, do now make my last will and testament, which is as follows:

I give my gold locket and beads, my silver tablespoon marked H O S, and all my household goods and clothing (except those articles which I have reserved and otherwise disposed of in the annexed papers written with my own hand), which I order to be sold.[2] And after my funeral charges and just debts are paid, it is my will that the remainder of the money shall be put out on interest, and that one half of the interest be given yearly for the support of the pastor of the First Congregational Church in Newport for the time being. And that the other half be given to the poor of said church. And if I have any money at my death, I give it to the use above mentioned. And I appoint and constitute Deacon Samuel Vinson of Newport, above said, as my sole executor of this my last will, putting entire confidence in him that he will faithfully execute the former.

In witness of the above as my last will and testament, I, the said Sarah, do hereunto set my hand and seal, this twenty-fifth day of October, A.D. 1794.

Sarah Osborn

Signed and sealed and declared to be her last will and testament in presence of witnesses,

Samuel Hopkins
Elizabeth Clarke
Mary Anthony

An Inventory of the Personal Estate of
Mrs. Sarah Osborn, Late of Newport, Deceased, Taken by Us,
the Subscribers, the 22nd Day of August 1796

one old maple desk: four dollars

old kitchen chairs: two dollars, seventy cents

two old windsor chairs, one of them very much broken: fifty cents

one old two-armed chair: fifty cents

one old feather bed, bolster, four small pillows, and underbed: seven
   dollars

one old bedstead rods and rails: one dollar

three old blankets, two of them very old: forty cents

one flannen sheet,[3] one holland sheet, and three old tow cloth sheets:[4]
  one dollar and sixty-five cents

one old woolen coverlid,[5] three old pillowcases, and two old bolster
  cases: five cents

one old suit, curtains, valence, and one side of an old gown: one dollar

one old candlestand, one old chest, one old tea table: one dollar, twelve
  cents

one old fire screen, one old bottle case, one old stew: twenty cents

one old corner cupboard and a parcel of old crockery: fifty cents

one old brush, four small sugar boxes, and two old small pails: twenty-
  five cents

Doctor Guyse's likeness: forty cents

one small looking glass: twenty-five cents

one small writing desk and a number of manuscripts: twenty-five cents

two stone and two earthen pots: thirty cents

one old $\frac{1}{2}$ barrel, one old pair of bellows, and one old shovel: fifteen
  cents

one pair small handirons and one earthen pan: five cents

one old coffee mill, candlestick lamp, and some old knives and forks:
  twelve cents

a parcel of old tinware: six cents

seven old pewter: seventy-five cents

three small skillets, pipe box, saltbox, and two knife boxes: fifty cents

one old folding board and some pieces of boards for screen: fifteen cents

one quarto Bible: one dollar

one octavo Bible: fifty cents

four pamphlets and Patten's *Answer to Paine:* twenty cents[6]

one paper pins, two old combs, comb, brush, and one pair old spectacles:
  twenty cents

one old Gown (one dollar), one old skirt and some pieces of skirt and
  one old handkerchief: thirty-three cents

six small old towels and a bit of old gown: twenty cents

one small old trammel,[7] hammer, and hourglass: twenty-five cents

Wearing apparel: two dollars

one old gold necklace and locket: five dollars

Old silver spoon: one dollar, ninety-five cents

Cash: six dollars, ninety cents

A parcel of old trumpery and a few pieces of new cloth: thirty cents

ABBREVIATIONS

ARCHIVAL LOCATIONS

AAS   American Antiquarian Society, Worcester, Massachusetts.

BL   Beinecke Rare Book and Manuscript Library, Yale University, New Haven, Connecticut.

BPL   Boston Public Library, Boston, Massachusetts.

CHS   Connecticut Historical Society, Hartford, Connecticut.

HSP   Historical Society of Pennsylvania, Philadelphia, Pennsylvania.

MHS   Massachusetts Historical Society, Boston, Massachusetts.

NHS   Newport Historical Society, Newport, Rhode Island.

RIHS   Rhode Island Historical Society, Providence, Rhode Island.

SML   Sterling Memorial Library, Yale University, New Haven, Connecticut.

SARAH OSBORN'S MANUSCRIPTS

Sarah Osborn's writings have been preserved in the following collections: SO, Diaries, 1753–1772, NHS; SO, Diaries and Memoir, 1757–1769, BL; SO, Letters, 1743–1770, 1779, AAS; SO, Diaries, 1754, 1760–1761, CHS; and SO, 5 Letters, 1769–1770, Simon Gratz Manuscript Collection, HSP. The diaries are cited by date in the endnotes. For locations, see the list below.

Memoir (1743): BL.

Diaries

July 8, 1753–March 1, 1754   Cover marked "No. 14," NHS.

March 5–October 16, 1754   Cover marked "No. 15," CHS.

January 1–May 7, 1757   Cover marked "No. 20," NHS.

May 9–November 6, 1757   Cover marked "No. 21," BL.

February 19–April 2, 1758   No cover, NHS.

November [no date] 1759–April 30, 1760   No cover, NHS.

June 22, 1760–January 18, 1761   Cover marked "No. 27," CHS.

September 28, 1761–February 18, 1762   Cover marked "No. 29," BL.

February 21–April 29, 1762   Cover marked "No. 30," BL.

January 11–June 2, 1767   No cover, NHS.

FIRST CHURCH OF CHRIST RECORDS

The First Church of Christ in Newport was later known as the First Congregational Church, and its records are catalogued under the later name.

FCCR-BM   First Congregational Church, Records of Baptisms and Marriages, 1744–1821, Vault A, no. 832, NHS.

FCCR-CB   First Congregational Church Records, Committee Book, 1743–99, Vault A, no. 836B, NHS.

FCCR-418, Folder 4   Records of the First Congregational Church of Newport, MSS 418, Folder 4: Contribution Book, 1763–75, RIHS.

FCCR-418, Folder 5   Records of the First Congregational Church of Newport, MSS 418, Folder 5: Contribution Book, 1775–76, 1780, 1805–7, RIHS.

FCCR-418, Folder 6   Records of the First Congregational Church of Newport, MSS 418, Folder 6, RIHS.

FCCR-418, Folder 9   Records of the First Congregational Church of Newport, MSS 418, Folder 9, RIHS.

FCCR-DRC   First Congregational Church Records, Documents Relating to the Church, 1729–99, Vault A, Box 40, Folder 1, NHS.

FCCR-1743–1831   First Congregational Church Records, 1743–1831, Vault A, no. 833, NHS.

PEOPLE

JE   Jonathan Edwards

JF   Joseph Fish

SA   Susanna Anthony

SH   Samuel Hopkins

SO   Sarah Osborn

PUBLICATIONS

Bushman, *GA*   Richard L. Bushman, ed. *The Great Awakening: Documents on the Revival of Religion, 1740–1745* (New York: Atheneum, 1970).

CH   Thomas Prince, ed., *The Christian History: Containing Accounts of the Revival and Propagation of Religion in Great-Britain & America* (Boston: S. Kneeland and T. Green, 1743–45).

FL   *Familiar Letters, Written by Mrs. Sarah Osborn and Miss Susanna Anthony,*

Late of Newport, Rhode-Island [ed. Elizabeth West Hopkins] (Newport: Newport Mercury, 1807).

LD   Franklin Bowditch Dexter, ed., *The Literary Diary of Ezra Stiles*, 3 vols. (New York: Scribner's, 1901).

NM   *Newport Mercury* (Newport, R.I.).

Kramnick, *PER*   Isaac Kramnick, ed., *The Portable Enlightenment Reader* (New York: Penguin, 1995).

SH, *Life and Character*   Samuel Hopkins, *The Life and Character of Miss Susanna Anthony* (Worcester, Mass.: Leonard Worcester, 1796).

SH, *Memoirs*   Samuel Hopkins, *Memoirs of the Life of Mrs. Sarah Osborn* (Worcester, Mass.: Leonard Worcester, 1799).

SO, *Nature*   Sarah Osborn, *The Nature, Certainty and Evidence of True Christianity* (Boston: Samuel Kneeland, 1755).

WJE   *Works of Jonathan Edwards*, 26 vols. (New Haven: Yale University Press, 1957–2008), Perry Miller, John E. Smith, and Harry S. Stout, general editors.

WJE Online   *Works of Jonathan Edwards* Online (Jonathan Edwards Center, Yale University, 2008–), http://edwards.yale.edu/archive.

WSH   Edwards Amasa Park, ed., *The Works of Samuel Hopkins*, 3 vols. (Boston: Doctrinal Tract and Book Society, 1865).

SCRIPTURAL ABBREVIATIONS

Old Testament/Hebrew Bible

Genesis	Gn
Exodus	Ex
Leviticus	Lv
Numbers	Nm
Deuteronomy	Dt
Joshua	Jo
Judges	Jgs
Ruth	Ru
1 Samuel	1 Sm
2 Samuel	2 Sm
1 Kings	1 Kgs
2 Kings	2 Kgs
1 Chronicles	1 Chr
2 Chronicles	2 Chr
Ezra	Ezr

Nehemiah	Neh
Esther	Est
Job	Jb
Psalms	Ps
Proverbs	Prv
Ecclesiastes	Eccl
Song of Solomon	Sg
Isaiah	Is
Jeremiah	Jer
Lamentations	Lam
Ezekiel	Ez
Daniel	Dn
Hosea	Hos
Joel	Jl
Amos	Am
Obadiah	Ob
Jonah	Jon
Micah	Mi
Nahum	Na
Habakkuk	Hb
Zephaniah	Zep
Haggai	Hg
Zechariah	Zec
Malachi	Mal

New Testament

Matthew	Mt
Mark	Mk
Luke	Lk
John (Gospel)	Jn
Acts of the Apostles	Acts
Romans	Rom
1 Corinthians	1 Cor
2 Corinthians	2 Cor
Galatians	Gal
Ephesians	Eph
Philippians	Phil
Colossians	Col
1 Thessalonians	1 Thes

2 Thessalonians	2 Thes
1 Timothy	1 Tm
2 Timothy	2 Tm
Titus	Ti
Philemon	Phlm
Hebrews	Heb
James	Jas
1 Peter	1 Pt
2 Peter	2 Pt
1 John (Epistle)	1 Jn
2 John (Epistle)	2 Jn
3 John (Epistle)	3 Jn
Jude	Jude
Revelation	Rev

APPENDIX: LOCATIONS OF SARAH OSBORN'S WRITINGS INCLUDED IN THIS VOLUME

ALL BUT ONE OF SARAH OSBORN's letters to Joseph Fish are transcribed from the AAS, and her letters to Samuel Hopkins are transcribed from the HSP. Unless otherwise indicated below, all of Osborn's diary entries are reprinted from her manuscripts at CHS, BL, or NHS. A few diary entries have been reprinted from SH, *Memoirs,* because the originals do not exist.

CHAPTER ONE

Letter from SO to Eleazar Wheelock (May 5, 1742) in the Eleazar Wheelock Papers, Dartmouth College, Hanover, N.H. A microfilm copy is available at Wheaton College, Wheaton, Ill., Reel 1, item 742305.

CHAPTER TWO

SO, Memoir, 1743, BL.

CHAPTER THREE

Osborn's account of her son's death can be found in SH, *Memoirs,* 65–70.

Her undated letter to Susanna Anthony can be found in *FL,* 49–51.

The diary entry for November 14, 1756, can be found in SH, *Memoirs,* 196–98.

CHAPTER FOUR

This chapter includes several diary entries reprinted by SH in *Memoirs:*

May 10, 1744 (p. 63)
May 27, 1745 (pp. 92–93)
July 28, 1745 (pp. 97–98)
November 1745 (pp. 93–96)
February 9, 1752 (pp. 112–14)

APPENDIX

CHAPTER FIVE

SO, *Nature.*

CHAPTER SIX

The following diary entries have been reprinted from SH, *Memoirs:*

December 21, 1757 (pp. 218–19)
November 1, 1758 (pp. 234–35)

CHAPTER EIGHT

The following diary entries have been reprinted from SH, *Memoirs:*

January 11, 1761 (pp. 262–64)
February 19, 1761 (pp. 267–70)
April 2, 1761 (p. 270)
October 27, 1763 (pp. 308–9)

CHAPTER NINE

The following diary entries have been reprinted from SH, *Memoirs:*

June 7, 1764 (pp. 320–21)
July 19, 1764 (p. 322)
July 27, 1768 (pp. 342–43)

CHAPTER TEN

The letter from SO to "Deacon ——," 1769: this letter appears in *FL*, July 9, 1769.

The letter from SO to SA, May 19, 1770, is reprinted from HSP.

The letter from SO to William Vinal, circa 1771–74, appears in the Records of the First Congregational Church of Newport, MSS 418, Folder 9, RIHS.

CHAPTER ELEVEN

The undated letter from SO to JF appears in *FL*, 154–60.

CHAPTER TWELVE

The Employment and Society of Heaven is reprinted from SH, *Memoirs*, 374–80.

May 15, 1753, is reprinted from SH, *Memoirs*, 123–27.

CHAPTER THIRTEEN

Sarah Osborn's Will and Inventory can be found in Probate Book No. 3, pp. 11–12, Newport City Hall, Newport, R.I.

NOTES

Citations are given in these notes to Osborn's works; in cases where the text quoted is reprinted in this volume, I follow my edited version with regard to spelling, punctuation, capitalization, and emphasis.

INTRODUCTION

1. SO, Memoir. For more on Osborn, see SH, *Memoirs*, *FL*, and Catherine A. Brekus, *Sarah Osborn's World: The Rise of Evangelical Christianity in Early America* (New Haven: Yale University Press, 2013).

2. SH, *Memoirs*, 358.

3. SO, *Nature.* SH, *Memoirs.* Elizabeth West Hopkins was Samuel Hopkins's wife, and although not named on the title page of *FL*, she was clearly the editor. See Elizabeth Hopkins to Levi Hart, January 12, 1787, Gratz Collection, Case 8/Box 23, American Colonial Clergy Collection, HSP.

4. SO, Memoir.

5. We have no way to measure literacy except to count how many women could sign their names on wills or other legal documents. My figures represent women's literacy around 1743, the year that Osborn wrote her memoir. Female literacy rose throughout the eighteenth century, increasing to as high as 65 percent in Boston between 1758 and 1762. See Kenneth A. Lockridge, *Literacy in Colonial New England: An Inquiry into the Social Context of Literacy in the Early Modern West* (New York: Norton, 1974), 40–41; Joel Perlmann and Dennis Shirley, "When Did New England Women Acquire Literacy?," *William and Mary Quarterly* 48, no. 1 (1991): 50–67; Linda Auwers, "Reading the Marks of the Past: Exploring Female Literacy in Colonial Windsor, Connecticut," *Historical Methods* 13 (1980): 204–14; E. Jennifer Monaghan, "Literacy Instruction and Gender in Colonial New England," in *Reading in America: Literature and Social History,* ed. Cathy N. Davidson (Baltimore: Johns Hopkins University Press, 1989), 53–80; and Gloria L. Main, "An Inquiry into When and Why Women Learned to Write in Colonial New England," *Journal of Social History* 24 (1991): 579–89.

6. Cotton Mather, *Awakening Thoughts on the Sleep of Death* (Boston: T. Green, 1712), iii–iv.

7. SO, Diary, March 26, 1754.

8. D. Bruce Hindmarsh, *The Evangelical Conversion Narrative: Spiritual Autobiography in Early Modern England* (New York: Oxford University Press, 2005), 13.

9. Robert Southey, *Letters from England*, II (London: Longman, Hurst, Rees, Orme and Brown, 1814), 359.

10. See D. W. Bebbington, *Evangelicalism in Modern Britain: A History from the 1730s to the 1980s* (Boston: Unwin Hyman, 1989), 1–74.

11. John Locke, *Essay Concerning Human Understanding* (1690; rpt. London: Awnsham and J. Churchill, 1706), vol. 1, p. 51. Roy Porter, *The Enlightenment*, 2nd ed. (New York: Palgrave, 2001), 2. On evangelicalism and empiricism, see Bebbington, *Evangelicalism in Modern Britain*, Catherine A. Brekus, "Sarah Osborn's Enlightenment: Reimaging Eighteenth-Century Intellectual History," in *The Religious History of American Women: Reimagining the Past*, ed. Catherine A. Brekus (Chapel Hill: University of North Carolina Press, 2007), 108–41, Mark A. Noll, *The Rise of Evangelicalism: The Age of Edwards, Whitefield, and the Wesleys* (Downers Grove, Ill.: InterVarsity Press, 2003), David Hempton, *Methodism: Empire of the Spirit* (New Haven: Yale University Press, 2005), 52, Frederick A. Dreyer, *The Genesis of Methodism* (Bethlehem: Lehigh University Press, 1999), Brian Stanley, "Christian Missions and the Enlightenment: A Reevaluation," in *Christian Missions and the Enlightenment*, ed. Brian Stanley (Grand Rapids, Mich.: Eerdmans, 2001), 1–21.

12. On Christian experientialism, see Bernard McGinn, "The Language of Inner Experience in Christian Mysticism," *Spiritus: A Journal of Christian Spirituality* 1, no. 1 (2001): 156–71. Susan Schreiner, *Are You Alone Wise?: The Search for Certainty in the Early Modern Era* (New York: Oxford University Press, 2011), 209–60. On seventeenth- and eighteenth-century attitudes towards experience, see Martin Jay, *Songs of Experience: Modern American and European Variations on a Universal Theme* (Berkeley: University of California Press, 2005), 9–78.

13. SO, *Nature*, 3. SO, Memoir.

14. SO, Diary, July 8, 1753. SO, Memoir.

15. JE, *A Treatise Concerning Religious Affections*, in *WJE* 2: 93–461. JE, "Personal Narrative," in *WJE* 16: 792. Bruce Kuklick describes Edwards as "an experimental Calvinist": he believed that the "supernatural was conveyed in experience." Bruce Kuklick, *Churchmen and Philosophers: From Jonathan Edwards to John Dewey* (New Haven: Yale University Press, 1985), 32.

16. SO, Diary, February 11, 1757.

17. Bruce Hindmarsh, "Reshaping Individualism: The Private Christian, Eighteenth-Century Religion and the Enlightenment," in *The Rise of the Laity in Evangelical Protestantism*, ed. Deryck W. Lovegrove (New York: Routledge, 2002), 74; Harry S. Stout, *The Divine Dramatist: George Whitefield and the Rise of Modern Evangelicalism* (Grand Rapids, Mich.: Eerdmans, 1991), 205; Jerald C. Brauer, "Conversion: From Puritanism to Revivalism," *Journal of Religion* 58, no. 3 (July 1978): 241.

18. Josiah Smith, *A Sermon, on the Character, Preaching &c. of the Rev. Mr.*

Whitefield (1740), in *The Great Awakening: Documents Illustrating the Crisis and Its Consequences*, ed. Alan Heimert and Perry Miller (Indianapolis: Bobbs-Merrill, 1967), 65. SO, *Nature*, 3, 5–6.

19. On humanitarianism, see Norman Fiering, "Irresistible Compassion: An Aspect of Eighteenth-Century Sympathy and Humanitarianism," *Journal of the History of Ideas* 37, no. 2 (1976): 195–218; Daniel Wickberg, "Humanitarianism," in *Encyclopedia of American Cultural and Intellectual History*, ed. Mary Kupiec Cayton and Peter W. Williams (New York: Scribner's, 2001), vol. 2, pp. 689–97; Karen Haltunnen, "Humanitarianism and the Pornography of Pain in Anglo-American Culture," *American Historical Review* 100, no. 2 (April 1995): 303–34; Ava Chamberlain, "The Theology of Cruelty: A New Look at the Rise of Arminianism in Eighteenth-Century New England," *Harvard Theological Review* 85, no. 3 (1992): 335–56.

20. On this theme, see Mark A. Noll, *A History of Christianity in the United States and Canada* (Grand Rapids, Mich.: Eerdmans, 1992), 104–5.

21. SO, Diary, January 23, 1757, and October 31, 1753.

22. For accounts of housework in the eighteenth century, see Jane C. Nylander, *Our Own Snug Fireside: Images of the New England Home, 1760–1860* (New York: Knopf, 1993); Laurel Thacher Ulrich, *Good Wives: Image and Reality in the Lives of Women in Northern New England, 1650–1750* (New York: Oxford University Press, 1980), 13–34; and Alice Morse Earle, *Home Life in Colonial Days* (New York: Grosset and Dunlap, 1898).

23. SO to JF, March 7, 1767.

24. Undated entry at the end of Diary marked as "No. 15," CHS. Jer 20:9.

25. SO, Diary, July 29, 1753.

26. SO, Diary, August 2, 1757. SH, *Memoirs*, 174. SO, Diary, November 1, 1753. For an example of a notation made a year after the original prayer, see SO, Diary, March 6, 1758.

27. SO, Diary, September 12, 1754 ("broken body").

28. SO, Diary, January 2, 1762. See also SO, Diary, July 8, 1753, and March 17, 1754.

29. *FL*, 15. Letter from JF to SO, October 31, 1751, SML.

30. *FL*, 25.

31. Letter from SO to Eleazar Wheelock (May 5, 1742) in the Eleazar Wheelock Papers, Dartmouth College, Hanover, N.H. A microfilm copy is available at Wheaton College, Wheaton, Ill., Reel 1, item 742305. Letter to an unnamed "deacon" in *FL*, 162.

32. Hindmarsh, *Evangelical Conversion Narrative*, 74. An invaluable study of letter writing is Susan O'Brien, "A Transatlantic Community of Saints: The Great Awakening and the First Evangelical Network, 1735–1755," *American Historical Review* 91, no. 4 (October 1986): 811–32.

33. SO to JF, September 15, 1766, AAS. Occom's letter (dated December 6, 1765) is reprinted in Joanna Brooks, *The Collected Writings of Samson Occom, Mohegan: Leadership and Literature in Eighteenth-Century Native America* (New York: Oxford University Press, 2006), 74.

34. Anthony did not become a member of Osborn's church until 1742, but the editor of *FL* claims that they were corresponding as early as 1740. See *FL*, "Advertisement," 2.

35. *FL*, 31. SO, Diary, October 13, 1754. SH, *Life and Character*, 22, 25.

36. In 1746 Fish also preached the installation sermon for the new pastor of Osborn's church, the Reverend William Vinal. Joseph Fish, *Love to Christ a Necessary Qualification in a Gospel Minister* (Newport, R.I.: the Widow Franklin, 1747).

37. Letter from SO to JF, May 29, 1753, AAS. Barbara Lacey, "The Bonds of Friendship: Sarah Osborn of Newport and the Reverend Joseph Fish of North Stonington, 1743–1779," *Rhode Island History* 45 (November 1986): 126–36.

38. SO to JF, May 29, 1753, AAS. Letter from SO to JF, January 27, 1755, AAS. On Fish and his family, see Joy Day Buel and Richard Buel, Jr., *The Way of Duty: A Woman and Her Family in Revolutionary America* (New York: Norton, 1984).

39. William Patten, *Christianity the True Theology, and Only Perfect Moral System in Answer to "The Age of Reason": with an Appendix, in Answer to "The Examiners Examined"* (Warren, R.I.: Nathaniel Phillips, 1795). One of the unidentified pamphlets may have been Samuel Russell's *Man's Liableness to Be Deceiv'd about Religion, Shewn and Caution'd Against*, a book currently owned by the American Antiquarian Society which bears her signature.

40. SO, Diary, October 23, 1761. Since this book was not published in America until 1792, she must have read a copy imported from England. See Daniel Defoe, *The Family Instructor*, 13th ed. (London: Tho. Longman, Ch. Hitch, and L. Hawes, 1751). The first edition of this book was published in London in 1715.

41. It is possible that this was a longer tradition that was not recorded until the 1750s. Sheila Skemp, "A Social and Cultural History of Newport, Rhode Island, 1720–1765" (Ph.D. diss., University of Iowa, 1974), 32.

42. For a full list of books, see FCCR-DRC. Nathaniel Morton, *New-Englands Memoriall; or, A Brief Relation of the Most Memorable and Remarkable Passages of the Providence of God, Manifested to the Planters of New-England in America* (Cambridge, Mass.: Samuel Green and Marmaduke Johnson, 1669). SH, *Life and Character of the Late Reverend Mr. Jonathan Edwards* (Boston: S. Kneeland, 1765).

43. George C. Mason, ed., *Annals of the Redwood Library* (Newport: Redwood Library, 1891), 3.

44. On publishing during the revivals, see Elizabeth Carroll Reilly and David D. Hall, "Customers and the Market for Books," in *The Colonial Book in the Atlantic World*, ed. Hugh Amory and David D. Hall (New York: Cambridge University Press, 2000), 395. For references to Bunyan, see SO to JF, February 5, 1761, AAS. She also alluded to Bunyan in her diary on September 25, 1757, when she thanked God for "grace abounding to the chief of sinners."

45. Osborn mentioned *Token for Children* in her diary entries on April 28, 1760, and June 12, 1766. The book was originally published in England in 1671, but she probably read the American version that included material by Cotton Mather. James Janeway, *A Token for Children. Being an Exact Account of the Conversion, Holy and*

Exemplary Lives and Joyful Deaths of Several Young Children. To Which Is Added, A Token, for the Children of New England; or, Some Examples of Children, in Whom the Fear of God was Remarkably Budding before They Died; in Several Parts of New England (Boston: John Phillips, 1728). Charles Drelincourt, *The Christian's Defence against the Fears of Death* (Boston: Thomas Fleet and Charles Harrison, 1744). Osborn mentioned Drelincourt's book in her diary on October 19, 1760.

46. See SO, Diary, November 26, 1761, for her mention of Jonathan Edwards, *An Account of the Life of the Late Reverend Mr. David Brainerd* (Boston: D. Henchman, 1749). She mentioned Samuel Buell, *A Faithful Narrative of the Remarkable Revival of Religion, in the Congregation of East-Hampton, on Long-Island, in the Year of Our Lord 1764* (New York: Samuel Brown, 1766), in her diary on March 17, 1767.

47. Karl Heinrich von Bogatzky, *A Golden Treasury for the Children of God, Whose Treasure Is in Heaven* (London: J. Richardson and T. Field, 1762). According to World Cat, the first edition of this book was published in London in 1754. SO, Diary, April 30, 1762.

48. James Hervey, *Theron and Aspasio; or, A Series of Dialogues and Letters, upon the Most Important and Interesting Subjects* (London: Charles Rivington, for John and James Rivington, 1755).

49. SO, Diary, April 24, 1757.

50. For Osborn's comparison of herself to Bury, see SO, Diary, July 17, 1757. On Mather, see SO, Diary, April 8, 1762, where she quotes from Samuel Mather, *The Life of the Very Reverend and Learned Cotton Mather* (Boston: Samuel Gerrish, 1729), 16–17.

51. SO, Memoir. For the reference to Joseph Eliot, *A Copy of a Letter Found in the Study of the Reverend Mr. Joseph Belcher, Late of Dedham, since His Decease* (Boston: B. Green, 1725), see SO, Diary, September 23, 1757.

52. SO, Diary, November 26, 1761. Edwards, *An Account of the Life of the Late Reverend Mr. David Brainerd*, 258.

53. SO, Diary, December 21, 1759.

54. JE, "Miscellanies," in *WJE* 13: 20.

55. *An Account of the Life and Death of Mrs. Elizabeth Bury* (Boston: Green, Bushell, and Allen, 1743). Mrs. Housman, *The Power and Pleasure of the Divine Life* (Boston: S. Kneeland, 1755). Both books were originally printed in England: Bury in 1721 and Housman in 1744. Osborn mentioned Bury's book in a letter to JF on February 4, 1748, AAS, and also in her diary on July 17, 1757. She mentioned Housman in her diary on March 10, 1758.

56. *An Account of the Life and Death of Mrs. Elizabeth Bury*, 96, 63. SO, Diary, July 8, 1753. SO, Diary, January 17, 1760.

57. SH, *Life and Character*, 41.

58. SO, Diary, November 16–17, 1753.

59. SO, Diary, July 11, 1753.

60. Elizabeth Singer Rowe, *Devout Exercises of the Heart in Meditation and Soliloquy, Prayer and Praise* (London: R. Hett, 1738), 132. *The Journal of Esther Edwards*

Burr, 1754–1757, ed. Carol F. Karlsen and Laurie Crumpacker (New Haven: Yale University Press, 1984), 99. SO, Diary, July 18, 1749, CHS.

61. SO, Diary, October 3, 1757. She quotes these passages: Gn 48:15: "the God that has fed me all my life long"; Phil 4:19: "will supply all my needs"; Ps 119:116: "ashamed of my hope"; Heb 13:5: "he will never leave me nor forsake me." See also Jo 1:5.

62. I have borrowed the phrase "biblical story in miniature" from Hindmarsh, "Reshaping Individualism," 80.

63. For Jabez, see SO, Diary, January 20, 1757, March 15, 1757, and September 11, 1757. For Mary, see *FL*, 42.

64. SH, *Memoirs*, 50, quoting Jb 1:21. SO, Diary, May 20, 1757, quoting Jb 19:21 and Ps. 103:13.

65. SO, Diary, January 20, 1757, March 15, 1757, and November 25, 1760, quoting Hb 1:2 and 3:17–18.

66. SO, Diary, November 28, 1759. For other comparisons to Jacob, see SO, Diary, October 14, 1753, and July 18, 1754.

67. For Esther, see SO, Diary, August 6, 1753, and September 1, 1753.

68. On the biblical women who inspired early nineteenth-century evangelical women preachers, see Catherine A. Brekus, *Strangers and Pilgrims: Female Preaching in America, 1740–1845* (Chapel Hill: University of North Carolina Press, 1998), 219.

69. For Hannah, see SO, Diary, April 11, 1757, and April 20, 1757. For Mary, see SO, Diary, July 1, 1757, September 9, 1757, and February 7, 1757. Osborn identifies this woman as Mary Magdalene, not Mary of Bethany. The biblical accounts are not clear which Mary washed Christ's feet, but the Gospel of John identifies her as Mary of Bethany. See Jn 12:1–3.

70. For references to this story, see SO, March 10, 1757, February 18, 1757, and April 11, 1757. For the biblical accounts, see Mt 9:20–22, Mk 5:25–34, and Lk 8:43–48.

71. For images of Christ as a fountain, see SO, Diary, June 21, 1754, January 22, 1757, and April 20, 1757.

72. SO, cover of Diary marked "No. 21."

73. SO, cover of Diary marked "No. 15."

CHAPTER ONE. THAT PRECIOUS PROMISE

1. Rom 8:28.
2. Ex 14:15.
3. Is 54:13.
4. Is 54:4.

CHAPTER TWO. A MEMOIR

1. On this point, see Georges Gusdorf, "Conditions and Limits of Autobiography," in *Autobiography: Essays Theoretical and Critical*, ed. James Olney (Princeton: Princeton University Press, 1980), 44.

2. Mt 15:14, Ps 95:11.

3. Osborn crossed out these words: "lying in little trivial things, but I could not go on silently in it." In the margin she added, "They go astray from the womb, speaking lies," quoting Ps 58:3.

4. Rev 21:8.

5. In the margin: "I desire to be thankful I never escaped correction for the sin of lying."

6. Osborn may have attended the same boarding school in Peckham where Edward Harwood (1729–94), a well-known Dissenting minister, later served as a tutor. See *Dictionary of National Biography*, ed. Leslie Stephen and Sidney Lee (New York and London, 1891), vol. 25, pp. 102–3.

7. In the margin: "governed by a legal spirit here."

8. Mt 7:3–5, Lk 64:1–2.

9. Osborn crossed out the word "exceeding" before "vile."

10. Osborn crossed out the word "again" after "sin." The words "or rather what was ordered by infinite wisdom to that end" appear in the margin.

11. In the margin: "I mention this as a childish notion that I took such pleasure in touching them. I used to go secretly behind them for that purpose." Osborn refers to the story of the woman with the issue of blood who came behind Jesus to touch the hem of his garment (Mt 9:20).

12. The Reverend Nathaniel Clap (1669–1745) was the pastor of Newport's First Church. Freetown is in Bristol County, Mass. The book may have been Isaac Watts, *Honey Out of the Rock Flowing to Little Children That They May Know to Refuse the Evil and Chuse the Good* (Boston: T. Fleet and T. Crump, 1715).

13. In the margin: "self-love perhaps was the only cause."

14. At the end of this sentence she crossed out the words "and therefore frequently prayed that God would give me a sight of hell, even with my bodily eyes, or anything though [several words cannot be deciphered] . . . courage."

15. Gn 6:3.

16. In the margin: "bright moonlight."

17. The words "as I thought" are inserted above the line. They may have been added later.

18. Ibid.

19. In the margin: "O, how far may a hypocrite resemble a true Christian."

20. The words "the change was then wrought and" appear in the margin.

21. The words "as I thought" are inserted above the line. They may have been added later.

22. The words "it seemed to me" are inserted above the line.

23. The words "as a narrow bridge" are inserted above the line.

24. The word "again" is inserted above the line.

25. In the margin: "though I think I kept on praying, &c."

26. Dighton, Mass., is on the other side of the Taunton River.

27. In the margin: "Is it duty to let this criminal affair stand recorded?"

28. Jas 4:7–8.

29. The words "as I thought" are inserted above the line. They may have been added later. In the margin: "supposing all was well with me, God had forgiven me, etc."

30. The words "for whose sakes I write these lines" are inserted above the line.

31. The word "criminal" was added above the line.

32. The words "without disparagement to justice" were added above the line.

33. Osborn's parents belonged to the Second Church of Newport. The pastor was James Searing (1704–55).

34. The words "as I thought" (after "I see") were added above the line.

35. In the margin: "I was . . . led into all these things by example, yea trained up in them, being taught from a child to believe there was no sin in them." (The word after "was" is not decipherable.)

36. Osborn made significant revisions to her account of her parents' opposition to her first marriage. She crossed out three and a half lines after the words "at first they liked him." These words can be deciphered: "led me into offense very disobedient. Now I durst not say I was . . . so then I justified myself." The words "I thought" were added above the line. The words "to help get it" are crossed out.

37. The words "thirty pounds total" are crossed out. Osborn wrote that she was "exceedingly terrified" but then crossed out the word "terrified" and added "perplexed" above the line.

38. Prv 28:24, 19:26.

39. Osborn originally wrote, "I resolved again to," but then crossed out these words and added above the line, "I made resolutions that I would."

40. Osborn crossed out the words "yet had" after the words "I had." The words "or an entire breaking off from vanity" were added above the line.

41. She was seventeen years old.

42. 1 Cor 11:29.

43. In the margin: "And I thought of a truth that I did indeed give up both myself and it. I don't know how to reconcile these exercises of heart with being at total enmity."

44. The following words can be deciphered: "and the cold set in . . . he would get wood and help. The church assisted me . . . ."

45. Heb 2:3.

46. Jb 1:21.

47. The words "as I thought" were added above the line.

48. The following words can be deciphered: "And being intimate and . . . with those whose example was very bad, I found it exceeding . . . and by degrees followed them in many respects and . . . light by Sabbaths. And would make bold . . . excuses to absent myself from the public worship, employing myself about worldly things . . . gave myself a greater lease in my excuses till . . . sin. . . . crept in . . . ." The words "but at length" were also crossed out.

49. One line is crossed out here.

50. Osborn crossed out this sentence.

51. Osborn crossed out the following words at the end of the sentence, "Thus I decided conscience called me, as in all haste."

52. "N.B." is an abbreviation for "nota bene."

53. The following words can be deciphered: "But to go on, as I said, I, by many good peoples, and I thought myself to be indeed very good . . . ."

54. Osborn crossed out the words "church woman."

55. The words "or no essential" were added above the line.

56. In the margin: "it was for want of a seat I had left his meeting."

57. Osborn again crossed out the words "church woman."

58. Osborn crossed out the word "all," which she might have seen as an exaggeration.

59. After the word "works," Osborn crossed out the words "I had before been so fond of."

60. "all liars": Rev 19:20; "depart from me": Mt 25:41; "consider this": Ps 50:22; "he, that being often reproved": Prv 29:1; "ye have set at naught": Prv 1:25–26; "it is a fearful thing": Heb 10:31; "who among us": Is 33:14.

61. Ps 50:16.

62. A few words can be deciphered: "and . . . to read pray or . . . ."

63. The words "thought to do so" appear in the margin. These words echo her earlier account of her temptation to commit suicide, which raises the possibility that this may have been a second suicidal crisis.

64. "depart from me": Mt 7:23; "the door of mercy is shut against me": Lk 13:25; "you may yet obtain mercy": Heb 4:16, Rom 11:31; "he is a liar from the beginning": Jn 8:44, 1 Jn 2:22.

65. Prv 18:14.

66. The following words can be deciphered: "spoken . . . is the most acutest pain. It is possible the pain of . . . ."

67. The word "chosen" was added above the line.

68. The word "ever" was added above the line.

69. Eph 2:8.

70. In the margin: "Lord, what made it thus impossible but my legal spirit and unwillingness to accept freely? My inability was criminal and too obstinate, for I was then as . . . as . . . ." (two words are not decipherable).

71. 1 Cor 10:13. In the margin: "Sovereign mercy, then I cast anchor on divine faithfulness."

72. In the margin: "This is all old tenor language, and if I did not remember exercises of a better kind than is here expressed respecting God's glory, I should be staggered."

73. 1 Cor 11:29.

74. Joseph Stevens, *Another and Better Country, Even an Heavenly: In Reserve for All True Believers* (Boston: S. Kneeland, 1723).

75. "Come in, Lord Jesus": Gn 24:31; "I will come": Ps 5:7; "I am thine": 1 Kgs 20:4, Ps 119:94; "even so, Father, for so it seemed good in thy sight": Mt 11:26.

76. 1 Jn 4:19. In the margin: "My meaning was 'for it' and not 'first,' etc. I never had, etc."

77. Hos 14:4.

78. Sg 5:10, 16.

79. Lk 22:32.

80. Thomas Doolittle, *A Call to Delaying Sinners* (Boston: Benjamin Eliot, 1700). I have omitted her second use of the word "but" before "according" because it appears to have been a mistake.

81. She quotes Jn 20:25–28: "I was forced to cry out," and Jn 21:17: "Lord thou knowest all things."

82. After "unspeakable joy," Osborn crossed out the words "to hear the blessed Jesus say, 'daughter, thy sins are forgiven thee.'" She was quoting Mt 9:2, Mk 2:5, and Lk 5:20.

83. Ps 32:1–5: "Blessed is he whose transgression is forgiven, whose sin is covered. Blessed is the man unto whom the Lord imputeth not iniquity, and in whose spirit there is no guile. When I kept silence, my bones waxed old through my roaring all the day long. For day and night thy hand was heavy upon me: my moisture is turned into the drought of summer. Selah. I acknowledge my sin unto thee, and mine iniquity have I not hid. I said, I will confess my transgressions unto the Lord; and thou forgavest the iniquity of my sin. Selah."

84. Ps 73:25.

85. Osborn paraphrases Doolittle, *A Call to Delaying Sinners*, 140. His language was less extreme: "That when thou shall call me thereunto, I may practice this my resolution, through thy assistance, to forsake all that is dear unto me in this world, rather than to turn from thee to the ways of sin."

86. 2 Cor 12:9.

87. In the margin: "on further reflection, I think it was at this time, when writing my covenant engagements, that I [the word "think" is crossed out] know the 5th of Isaiah was applied, also from the fourth to the tenth verse."

88. The words "when writing, before I finished," appear in the margin. Several words are crossed out and indecipherable after the word "rejoicing."

89. Rom 8:35–36, 38–39.

90. She crossed out the word "presently" before the word "thought."

91. Mk 4:39.

92. In the margin: "though I should die with thee, yet will I not deny thee, etc." She quotes Mt 26:35.

93. Osborn crossed out the word "miracle" and substituted "some foretaste" above the line.

94. Osborn crossed out several words in this sentence. It originally read, "and

singing, dancing, and now and then playing a game at cards and telling romancing stories."

95. In the margin: "Oh! The woeful, bitter remains of total depravity and contrariety to God and strict holiness and a legal spirit. Lord, was there ever such a heart as mine?"

96. Osborn crossed out the following words: "And indeed, I was so comforted with the belief I had that his change out of a world of sin and sorrow was infinitely his gain, that I could not mourn, but found rather to have a secret joy that he was released."

97. People with the smallpox were quarantined.

98. In the margin: "from being unequally yoked."

99. Michaelmas was the feast of the archangel Michael, September 29. The term was commonly used to refer to the beginning of autumn.

100. 2 Cor 6:14.

101. An "Edomite" was an enemy of the Jews. See 1 Sm 22:18. In the midst of her cross out, Osborn did not scratch out the following words: "O! How many deliverances has God wrought out for me, both in spiritual and corporal things, but alas . . . ." In the margin she added: "I don't mean that I laid the means of grace aside and returned wholly to the world. I did not do this."

102. George Whitefield (1714–70), a British Anglican, was the most famous minister of the eighteenth century and a leader of the transatlantic revivals of the Great Awakening. Gilbert Tennent (1703–64) was a Presbyterian minister from New Jersey.

103. The word "justly" was added above the line.

104. Jer 3:22.

105. Is 44:22.

106. The original sentence read, "such as singing songs, dancing, playing at cards and foolish jesting," but she crossed out "playing at cards."

107. In the margin: "as to songs."

108. Osborn originally wrote, "singing, dancing, or playing at cards," but once again she crossed out the words "or playing at cards."

109. The words "if the Lord will" were added above the line.

110. The words "lost my evidences" were added above the line.

111. Ps 42:5, Ps 42:11, Ps 43:5.

112. Jb 1:21.

113. "Secret things belong to God": Dt 29:29; "my will is done": Mt 6:10. In the margin: "Improperly expressed. I heard no voice." (Osborn capitalized the word "I" in this sentence, which suggests that this comment was added later. She did not capitalize the word "I" in the main text of her memoir.) After the words "My will," she wrote above the line, "or God's."

114. Osborn originally wrote, "but it seemed to be set home," but she crossed out "it" and added "the words" above the line.

115. Osborn kept shop for Captain David Moore. See the letter from David Moore

to Eleazar Wheelock, May 6, 1742, Eleazar Wheelock Papers, Microfilm at Wheaton College, Wheaton, Ill., Reel 1, item 742306.2.

116. The words "which I earnestly entreated" were added above the line.

117. These words can be deciphered: "though as in all other respects thought him worthy of my affections . . . of it to a great degree but . . . ."

118. Mk 5:36. Osborn wrote, "when praying and agonizing with God," but then crossed out the words "and agonizing with God."

119. Eleazar Wheelock (1711–79).

120. In the margin: "how the remains of a legal spirit follow me from stage to stage."

121. The words "Block Island" are crossed out. Osborn seems to be saying that her mother discovered something while on a trip to Block Island (an island that is part of Rhode Island), but Osborn was able to conceal it again. In the margin, Osborn crossed out the words "note that I was persuaded to lend some there, but was betrayed."

122. Osborn identified this woman only as "poor Mrs."

123. These words echoed the covenant that she made with God.

124. God rejected Saul as king after he spared King Agag. See 1 Sm 15:9.

125. Mt 6:14.

126. Osborn crossed out the word "dutiful" and chose "obedient" instead.

127. Osborn wrote "a small present," but then she crossed out the word "small."

128. Hos 13:9.

129. Prv 28:13.

130. Osborn's mother refers to the story of the Prodigal Son (Lk 15:22), who was welcomed home by his father despite his profligacy.

131. Is 41:10.

132. Ex 14:15.

133. This sentence is in the margins.

134. Osborn crossed out a sentence here that reads, in part: "he had only . . . sheep, his house, and was very . . . ."

135. In eighteenth-century usage, a "mother-in-law" was a stepmother. Henry had four sons with his first wife, Margaret Miller (1700–1741), who died the year before his marriage to Sarah: Edward (born in 1724), Henry (born in 1725), John (born in 1728), and Samuel, who died in 1727 at the age of twenty-two months.

136. Is 54:13.

137. Osborn originally wrote "pleading that promise" but crossed out the words "that promise." Crossed out in the margin: "I don't think I was free from impulses here." She added the word "and" above the line in order to make her sentence coherent.

138. Osborn made significant edits to this sentence. The words "that I know of" were added above the line. The fact that Osborn capitalized her "I" in this sentence suggests that this phrase was added later.

139. This may have been Andrew Tyler (1719–75), who was appointed pastor of the church in Dedham, Mass., in 1743. Tyler was the author of *The Terms of Christianity*

Briefly Considered; and the Reasonableness of Them Illustrated (Boston: Edes and Gill, 1756).

140. In the margin: "Yet I found Christ was my only refuge."

141. Osborn crossed out a sentence here: "I was told by an intimate Christian friend."

142. Osborn did not identify this minister. Since she briefly considered joining Trinity Church, the Anglican congregation in Newport, she may have been acquainted with its pastor, the Reverend James Honeyman (1675–1750). Anglicans were skeptical of evangelical claims to religious certainty.

143. 2 Tm 2:19.

144. Rom 8:28–30. I have changed her words "and was much comforted" to "I was much comforted."

145. Rom 8:1.

146. Rom 8:38–39.

147. The words "in years past" appear in the margin.

148. Osborn was probably referring to Ps 81:8, 13.

149. Mt 23:23.

150. Is 65:5.

151. Isaac Watts, *Psalms of David, Imitated in the Language of the New Testament, and Applied to the Christian State and Worship,* 12th ed. (London: R. Hett and J. Brackston, 1740), 277.

152. Heb 13:5.

153. This diary no longer survives.

154. The "first table" was the first four of the Ten Commandments. The "second table" was the last six. See Ex 20.

155. Prv 14:20.

156. On the back cover, which is faded, she wrote: "I acknowledge God had been just if he had given me up to my own heart's lusts till I had filled up my measure. I . . . to reply against the glorious potter for thus forming me to be so vile, I adore the wisdom I cannot comprehend. O what a comfort is it. In the great day when all of our sins should be as . . . ." The rest is indecipherable.

CHAPTER THREE. A SON'S DEATH

1. Osborn's description of Samuel as her "only son" echoes several biblical passages. God spared Isaac, Abraham's "only son," as he lay upon the altar of sacrifice (Gn 22, Heb 11:17); Jesus healed the only son of a man whose only son had been possessed by an evil spirit (Lk 9:38); and Jesus also healed the "only son" of a widow (Lk 7:12). Osborn may also allude to the words of the prophet Jeremiah 6:26: "O daughter of my people, gird thee with sackcloth, and wallow thyself in ashes: make thee mourning, as for an only son, most bitter lamentation," or Amos 8:10: "I will turn your feasts into mourning . . . and I will make it as the mourning of an only son." The words "sick

unto death" echo the biblical descriptions of Epaphroditus, an associate of the apostle Paul's who had been "sick nigh unto death: but God had mercy on him," and Hezekiah, who had beseeched God for mercy when he had been "sick unto death." "I have heard thy prayer," God responded. "I have seen thy tears: behold, I will heal thee." On Hezekiah, see 2 Kgs 20, 2 Chr 32:24, and Is 38:1. On Epaphroditus, see Phil 2:27.

2. Ps 86:7.

3. Jer 30:8.

4. Joseph Alleine, *An Alarm to Unconverted Sinners* (1671; rpt. Philadelphia: B. Franklin, 1741).

5. Osborn refers to the story of Jacob wrestling in Gn 32:24–25. The King James Version says that Jacob wrestled with "a man," while other versions specify an "angel." Like many other early Americans, Osborn believed that Jacob had wrestled with God because of Jacob's words, "I have seen God face to face": Gn 32:30.

6. Osborn refers to the story of the woman of Canaan, who asked Jesus to heal her daughter. When Jesus said, "It is not meet to take the children's bread, and to cast it to dogs," she responded, "Truth, Lord: yet the dogs eat of the crumbs which fall from their masters' table." Jesus praised her great faith and healed her child. See Mt 15:22–28.

7. Jesus promised one of the thieves who was crucified next to him that they would rejoice together in paradise. Lk: 23:43.

8. Osborn compares herself to Job ("I was enabled to fill my mouth with arguments") and Jacob, who wrestled with God until he received a blessing. See Jb 23:4 and Gn 32:24–25.

9. Once again Osborn identifies herself with Job, who resigned himself to his suffering ("blessed his name, for he had given, and it was he who had taken": Jb 1:21).

10. Osborn compares herself to David, who resigned himself to the death of his child ("I then arose from my dead child and was quieted": 2 Sm 12:20).

11. Osborn refers to two biblical passages in this sentence. In the first, she remembers the comforting words of 1 Jn 16–18: "Hereby perceive we the love of God, because he laid down his life for us: and we ought to lay down our lives for the brethren. But whoso hath this world's good, and seeth his brother have need, and shutteth up his bowels of compassion from him, how dwelleth the love of God in him? My little children, let us not love in word, neither in tongue; but in deed and in truth." In the second, she remembers Ezekiel's warning to sinners (Ez 33:2–5): "Son of man, speak to the children of thy people, and say unto them, When I bring the sword upon a land, if the people of the land take a man of their coasts, and set him for their watchman: If when he seeth the sword come upon the land, he blow the trumpet, and warn the people; Then whosoever heareth the sound of the trumpet, and taketh not warning; if the sword come, and take him away, his blood shall be upon his own head. He heard the sound of the trumpet, and took not warning; his blood shall be upon him. But he that taketh warning shall deliver his soul."

12. Osborn strings together a series of comforting biblical quotations in this paragraph from Lam 3:24 (my only portion); Ps 73:25–26: "Whom have I in heaven but

thee? And there is none on earth I desire besides thee. Though my flesh and my heart fail, yet God is the strength of my heart and my portion forever"; and Rom 8:38–39: "though death separate from all things here below, it cannot separate between thee and me."

13. Heb 12:6.

14. Ps 119:75.

15. Ps 103:13.

16. Osborn refers to the death of Lazarus. Mary and Martha sent for Jesus when their brother Lazarus became ill, but Jesus did not arrive until four days after his death. Jesus wept with them and then resurrected Lazarus from the dead. See Jn 11.

17. Osborn refers to two biblical passages. In the first, Is 48:10, God promised to purify his chosen in "the furnace of affliction." In the second, Dn 3:1–30, God rescued Shadrach, Meshach, and Abednego when Nebuchadnezzar threw them into a fiery furnace for refusing to worship him.

18. Osborn remembers God's punishment of the Israelites for committing idolatry ("lest my heart be joined to idols": Hos 4:17). She also remembers Elkanah's words to his wife Hannah, who wept because she could not have children: "am not I better to thee than ten sons?" 1 Sm 1:8.

19. John Mason, *Spiritual Songs; or, Songs of Praise with Penitential Cries to Almighty God, upon Several Occasions,* 15th ed. (Boston: D. Henchman, 1742), 95.

CHAPTER FOUR. A HIDDEN GOD

1. Osborn includes the wrong reference. This passage is from Mt 7:7.

2. Prv 8:17.

3. Osborn quotes from Jb 19:21 twice in this entry: "thou hast touched me" and "pity me."

4. Osborn makes a dash instead of identifying this man by name.

5. This entry comes from SH, *Memoirs,* 93–96. Hopkins combined this entry with the entry for May 27, 1745 (Osborn's account of the Rev. Helyer's death). Clap died in October 1745, which means that this entry was written sometime afterward.

6. Osborn compares herself to Job (Jb 1:21).

7. Gn 42:36. Osborn echoes the cry of Jacob, who thought he had lost his son Benjamin. But he would soon discover that both Benjamin and another son, Joseph, were alive.

8. The Reverend William Vinal (1718–81) served as the pastor of the First Church of Newport from 1746 until his dismissal in 1768.

9. Jn 1:16.

10. Mt 14:31.

11. Elizabeth Bury, *An Account of the Life and Death of Mrs. Elizabeth Bury, who Died, May the 11th 1720. Aged 76. Chiefly Collected Out of Her Own Diary. Together with Her Elegy, by the Reverend Dr. Watts,* 4th ed. (Boston: Green, Bushell, and Allen, for D. Henchman, 1743), 39. Elizabeth Bury (1644–1720) was a British Dissenter whose diaries were published posthumously.

12. Osborn quotes from Acts 8:39 ("going on my way rejoicing") and implicitly compares herself to the Ethiopian eunuch who was baptized by Philip.

13. Rom 8:28.

14. Rebecca Fish (1738–66) and Mary Fish (1736–1818) both attended Osborn's school.

15. She had run out of space to write.

16. See George Whitefield's 1740 letter: "I received your long wished-for letter. It . . . knit my soul to you much more than ever." *The Works of the Reverend George Whitefield*, vol. 1 (London: Dilly, 1771), 184.

17. Jon 3:9.

18. "Molly" was Mary Fish's nickname.

19. Elizabeth Vinal was married to the Reverend William Vinal.

20. Sg 2:16.

21. The words "or unbelief" were added above the line. In the margin: April 15, 1760: "Time has shown me how needless these cares and fears were, for hitherto the Lord has helped me." She quotes from 1 Sm 7:12.

22. Mt 6:34.

23. Osborn refers to a story about Saint Basil (330–379). She may have read this story in John Flavel, *Divine Conduct or the Mystery of Providence* (London: Francis Tyton, 1678), 99.

24. Nabal was a rich man who insulted David and refused his request for provisions. See 1 Sm 25:3.

25. "Therefore all things whatsoever ye would that men should do to you, do ye even so to them" (Mt 7:12).

26. Osborn stopped writing the entry for October 30 with the words "clear the eye of faith." She began the entry for October 31 in midsentence, "that it may behold thee . . ." I have combined these two entries for clarity.

27. The words "'tis good for me to be here" are a reference to the Transfiguration of Jesus (Mt 17:4, Mk 9:5, Lk 9:33), when God reveals Jesus to be his son.

28. The entry for Saturday, November 17, begins in midsentence from the previous day's entry at the words "that he may not accomplish his designs."

29. Osborn refers to the story of Mary and Martha (Lk 10:38–42). Martha complained that Mary sat at the feet of Jesus instead of helping to serve, but Jesus praised Mary for choosing the "good part."

30. Osborn echoes the words of Moses and David. See Ex 3:11, 1 Sm 18:18, 2 Sm 7:18, 1 Chr 17:16, 1 Chr 29:14, 2 Chr 2:6.

31. Isaac Watts, *Hymns and Spiritual Songs*, 16th ed. (Boston: D. Henchman, 1742), Book 1, 18.

32. Osborn refers to Bobey (1744–?), a slave boy. Based on her assertion that he was ten years old and had lived with them "from the cradle," she had owned him since 1744.

33. Nathaniel Eels (1710–86) was a Congregationalist minister in Stonington,

Conn. His wife was Mary Eels (?–1791). Ancestry.com, *Connecticut, Church Record Abstracts, 1630–1920* [database online], Provo, Utah, 2013.

34. Parts of her letter are written in the margins.

35. Benjamin Pabodie (Peabody) (1717–92) was the deacon of the First Church. His half sister, Rebecca Pabodie (1704–83), was married to Joseph Fish.

36. The Reverend Samuel Tobey (1715–81) was the pastor of the Congregational Church in Berkley, Mass., from 1735 until 1781. See Enoch Sanford, *History of the Town of Berkley, Mass.: Including Sketches of the Lives of the Two First Ministers, Rev. Samuel Tobey, and Rev. Thomas Andros* (New York: Kilbourne Tompkins, 1872). Osborn never mentioned the name of her first husband's brother.

37. Eph 3:19.

38. George Whitefield (1714–70) was a famous British Anglican evangelist who led revivals throughout the Atlantic world. See Harry S. Stout, *The Divine Dramatist: George Whitefield and the Rise of Modern Evangelicalism* (Grand Rapids, Mich.: Eerdmans, 1991). He preached on the following texts in Newport: "To know the love of Christ": Eph 3:19; "Behold the bridegroom cometh": Mt 25:6; "Blessed and holy is he who has part in the first resurrection": Rev 20:6; "I am the way": Jn 14:6; "Awake thou that sleepeth": Eph 5:14.

39. I have silently added the full words to this sentence. There is a hole in the page. The words "under" and "I will be" are obscured in the original.

CHAPTER FIVE. THE NATURE, CERTAINTY, AND EVIDENCE OF TRUE CHRISTIANITY

1. For the story of the publication of Osborn's letter, see SH, *Memoirs*, 159.

2. For a fuller discussion of women's writing in the eighteenth century, see Catherine A. Brekus, *Sarah Osborn's World: The Rise of Evangelical Christianity in Early America* (New Haven: Yale University Press, 2013), chapter 6.

3. SO, *Nature*, title page. 1 Cor 1:27.

4. Jn 5:40.

5. The term "Rock of Ages" is not found in the King James Version of the Bible, though some commentators translate the words of Is 26:4, "everlasting strength," as "everlasting rock." Osborn may have been quoting from Isaac Watts, *Hymns and Spiritual Songs*, 16th ed. (Boston: D. Henchman, 1742), Book 1, 18.

6. Jn 9:25, 1 Cor 5:17.

7. 1 Sm 27:1, Jas 2:7.

8. Mt 27:46, Mk 15:34, Ps 22:1.

9. Mi 7:19.

10. Osborn distinguishes herself from the Strict Congregationalists, also known as the Separates, who argued that "Assurance is of the essence of faith." *The Result of a Council of the Consociated Churches of the County of Windham* (Boston, 1747), 17. Osborn also had a robust sense of assurance, but she did not want to be associated with the most radical wing of the revivals, especially because Separates had split Joseph Fish's church.

See Joy Day Buel and Richard Buel, *The Way of Duty: A Woman and Her Family in Revolutionary America* (New York: Norton, 1984), 14–18.

CHAPTER SIX. ZION'S TROUBLES

1. Osborn listed the wrong biblical citation. The correct citation is 1 Jn 2:15.

2. Isaac Watts, *The Psalms of David*, 7th ed. (Philadelphia: B. Franklin, 1729), 256.

3. Heb 13:5.

4. Is 41:10, Mt 14:24, Mk 6:50, Jn 6:20.

5. Jo 9:25, Jgs 10:15, Jgs 19:24, 2 Sm 10:12, 1 Sm 3:18, 2 Sm 15:26, 2 Sm 24:22, Jer 26:14.

6. Osborn may have been thinking of several biblical texts, including Jo 9:25, Jgs 10:15, Jgs 19:24, 2 Sm 10:12, 1 Sm 3:18, 2 Sm 15:26, 2 Sm 24:22, Jer. 26:14.

7. Mt 26:22.

8. 2 Cor 12:9, Jo 14:11, Is 26:20.

9. Is 54:10.

10. Osborn left a space here and resumed writing later in the evening.

11. The words "Mrs. Mary Allen died . . . I hope she is gone to rest" appear in the margin. Mary Franklin (circa 1732–57) was the daughter of Ann Smith Franklin (1696–1763), the printer of the *Newport Mercury* and the widow of James Franklin (1697–1735), who was Benjamin Franklin's brother. Mary Franklin Allen married William Allen in 1752. Ancestry.com, *Rhode Island, Vital Extracts, 1636–1899* [database online], Provo, Utah, 2014.

12. Ps 119:71.

13. Newport held lotteries in order to raise money for civic improvements.

14. This sentence appears in the margin.

15. This sentence appears in the margin. Peggy Lion may be Margaret Lyon, who married Edward Harris in Newport's Trinity Church in 1758. Ancestry.com, *Rhode Island, Vital Extracts, 1636–1899* [database online].

16. This sentence appears in the margin. John Osborn (1728–1759) was the son of Henry Osborn and Margaret Miller. He married Abigail Grey on June 19, 1748. Ancestry.com, *Rhode Island, Vital Extracts, 1636–1899* [database online].

17. Ps 41:1.

18. The Reverend William Vinal.

19. Osborn may have been referring to the defeat of the French at Fort William Henry in March 1757.

20. Moses "stood in the gap" on Mount Sinai for forty days and nights in order to prevent an angry God from destroying the Israelites.

21. James Hervey, *Theron and Aspasio; or, A Series of Dialogues and Letters, upon the Most Important and Interesting Subjects* (London: Charles Rivington, for John and James Rivington, 1755), 1: 70.

22. Osborn used the word "profession" as a synonym for "profession of faith."

23. This sentence appears in the margin.

24. Phillis was the slave of Timothy Allen (1713–92), a silversmith in Newport. He was a member of the Second Church of Newport. *LD* 1: 84, 140, 327, 428, 504. Phillis had two children: Bobey, who was owned by Osborn, and another child who was not named. We know that Phillis had two children only because of a brief entry in Sarah's diary. Praying for Phillis, she wrote: "O appear for Her offspring, both of them." SO, Diary, December 15, 1761. The other child may have belonged to Timothy Allen, Phillis's master. Phillis seems to have been married to a man named Gosper, a slave. Gosper is mentioned in SO, Diary, October 19, 1761. Gosper was probably Bobey's father. See SO, Diary, December 7, 1761. I assume that Phillis and Gosper were married; otherwise the church would not have accepted her as a full member. She was baptized and admitted to full membership in the First Church of Newport on June 26, 1757. See FCCR-BM. Phillis is listed as a member of the women's society in SO, Diary, December 4, 1761, and SO, Diary, January 2, 1762.

25. This sentence appears in the margin. The identity of this woman is not clear, and she is not mentioned in Osborn's other writings. She may have been Elizabeth Gardiner, who married Clark Brown in Newport's Second Baptist Church on December 4, 1740. Ancestry.com, *Rhode Island, Vital Extracts, 1636–1899* [database online].

26. Edward (1724–57) was the son of Henry Osborn and Margaret Miller.

27. Osborn was preparing for the monthly celebration of the Lord's Supper at the First Church of Newport.

28. This sentence appears in the margin.

29. "Believest thou I am able to do this?": Jn 1:50, 11:26; "Lord, I believe": Jn 11:26–27; "Help thou my unbelief": Mk 9:24.

30. Henry seems to have been hired to be a warden who stood watch over Newport's harbor in case of French attack.

31. Osborn refers to miracles that God performed: Mt 3:9, Jn 2:9, 1 Kgs 17:15–16, 1 Kgs 17:4–6, Mt 15:34–38, Mk 6:40–42, Lk 9:16–17, Jn 6:10–12.

32. Osborn compares herself to Mary of Magdala ("heal my infirmities": Lk 8:2) and the woman with the bloody issue ("stanch the issue of my corruption": Lk 8:44), both of whom were cured by Jesus.

33. Phillis was baptized and admitted to full membership in the First Church of Newport on June 26, 1757. See FCCR-BM.

34. The words in parentheses appear in the margin. John and his wife Abigail had four children. It is not clear which child Sarah and Henry considered taking.

35. In the margin: "when I wrote this, it was said the earl of Loudon was gone against Cape Breton."

36. Mt 16:18.

37. Osborn refers to the story of Moses leading the Israelites out of their captivity in Egypt by parting the Red Sea with his staff.

38. Cape Breton Island, Nova Scotia, was the site of the French fortress of Louisburg.

39. The emphasis is in the original.

40. The book of Revelation refers to a Seventh Angel who blows the final trumpet that signals the end of the world (Rev 11:15).

41. In the margin: "July 26, 1757, Blessed be God, Cape Breton taken again."

42. Jacob wrestled with God until he received a blessing (Gn 32:24–25).

43. Rebecca Fish (1738–66) was the daughter of Joseph Fish (1705–81) and Rebecca Pabodie Fish (1704–83).

44. "Sheol" refers to the grave or the underworld.

45. In August of 1757, General Louis-Joseph de Montcalm and his troops traveled to Fort William Henry in New York. The British troops at the fort surrendered on August 9, 1757.

46. Ps 46:10

47. Mk 4:37–39.

48. Edward Osborn (1724–57) was married to Mary Young on April 2, 1747. Ancestry.com, *Rhode Island, Vital Extracts, 1636–1899* [database online]. There is no record of any children, and Osborn does not mention any.

49. In the margin: "Blessed be God, this was a mistake. The enemy was gone back."

50. There are many times in the Bible when God promises not to forsake his people. For a few examples, see 1 Sm 12:22, Dt 31:8, Hb 13:5.

51. "Hitherto thou shalt come, and no further": Jb 38:11. For a few biblical examples of God being provoked to anger, see Dt 9:18, Is 1:4, 1 Kgs 14:22, 1 Kgs 15:30, 1 Kgs 16:2, 1 Kgs 16:26, 1 Kgs 21:22, 2 Kgs 21:15.

52. In the margin: "All this day our people has been mustering, drawing lots, and preparing to go against the enemy. The Lord forgive sins of the day and go with them."

53. Death is "the King of Terrors."

54. Osborn refers to Rom 7:23: "law of my members."

55. The words "Almey Greenman, September 15 1757" appear in the margin. I have not been able to locate any information on Almey (or "Almy") Greenman. There are several girls named Greenman who lived in or near Newport at this time, including Abigail Greenman (1740–?) and Anna Greenman (1741–?). Ancestry.com, *Rhode Island, Vital Extracts, 1636–1899* [database online].

56. Osborn compares Phillis to the Ethiopian eunuch who "went on his way rejoicing" (Acts 8:39). The eunuch declared his faith in Christ and was baptized by Philip.

57. Osborn probably refers to her mother and her mother's second husband. Osborn's father had died in 1739.

58. Joseph Eliot, *A Copy of a Letter, Found in the Study of the Reverend Mr. Joseph Belcher, Late of Dedham, since His Decease* (Boston: B. Green, 1725), 3.

59. The words inside the parentheses are crossed out in the manuscript.

60. Benjamin Pabodie (Peabody) was the deacon of the First Church. His half sister, Rebecca Pabodie, was married to Joseph Fish.

61. Mt 6:10, Lk 11:2.

62. The name of the privateer may have been the *Governor Tompkins*. This was the

name of a privateer during the War of 1812. George Coggeshall, *History of the American Privateers* (New York: the author, 1861), 140.

63. Dn 4:35.

64. Be of good courage: Nm 13:20, Dt 31:6–7, Dt 31:23, Jo 1:6, Jo 1:9, Jo 1:18, Jo 10:25, 2 Sm 10:12, 1 Chr 19:13, 1 Chr 22:13, 1 Chr 28:20, Ezr 10:4, Ps 27:14, Ps 31:24, Is 41:6.

65. Ebenezer Erskine, *The King Held in the Galleries* (Edinburgh: John Brown, 1734).

66. Mt 17:20.

67. Osborn refers to one of Johnny and Abigail's children.

68. Ps 37:3.

69. The words in parentheses appear in the margin. It is not clear why Henry did not see his "way clear" to baptize his sons. It was common in the eighteenth century to refer to a child as "it."

70. Added at the bottom of the page: "April 12, 1759. Thanks be to God, he heard and has answered, made those kind and generous whom I feared. O, that I could ever trust him."

71. Osborn refers to her step-grandchild.

72. Mk 4:39.

73. The Osborns planned to move, probably because they could no longer afford their former rent.

74. Jo 1:9.

75. Added later: "I now record that April 13, 1759, blessed be God, our rent has been paid the year past with ease amidst all my fears."

76. Is 54:10, Ps 27:1.

77. Sarah and Henry Osborn paid for their pew in the First Church. See the lists of pew assessments in FCCR-DRC. In addition, the women's society collected money for charity. See First Congregational Church Records, Osborne House, Vault A, #1999, NHS.

CHAPTER SEVEN. OPEN MY HAND AND HEART

1. SO, Diary, December 17, December 29, 1759, January 2, 1760.

2. Mary Fish married the Reverend John Noyes on November 16, 1758. See Joy Day Buel and Richard Buel, Jr., *The Way of Duty: A Woman and Her Family in Revolutionary America* (New York: Norton, 1984), 25.

3. The sentence in parentheses appears in the margin.

4. Ps 41:1: "Blessed is he that considereth the poor: the Lord will deliver him in time of trouble."

5. Osborn probably refers to herself, Henry, their two grandchildren, and Almey Greenman.

6. Osborn refers to Fish's two daughters, Mary Fish Noyes (1736–1818) and Rebecca Fish (1738–66). Mary married John Noyes of New Haven in 1758. John's father

was the Reverend Joseph Noyes (1688–1761), pastor of the Center Church of New Haven, and his mother was Abigail Pierpont Noyes (1696–1768).

7. The Reverend Nathaniel Eels (1710–68) of Stonington, Conn., and his wife Mary. The identity of "cousin Hewitt" is not clear.

8. Sakonnet is in Rhode Island.

9. Elizabeth Fisher Vinal (1719–59) married the Rev. William Vinal (1718–81) in 1746.

10. The Reverend Othniel Campbell (1695–1778) was pastor of the Congregational Church in Tiverton, R.I.

11. Osborn cites 1 Cor 2:9: "But as it is written, Eye hath not seen, nor ear heard, neither have entered into the heart of man, the things which God hath prepared for them that love him."

12. Osborn refers to the verse, "In that hour Jesus rejoiced in spirit, and said, I thank thee, O Father, Lord of heaven and earth, that thou hast hid these things from the wise and prudent, and hast revealed them unto babes: even so, Father; for so it seemed good in thy sight" (Lk 10:21).

13. This postscript appears in the margin. Osborn mentions two of Vinal's children, Becky Vinal and Sarah (Sally) Vinal (1754–?). I have not been able to find a birth record for Becky. Her full name may have been Elizabeth, who was born to William and Elizabeth Vinal in 1748.

14. Thanksgiving did not become a national holiday until 1863, but days of thanksgiving were often proclaimed by churches and colonial governments.

15. King George II (1683–1760) was the ruler of England from 1727 to 1760.

16. William Pitt (1708–78) was Great Britain's secretary of state during the French and Indian War. He served as prime minister of England from 1766 to 1768.

17. Frederick the Great (1712–86).

18. General James Wolfe (1727–59) and Field Marshal Jeffery Amherst (1717–97).

19. Crossed out: "Thanks be to God for discovering and preventing the cursed plot of Quebec being put in execution."

20. Heb 13:5.

21. Is 41:10.

22. Jo 1:9.

23. Mrs. Tweedy may have been Mercy Tillinghast Tweedy, the mother of Sarah Tweedy (1739–?), one of Osborn's former students. See SO, Diary, November 14, 1760. Mercy Tillinghast married John Tweedy in 1732.

24. The words in parentheses appear in the margin. I could not find any genealogical record for a James Leach in Newport. He may have been the James Leach who was born in Hampton, Conn., in 1729. Ancestry.com, *Connecticut, Church Record Abstracts, 1630–1920* [database online], Provo, Utah, 2013. The Osborns rented part of the Leaches' house.

25. It is possible that Ruth Gibbs was the daughter of George and Hannah Gibbs

of Newport, birthdate unknown. See Ancestry.com, *Rhode Island, Vital Extracts, 1636–1899* [database online], Provo, Utah, 2014.

26. The sentence in parentheses appears in the margin. Sarah Hacker (1752–59) was the daughter of Caleb Hacker, who seems to have been a member of the First Church (see FCCR-1743–1831). His wife was a member of the women's society. See SO, Diary, January 2, 1762. Sarah Hacker died of her illness. See SO, Diary, December 18, 1759.

27. 2 Cor 12:9, 2 Kgs 4:26, Mt 10:25.

28. This sentence appears in the margin.

29. Osborn refers to John's family.

30. The words in parentheses appear in the margin. Gardner Thurston (1721–1802) was the pastor of the Second Baptist Church of Newport. It is not clear whether this money was given as charity or as a payment. Several Thurston children attended Osborn's school.

31. This sentence appears in the margin. Osborn refers to James Janeway, *Invisibles, Realities, Demonstrated in the Holy Life and Triumphant Death of Mr. John Janeway* (London, 1674; rpt. Boston: J. Blanchard, 1742).

32. Mt 15:28.

33. The words in parentheses appear in the margin. Captain David Moore was a member of Osborn's church. The "doctor's lady" was probably Mary Prentice Gray, the wife of Ebenezer Gray, also a member of Osborn's church. Both Moore and Gray paid pew assessments that placed them in the top 1 percent of the church. See the pew assessments in FCCR-DRC. David Moore mentioned Sarah Osborn tending shop for him in a letter he wrote to Eleazar Wheelock, May 6, 1742, in the Eleazar Wheelock Papers, Dartmouth College, Hanover, N.H. A microfilm copy is available at Wheaton College, Wheaton, Ill., Reel 1, item 742305.

34. In the margin: "I was misinformed: the town had then not taken it, but have since, in justice to her."

35. Ezra Stiles made a mistake when speaking to Osborn. Mary Fish Noyes did give birth to a daughter in 1760, but the baby died four days later. Stiles (1727–95) was the pastor of the Second Church of Newport. He became the president of Yale in 1778.

36. Fort George was also known as Fort Duquesne and Fort Pitt. It was located in present-day Pittsburgh, Pa.

37. This sentence appears in the margin.

38. John Maxson was the pastor of Seventh-Day Baptist Church.

39. Osborn did not spell out Stiles's name in her letter, but wrote only "Mr. St."

40. William Vinal (1718–81) became pastor of the First Church of Newport in 1746.

41. Susanna Anthony volunteered to be the Vinals' housekeeper after Elizabeth Vinal died.

42. Newport sold lottery tickets to raise money to build a granary, a storehouse for grain. Abigail Osborn was John's widow.

43. A major fire destroyed more than three hundred houses in Boston on March 23, 1760. http://www.massmoments.org/moment.cfm?mid=86, accessed July 13, 2015.

44. The words in parentheses appear in the margin. Mrs. Mason was probably Mary Mason (circa 1736–92), who left Trinity Church (Newport's Anglican church) to become a member of the First Church in 1775. See the Admissions List, 1744–1796, in FCCR-BM. See also Ancestry.com, *U.S., Newspaper Extractions from the Northeast, 1704–1930* [database online], Provo, Utah, 2014. Mrs. Haggar was the wife of William Guise Haggar (1738–?), Sarah Osborn's nephew. In 1771, William Haggar was listed as a "halfway member" of the Second Church of Newport who could not yet take communion. *LD* 1: 83. I have not been able to find any information on Kitty King or Mrs. Short, whose names do not appear in the records of the First Church of Newport.

45. Osborn compares herself to the woman with the bloody issue who was healed when she touched the hem of Christ's garment (Mt 9:20, Mt 14:36).

46. Prv 23:26.

47. Osborn compares herself to the Prodigal Son, whose father forgave him and dressed him in his best robe (Lk 15:22–24).

48. Osborn compares herself to Jonah, who was swallowed by a whale when he refused to heed God's call to preach to the sinful people of Ninevah. See the book of Jonah.

49. Hos 2:7. Osborn compares herself to the Israelites who "murmured" against God. See Dt 1:27, Ps 106:25.

50. Mt 6:10, Mt 26:42, Lk 11:2.

51. Heb 13:5.

52. The French were defeated by the British at Quebec in May 1760.

53. Ps 71:11.

54. The words in parentheses appear in the margin. Samuel Parks and Benjamin Hawkins were convicted of piracy and executed on August 21, 1760. http://gaspee.org/18thRIPrivateers.pdf, accessed July 15, 2015. See also William P. Sheffield, *An Address Delivered before the Rhode Island Historical Society* (Newport: Sanborn, 1883), 39.

55. Osborn compares herself to Peter, who asks the risen Jesus about the future of the disciple John after Jesus predicts Peter's martyrdom. She cites Jn 21:21 ("Lord, and what shall this man do?") and Ps 63:8 ("follow hard").

56. Osborn quotes Rev 12:10 by describing Satan as "the accuser of the brethren."

57. Crossed out: "reaping a harvest."

58. Osborn cites Rom 7:23: "But I see another law in my members, warring against the law of my mind, and bringing me into captivity to the law of sin which is in my members."

59. Mal 1:10.

60. Jn 14:23.

61. Prv 19:18.

62. This paragraph appears in the margin.

63. The criminal alludes to Eph 2:5: "Even when we were dead in sins, hath quickened us together with Christ, (by grace ye are saved)."

64. In the margin: "A disappointment in the flour. 'Tis so bad we cannot use it at all, but I trust God will still be kind and constrain him to do us justice."

65. Abigail (Nabby) Chesebrough (1734–1807) was the daughter of David Chesebrough, a wealthy slave trader in Newport. When Chesebrough died in 1782, Ezra Stiles estimated that he was worth ten thousand pounds sterling. See *LD* 3: 11. The Chesebrough family had once belonged to Osborn's church, the First Church of Christ. It is not clear when they left, but it was before 1753. They were assigned a church pew at the First Church in 1744, but not in 1753. Abigail became a full member of the Second Church of Christ in 1756. *LD* 1: 53. Abigail could afford to be generous because she had secretly married Alexander Grant, Esq., the son of a British nobleman, in October 1760. See SO, Diary, November 16, 1760.

66. The first two sentences of this paragraph appear in the margin.

67. Added later: "I find my dear friend was married on October 6 as she herself told me this day, November 15."

68. John Maxson was the pastor of Seventh-Day Baptist Church.

69. On November 5, 1605, in England, Guy Fawkes was arrested before he was able to blow up King James I. November 5 became a British holiday commemorating the foiling of what became known as the Gunpowder Plot.

70. Lk 12:19.

71. Osborn had sent her slave, Bobey, to live with her former brother-in-law, whose last name was Wheaten, in Berkley, Mass. For more on Bobey, see chapter 4.

72. The second and third sentences in this paragraph appear in the margin. Miss Davis may have been Mary Davis, a widow who belonged to the Second Church. See *LD* 1: 327.

73. Osborn cites Is 2:22 to emphasize that she should trust God rather than mere man, "whose breath is in his nostrils."

74. Osborn compares Habakkuk and Jonah. While Habakkuk responded to God's judgment with faith, Jonah fled from his call to preach the destruction of Ninevah. See the book of Habakkuk and the book of Jonah.

75. Mordecai overheard a plot to kill the king while sitting at the gate (Est 5:14).

76. Is 41:10.

77. Mk 6:22–23, Jn 11:12, Jn 14:13, Jn 15:16.

78. Mk 5:34, Lk 8:48. The emphasis is mine.

79. Lk 5:20, Lk 7:48, Mk 2:5.

80. Lk 13:12–13.

81. Ps 84:11.

82. Ibid.

83. Crossed out: "of abundance and a fullness of redundance."

84. The sentence in parentheses appears in the margin. Elizabeth Henshaw

Seabury (1740–?) was admitted to the First Church of Christ in 1761. Ancestry.com, *Rhode Island, Vital Extracts, 1636–1899* [database online]. She was the daughter of Samuel Henshaw of Boston. She married John Seabury of Newport in 1758 (see *Vital Records of Rhode Island, 1636–1850: Births, Marriages and Deaths*, vol. 8: Episcopal and Congregational [Providence, R.I.: Narragansett Historical Publishing, 1896]).

85. Acts 16:18.

86. The words in parentheses appear in the margin. Mrs. Coggeshall was Abigail Wanton Coggeshall (1702–70), the wife of Nathaniel Coggeshall (1701–84), the deacon of the First Church of Christ. On their marriage, see *Rhode Island Historical Magazine* 5 (July 1884): 217. Coggeshall owned a distillery, and he was one of the wealthiest members of the church. In comparison to the ten pounds that Henry Osborn paid for his pew in 1753, Nathaniel Coggeshall and his sons were assessed twenty-two pounds. See the 1753 pew assessments in FCCR-DRC. Nathaniel was the great-grandson of John Coggeshall (1601–47), the first president of the Colony of Providence Plantations. On Nathaniel Coggeshall's leadership in the church, see FCCR-CB. Sarah Osborn mentions Mrs. Coggeshall as a member of her women's society in SO, Diary, January 28, 1762.

CHAPTER EIGHT. GLORIFY THYSELF IN ME

1. Osborn left his name blank.

2. Osborn refers to biblical depictions of the sinfulness of Jerusalem. See Lam 1:8, Dn 9:16. She may also refer to John Bunyan, *The Jerusalem Sinner Saved* (1688; rpt. London: John Marshall, 1728).

3. Reformed Protestants rejected the Catholic practice of intercessory prayers for the dead.

4. Mary Fish Noyes gave birth to Joseph Noyes in 1761. See Joy Day Buel and Richard Buel, Jr., *The Way of Duty: A Woman and Her Family in Revolutionary America* (New York: Norton, 1984), 33.

5. Osborn refers to Is 48:10: "Behold, I have refined thee, but not with silver; I have chosen thee in the furnace of affliction."

6. This letter has disappeared.

7. Osborn refers to Ps 141:5: "Let the righteous smite me; it shall be a kindness: and let him reprove me; it shall be an excellent oil, which shall not break my head: for yet my prayer also shall be in their calamities."

8. Benjamin Peabody, or "Pabodie" (1717–94), was a deacon of the First Church of Christ. He married Abigail Lyon (1720–1804) in 1745. Ancestry.com, *U.S., Find a Grave Index, 1600s–Current* [database online], Provo, Utah, 2012. *Newport Historical Magazine* 3 (July 1882): 218. Godfrey Memorial Library, comp., *American Genealogical-Biographical Index (AGBI)* [database online], Provo, Utah, 1999.

9. Osborn compares Susanna Anthony to Jacob, who wrestled with God until he received a blessing (Gn 32:24–26).

10. David Brainerd (1718–47) was a missionary to Native Americans who died young. His life was memorialized in Jonathan Edwards, *An Account of the Life of the Late*

Reverend Mr. David Brainerd, Minister of the Gospel, Missionary to the Indians (Boston: D. Henchman, 1749). Eliab Byram (1718–54) was a Presbyterian minister from New Jersey who traveled with David Brainerd. John McClintock and James Strong, eds., *Cyclopedia of Biblical, Theological and Ecclesiastical Literature, Supplement* (New York: Harper and Publishers, 1885), 1: 712.

11. Osborn refers to the Strict Congregationalists, more popularly known as the Separates.

12. Mary Eels, the wife of the Reverend Nathaniel Eels (1710–68) of Stonington, Conn.

13. This woman was a member of Newport's Second Baptist Church, which was led by Gardner Thurston (1721–1802).

14. Itinerant preaching was controversial during the eighteenth century. See Timothy D. Hall, *Contested Boundaries: Itinerancy and the Reshaping of the Colonial American Religious World* (Durham: Duke University Press, 1994).

15. Osborn quotes from 2 Tm 4:3: "For the time will come when they will not endure sound doctrine; but after their own lusts shall they heap to themselves teachers, having itching ears."

16. On Fish's battles with the Strict Congregationalists, who separated from his church, see *Old Light on Separate Ways: The Narragansett Diary of Joseph Fish, 1765–1776*, ed. William S. Simmons and Cheryl L. Simmons (Hanover, N.H.: University Press of New England, 1982).

17. Osborn alludes to 1 Pt 5:8: "Be sober, be vigilant; because your adversary the devil, as a roaring lion, walketh about, seeking whom he may devour."

18. 1 Cor 10:13.

19. Ps 103:13.

20. 2 Cor 12:9.

21. Gosper was probably Phillis's husband. Molly Allen may be "Mary Allen" (1745–?) who was the daughter of Timothy Allen, Phillis's master. Ancestry.com, *Rhode Island, Vital Extracts, 1636–1899* [database online], Provo, Utah, 2014. Timothy Allen and his family belonged to the Second Church.

22. Ps 115:1.

23. Mt 25:45.

24. Osborn quotes 1 Kgs 2:20 ("say me not, 'Nay'"), in which Bathsheba asks her son Solomon not to deny her petition.

25. Daniel Defoe, *The Family Instructor in Three Parts*, 15th ed. (London: C. Hitch and L. Hawes, G. Keith, W. Johnston, and T. Longman, 1761).

26. Osborn quotes Jo 24:21–22, in which the Israelites promise to serve God.

27. Osborn quotes Mt 18:26, 29: "Have patience with me, and I pay you all."

28. Osborn cites the parable of the ten virgins (Mt 25:21, 23) who waited for the bridegroom.

29. Mt 25:21, 23.

30. A theater company performed in Newport in 1761. *The Colonial American*

Stage 1665–1774: A Documentary Calendar, ed. Odai Johnson (Madison, N.J.: Fairleigh Dickinson University Press, 2001), 213.

31. Osborn refers to the Prodigal Son, who "filled his belly with the husks that the swine did eat" (Lk 15:16).

32. James Burgh, *Britain's Remembrancer: Being Some Thoughts on the Proper Improvement of the Present Juncture, the Character of this Age and Nation* (London: M. Cooper, 1746). Samuel Pike and S. Hayward, *Some Important Cases of Conscience Answered, at the Casuistical Exercise,* 3rd ed. (Boston: Green and Russell, 1757).

33. Osborn compares herself to several self-righteous biblical characters. She refers to Lk 18:11: "The Pharisee stood and prayed thus with himself, God, I thank thee, that I am not as other men are, extortioners, unjust, adulterers, or even as this publican." She also compares herself to Jehu, who viciously slaughtered large numbers of his enemies (2 Kgs 10:16), and she cites Jesus's warning not to "beholdest thou the mote that is in thy brother's eye, but considerest not the beam that is in thine own eye" (Mt 7:3–5, Lk 64:1–2). She also cites Is 65:5: "stand by thyself, come not near to me; for I am holier than thou," and 1 Cor 10:12: "Wherefore let him that thinketh he standeth take heed lest he fall." She also compares herself to Absalom, who rebelled against his father David (2 Sm), and Adonijah, who tried to usurp the throne from his brother Solomon and was put to death (1 Kgs 2: 13–25).

34. 2 Cor 12:9, Jo 1:5.

35. Osborn compares herself to David, who fell into despair and became convinced that God would allow Saul to kill him. See 1 Sm 27:1.

36. The Reverend John Gano (1727–1804), a Baptist, did not publish any of his sermons. Osborn is probably quoting a sermon that he delivered in Newport on Rom 9:15: "For he saith to Moses, I will have mercy on whom I will have mercy, and I will have compassion on whom I will have compassion."

37. Osborn refers to her correspondence with Eliphal Prentice (about 1717–66). See SO to Mrs. Oliver Prentice, July 12, 1755, AAS. Eliphal Noyes married Oliver Prentice in 1743. See Ancestry.com, *Connecticut, Town Marriage Records, Pre-1870 (Barbour Collection)* [database online], Provo, Utah, 2006. Oliver Prentice became the pastor of North Stonington Separate Church in 1753. Alvah Hovey, *A Memoir of the Life and Times of the Rev. Isaac Backus* (Boston: Gould and Lincoln, 1859), 109.

38. The Reverend Othniel Campbell (1695–1778) was pastor of the Congregational church in Tiverton, R.I.

39. There seem to have been many "women's societies" associated with Protestant churches in the eighteenth century. For example, George Whitefield organized a women's society in Philadelphia in 1741. See Janet Moore Lindman, "Wise Virgins and Pious Mothers: Spiritual Community among Baptist Women of the Delaware Valley," in *Women and Freedom in Early America,* ed. Larry D. Eldridge (New York: New York University Press, 1997), 136.

40. The full text is: "And if the righteous scarcely be saved, where shall the ungodly and the sinner appear?" (1 Pt 4:18).

41. Jb 34:13.

42. Osborn crossed out the words "our servant" after the word "keep." Bobey was born around 1744 (see chapter 4). His mother, Phillis, was owned by Timothy Allen. His father seems to have been a slave named Gosper. On Phillis, see chapter 6.

43. This sentence appears in the margin.

44. 2 Pt 2:20.

45. By "guile," Osborn means "devious."

46. Ps 101:1.

47. Osborn alludes to the return of Jesus "as a thief in the night" (1 Thes 5:2 and 2 Pt 3:10).

48. Osborn quotes from Is 63:1. This passage describes the victory of God over Edom, the enemy. Bozrah was the capital of Edom.

49. Osborn never names Bobey's father, but he was probably Gosper, whom she mentions with Phillis in SO, Diary, October 19, 1761.

50. Is 54:10.

51. Heb 13:5.

52. Osborn cites the same scripture as she did after the death of her son Samuel: "Then said Elkanah her husband to her, Hannah, why weepest thou? and why eatest thou not? and why is thy heart grieved? am not I better to thee than ten sons?" (1 Sm 1:8).

53. Osborn cites the words of Jacob in Gn 42:36.

54. Osborn crossed out the word "continually" after "me."

55. By "amused," Osborn means "perplexed."

56. Heb 13:5, Jo 1:5.

57. Osborn refers to the story of the wicked servant who did not improve his talents (Lk 19:20–23). On one hand, she is concerned about failing to make the most of her ownership of Bobey, but on the other hand, she is also concerned about greed.

58. Osborn alludes to 1 Pt 4:19: "Wherefore let them that suffer according to the will of God commit the keeping of their souls to him in well doing, as unto a faithful Creator." Based on this passage, Osborn decided not to sell Bobey, but unfortunately there is no record of what happened to him in the future. Osborn may have continued to hire him out, which would explain her greater financial security in 1762.

59. These sentences appear in the margin: "It was the gift of many good earthly friends. Also it was to me as something saved from shipwreck when all the rest was cast over." According to a letter that she wrote to JF on June 4, 1754 (see chapter 4), Osborn raised Bobey from his birth in 1744. Bobey seems to have been given to her and Henry as a gift soon after their bankruptcy in 1743.

60. Osborn compares Bobey to the centurion's servant in Lk 7:2–7, whom Jesus healed.

61. Rom 8:15, 23.

62. Osborn used the same biblical language (Ps 22:10) when writing about her son Samuel in her memoir: "I oft pleaded for covenant blessings to be bestowed on him since he had been cast upon God from the womb." See chapter 2.

63. Osborn alludes to Ez 37:26: "Moreover I will make a covenant of peace with them; it shall be an everlasting covenant with them: and I will place them, and multiply them, and will set my sanctuary in the midst of them for evermore."

64. Osborn quotes from Ps 68:31: "Princes shall come out of Egypt; Ethiopia shall soon stretch out her hands unto God."

65. This passage makes it clear that Phillis had two children.

66. Most Protestants in early America did not treat Christmas as a special day, but Trinity Church in Newport (the Anglican church) would have celebrated it.

67. Osborn may refer to Phillis.

68. Osborn refers to Mt 9:15: "And Jesus said unto them, Can the children of the bridechamber mourn, as long as the bridegroom is with them? but the days will come, when the bridegroom shall be taken from them, and then shall they fast."

69. The fact that Phillis attended this women's society meeting suggests that she and Sarah made peace after their fight over selling Bobey. Several women on this list can be identified as members of the First Church, and some of the others can be tentatively identified as members. The members include Mrs. Fairbanks, Mrs. Hannah Lamb, Mrs. Abigail Lyon Peabody, Mrs. Mary Anthony, Susanna Anthony, Molly (Mary) "Donnely" (Donnelly), and Phillis. Hannah Lamb was admitted to the First Church in 1748 (see FCCR-BM). She and Mrs. Fairbanks, both widows, frequently received charity from the church (see FCCR-CB). Mrs. Glading may have been Mary Glading, the wife of Josiah Glading, who was admitted to the church in 1771 (see List of Admissions, 1744–1796, FCCR-BM). Mrs. James may have been the wife of John James, who was listed on the seating chart for 1744 (see FCCR-CB). Mrs. Henshaw may have been the wife of Mr. Henshaw, who paid a pew assessment in 1755 (see FCCR-1743–1831). "Hacker" was listed in the 1753 pew assessments (see FCCR-BM). Mrs. Hacker was probably the wife of Caleb Hacker, whose six children were baptized at the First Church (see *Vital Records of Rhode Island, 1636–1850: Births, Marriages and Deaths*, vol. 8: Episcopal and Congregational [Providence, R.I.: Narragansett Historical Publishing, 1896]). Mrs. Abigail Lyon Peabody (1720–1804) was the wife of Benjamin Peabody (1717–92), the deacon of the First Church. Mrs. Anthony was probably Sarah Anthony, the wife of John, who transferred to the church from Bristol in 1763 (see List of Admissions, 1744–1796, FCCR-BM). Mary Anthony (d. 1810) was admitted to the church in 1771 (see List of Admissions, 1744–1796, FCCR-BM). Molly (Mary) Donnelly (1725–1810) became a member of the First Church in 1762 (see FCCR-BM, and *Rhode Island Vital Records: Births, 1590–1930, from Newport Common Burial Ground Inscriptions*, ed. Alden G. Beaman [Princeton, N.J.: Alden G. Beaman, 1987], New Series, vol. 11). Mary Allen is probably the same person as the "Molly Allen" whom Osborn mentions in her diary on October 19, 1761. Mrs. "Daves" may have been Mary Davis, a widow who belonged to the Second Church (see *LD* 1: 327). Osborn mentions her in SO, Diary, November 13, 1760. Mrs. Ross may have been Bathsheba Ross (1738–91), the wife of William Ross (*Rhode Island Vital Records*, vol. 11). Mrs. "Creapman" may have been Mrs. Chipman, the wife of Handly Chipman (FCCR-1743–1831).

70. This sentence appears in the margin. John Guyse (1680–1761) was her mother's brother. He was a well-known Dissenting minister in England. See "Guyse, John," in *The Dictionary of National Biography* (Oxford: Oxford University Press, 1964), 8: 837.

71. These words appear in the margin: "and to relieve any necessitous, distressed poor as God gives leave and opportunity. Lord, let this little fund be as the widow's cause." Osborn compares herself to the widow described in the gospels of Mark and Luke who gave away her two mites, all that she owned (Mk 12:42–43, Lk 21:2–3).

72. Osborn compares herself to Mary of Bethany, who sat at the feet of Jesus instead of helping her sister Martha to serve. Jesus told Martha that Mary had "chosen that good part, which shall not be taken away from her" (Lk 10:42).

73. The words in parentheses appear in the margin.

74. James Leach and his wife (whose first name is unknown) were the Osborns' landlords.

75. Osborn promises to follow biblical law by setting apart a fifth of her legacy for religious purposes. See, for example, Lv 27:31.

76. This sentence appears in the margin.

77. Mt 6:34.

78. This sentence appears in the margin. Osborn offered to care for Johnny so that Abigail, John Osborn's widow, could find employment. The Osborns had already taken in two of Abigail and John's other children, Sally (Sarah) and another child whose name is unknown. The identity of Mrs. Wanscoat is not clear. She was not a member of the First Church.

79. Osborn refers to two stories about the power of fasting to move God: the healing of a child who was possessed by the devil (Mt 17:15–21) and Esther's determination to save her people from destruction (Est 4:16).

80. Osborn quotes from Is 45:19: "I have not spoken in secret, in a dark place of the earth: I said not unto the seed of Jacob, Seek ye me in vain: I the Lord speak righteousness, I declare things that are right."

81. Mrs. Margaret Sylvester Chesebrough (1719–82) was the second wife of David Chesebrough. They married in 1749. Her portrait was painted by Joseph Blackburn. See http://www.metmuseum.org/collection/the-collection-online/search/10175.

82. The edges of this letter are ripped. I have filled in missing words with brackets.

83. Osborn refers to several passages in the Bible of direct calls from God. For example, when an angel of the Lord called to Abraham, Abraham answered, "Here am I." See Gn 22:11, Gn 31:11, Gn 46:2, Ex 3:4, 1 Sm 3:4–8, Is 6:8.

84. Rhoda Wilcox was baptized and accepted into full communion at the First Church of Christ in Newport on May 30, 1762. See FCCR-BM. When Osborn writes, "God is now, we trust, saying to her, 'return,'" she refers to Is 44:22.

85. In a letter to JF dated November 2, 1761, Osborn mentions that she might show one of his letters about the Separates to the women's society. She was reluctant to allow Separates into the society.

86. This letter is written on scraps of paper.

87. The women's society met on Thursday afternoons.

88. Osborn refers to the description of Pentecost in Acts 2: 1–4.

CHAPTER NINE. REVIVE THY WORK

1. SO to JF, undated letter, probably written in 1765.

2. SO, Diary, April 14, 1767.

3. Osborn cites Is 1:12, a description of God's anger towards the rebellious, sinful people of Sodom and Gomorrah.

4. Another group of Separate Baptists had left Fish's church in Stonington, Conn.

5. Osborn cites Ps 89:33: "Nevertheless my lovingkindness will I not utterly take from him, nor suffer my faithfulness to fail."

6. Little Rest, R.I.

7. Osborn writes "neighborhood," not "neighbor."

8. The Osborns rented their house from Mrs. Leach. Osborn accuses her landlord of stealing from her.

9. Joseph Eliot, *A Copy of a Letter, Found in the Study of the Reverend Mr. Joseph Belcher, Late of Dedham, since His Decease* (Boston: B. Green, 1725), 3.

10. Several words here are obscured by a brown stain.

11. Osborn refers to Rev 3:12: "Him that overcometh will I make a pillar in the temple of my God," and also Zec 3:9, when God promises to pardon iniquity: "Behold, I will engrave the graving thereof, saith the Lord of hosts, and I will remove the iniquity of that land in one day." Osborn also refers to 1 Sm 7:12: "Then Samuel took a stone, and set it between Mizpeh and Shen, and called the name of it Ebenezer, saying, Hitherto hath the Lord helped us." She hopes to be like Ebenezer, the monument that Samuel erected to commemorate the Israelites' victory over the Philistines.

12. This letter has no salutation.

13. Osborn cites the prophetic words of Ez 21:27.

14. Gardner Thurston (1721–1802) was the pastor of the Second Baptist Church of Newport.

15. This account was not included with Osborn's surviving letters and could not be found.

16. Osborn mentions that she "enclosed" an account, but it does not survive.

17. Nathaniel Eels (1710–68) was a Congregationalist minister in Stonington, Conn. Levi Hart (1738–1808) was pastor of the Second Congregational Church in Preston, Conn.

18. The side of the page is torn. I have added the word "long."

19. No enclosure survives.

20. The sentence trails off because the page is ripped.

21. Osborn invokes the biblical narrative of Uriah, whom King David arranged to have killed after impregnating Uriah's wife, Bathsheba. Uriah was shot by archers. David instructed his military leaders: "Set ye Uriah in the forefront of the hottest battle, and retire ye from him, that he may be smitten, and die" (2 Sm 11:15, 24). By expressing

her respect for "the ark"—a symbol of priestly authority in ancient Israel—and her dread at "giving [it] a presumptuous touch," Osborn emphasizes that she does not wish to usurp ministerial authority. See 1 Sm 4:13 and 1 Chr 13:9–10.

22. Osborn alludes to Jesus's description of the multitudes in Nazareth as "scattered abroad, as sheep having no shepherd" (Mt 9:36). She also refers to the "distinguishing badge" of Christian love. Jn 13:35: "By this shall all men know that ye are my disciples, if ye have love one to another."

23. Samuel Buell had preached in Newport on Hos 6:3: "Then shall we know, if we follow on to know the Lord: his going forth is prepared as the morning; and he shall come unto us as the rain, as the latter and former rain unto the earth."

24. Nathaniel Coggeshall (1701–84) was a deacon of the First Church.

25. Osborn refers to the biblical description of the men and women waiting to be healed in the pool of Bethesda: "In these lay a great multitude of impotent folk, of blind, halt, withered, waiting for the moving of the water" (Jn 5:3).

26. Fish may have suggested that Osborn should write to Vinal asking for the names of ministers who could help with her meetings.

27. Osborn leaves the name blank.

28. Mrs. Hutcherson (or Hutchinson) may have been a member of Trinity Church. Osborn's description of her and her friends as "holy sisters" suggests that they may have been Anglican. It is clear from this letter that Mrs. Hutcherson opposed Osborn's meetings for blacks.

29. Osborn hopes that Hutcherson's daughter has true religion within her, "the root of the matter." She cites Jb 19:28: "But ye should say, Why persecute we him, seeing the root of the matter is found in me?"

30. Osborn compares Fish to the biblical Jacob, the father of Joseph. Mary Fish Noyes gave birth to Joseph Fish's grandson, Joseph Noyes, in 1761. Osborn cites Gn 49:22: "Joseph is a fruitful bough, even a fruitful bough by a well; whose branches run over the wall."

31. This letter seems to have been sent with the previous one.

32. William Vinal.

33. Osborn means that Vinal had come to pray with the women's society only twice: once to pray with a delirious woman, and on another occasion that she had mentioned in a previous letter.

34. This was a frequent image in Buell's sermons. See, for instance, Samuel Buell, *The Import of the Saint's Confession, That the Times of Men Are in the Hand of God* (New London, Conn.: T. Green and Son, 1972), 11.

35. Osborn leaves Vinal's name blank. Once again she alludes to Mt 9:36: "But when he saw the multitudes, he was moved with compassion on them, because they fainted, and were scattered abroad, as sheep having no shepherd."

36. This letter continues on the same page as the former.

37. Osborn indicates that she has dismissed her meetings without prayer to emphasize her deference and to acknowledge that she is uncertain whether public prayer

falls within the scope of her authority. The next year, however, she writes that she "dared not omit praying" in her meetings (see SO, Diary, April 24, 1767).

38. The letter continues on the same page.

39. The letter continues on the same page.

40. Osborn compares herself to Jonah, who fled from his errand by sea when God called him to preach. Jonah was swallowed by a "great fish" and vomited on shore; later a plant or "gourd" grew up suddenly to shade him from the sun (Jon 1–4). Osborn adapts the narrative to express her own trials and to affirm God's mercy.

41. Osborn suggests that the Holy Spirit (the "Comforter") has demonstrated his power to her and will protect her. She cites Is 64:1–3: "Oh that thou wouldest rend the heavens, that thou wouldest come down, that the mountains might flow down at thy presence, As when the melting fire burneth, the fire causeth the waters to boil, to make thy name known to thine adversaries, that the nations may tremble at thy presence! When thou didst terrible things which we looked not for, thou camest down, the mountains flowed down at thy presence."

42. The correct reference is 2 Jn 4.

43. Osborn refers to several biblical passages ("I am with thee"), in which God promises to bless and protect his covenant people. Gn 26:3, Gn 31:3, Ex 3:12, Dt 31:23, Jo 1:5, Jo 3:7, Jgs 6:16, 1 Kgs 11:38, Is 43:2. Osborn also refers to several examples of holy people who answered direct calls from God with the words "here am I," including Abraham, Jacob, Moses, Samuel, and Isaiah: Gn 22:11, Gn 31:11, Gn 46:2, Ex 3:4, 1 Sm 3:4–8, Is 6:8.

44. By "professor," she means one who professes Christ, a believer.

45. As the next letter makes clear, the deacon wanted to move the meetings for blacks to his house.

46. Eccl 9:10.

47. Osborn crosses out the rest of Mr. B's name. His identity is unclear.

48. By law, slaves in Newport were required to return to their masters' houses by nine o'clock in the evening.

49. Osborn refers to 2 Pt 3:9: "The Lord is not slack concerning his promise, as some men count slackness; but is longsuffering to us-ward, not willing that any should perish, but that all should come to repentance."

50. Osborn never identifies the "Jew" in this or other entries. It is possible that a Jewish resident of Newport owed her money, perhaps for sewing or baking. Colonial Rhode Island was a haven for religious dissent, and Jews settled in Newport during the mid-seventeenth century. In 1763, the Jewish residents of Newport erected the Touro Synagogue, now the earliest surviving Jewish synagogue in North America. Osborn refers to 2 Sm 19:14: "And he bowed the heart of all the men of Judah, even as the heart of one man."

51. Abner helped rally and consolidate political support for King David of Israel. For Osborn's reference, see 2 Sm 3:12.

52. Osborn refers to Mt 14:33: "Of a truth thou art the Son of God."

53. "Touch not my anointed and do my prophets no harm": 1 Chr 16:22, Ps 105:15; Satan's wiles: Eph 6:11; "if any love father and mother more than me, he is not worthy of me": Mt 10:37.

54. The names appear in the margin.

55. When Osborn writes "not I," she may refer to Gal 2:20: "I am crucified with Christ: nevertheless I live; yet not I, but Christ liveth in me: and the life which I now live in the flesh I live by the faith of the Son of God, who loved me, and gave himself for me," or Ps 115:1: "Not unto us, O Lord, not unto us, but unto thy name give glory, for thy mercy, and for thy truth's sake." She also quotes 1 Cor 15:10: "But by the grace of God I am what I am: and his grace which was bestowed upon me was not in vain; but I laboured more abundantly than they all: yet not I, but the grace of God which was with me."

56. This sentence appears in the margin.

57. Osborn may mean that she needs the money to pay her landlord.

58. She refers to a verse from Nm 6:5: "he shall be holy, and shall let the locks of the hair of his head grow."

59. Osborn refers to the Reverend Vinal, who seems to have been opposed to her meetings.

60. Samuel Mather, *The Life of the Very Reverend and Learned Cotton Mather* (Boston: Samuel Gerrish, 1729).

61. Osborn cites Eccl 10:1: "Dead flies cause the ointment of the apothecary to send forth a stinking savour: so doth a little folly him that is in reputation for wisdom and honour."

62. Mather, *Life of the Very Reverend and Learned Cotton Mather*, 16–17.

63. Osborn had often used corporal punishment to discipline her students. For an example, see SO, Diary, August 10, 1760.

64. Mather, *Life of the Very Reverend and Learned Cotton Mather*, 25.

65. Her nephew was William Guise Haggar (1738–?). In 1771, he was listed as a "halfway member" of the Second Church of Newport who could not yet take communion. *LD* 1: 83. "N. C." may have been Nathaniel Coggeshall, Jr., the deacon's son. The identity of Sammy Gibbins is not clear. He was not a member of Osborn's church.

66. Osborn is probably referring to her granddaughter, Sally, who joined the First Church in 1773. The identity of "Ishmael" is not clear. He may have been a slave. In the biblical text Ishmael refers to a son of Abraham who was not part of his covenant with God. See Genesis 21.

67. Osborn is probably referring to Elisha Gibbs and Sarah Rossey, whom she mentions in the next entry. Two other people were also admitted to the First Church in 1767: Joseph Clark, Jr., and Lydia Gibbs (the wife of Elisha). See FCCR-BM.

68. An unnamed woman had lost her husband. Osborn refers to two biblical texts about the "widow's God." "A father of the fatherless, and a judge of the widows, is God in his holy habitation" (Ps 68:5). "Pure religion and undefiled before God and the Father is this, to visit the fatherless and widows in their affliction, and to keep himself unspotted from the world" (Jas 1:27).

69. Ps 119:71.

70. Osborn cites Is 49:16, part of a long passage emphasizing God's compassion: "Behold, I have graven thee upon the palms of my hands; thy walls are continually before me."

71. Osborn's concern with transgressing her "line," especially with respect to the matter of public prayer, reflects her sensitivity to traditional Christian teaching about women, particularly Paul's injunctions that women should be silent in the church and defer to men as their "heads." See 1 Cor 4:34–35 and 1 Cor 11.

72. Osborn cites Jn 21:11: "Simon Peter went up, and drew the net to land full of great fishes, an hundred and fifty and three: and for all there were so many, yet was not the net broken."

73. Mrs. Chesebrough was the wife of David Chesebrough, a wealthy slave trader in Newport. They belonged to the Second Church of Christ in Newport. Abigail Chesebrough Grant (1734–1807) was the daughter of David Chesebrough and the wife of Sir Alexander Grant of Scotland. See *LD* 1: 53, 32.

74. Osborn reads Philemon 1:13 as suggesting that Onesimus served Paul in the place of Philemon. If Philemon returned, Onesimus would no longer need to serve Paul. Here she suggests that she would like to cede control of her meetings to a minister.

75. By "church folks," Osborn means Anglicans, or members of the Church of England.

76. Osborn refers to 2 Kgs 4:10: "Let us make a little chamber, I pray thee, on the wall; and let us set for him there a bed, and a table, and a stool, and a candlestick: and it shall be, when he cometh to us, that he shall turn in thither."

77. By "church folk" she means Anglicans.

78. William Guise Haggar (1738–?).

79. The women's society met on Thursdays at Osborn's house, and apparently Baptist women held their own meeting on Friday evenings. To prevent this, Osborn invited the members of the women's society to join the men's meeting that took place at her house on Friday evenings.

80. The father of Polly Evans had died the week before.

81. This sentence appears in the margin. Vinal seems to have accused Clark of being sympathetic to the Baptists, but he was admitted to the church in 1767. See FCCR-BM.

82. In Ex 18:18, Jethro advises Moses: "Thou wilt surely wear away, both thou, and this people that is with thee: for this thing is too heavy for thee; thou art not able to perform it thyself alone."

83. Osborn quotes the words of Jesus: "He that findeth his life shall lose it: and he that loseth his life for my sake shall find it" (Mt 10:39, Mt 16:25, Mk 8:35, Lk 9:24).

84. Matthew Henry, *Directions for Daily Communion with God*, 4th ed. (Boston: Thomas Crump, 1717), 106.

85. Osborn cites 1 Cor 1:27: "But God hath chosen the foolish things of the world

to confound the wise; and God hath chosen the weak things of the world to confound the things which are mighty."

86. Osborn reminds Fish that God instructed Moses to call together seventy elders to stand with him (Nm 11:16).

87. Osborn refers to a story in Lk 5:4. After Jesus instructed Simon Peter where to put down his net, he pulled up so many fish that the net broke.

88. Osborn assures Fish that sending letters through Mr. Mumford does not cost her anything. In 1775, Ezra Stiles described Mumford as "the old Postrider." *LD* 2: 554.

89. Osborn wrote to the Rev. William Vinal about Joseph Clark, Jr., who was admitted to membership in the First Church in 1767. Vinal seems to have suspected Clark of Baptist sympathies. The "disapproved" was probably the Reverend Gardner Thurston.

90. Osborn cites identical passages in 2 Kgs 19:28 and Is 37:29: "Because thy rage against me and thy tumult is come up into mine ears, therefore I will put my hook in thy nose, and my bridle in thy lips, and I will turn thee back by the way by which thou camest."

91. Osborn cites Mt 10:16: "Behold, I send you forth as sheep in the midst of wolves: be ye therefore wise as serpents, and harmless as doves."

92. Samuel Buell, *A Faithful Narrative of the Remarkable Revival of Religion, in the Congregation of East-Hampton, on Long-Island* (New York: Samuel Brown, 1766).

93. In the margin: "O, let dear Easthampton remember with joy the liberty that they had at the throne of grace on the memorable 18 of March 1764."

94. The Stamp Act was repealed on March 18, 1766.

95. Heb 13:5.

96. This sentence appears in the margin.

97. This number is crossed out in the text.

98. Osborn seems to have sold cookies after her meetings in order to make money.

99. Osborn refers to God's promise to bless Isaac (Gn 26:3).

100. A pistareen was a silver coin from Spain. Because of the shortage of currency, colonial Americans sometimes used currency from other countries. There were many women in Newport with the last name of "Champlain," and the identity of this Mrs. Champlain is unclear.

101. Osborn does not list the title of this book.

102. In his edited version of this entry, Samuel Hopkins deleted the words "though I should labor in vain all my days, as even thy ministers have done." Apparently he did not like her comparison of herself to a minister. See SH, *Memoirs,* 333.

103. Ps 50:23.

104. Osborn refers to the story of Simon Peter, who fished all night and caught nothing until Jesus told him where to place his nets. See Jn 21:3–6, Lk 5:5–6.

105. Osborn refers to the Israelites who "murmured" against God's will (Nm 14:27, Dt 1:27, Ps 106:25), and also those who "murmured" against Jesus (Jn 6:61, Jn 7:12,

1 Cor 10:10). She also refers to Heb 12:11–12: "Now no chastening for the present seemeth to be joyous, but grievous: nevertheless afterward it yieldeth the peaceable fruit of righteousness unto them which are exercised thereby. Wherefore lift up the hands which hang down, and the feeble knees."

106. When God asks Solomon what he would like, Solomon asks for an understanding heart. See 1 Kgs 3:9–12.

107. Joshua's resolution was to serve the Lord (see Jo 24:15).

108. Isaac Watts, *Horae Lyricae: Poems, Chiefly of the Lyric Kind, in Three Books,* 9th ed. (Boston: Rogers and Fowle, 1748), Book 1, 48. Osborn quotes from memory. The original hymn says "this rebel heart," not "these rebel hearts."

109. Osborn cites Jer 31:18 and Lam 5:21.

110. 2 Cor 5:17.

111. This is the end of the sentence, though it is incomplete.

112. Both Mrs. Henshaw and Mrs. Peabody had been members of the women's society since 1762 or earlier. See SO, Diary, January 2, 1762. Mrs. Henshaw may have been the wife of Mr. Henshaw, who paid a pew assessment in 1755. See FCCR-1743–1831. Abigail Lyon Peabody (1720–1804) was the wife of Deacon Benjamin Peabody.

113. Osborn refers to Mt 6:5: "And when thou prayest, thou shalt not be as the hypocrites are: for they love to pray standing in the synagogues and in the corners of the streets, that they may be seen of men."

114. Osborn cites Dt 5:7, Mk 12:32, 1 Cor 8:4, Acts 4:12.

115. Osborn cites 1 Cor 16:22: "all that loves thee not, be anathema Maranatha." The phrase "anathema Maranatha" means that those who did not love Jesus would be cursed. The people of Meroz were cursed for failing to help the Israelites fight against Sisera. See Jgs 5:23.

116. Osborn uses three biblical images to emphasize her weakness and dependence on God: "this poor wild ass's colt" (Jb 11:12), "this ram's horn" (Dn 8:7), and "this clay and spittle" (Jn 9:6).

117. Osborn mistakenly lists the day as Wednesday instead of Thursday.

118. Albro Anthony (1762–1834) was the child of John and Sarah Anthony, who became members of the First Church of Christ in 1763. See FCCR-BM. On Albro, see Ancestry.com, *U.S., Find a Grave Index, 1600s–Current* [database online], Provo, Utah, 2012.

119. This sentence is added in the margin.

120. Say me not, "nay": 1 Kgs 2:17, 20. Osborn also cites identical verses from Mt 7:7 and Lk 11:9: "Ask, and it shall be given you; seek, and ye shall find; knock, and it shall be opened unto you."

121. Osborn quotes Mk 5:34, Lk 7:50, and Lk 8:48: "go in peace." She also quotes Ps 6:9: "The Lord hath heard thy voice, thy supplication."

122. Ps 115:1.

123. Abraham repeatedly pleaded with God until God agreed not to destroy Sodom if he could find ten righteous men there. See Gn 18:22–33.

124. In the margin: "May 25: and so he has."

125. In the margin: "relating to Friday evenings." Adult white men met at the Osborns' house on Friday evenings.

126. Joseph Fish's daughter Rebecca Fish Douglas died in 1766.

127. This "packet" no longer survives.

128. There is a blotched word between "those . . . things."

129. Osborn discusses Vinal in this passage.

130. Osborn's meaning is not clear, but she seems to be suggesting that she did not invite Vinal to her meetings because he resented being asked for anything.

131. Osborn quotes the words "restless sin and raging hell" from Isaac Watts, *Hymns and Spiritual Songs*, 17th ed. (London: Ware et al., 1751), 27.

132. Osborn refers to Jeremiah's lament that the Israelites would "rush as the horse into battle" instead of repenting for their wickedness. See Jer 8:6.

133. Osborn quotes Gn 20:6: "I withheld thee." After Abimelech took Sarah to be his wife, God withheld him from touching her and prevented him from committing a sin. Sarah was already married to Abraham.

134. Osborn did not subscribe to Joseph Fish's book, *The Church of Christ a Firm and Durable House* (New London: Timothy Green, 1767), because of its criticism of Baptists. She did not want to offend the Reverend Thurston or her other Baptist friends. Yet she also assures Fish that her meetings are no longer open to Baptists.

135. There is a word between "of" and "consolation" that is obscured by a hole in the page.

136. Osborn quotes Ps 23:6.

137. The two blacks who were admitted to the First Church in 1768 were Bristol Coggeshall, enslaved to Nathaniel Coggeshall, the deacon; and Obour Tanner, enslaved to James Tanner. The white woman was Sarah Balch, the wife of Timothy Balch. Timothy Balch was a member of the First Church Committee, which managed the church's financial affairs. See FCCR-BM.

138. Osborn refers to Lk 24:32: "And they said one to another, Did not our heart burn within us, while he talked with us by the way, and while he opened to us the scriptures?" The disciples had walked and talked with the resurrected Jesus without realizing his identity, but their hearts had "burned within them."

139. Osborn refers to Vinal's failure to support her meetings, especially for blacks.

140. Mk 6:22–23, Jn 11:12, 14:13, Jn 15:16.

141. Osborn assures herself that Jesus will conquer her enemies just as he saved Esther and the Jews from Haman, who wanted to destroy them. See the book of Esther.

142. Is 45:17, Is 50:7, Is 54:4, 1 Pt 2:6.

CHAPTER TEN. GREAT INFLUENCE

1. *LD* 1: 41, 44.

2. This poem, "The Employment and Society of Heaven," is reprinted in chapter 12.

3. FCCR-BM, March 5, 1784.

4. Major Jonathan Otis (1723–91) was a silversmith in Newport who belonged to the Second Church of Christ.

5. "Mrs. Hubbard" may be Sarah Hubbard, the wife of Leverett Hubbard, who was the brother-in-law of Ezra Stiles. Stiles recorded a visit from the Hubbards, who lived in New Haven, in May of 1769. *LD* 1: 10.

6. The ellipsis marks an indecipherable word in Osborn's letter. She mentioned the name of the place: "at [indecipherable word]."

7. Osborn probably refers to Mary Noyes's sister-in-law. Mary's only sister, Rebecca Fish Douglas, had died in 1766.

8. Heb 13:5.

9. Mary Fish Noyes's mother-in-law, Abigail Pierpont Noyes (1696–1768), had died in October 1768.

10. Reverend Punderson Austin (1743–73) and Reverend Ephraim Judson (1737–1807). On Judson, see William Buell Sprague, *Annals of the American Pulpit: Trinitarian Congregational* (New York: Robert Carter, 1857), 1: 20. For a biographical sketch of Punderson Austin, see Franklin Bowditch Dexter, *Biographical Sketches of the Graduates of Yale College, with Annals of the College* (New York: Henry Holt, 1896), 2: 727–28.

11. The page is torn on the bottom and two lines have been cut off.

12. Ezra Stiles led religious meetings at Osborn's house.

13. Osborn writes this postscript in the margin.

14. Osborn refers to the Reverend Vinal.

15. The words in parentheses were added in the margin.

16. This parenthetical aside appears in the margin. Hopkins argued that only full church members should be allowed to have their infants baptized. See Joseph A. Conforti, *Samuel Hopkins and the New Divinity Movement: Calvinism, the Congregational Ministry, and Reform in New England between the Great Awakenings* (Grand Rapids, Mich.: Eerdmans, 1981), 82.

17. The Reverend Nathaniel Clap (1669–1745) and the Reverend Jonathan Helyer (1719–45) were previous pastors of the First Church of Newport.

18. Hopkins had three daughters: Elizabeth (1755–90), Joanna (1757–86) and Rhoda (1766–92).

19. Isaac may have been a child in her school.

20. Osborn alludes to Ez 1:16: "The appearance of the wheels and their work was like unto the colour of a beryl: and they four had one likeness: and their appearance and their work was as it were a wheel in the middle of a wheel." She cites this passage to suggest that they should trust in God's providence.

21. This letter was reprinted in *FL,* 160–66. The original does not survive, and the editors of the volume decided not to identify the deacon by name. This letter may have been addressed to Nathaniel Coggeshall (1701–84), the deacon of the First Church.

22. Prv 16:18.

23. Jas 4:6, 1 Pt 5:5.

24. Mt 11:26.

25. Osborn refers to the Parable of the Talents (Mt 25:26): the slothful servant hid his talent in the earth instead of increasing it.

26. Osborn quotes Ps 141:5: "Let the righteous smite me; it shall be a kindness: and let him reprove me; it shall be an excellent oil, which shall not break my head."

27. Osborn refers to Est 3:2. Mordecai refused to bow down in front of Haman.

28. Osborn quotes from Is 43:10, 43:12, 44:8 ("ye are my witnesses"), Jn 14:19 ("because I live, ye shall live also)," and 1 Sm 22:23 ("with me, thou shalt be in safeguard").

29. This may be Joseph Clark, Jr., who was baptized and accepted as a full member of the First Church of Christ in 1767. See FCCR-BM.

30. The part of the sentence beginning with "and is" appears in the margin.

31. This sentence appears in the margin.

32. Osborn compares herself to the biblical Sarah (Gn 11:30), who conceived a child in her old age after a lifetime of being barren.

33. Osborn cites 1 Cor 1:27: "But God hath chosen the foolish things of the world to confound the wise; and God hath chosen the weak things of the world to confound the things which are mighty."

34. Osborn draws a parallel between Hopkins and Jesus. She refers to the story of the centurion who tells Jesus, "Lord, I am not worthy that thou shouldest come under my roof" (Mt 8:8, Lk 7:6).

35. "Molly" may have been Osborn's close friend Mary Mason (circa 1736–92), who left Trinity Church (Newport's Anglican church) to become a member of the First Church in 1775. See FCCR-BM. For more on Mason, see *FL*, 156–57. See also SH to Levi Hart, April 23, 1787, HSP.

36. The Reverend Samuel Buell (1716–98) of East Hampton, N.Y., was one of Osborn's friends. He often signed his letters, "yours in the Lord of love." See, for example, Samuel Buell to Eleazar Wheelock, September 30, 1765, available online: https:// collections.dartmouth.edu/occom/html/normalized/765530-3-normalized.html.

37. In 1769, the Reverend William Hart of Saybrook, Conn., published a scathing indictment of Hopkins's theology. William Hart, *Brief Remarks on a Number of False Propositions, and Dangerous Errors, Which Are Spreading in the Country* (New London, Conn.: Timothy Green, 1769).

38. West and Brown were probably members of the First Church of Christ.

39. Unsigned letter to William Vinal, circa 1771–74, Records of the First Congregational Church of Newport, MSS 418, Folder 9, RIHS. Though this letter is not signed, it is written in Osborn's handwriting, and internal clues show that it is hers. For example, Osborn explains that she had seen Vinal drunk when she was still able to walk to his house. The letter probably dates from 1771, when Vinal claimed that his confession of drunkenness "was extorted from him, while through bodily infirmity, and weakness of mind, he knew not what he did, and confessed what he never was really guilty of." FCCR-BM, September 6, 1771.

40. Osborn refers to several verses in Romans and Galatians that describe love as "the fulfilling of the law" (see Rom 13:8–10, Gal 5:14). "Deacon Coggeshall" was Nathaniel Coggeshall (1701–84), and "Mr. Baltch" was Timothy Balch (1726–76), who both were members of the First Church Committee. A church council of outside ministers was called in 1774 to investigate Vinal's charges that the First Church had treated him "revengefully." Vinal had also accused Osborn, Balch, Coggeshall, Susanna Anthony, and James Tanner of "immoralities." In the words of the council, "with relation to the charge of some or other immoralities, exhibited against several members of this church, viz., Deacon Coggeshall, Mr. Tanner, Mr. Balch, Mrs. Osborn, and Miss Susa Anthony: we judge that nothing has been said, which lamisheth [blemisheth] their Christian character." See FCCR-BM.

41. Osborn crossed out the words "those things which you have confessed" and substituted "the effects of spirituous liquor."

42. Prv 28:13.

CHAPTER ELEVEN. ALL THAT HATH BEFALLEN US

1. SH, *Memoirs*, 355; SH to Mrs. Pemberton, January 7, 1778, MHS.

2. Osborn dictated this letter to a friend. It is not written in her handwriting.

3. By using the word "captivity," Osborn compares her experiences during the Revolutionary War to the enslavement of the Israelites in Egypt.

4. Deacon Nathaniel Coggeshall (1701–84). It is not clear which "Mr. Brown" attended worship at Osborn's house. The 1753 pew assessments include both Josiah Brown and Thomas Brown. See FCCR-1743–1831.

5. The neighbor may have been Mary Mason (circa 1736–92).

6. Osborn alludes to three stories of God's miraculous intervention: Gn 7:7, Dn 3:20–26, and Dn 6:22. By referring to "God's little remnant," she suggests that the end of the world is approaching, and a faithful remnant will do battle with Satan (Is 1:9, Rom 11:5, Rev 12:17).

7. The British turned the First Church of Christ into a barracks and a hospital.

8. Ex 5:2.

9. Jehu refused to make peace until he had destroyed God's enemies, including Jezebel. Osborn imagines that God is like Jehu, punishing Americans for their sins. Osborn cites 2 Kgs 9:19.

10. Osborn cites a passage from the book of Revelation (Rev 22:11) to suggest that God would be just to punish the wicked.

11. The first name is indecipherable. David Chesebrough (1701–82), a wealthy slave trader in Newport. The Reverend Nathaniel Eels (1710–68) of Stonington, Conn.

12. Deacon Benjamin Peabody (1717–94).

13. Several words cannot be recovered because of a hole in the page.

14. This letter appears in *FL*, 154–60. It was probably composed in 1780.

15. Osborn quotes God's words to Job in the whirlwind (Jb 38:11), when God asserts power over all things.

16. Osborn refers to Samuel's erection of a stone that he called "Ebenezer" (1 Sm 7:12). The stone marked the place of victory over the Philistines.

17. Osborn refers to God's promise to Elijah that all of Israel had not forsaken God's covenant (1 Kgs 19:14–18, Rom 11:14).

18. 2 Tm 2:19.

19. Jn 6:37.

20. Joseph Eliot, *A Copy of a Letter, Found in the Study of the Reverend Mr. Joseph Belcher, Late of Dedham, since His Decease* (Boston: B. Green, 1725), 3.

21. Jn 17:24.

22. Mt 28:20.

CHAPTER TWELVE. VISIONS OF HEAVEN

1. SH, *Memoirs*, 363.

2. Since the original of this poem does not survive, we do not know whether Osborn wrote it or a friend transcribed it. I have edited the version that appears in SH, *Memoirs*, to get rid of his frequent use of contractions ("form'd," "forgiv'n," "glorify'd").

3. Mt 19:14.

4. Mt 25:21, 23.

5. Lk 13:27.

6. Mt 25:34.

7. Gn 42:36.

CHAPTER THIRTEEN. SARAH OSBORN'S WILL AND INVENTORY

1. Stephen West, ed., *Sketches of the Life of the Late Rev. Samuel Hopkins* (Hartford: Hudson and Goodwin, 1805), 104.

2. The "annexed papers" do not survive.

3. "Flannen" was flannel.

4. Tow cloth was a heavy linen fabric.

5. A "coverlid" was a bedspread.

6. William Patten, *Christianity the True Theology, and Only Perfect Moral System in Answer to "The Age of Reason:" with an Appendix, in Answer to "The Examiners Examined"* (Warren, Rhode-Island: Nathaniel Phillips, 1795). Patten (1763–1839) was the pastor of the Second Congregational Church of Newport.

7. A "trammel" was a net.

ACKNOWLEDGMENTS

I have learned many things from reading Sarah Osborn's manuscripts, not the least of which is the importance of community.

Without the help of the librarians at many different archives, I would never have been able to write this book. I am grateful to the staffs of the American Antiquarian Society, the Newport Historical Society, the Rhode Island Historical Society, the Connecticut Historical Society, the Beinecke Rare Book and Manuscript Library at Yale University, the Historical Society of Pennsylvania, and the Archives and Special Collections department of the Buswell Memorial Library at Wheaton College.

I am also grateful to the Newport Historical Society, the Beinecke Rare Book and Manuscript Library at Yale University, the American Antiquarian Society, the Rhode Island Historical Society, the Historical Society of Pennsylvania, and the Connecticut Historical Society for expert research assistance and for permission to publish Sarah Osborn's manuscripts.

This is my second time publishing with Yale University Press, and each time has been a pleasure. I am grateful to Christopher Rogers, my editor, for his support, and to Heather Gold and Erica Hanson for their patient guidance through the publication process. I am especially delighted that Susan Laity agreed to work with me on a second book about Sarah Osborn. Eliza Childs has been an immensely helpful copyeditor, poring over my transcriptions of Osborn's writings with a keen eye for detail. She has made this a better book.

I began this book while teaching at the University of Chicago Divinity School; I finished it after moving to Harvard Divinity School. I am grateful to both institutions for providing research assistance. Amy Artman, Philippa Koch, and Ryan Tobler—excellent historians in their own right—helped with numerous facets of this book. My students at both Harvard and Chicago, including Christopher Allison, Carleigh Beriont, Paul Chang, Helen Kim, Erik Nordbye, Emily

Romeo, Kit Shields, Kyle Wagner, and Tom Whittaker, have taught me much about American religion.

Many trusted colleagues have encouraged me during the many years that I have spent researching Sarah Osborn's life, including Elizabeth Alvarez, Jon Butler, Jonathan Ebel, Curtis Evans, Martin Marty, Seth Perry, and Tom Tweed. I am grateful to Bruce Hindmarsh and Mark Noll for sharing their vast knowledge of eighteenth-century evangelicalism with me, and to Kathryn Lofton for her keen intelligence and friendship. David Holland and Laurel Ulrich offered crucial advice as I was finishing the book. Clark Gilpin has been an exemplary colleague, a model of judiciousness, and a good friend. To Harry Stout, who introduced me to the history of early American religion, I owe a greater debt than I can ever repay. His influence has left a mark on all my scholarship.

My colleagues at Harvard Divinity School—including Ann Braude, David Hempton, David Holland, Karen King, Kevin Madigan, Dan McKanan, and Stephanie Paulsell—have been valuable conversation partners. I will always be deeply grateful to David Hempton for making the phone call that brought me to Harvard.

Ellen and Phillip Boiselle have been treasured friends for more than two decades, never letting me forget what matters most. I am grateful to Kevin and Carol Sontheimer for their encouragement, and to my mother and my late father for always believing in me. My husband, Erik, and our daughters, Claire and Rachel, have given me the gifts of kindness, laughter, wisdom, and love.

This book is dedicated to my godmother and my grandmother, two women whose lives inspired me and whose memories I hold dear.

INDEX

As indicated in the Note on the Text, Osborn used thousands of scriptural citations in her writings, more than could be indexed here. A guide to all of Osborn's citations can be found at http://yalebooks.com/sarah-osborns-writings.